STAGED PROPERTIES
MODERN ENGLISH

This collection of essays studies the material, economic, and dramatic roles played by stage properties in early modern English drama. The received wisdom about the commercial stage in Shakespeare's time is that it was a bare one, uncluttered by objects. *Staged Properties* offers a timely critique of this view. In a series of provocative essays, the volume's contributors offer valuable evidence and insight into the modes of production, circulation and exchange that brought such diverse properties as sacred garments, household furnishings, pawned objects and even false beards onto the stage. Departing from previous scholarship, which has focused solely on the symbolic or iconographic aspects of props, these essays explore their material dimensions, and in particular, their status as a special form of property. In the process, the volume reflects upon what the material history of stage props may tell us about the changing demographics, modes of production and consumption, and notions of property that contributed to the rise of the commercial theatre in London.

JONATHAN GIL HARRIS is Robert Ryan Professor of the Humanities and Associate Professor of English at Ithaca College. He is the author of *Foreign Bodies and the Body Politic: Discourses of Social Pathology in Early Modern England* (1998), as well as numerous articles on Renaissance drama and culture.

NATASHA KORDA is author of *Shakespeare's Domestic Economies: Gender and Property in Early Modern England* (2002), and numerous essays on early modern drama and stage history. She is Associate Professor of English and Women's Studies at Wesleyan University.

STAGED PROPERTIES IN EARLY MODERN ENGLISH DRAMA

JONATHAN GIL HARRIS

Ithaca College

AND

NATASHA KORDA

Wesleyan University

CAMBRIDGE UNIVERSITY PRESS
Cambridge, New York, Melbourne, Madrid, Cape Town, Singapore, São Paulo

Cambridge University Press
The Edinburgh Building, Cambridge CB2 2RU, UK

Published in the United States of America by Cambridge University Press, New York

www.cambridge.org
Information on this title: www.cambridge.org/9780521813228

© Cambridge University Press 2002

First published 2002
This digitally printed first paperback version 2006

A catalogue record for this publication is available from the British Library

Library of Congress Cataloguing in Publication data

Staged properties in early modern English drama / edited by Jonathan Gil Harris
and Natasha Korda.
p. cm.
Includes bibliographical references and index.
ISBN 0 521 81322 0
1. English drama – Early modern and Elizabethan, 1500–1600 – History and criticism.
2. Shakespeare, William, 1564–1616 – Stage history – To 1625.   3. English drama – 17th
century – History and criticism.   4. Stage props – England – History – 16th century.   5. Stage
props – England – History – 17th century.   I. Harris, Jonathan Gil.   II. Korda, Natasha.
PR658.S597 S73   2002   792'.0942'0931 – dc21   2002067370

ISBN-13 978-0-521-81322-8 hardback
ISBN-10 0-521-81322-0 hardback

ISBN-13 978-0-521-03209-4 paperback
ISBN-10 0-521-03209-1 paperback

Contents

Illustrations

Notes on contributors

DOUGLAS BRUSTER, Associate Professor at the University of Texas at Austin, is the author of *Drama and the Market in the Age of Shakespeare* (1992), the inaugural volume in Cambridge University Press's Studies in Renaissance Literature and Culture series. He is the textual editor of *The Changeling* for the forthcoming Oxford University Press edition of *The Complete Works of Thomas Middleton*, and has published widely on Shakespeare and early modern drama in England in a variety of journals.

WILL FISHER is Assistant Professor of English at Lehmann College, City University of New York. He is currently at work on a book-length project called *Prosthetic Goods: Subjects/Objects in Early Modern England*. He has published in *Textual Practice* and *ELH*.

JUANA GREEN is Assistant Professor of English at Clemson University. She is at work on a book-length manuscript, *Custard, Carousing Cups, Hankies and Hats: Materializing Desire in Early Modern City Comedy*, which examines the important roles dramatic objects perform in the cultural work necessary to construct gender, identity, and nationality in early modern England.

JONATHAN GIL HARRIS is Robert Ryan Professor of the Humanities and Associate Professor of English at Ithaca College. The author of *Foreign Bodies and the Body Politic: Discourses of Social Pathology in Early Modern England* (Cambridge, 1998) as well as many essays on early modern English drama and culture, he is now at work on a project entitled *Etiologies of the Economy: Dramas of Mercantilism and Disease in Shakespeare's England*.

NATASHA KORDA is Associate Professor of English and Women's Studies at Wesleyan University. She is the author of *Shakespeare's Domestic Economies: Gender and Property in Early Modern England* (University of

Pennsylvania Press, 2002), and many essays on early modern literature, drama, and stage history.

LENA COWEN ORLIN is Research Professor of English at the University of Maryland, Baltimore County and Executive Director of Shakespeare Association of America. The author of *Private Matters and Public Culture in Post-Reformation England* (Cornell, 1994), and editor of *Elizabethan Household: An Anthology* (Folger Institute, 1995) and *Material London* (Pennsylvania, 2000), she is at work on a study of domestic space and household objects in early modern England.

CATHERINE RICHARDSON is a Lecturer at the Shakespeare Institute in Birmingham. She is currently preparing a book-length manuscript on property, drama, and probate inventories.

SASHA ROBERTS is Lecturer in the School of English at the University of Kent at Canterbury. Co-editor of *Women Reading Shakespeare, 1660–1900* (1997) with Ann Thompson, author of *Writers and their Work: Romeo and Juliet* (1998) and articles on early modern texts, readers, and visual arts, she is currently completing a book called *Shakespeare's Poems and Domestic Culture: Gender, Reading, and Space in Early Modern England*.

PETER STALLYBRASS is Professor of English and of Comparative Literature and Literary Theory at the University of Pennsylvania. With Allon White, he wrote *The Politics and Poetics of Transgression* (Routledge and Cornell, second edition, 1990), and he has co-edited *Staging the Renaissance: Studies in Elizabethan and Jacobean Drama* (Routledge, 1991), *Subject and Object in Renaissance Culture* (Cambridge, 1996), and *Language Machines: Technologies of Literary and Cultural Production* (Routledge, 1997). He has just completed a book with Ann Rosalind Jones entitled *Renaissance Clothing and the Materials of Memory* (Cambridge, 2000).

VALERIE WAYNE is Professor of English at the University of Hawai'i at Manoa. She is the editor of *The Matter of Difference: Materialist Feminist Criticism of Shakespeare* (Harvester Wheatsheaf and Cornell, 1991), a Renaissance text on marriage by Edmund Tilney called *The Flower of Friendship* (Cornell, 1992), and Thomas Middleton's play *A Trick to Catch the Old One*, which will appear in Oxford's *Collected Works of Thomas Middleton*, for which she also serves as an Associate General Editor. Her current projects are an edition of *The Winter's Tale* for the Bedford Shakespeare Series and an edition of *Cymbeline* for the Arden Shakespeare, third series.

PAUL YACHNIN is Tomlinson Professor of Shakespeare Studies at McGill University. His first book, *Stage-Wrights: Shakespeare, Jonson, Middleton, and the Making of Theatrical Value*, was published in 1997 by University of Pennsylvania Press; his second, *The Culture of Playgoing in Elizabethan London: A Collaborative Debate* (co-authored by Anthony Dawson), was published by Cambridge in 2001. He is also one of the editors of the forthcoming *Complete Works of Thomas Middleton* (Oxford University Press).

CHAPTER I

Introduction: towards a materialist account of stage properties

Jonathan Gil Harris and Natasha Korda

props (pr: ops) *sb. pl. Theatrical slang.* [Short for *properties.*]
1. a. Stage requisites: see PROPERTY 3.
1841 *Spirit of Times* 16 Oct 396/2 There we subsisted by *spouting*, not Shakespeare, but our dresses and props.

The *OED*'s earliest recorded use of "props" is revealing. Props are modeled in this Victorian exemplum as a diversion, and a ludicrous one, from Shakespeare's plays; unlike the latter, it is implied, props (or costumes) are hardly worth "*spouting*" about. The *OED* citation points to a devaluation of stage properties that is by no means confined to 1841. Subsequent criticism of early modern English drama has if anything intensified this disregard, although perhaps more by omission than commission: props have barely rated more than a passing mention in the vast majority of studies of Shakespeare and his contemporaries.

This neglect finds an objective correlative in the semantic baggage that attaches to the term. "Props" is derived from "property," as the *OED* points out. Yet the term has also acquired some of the connotations of "prop" in the sense of "an object placed *beneath or against* a structure" (emphasis added). The latter meaning certainly resonates with the tendency to regard stage properties as theatrical prostheses, strictly ancillary to and "beneath or against" the main structure, the play-text. Yet the etymological derivation of props should give the materialist critic pause. When props are regarded as *properties*, they may no longer seem to be so trifling: as objects owned by acting companies, impresarios, and players, as objects belonging to – proper to – the institution of the theatre, stage properties encode networks of material relations that are the stuff of drama and society alike.

We should make clear that by stage properties, we mean *all* the moveable physical objects of the stage. As the contributions to this volume demonstrate, early modern English theatrical furniture, costumes, and hand properties were all implicated within a complex, shifting ensemble of property relations that both theatre history and dramatic literary criticism have been inclined to overlook. In this introductory essay, we offer historiographical explanations for the critical neglect of stage properties. We then propose ways in which specifically materialist analyses of theatrical objects might furnish new and invaluable information about the institution of the early modern London public stage, its play-texts, its modes of cultural as well as theatrical production, and the larger social and economic contexts in which it was embedded.

THE MYTH OF THE BARE STAGE

One of modern theatre history's enduring shibboleths is that the Shakespearean stage was a bare one. This assessment, of course, has never been considered to apply to all theatrical production of the period. It has been long acknowledged, for example, that Stuart court masques and even the children's company plays involved elaborate scenery, machinery, costumes, and props.[1] Yet a whiff of decadence has attached to these stage objects; they are often invoked so they may be reviled, whether as signs of James's and Charles's Neronian excesses – extravagantly masquing while the country burned – or as evidence of the poor taste of the élite private theatergoers, in craven thrall to spectacle and effects, rather than pure poetry. By contrast, the early modern English public stage has customarily been considered to be altogether empty of visual ornament, occupied instead by the comparative immateriality of the playwright's language. There is still a pronounced tendency to valorize the Shakespearean stage as a simple "wooden O" appealing to its audiences' minds rather than their senses, or to their ears rather than their eyes. Many primers on Shakespeare, for example, routinely inform their readers that his contemporaries went to *hear* rather than *see* plays – the implication being that public theatergoers were thoughtful auditors, not mindless spectators.

This view founders, however, on the jagged rocks of historical evidence. Such evidence includes the eyewitness accounts of contemporary theatergoers, the play-scripts themselves, the inventories of tiring-house costumes and properties kept by theatrical companies and entrepreneurs, and even the writings of anti-theatricalist Puritan divines. All these furnish innumerable reminders that early modern London playgoers did not just *hear* plays; they also upheld the original, Greek root of "theatre " – *theasthai*, meaning to watch.

The few recorded responses of individual spectators of Shakespeare's plays repeatedly note their stage properties. Samuel Rowlands, for example, was struck by Richard Burbage's constant caress of his stage-dagger in performances of *Richard III*. Recalling an actor's performance of Malvolio, Leonard Digges notably remembered his costume too, referring to him as "that cross gartered gull." Simon Forman's attention was captured by numerous stage properties, including a chair in *Macbeth*, the bracelet and chest of *Cymbeline*, and Autolycus's "pedlers packe" in *The Winter's Tale*.[2] Play-scripts often explicitly confirm spectators' investment in the visual dimension of performance. In *Pericles*, Gower announces that he is come not only "To glad your ear," but also to "please your eyes"; in the Prologue to *No Wit, No Help Like a Woman's*, Thomas Middleton notes of playgoers that "Some in wit, some in shows / Take delight, and some in clothes."[3] Indeed, stage apparel seems to have held a particular fascination for early modern spectators. In *The Gull's Horn Book*, Thomas Dekker instructs playgoing gallants that "by sitting on the stage, you may, with small cost... examine the play-suits' lace, and perhaps win wagers upon laying 'tis copper."[4]

While critics have recently begun to reevaluate the importance of clothes and costumes within the nascent entertainment industry of the public theatre,[5] many other types of stage property remain neglected. That the public stage was populated not just by extravagant costumes, but by other eye-catching objects as well, is attested by Philip Henslowe's well-known, and doubtless incomplete, 1598 inventory of the Admiral's Men's properties (see appendix at the end of the volume). The latter includes not only a number of fairly humble, functional objects, such as "an elm bowl," a "pair of rough gloves," and "one plain crown," but also a quite staggering array of properties obviously designed to impress the eye: "one Hell mouth"; "one pair of stairs for *Phaëton*"; "two moss banks"; "one tree of golden apples"; "one great horse with his legs"; "one cauldron for *The Jew*"; "the cloth of the sun and the moon"; and, perhaps most impressive, "the city of Rome."[6]

Stage directions offer another invaluable and neglected source of information about theatrical properties.[7] The props listed in the stage directions of George Peele's *The Battle of Alcazar*, for example, performed by the Admiral's Men in the late 1580s, include "raw fleshe" impaled upon a character's sword, "dead mens heads in dishes," and, in the induction to the final act, a tree from which Fame descends, several crowns, a blazing star, and fireworks.[8] The stage directions for the spectacular funeral of Zenocrate in *Tamburlaine Part Two*, in the Admiral's repertory at much the same time as Peele's play, demand the simulated burning of an entire town.[9] Plays performed by other companies likewise entailed the display of visually striking properties and effects. The stage direction in 4.3 of *The Lady's Tragedy*, performed by the King's Men in 1613, expressly calls for a "tomb here discovered, *richly* set forth" (emphasis added);[10] Thomas Heywood's *Age* plays, performed by the Queen Anne's Men at the Red Bull in 1610–12, demand an abundance of lavish properties and effects such as a "sea-horse" ridden by Neptune, the colossal Trojan horse of the Greeks, a "raine-bow," "burning weapons," and, the *pièce de résistance*, a flying, flaming bed.[11]

As the properties called for in these stage-directions make quite clear, the objects of the early modern stage were often intended not merely to catch, but to overwhelm the eye by means of their real or apparent costliness, motion, and capacity to surprise. In performances of plays in all the public theatres, dazzling properties were exposed in the discovery space, wheeled onto the main playing area, raised through trapdoors, or – much to Ben Jonson's annoyance – lowered from the heavens (the conventional "creaking throne [that] comes down, the boys to please").[12] Despite the relative absence of scenery, Henslowe's city of Rome notwithstanding, the public playhouse supplemented the visual impact of its costumes and props with its spectacular architecture, whether wooden, painted, or even human. The gallery could serve as the wall of a city or a castle; the brightly painted canopy "or counterfit heauen ouer the stage," as John Higgins called it in his *Nomenclator* (1584), was where "some god appeared or spoke";[13] the wooden pillars supporting the heavens, which the Dutch tourist Johannes De Witt praised as "painted in such excellent imitation of marble that it is able to deceive even the most cunning," may well have doubled as the columns of Greek temples, Roman palaces, or *Tamburlaine*'s "stately buildings of fair Babylon" with their "lofty pillars."[14] Even the audience themselves could be co-opted for the spectacular display of the playhouse's materiality, as is made clear by the extended conceit of 1.2 of Middleton and Dekker's *The Roaring Girl* (1611), which transformed the Fortune theatre into Sir Alexander Wengrave's private library, and the colorfully clad audience members into its diverse books.[15] If the play was the thing, therefore, this was in part because the *staging* of the play often entailed a variety of marvelous, eye-catching things.

The widespread erasure of the visual dimensions of the public stage in modern theatre criticism, coupled with the glorification of its playwrights' supposedly accessory-less poetic inspiration and powers of imagination, has a long history. Although most forcefully articulated during the Romantic period, its roots can be traced back, paradoxically, to the Puritan anti-theatrical writers who made it their business to attack the visual excess of the Elizabethan stage. The discourses of this tradition have been extensively plotted by literary as well as theatre historians, most notably Jonas Barish in his magisterial *The Antitheatrical Prejudice*. Particularly suggestive for our purposes is Barish's analysis of how early modern English anti-theatricality was fueled in large part by a Protestant disdain for the supposedly "theatrical" accessories of Catholic ritual such as relics, priests' vestments and, most especially, the sacrament of the Eucharist. Barish explains how the "hardening Protestant attitude toward the Eucharist itself sprang from a distrust of visible and sensible things. The idea that so much supernatural potency lay in an inert biscuit, or that anything so palpable and localized in space could wield so much enormous leverage in the spiritual world, was one that the reformers could not accept... It had been turned into a thing of spectacle, to be gazed upon and marveled at."[16] As Barish's remarks intriguingly hint, Protestant iconoclasm and antipathy to the theatre operated in tandem with a pronounced hostility to *objects*: the props of religious and dramatic ritual alike served – as did the paltry Eucharist biscuit – to distract attention from more godly, hidden truths, by virtue of their very visibility. Indeed, the *OED*'s list of definitions for "object" suggests that one of the dominant meanings of the word in early modern England was "something placed before the eyes, or presented to the sight."[17]

   In his well-known invectives against the evils of the Elizabethan stage, Stephen Gosson repeatedly warns against the distracting power of its visible objects. Some six years after the opening of the Theatre and the Curtain in 1576, he complained about "the masse of expences in these spectacles that scarce last like shooes of browne paper,"[18] an assessment that speaks to the power of the theatre's visual details even as it endeavors to belittle these as flimsy ephemera. "Sometime," Gosson tells his readers,

...you shall see nothing but the adventures of an amorous knight, passing from countrie to countrie for the loue of his lady, encountering many a terrible monster made of broune paper, & at his retorne, is so wonderfully changed, that he can not be knowne but by some posie in his tablet, or by a broken ring, or a handkircher, or a piece of a cockle shell, what learne you by that? When ye soule of your plays is... meere trifles... what are we taught?

Complaining that "the statelynes of the preparation drownes ye delight which the matter affords," Gosson proceeds to ask: "what delight... hath the sight of 600. mules in *Clytemnestra*; or 3000. cuppes in the *Troian horse?*"[19] In these passages, Gosson's anti-theatricalism expresses itself in an outrage directed less at drama as such, than at props' potential to displace or obstruct dramatic meaning due to their very visibility: the mere sight of those impressively inexplicable six hundred mules and three thousand cups – doubtless exaggerated figures – gets in the way of, even usurps, the ineffable "soule of your plays."

Gosson's animus against the visible dimensions of theatre was reiterated nearly half a century later by the Puritan William Prynne, who professed in 1633 to be disturbed by the "overcostly gawdinesse" of stage apparel.[20] Yet there is much more than a knee-jerk, religious aversion to the visible object at work in these outbursts. Significantly, Gosson's and Prynne's disdain for stage properties betrays a hostility to their extra-dramatic economic freight, the uneffaced signs of their costs and histories of production. Note Prynne's irritation at costumes' "overcostliness," or Gosson's at both the expensive "statelynes of the preparation" and the "broune paper" monster that flaunts not just its artificiality, but also the cheap and disposable materials out of which it was manufactured. Hence the anti-theatricalists' pointedly Puritan distrust of the visible is motivated, at least in these passages, just as much by the distracting glimpses stage properties afford of their material, economic histories as by their sensible objecthood.

For Gosson and Prynne, the economic histories that stage properties bring to visibility entail two related yet distinct dimensions: the conspicuous consumption of superfluous, perishable commodities by actors and/or theatre companies; and, perhaps more importantly, processes of production not necessarily confined to the companies, involving non-theatrical artisanal labor. Interestingly, the anti-theatricalists' aversion to this latter dimension of props' economic histories seems often to have been shared by playwrights. Ben Jonson repeatedly felt himself to be in competition with stage materials, their designers, and their artisanal manufacturers.[21] Even the relatively stage-property-friendly Thomas Dekker asserts in *The Magnificent Entertainment* (1603) that "the Soule that should giue life, and a tongue" to plays is breathed "out of Writers pens," but that "the limnes of it ly at the hard-handed mercy of Mycanitiens [i.e. mechanicals] . . . Carpenters, Ioyners, Caruers, and other Artificers sweating at their Chizzells."[22] The attention Dekker focuses here not only on the materials of stage performance, but also on their histories of manufacture by callous, sweating "Mycanitiens" and "Artificers," underscores how stage properties potentially introduce into any play a plurality of makers, a multiplicity of meanings, and alternate tales of the body or of artisanal labor. These tales lead away from the playwright's scripted drama and into what anthropologist Arjun Appadurai terms the "social lives of things"[23] – the refractory histories of production, ownership, and exchange that constitute objects' trajectories through time and space.

Literary criticism of early modern drama in general and of Shakespeare's plays in particular has belittled or ignored these histories. In the process, it has worked to articulate a related sequence of oppositions or hierarchies, privileging the aesthetic over the economic, the textual over the theatrical, the ineffable over the material, the human over the mechanical, the subject over the object. Shakespeare has played a crucial yet contradictory role in the evolution of these distinctions, inasmuch as he and his plays have been variously aligned with both negative and positive poles in all the above oppositions. Initially cast as a base artisan inhabiting a commercial, theatrical world of trifling objects, Shakespeare came to be refashioned by later generations of critics, especially the Romantics, as the peerless representative of a transcendent dramatic literature whose native habitat, the individual imagination, disdains vulgar physical accoutrements.

THE RISE OF PROP-FREE SHAKESPEARE

The earlier, negative version of Shakespeare informs much of Thomas Rymer's legendarily splenetic censure of *Othello* in his *Short View of Tragedy* (1692). To support his contention that Shakespeare was "out of his element" in writing tragedy, Rymer repeatedly equates him with those "Carpenters, Coblers, and illiterate fellows," the artisanal players of medieval drama who "found that the Drolls, and Fooleries interlarded by them, brought in the rabble...so they got Money by the bargain." The medieval players' commercial acumen was emulated and even outdone by Shakespeare who, Rymer asserts with the help of a nimble equivocation on the double meaning of "master" as authority and as skilled artisan, "was a great Master in this craft." To Rymer's eyes, of course, the transformation of drama into money-making, artisanal "craft" can only be seen as "un-hallowing the Theatre, profaning the name of Tragedy." This language is markedly redolent of Puritan invectives against the materiality of the Catholic church, profaned by idolatrous props such as the Eucharist biscuit and priests' vestments. So it is no surprise that Rymer should proceed to attribute Shakespeare's baseness not only to the "Fooleries" of artisanal culture, but also to the distracting primacy of stage properties on the Elizabethan stage. In what is perhaps his most withering criticism of *Othello*, Rymer exclaims: "So much ado, so much stress, so much passion and repetition about an Handkerchief! Why was not this call'd the *Tragedy of the Handkerchief*? What can be more absurd...?" And he continues: "we have heard of *Fortunatus his Purse*, and of the *Invisible Cloak*, long ago worn threadbare, and stow'd up in the Wardrobe of obsolete Romances: one might think, that were a fitter place for this Handkerchief, than that it, at this time of day, be worn on the Stage, to raise every where all this clutter and turmoil."[24] One might note here that if the Elizabethan stage looks bare to the modern theatre historian, this early modern observer viewed it as positively "cluttered." The stage properties Rymer singles out, moreover, are not unconnected to his earlier critique of commercially oriented stage "craft." The handkerchief, purse, and threadbare cloak serve as synecdoches not only for Shakespeare's "unhallowed" or "profane" theatre, in which mere clutter has supplanted classical tragedy, but also for the economic world of artisanal production, commerce, and traffic in goods to which Rymer dismissively consigns that theatre.

The animus Rymer expresses against stage properties was by no means confined to those of a Puritan bent. In the introduction to his 1723 edition of Shakespeare's plays, the Catholic Alexander Pope displays a similar hostility towards stage properties. Unlike Rymer, however, Pope persistently sets up both artisanal culture and the stage clutter it produces as the vulgar domains from which the playwright's career, themes, and texts alike need to be rescued. A distinction must be drawn, Pope insists, "between the real merit of the Author, and the silly and derogatory applauses of the Players," which only reflect the fatuous tastes of the paying audience members. Observing censoriously that for commercial reasons Shakespeare's early comedies pandered to such audiences, locating "their Scene among *Tradesmen* and *Mechanicks*," Pope salutes the playwright's transcendence of this base artisanal world in his later, more mature work. Even if Shakespeare successfully escaped the squalor of economic themes and his theatre's commercial imperatives, however, editorial work still needs to be done to purge his play-scripts of any trace of the contaminating materiality and labor of the stage. Pope complains that "the notes of direction to the *Property-men* for their *Moveables*, and to the *Players* for their *Entries*, are inserted into the Text, thro' the ignorance of the Transcribers"; to make his point, he singles out in a footnote that much debated line about Falstaff's death in *Henry V*, "His nose grew as sharp as a pen, and *a table of Greenfield's*, &c" (2.3.17), and proposes that the mysterious "table" is in fact a stray stage property.[25] By evicting such trespassers, Pope suggests, Shakespeare's plays may be successfully converted from unruly theatrical spectacles for and by the vulgar into disciplined texts of sublime, dramatic literature whose meanings are unsullied by the disruptive effects of stage properties, their handlers, or their makers.

Pope's attempts to distill a "pure," literary Shakespeare from the dross of the theatrical and the economic were repeated with far greater alacrity by the Romantics. Indeed, the baleful flame of a residual Puritanical anti-theatricalism flickers strongly in much Shakespeare criticism of the period. Samuel Taylor Coleridge makes this quite explicit with his decidedly ambiguous definition of "theatre," which he characterizes as "the general term for all places thro' the ear or eye in which men assemble in order to be amused by some entertainment presented to all at the same time. Thus, an old Puritan divine says: 'Those who attend public worship and sermons only to amuse themselves, make a theatre of the church, and turn God's house into the devil's. *Theatra aedes diabololatricae.*' "[26] Complaining about an actor's performance of Macbeth, Charles Lamb speaks yet more transparently of "the discrepancy I felt at the changes of garment which he varied, – the shiftings and re-shiftings, like a Romish priest at mass."[27] Both Coleridge and Lamb were reacting largely against the illusionist proscenium theatre of their age, whose extravagant, highly ornate visual tableaux they considered to detract from the sublimity of Shakespeare's poetry. For them, the only solution was to take Shakespeare out of the contemporary public theatre and reinstate him in the private study of the individual reader. Such a relocation was repeatedly justified by appeals to a nostalgic misconception of the early modern stage, one that left it looking a little like Coleridge's own study. In his lectures of 1811–12, Coleridge asserted that the accidents of Shakespeare's stage had forced the playwright "to rely on his own imagination, and to speak not to the sense, as was now done, but to the mind. He found the stage as near as possible a closet, and in the closet only could it be fully and completely enjoyed."[28] Initiating the remarkably tenacious trend of citing *Henry V*'s Chorus to support the image of the bare "Wooden O" filled only by text and imagination, Coleridge maintained that the Elizabethan theatre "had no artificial, extraneous inducements – few scenes, little music – and all that was to excite the sense in a high degree was wanting. Shakespeare himself said, 'We appeal to your imaginations; by your imagination you can conceive this round O to be a mighty field of monarchs and if you do not, all must seem absurd.' "[29]

What is particularly striking about the Romantics' Shakespearean stage of and for the imagination, though, is how it repeatedly evinces a scorn not just for sense-exciting performance or spectacle, but specifically for the stage property. Like Stephen Gosson, many of the Romantics regarded theatrical objects as usurping the soul or, to use their own terminology, the *ideal* of Shakespeare's plays. Lamb was most forthright in his hostility to the stage property:

The reading of a tragedy is a fine abstraction. It presents to the fancy just so much of external appearances as to make us feel that we are among flesh and blood, while by far the greater and better part of our imagination is employed upon the thoughts and internal machinery of the character. But in acting, scenery, dress, the most contemptible things, call upon us to judge of their naturalness.

Lamb's discussions of individual plays repeatedly circle back to the "contemptible" nature of theatrical "things." He says of *The Tempest* that "it is one thing to read of an enchanter, and to believe the wondrous tale while we are reading it; but to have a conjuror brought before us in his conjuring-gown..." And of *King Lear*, which he famously pronounced unperformable, he observes that "the sublime images, the poetry alone, is that which is present to our minds in the reading...So to see Lear acted, – to see an old man tottering about the stage with a walking-stick...has nothing in it but what is painful and disgusting."[30] Like Gosson's objections to cups and mules, Lamb's animus against conjuring-gowns, walking-sticks and the body of the "tottering" actor is driven by a conviction that these constitute unwelcome physical distractions from a much more valuable immateriality, in this case "the poetry present in our minds."

That this Romantic hostility to the stage property involved more than a disdain for the visible and, like Gosson's or Dekker's observations about theatrical objects, entailed also an aversion to its material history, is evident from a review by William Hazlitt of an 1818 performance of *A Midsummer Night's Dream*:

All that is fine in the play, was lost in the representation. The spirit was evaporated, the genius was fled; but the spectacle was fine: it was that which saved the play. Oh, ye scene-shifters, ye scene-painters, ye machinists and dress-makers, ye manufacturers of moon and stars that give no light...rejoice! This is your triumph; it is not ours... Poetry and the stage do not agree together. The attempt to reconcile them fails not only of effect, but of decorum. The *ideal* has no place on the stage, which is a picture without perspective; everything there is in the foreground. That which is merely an airy shape, a dream, a passing thought, immediately becomes an unmanageable reality... Thus Bottom's head in the play is a fantastic illusion, produced by magic spells: on the stage it is an ass's head, and nothing more; certainly a very strange costume for a man to appear in.[31]

Hazlitt's extended complaint betrays a deep-rooted hostility to the economic dimensions of theatrical production. The "spirit" or "airy shape" of his cherished *"ideal"* play – or rather, play-*script* – has been punctured by the contrivances of mere "manufacturers" such as "scene-shifters," "scene-painters," "machinists" and "dress-makers," an uncanny repetition of the play's own subordination of fairy spirits to the carnivalesque misrule of so-called rude mechanicals. As his remarks about the still ruder "manufacturers" make quite clear, what Hazlitt sees in the objects of the stage is not just their physical materiality, but also their pre-stage histories. These point decisively away from the "fantastic illusion" of the play: artifice presumes artificers and hence narratives of mechanical labor that compete with the sublime "dreams" of the poet. It is such narratives, we would argue, that constitute the "unmanageable reality" Hazlitt complains of. The phrase suggestively captures something of the refractory nature of stage properties. Like Snout's crude "rough-cast" wall in the play of Pyramus and Thisbe, theatrical objects always potentially refuse to be subordinated to the *logos* of the play in which they appear and instead make visible, by virtue of their conspicuous fabricatedness, alternate dramas of manufacture and the body.

TWENTIETH-CENTURY DEMATERIALIZATIONS

Hazlitt's invective against the spirit-evaporating "unmanageability" of stage properties hints at a generalized resistance of theatrical matter to domestication by and within "airy shapes." But his language evinces also a quite historically specific structure of feeling: his derogatory term "machinist" expresses an anxiety about a world in which the machine more than its operator has become the motor of production, thereby enabling the mass manufacture and consumption of disposable commodities. This anxiety arguably intensified in twentieth-century theatrical discourse.[32] Modernist theatre criticism was particularly haunted by the specter of the machine, which it sought to exorcize by repeated appeals to a higher power: early modern public stagecraft.[33] Take, for example, Harley Granville-Barker's idealization of Elizabethan public theatre in opposition to the Jacobean masque:

The Elizabethan drama made an amazingly quick advance from crudity to an excellence which was often technically most elaborate. The advance and the not less amazing gulf which divides its best from its worst may be ascribed to the simplicity of the machinery it employed. That its decadence was precipitated by the influence of the Mask and the shifting of its center of interest from the barer public stage to the candle-lit private theatre, where the machinery of the Mask became effective, it would be rash to assert; but the occurrences are suspiciously related. Man and machine (here at any rate is a postulate, if a platitude!) are false allies in the theatre, secretly at odds; and when man gets the worst of it, drama is impoverished; and the struggle, we may add, is perennial. No great drama depends upon pageantry. All great drama tends to concentrate upon character; and, even so, not upon picturing men as they show themselves to the world like the figures on a stage – though that is how it must ostensibly show them – but on the hidden man.[34]

A whiff of Papist "candle-lit" ritual arguably lurks in Granville-Barker's remarks about the "decadent" private stage and its machinery: the latter gets in the way of, even replaces, what he regards as the true stuff of theatre – "the hidden man," or interior Protestant subject. Far more noticeable than any residual anti-Catholic anti-theatricality, however, is Granville-Barker's anxiety about the relationship between human and machine, which suggests an intensification of Hazlitt's disdain for the "machinist." In this context, his use of the adverb "technically" is quite striking. Elizabethan drama is for Granville-Barker "technically most elaborate" not because of its props, machines or physical special effects, but because of its *meta*physical, or psychological, sophistication. Here we can glimpse how the notion that the Elizabethan public stage was a theatre of subjects rather than objects, of "hidden men" rather than "pageantry," served as a consoling myth and rallying point for a precarious post-Romantic humanism threatened by the impersonality of mechanical production.[35]

In marked contrast to Granville-Barker's disdain for machinery and spectacle, however, another strain of modernist theatre scholarship displayed more sympathy to stage objects. In *The Origin of German Tragic Drama* (1919), Walter Benjamin placed considerable emphasis on the role played by the props of baroque *Trauerspiel*, or mourning-drama. Benjamin saw reflected in this genre (whose most typical specimen, although non-German, he considered to be Shakespeare's *Hamlet*) the defining feature of his own capitalist society – what he called *das Primat des Dinghaften vor dem Personalen*, the dominance of things over sentiment, of the reified over the personal: "if tragedy is completely released from the world of things, this world towers oppressively over the horizon of the *Trauerspiel* . . . there is no getting away from the stage property."[36] Benjamin's reading of the baroque stage property arguably preserves the terms of the Romantic oppositions between subject and object, humans and mechanical things. Nevertheless, his sympathetic account of how "the life of [the] apparently dead" prop of *Trauerspiel* punctures any dramatic illusion of pure ideality by anchoring the play in the "profane world" of historical contingency not only contains the seeds of his later support for Bertolt Brecht's materialist theatre of alienation;[37] it also provides a potentially fruitful starting point for theorizing the social as well as dramatic lives of stage properties.

Benjamin's notes on the baroque stage property, however, were overwhelmingly ignored by subsequent twentieth-century theatre historians and literary critics.[38] Even the few scholarly studies devoted to early modern costumes, props, and scenery displayed a modicum of nervousness about the materiality of stage materials, frequently disciplining them and harnessing their meanings to those of the play-text by focusing exclusively on their functional and symbolic dimensions. This is the methodological orientation of the only two book-length studies of Elizabethan stage properties, Felix Bossonet's *The Function of Stage Properties in Christopher Marlowe's Plays* (1978) and Frances Teague's important *Shakespeare's Speaking Properties* (1991). Valuable as these studies are, they largely ignore theatrical objects' specifically material dimensions. When properties "speak" to audiences, Teague argues, they communicate not their extra-dramatic histories, but "significant presentational image clusters" that stand in centripetal relation to the symbolic dimensions of the entertainments in which they appear.[39]

James Calderwood's influential work on metatheatricality and early modern stage properties provides a particularly good illustration of this dematerializing tendency. In *Shakespearean Metadrama* (1971), Calderwood considers the status of a common early modern prop, the three-legged joint stool, in the scene where Lady Macbeth chides her husband for his embarrassingly public reaction to Banquo's ghost. Calderwood's remarks are worth quoting at some length.

"Why do you make such faces?" Lady Macbeth demands; "When all's done, / You look but on a stool." To be sure, and yet all the audience in the Globe has been looking on is but a stool too. This sudden casting of doubt on the nature and identity of the most innocent of stage props may cause us to wonder naively to whom the stool belongs. Is it the property, quite literally the stage property, of Shakespeare's acting company, the King's Men, or is it fully absorbed into the dramatic fiction where it becomes part of the furnishings of Macbeth's castle, an item on his steward's inventory? For the play to succeed as realistic illusion the audience must regard the stool as Macbeth's, which means fictionalizing in their imaginations an object that remains incorrigibly what it was before the play began. The process is analogous to the absorption of language into a literary work. For the language the poet uses comes as drab and gross from the everyday world as Macbeth's joint stool; but it has been transformed by the poetic imagination into a self-enclosed complex of meaning that abandons its referential dependence on the world outside. The joint stool in *Macbeth* undergoes one further transformation – from an object in the Globe theatre to an object in *Macbeth*'s castle to the hallucinated ghost of Banquo. Now Macbeth owns it uniquely; it has been wholly interiorized by the fictive world and no longer bears any likeness to its original form; there is no way back from Banquo's ghost to the joint stool owned by the King's Men. Nor is there any route by which we can return from the language of *Macbeth*, whose meanings are uniquely contained in their own ghostly linguistic forms, to the language of Jacobean England from which it came. This is true partly because just as the joint stool becomes Macbeth's by virtue of its insertion into a fictional context – its environment changing but not itself – so language is reconstituted by Shakespeare in *Macbeth* not through any material alteration in words but by virtue of their contextual relations.[40]

Calderwood's argument entails a two-step transubstantiation of the joint stool: the "drab and gross" materiality of the stage property, owned (or so he presumes) by the King's Men, is "fully absorbed into the dramatic fiction where it becomes part of the furnishings of Macbeth's castle," and thus becomes apparently less material insofar as it is now merely a fictional joint stool. In order for its transubstantiation to be complete, however, the joint stool must undergo "one further transformation": its fleshly materiality must be rendered ghostly spirit, the spirit not of an object but of a subject, Banquo. This final transformation, whereby Macbeth takes possession of the joint stool by interiorizing it, likewise allows it to be "wholly interiorized by the fictive world" of the play. Notably, Calderwood believes that the turnstile through which *Macbeth*'s piece of furniture passes can rotate in only one direction: "there is no way back from Banquo's ghost to the joint stool owned by the King's Men."

Yet as we have shown here, and as Stephen Gosson already knew, early modern English stage properties repeatedly found ways to reverse the dematerializing trajectory plotted by Calderwood. Indeed, theatrical objects have a habit of drawing attention to themselves as things with material lives surplus to the "fictive worlds" into which they have been enlisted. If stage properties "speak," to borrow Frances Teague's suggestive coinage, what they communicate often departs from the script of the Hazlittian "ideal." Instead of regarding Gosson as just a Puritan crackpot or killjoy, therefore, we might take seriously his claims about Elizabethan theatrical properties, and acknowledge their power to puncture dramatic illusion by pointing to alternate social dramas of economic production, exchange, and ownership. It is these latter dramas that the essays of *Staged Properties in Early Modern English Drama* attempt to bring to critical visibility, employing a variety of materialist methods of analysis.

REMATERIALIZING THE STAGE PROPERTY

It is perhaps surprising that, to date, avowedly materialist criticism of early modern drama has tended to reinforce the Romantic preference for dramatic text or character over theatrical objects. Though singularly concerned with the emergence of institutions of private property on the stage of history, such criticism has yet to offer a cogent account of stage properties. Andrew Sofer's important forthcoming study, *The Stage Life of Props*, pays attention to the materiality of objects "within the unfolding spatio-temporal event in the playhouse."[41] Yet the extent to which the objects of the early modern English playhouses participated within larger material networks of property relations off- as well as onstage remains largely ignored. Materialist critics of early modern drama have adroitly countered Romanticist fallacies of the "internal machinery of characters."[42] In a perhaps typical case of critique serving unwittingly to reinscribe other conventional hierarchies of value, however, materialists' failure to pay attention to stage properties has helped buttress the illusion that the early modern theatre was invested exclusively, if problematically, in the "inner world" of the subject.

Recently, however, the critical tide has begun to turn. Early modern scholarship has become obsessed with materiality; the trickle of studies of material culture that began in the 1980s has turned into a veritable flood at the millennium.[43] In the process, theatrical objects have increasingly joined subjects as privileged sites of materialist critical inquiry. In *Drama and the Market in the Age of Shakespeare* (1992), for example, Douglas Bruster explores the interrelations of stage properties and the personal in plays from *Jack Juggler* (1555) through *Bartholomew Fair* (1614).[44] As Margreta De Grazia observes in the important recent collection *Subject and Object in Renaissance Culture* (1996), early modern conceptions of identity always required external things: "subjectivity effects," she argues, were inextricably entwined with "personal effects."[45] Yet the objects of the early modern English public stage were not merely indispensable adjuncts to or determinants of Hamlet's legendary interiority, "that within which passeth show." As De Grazia's essay itself makes clear, Renaissance objects also materialized changing conceptions of property and constellations of property relations. In what ways, then, might materialist dramatic criticism offer accounts of specifically theatrical objects that do not simply subsume the latter within the post-Romantic problematic of the subject?

Materialism, of course, is not monolithic. It boasts numerous, occasionally conflicting traditions, and the current wave of scholarship on early modern material culture is no exception.[46] For strategic purposes, it will be useful to distinguish between five methodologically discrete yet overlapping materialist approaches to Renaissance objects, each of which offers productive points of departure for the essays in this volume.

The first entails the qualitative analysis of the stuff of material culture. This approach reflects the dominant methodological strain of the new historicism, which since Stephen Greenblatt's *Renaissance Self-Fashioning* (1980) has sought to disclose the contours and faultlines of cultural formations through nuanced accounts of synecdochic microdetail – a strategy redolent of the "thick description" famously advocated by cultural anthropologist Clifford Geertz.[47] In contrast to the preoccupation with the subject that distinguished early new historicist work, qualitative analysis of early modern material culture has increasingly focused on the object, thanks in no small part to a growing engagement with Michel de Certeau's theorization of the "everyday."[48] This engagement is exemplified by Patricia Fumerton and Simon Hunt's edited collection *Renaissance Culture and the Everyday* (1999), which takes as its starting point de Certeau's dictum that everyday practices and their objects transform rather than simply reproduce social structures and cultural systems. Through detailed descriptions of objects such as buck-baskets and embroidered psalmbooks, the volume's essays seek to show that early modern materials are not simply static things, but points of intersection for myriad relations of property and power.[49]

In focusing on the material attributes or properties of particular objects, however, exclusively qualitative analyses risk ignoring the larger economic frameworks within which such objects are situated. In tandem with this approach, therefore, materialist criticism has also begun to undertake quantitative analysis of patterns of production, consumption, and ownership of the world of goods. Such analysis has a rich tradition within social history, as is evidenced by the work of Joan Thirsk and, more recently, of Susan Staves, Carole Shammas, and Amy Erickson.[50] These scholars have ably demonstrated the importance of quantitative analyses in determining what kinds of property passed through the hands of ordinary men and women in the period. In the case of materialist literary and dramatic criticism, quantitative analysis can yield insight into the divergences as well as the convergences of the text and its material contexts. Several contributors to this volume have begun to review archival documents of stage-history through a recognizably quantitative lens.[51] As the work of Douglas Bruster, Lena Cowen Orlin, Peter Stallybrass and Natasha Korda shows, statistical analysis offers materialist critics a convenient way of illuminating histories that have been excluded from literary or dramatic representation.

Much of the recent scholarship on the early modern world of goods, however, has avoided theoretical reflection on what constitutes materiality. As a consequence, there has been a pervasive tendency to equate the "material" with the "physical." This equation unwittingly inverts the valences of the traditional Aristotelian opposition between "form" and "matter," according to which form is actuality and matter potentiality (*dynameos*). Aristotle thus understood materiality as a synonym not for physical presence, but for dynamic process; matter, in his analysis, is always *worked upon*. Marx attributed the same meaning to matter in his "Thesis on Feuerbach," in which he criticized Feuerbach for understanding matter "only in the *form* of the *object*."[52] Marx, by contrast, understood the materiality of objects to embrace as well the domain of labor and *praxis*, and thus to entail social relations of *production* – relations, Marx argued, that are effaced in the commodity form. Increasingly, scholarship on early modern material culture is returning to Marx's more dynamic, labor-oriented theories of materiality.[53]

These first three types of object analysis often privilege the synchronic, offering snapshots of a cultural moment. Diachronic materialist approaches to early modern culture seek to bring to visibility changing relations of economic and ideological production; in the process, they tend to make critical use of Marx's narratives of historical change, but in ways that avoid the teleological determinism and reductive economism of the latter. Recent materialist accounts of historical change in early modern England have often been critically interarticulated with Michel Foucault's archaeological studies of knowledge, according to which an object is less a thing anterior to discourse and power than an effect of them.[54] A particularly good example of this more diachronic materialist approach to early modern culture is Richard Halpern's *Poetics of Primitive Accumulation: the Genealogy of Capital in Renaissance Culture* (1991), which provocatively adapts Marx's study of the early modern economic preconditions for capitalism in order to illuminate the textual formations that prefigured it.[55] Halpern does not explicitly analyze physical objects in his study; but the approach to primitive capital accumulation that his argument models suggests how early modern property may be read not only in terms of changing relations of economic production, but also as a discursive effect, or Foucauldian "object," of changing organizations of knowledge and power.

Perhaps the newest development in criticism of early modern material culture and property, and one exemplified particularly well by many of the contributions to this volume, involves a somewhat different type of diachronic analysis: the study of processes of institutional exchange. This type of analysis has been foreshadowed by Stephen Greenblatt's evocative account in *Shakespearean Negotiations* (1988) of the migration of religious properties from the vestries of dissolved monasteries to the tiring-houses of theatres.[56] The most comprehensive theorization of objects' material trajectories of exchange is to be found in Arjun Appadurai's edited collection, *The Social Life of Things* (1986). The majority of the volume's contributions analyze objects and social processes well outside the orbit of early modern English studies (e.g. the history of cloth in Raj-era India and the circulation of *qat* plant in post-colonial northeast Africa). Nonetheless, their shared methodology is highly suggestive for scholars of early modern material culture. Objects, in Appadurai's words, possess "life histories" or "careers" of exchange that invest them with social significance and cultural value. According to this view, objects do not simply acquire meaning by virtue of their present social contexts; rather, they impart significance to those contexts as a result of the paths they have traced through time and space. The significance a particular object assumes thus derives from the differential relation of its present context to its known or assumed past, and potential future, contexts. In order to read the meanings of any object, then, it becomes necessary to trace its "cultural biography" as it "moves through different hands, contexts, and uses." It is "things-in-motion," as Appadurai puts it, "that illuminate their human and social context[s]."[57] Appadurai's choice of phrase might have a particular resonance for the scholar of early modern drama, for Shakespeare uses it – to similar effect – in *Troilus and Cressida*: "things in motion sooner catch the eye / Than what stirs not" (3.3.183–4).

These five strands of materialist criticism are by no means mutually exclusive. Although there are obvious ways in which (for example) a committedly positivist quantitative analysis of objects might come into conflict with a Foucauldian account of discursive production, the various strands we have sketched here can also be mutually reinforcing. In collating the various contributions to *Staged Properties*, we have sought to highlight the ways in which seemingly divergent materialisms can work together to broaden and deepen our understanding of stage properties, the plays in which they appear, the institutions and agents that own them, and the social, economic and cultural contexts in which they are embedded – including the changing configurations of property that their social and dramatic lives disclose.

Our principle of organization has been to group the essays in four sections, each of whose contributions embody different, though highly complementary, materialist approaches to a specific issue pertaining to stage properties. In the process, numerous unforeseen links and new opportunities for materialist critical dialogue emerge. The essays in the opening part, "Histories," offer two very different ways of understanding early modern stage properties and historical shifts within their types, meanings, and economic contexts. In "Properties of skill: product placement in early English artisanal drama," Jonathan Gil Harris considers diachronic shifts in the phenomenology and meanings of props in light of two quite distinct discourses of property: property as public membership within a corporate body, and property as privately owned capital asset. Harris shows how these two discourses are made visible in early English drama through metatheatrical episodes that in certain respects anticipate the twentieth-century practice of product placement. Many of the props of the late medieval cycle plays advertise themselves as products of a guild economy in which the property of artisanal skill was understood to constitute public membership within a fraternity or corporate network of social relations. By contrast, the props of the Elizabethan professional theatre companies demand to be seen largely as a nascent form of capital; they often functioned as profitable investments by means of which joint-stock theatre companies or their principals could advance their wealth and social standing. Props were no longer emblems of artisanal skill, in other words, but private assets – a shift illustrated by the stage properties of Dekker's *The Shoemaker's Holiday*. Despite the play's artisanal theme, Harris argues, its props advertise less the products and corporate fraternal relations of the guild than the social mobility afforded the private investor by theatrical stock.

Douglas Bruster's contribution, "The dramatic life of objects in the early modern theatre," offers a materialist history of early modern stage properties centered on form. Surveying the kinds of hand properties in early modern plays and how such plays employ them, Bruster passes over the "thick description" that has characterized so much criticism of objects to date, as well as the economic mode of analysis undertaken by Harris. By describing hand props in a more general way, he seeks to give context to this quantitative detail, at the same time deepening our understanding of the material properties of the early modern play-house. In the process, Bruster provides provocative answers to a variety of important questions: were hand properties a constant across genres, playwrights, and decades? Or were there significant differences in the numbers and kinds of props that appeared in early modern plays? If there were differences, what produced them? How, finally, might such differences influence our reading of the more familiar objects in Shakespeare's plays?

The remaining essays of the volume are divided into sections that reflect the traditional categories of stage properties: furniture, costumes, and hand properties. This taxonomy was of course foreign to Shakespeare and his contemporaries, and has been contested in our own time.[58] We utilize it here, however, to draw more effective attention to the multiple ways in which materialist criticism can complicate the conventional categories within which stage objects, early modern as well as contemporary, tend to be placed.

The essays in part II, "Furniture," consider problems raised by what Christopher Sly in *The Taming of the Shrew* calls "household stuff." In her essay "Things with little social life (Henslowe's theatrical properties and Elizabethan household fittings)," Lena Cowen Orlin employs a mixture of quantitative and qualitative analysis to interpret early modern domestic "fittings" or fixtures. The latter constitute a unique category of property that has been overlooked by the traditional binary distinction between "real" property and moveables, each of which is represented in its own class of documents. Because fittings are not included in inventories, they have a largely hidden history despite their sometimes quite significant presence in the domestic environment. Orlin argues that this overlooked category can help illuminate a longstanding theatrical problem: the infamous inventory of stage properties in Henslowe's diary is in theatrical terms comparable to a list of household "fittings," and that is why it notoriously omits "moveables" such as pots, purses and all the other objects that plays required.

The next two essays, Catherine Richardson's "Properties of domestic life: the table in Heywood's *A Woman Killed with Kindness*" and Sasha Roberts's " 'Let me the curtains draw': the dramatic and symbolic properties of the bed in Shakespearean tragedy," focus on two significant household properties employed in early modern drama. Examining

Thomas Heywood's *A Woman Killed With Kindness* in relation to probate inventories for the provincial bourgeoisie, Richardson poses suggestive questions about the relationship between the furniture explicitly called for in stage directions and commonly possessed items in inventories: how "real" are the former to their audiences? What tensions are there between a stage-table's symbolic meanings (evoked by the past experience of domestic interiors that it signals to the audience's imagination) and the visual and spatial construction of its material presence? By examining the domestic stage property as a focus for the audience's imagination and memory, Richardson argues, new light may be shed on its function in the operation of the domestic play's moral project.

Roberts likewise undertakes an interdisciplinary analysis of another important domestic property: the early modern bed. Whereas Richardson's analysis makes effective use of the methods of quantitative analysis to illuminate the dramatic role of the table as a domestic property, Roberts qualitatively investigates the symbolic function of the bed in Shakespearean drama. Yet her approach to symbolism and function differs from that of traditional theatre historians in that she turns to the material and cultural history of the bed not simply as an explanatory key through which to understand the symbolic use of wedding sheets, bridal beds and deathbeds in Shakespeare's plays, but rather as an occasion to question the methodological problems posed by interdisciplinary analyses of the symbolic function of stage properties. Her astute analysis of the unique status of the stage-bed as a discovery space or "stage-within-a-stage" likewise illuminates the ways in which stage properties may function to map the symbolic coordinates of spatial relations, in this case, the disruptions and collisions of the private and the public.

Part III, "Costumes," offers three different perspectives on one of the most important species of stage property in the first English commercial theatres. In "Properties in clothes: the materials of the Renaissance theatre," Peter Stallybrass extends his work on early modern textiles to demonstrate the economic significance of clothes for the early modern English stage. Costumes were any theatre company's most expensive investment – a term that hints at the uniquely early modern nexus of commerce and clothes. Prior to the advent of modern banking systems, early modern English people hoarded and circulated clothes as forms of convertible wealth. Such practices were crucial to the fortunes of theatrical entrepreneurs such as Philip Henslowe, whose pawnbroking business not only centered on clothes, but also helped provide his own playing company with a ready supply of costumes. Henslowe's commercial practices find many counterparts in Renaissance drama, which frequently stages the pawning of clothes or their theft or exchange. At both a dramatic and an economic level, then, the theatre of Henslowe and his contemporaries was founded on what Stallybrass terms the "regulated vagrancy of moveable goods."

Natasha Korda likewise pays particular attention to cloth and clothing in, "Women's theatrical properties," using these as the gateway to a feminist materialist understanding of women's elusive involvement in the early modern theatre. While some recent scholarship has focused on women's roles as theatrical spectators, such scholarship, in casting women in the familiar role of consumers, leaves undisturbed the governing assumption that women played no part in early modern theatrical production. Korda reexamines a variety of documents of Elizabethan stage history in order to show how women were involved in the manufacture, circulation and exchange of clothing, cloth and other properties. She examines evidence suggesting that women participated in the production of costumes and properties as sempstresses, silkwomen (who made props as well as costumes), lacemakers, head tirers, wigmakers, linen drapers, and as makers of smaller stage properties.

In "Staging the beard: masculinity in early modern English culture," Will Fisher focuses on another worn property that, in its prosthetic relation to the body, problematizes conventional understandings of the category of costume: the stage beard. Theatrical, literary and artistic representations of beards helped to fashion a historically specific vision of masculinity by fashioning a historically specific ideal of the male body. Facial hair was not, however, simply a means of constructing sexual differences between men and women. It was also the marker of difference between men and boys; in other words, boys were quite literally a different gender from men in the Renaissance. By casting light on the children's companies and their use of prosthetic facial hair – for the boy actors were as much "in drag" when playing the parts of men as they were when playing the parts of women – Fisher's essay contributes to our understanding of the ways in which stage properties construct, to use Judith Butler's resonant phrase, "bodies that matter."

The final part, "Hand Properties," supplements Douglas Bruster's essay with the "thick description" that his general account of hand properties necessarily eschews. Juana Green's "Properties of marriage: proprietary conflict and the calculus of gender in *Epicoene*" examines how a specific set of hand properties within a play – the animal-shaped drinking mugs of Jonson's *Epicoene* – stages conflicted assumptions and anxieties about marital property relations. In exchange for his wife's portion, Captain Otter has relinquished control of their middle-class household to her, and their topsy-turvy marriage serves as an object of satire in the play; indeed, read in relation to early modern ideological discourses of conduct that attempt to regulate gender behavior, the play constructs Mrs. Otter as a stereotypical shrew. Yet the play's use of the carousing cups arguably complicates such a reading. By offering qualitative thick description of the carousing cups' materiality – that is, by reading them in relation to discourses against drunkenness, and locating them within early modern English laws governing property and its transmission – Green demonstrates how the stage properties of *Epicoene* problematize the role of property in marriage.

Valerie Wayne's essay, "The woman's parts of *Cymbeline*," examines three other hand properties implicated in marital relations: the manacle that Posthumus gives to Innogen, the ring that Innogen gives to Posthumus, and the bloody cloth that Posthumus takes as "proof" of Innogen's murder. In contrast to Green's historicist contextualization of carousing cups, Wayne employs Arjun Appadurai's anthropological model of value and commodity exchange to trace the careers of hand properties *within* Shakespeare's play. The shifting significations of *Cymbeline*'s marital properties are tethered to the changing commodity forms that each variously assumes during the course of the action – gift, prize, and item of theft. Regardless of the form they take, however, the props always materialize female sexuality, metonymically standing in for what the play calls Innogen's "woman's part." By tracing not only the fluctuating values of *Cymbeline*'s hand properties within the play but also their visible careers within subsequent stage productions and illustrations, Wayne sheds invaluable light on the complexity of theatrical commodity forms, as well as their interarticulation with female sexuality.

In "Wonder-effects: Othello's handkerchief," Paul Yachnin considers Shakespeare's most notorious hand property, the small piece of cloth so reviled by Thomas Rymer. In a critically nuanced discussion of possession – as both a type of property relation and an affective response to an object – Yachnin delineates two historically different modes of wonder. Theatrical wonder, he notes, entails the largely collective experience of an audience who neither own nor are owned by the entertainment they are watching; by contrast, literary and critical wonder, in which "a possession ... possesses the possessor," discloses the antinomies of the modern individuated subject. *Othello* is an illuminating text in this regard, inasmuch as it is *both* theatrically wonderful *and* critical of how magical properties can generate wonder by "possessing" the individuated eye. The modern literary wonder-effects with which Shakespeare's plays have been associated since the nineteenth century, therefore, are anticipated by *Othello*'s representational strategies, including its deployment of the handkerchief. Thus, if Harris examines stage properties' pre-theatrical lives, and Wayne concentrates on their lives within a single play, Yachnin draws our attention to the *afterlives*, rhetorical as much as social, of the early modern theatre's objects. As such, his essay provides a fitting conclusion to the volume.

The essays in this volume display considerable diversity in subject matter, choice of plays, and methodological approach. What all the contributions to *Staged Properties in Early Modern English Drama* share, however, is a materialist investment in the complex, multifaceted dimensions of theatrical objects, those pieces of external "machinery" so dreaded by Lamb, Hazlitt and their post-Romantic successors. Machinery implies more than simple physicality; after all, it must also *move*, in space and in time. This quality of stage properties is even more suggestively captured by the early modern term "moveable," which designated personal as opposed to "real" property. The volume's title works to convey something of the movements of the Elizabethan stage's "moveables" and other properties. The latter were self-consciously *staged*, not just in the obvious sense of being deployed on stage, but also in the more general sense of moving through many *stages* of their theatrical and extra-theatrical lives. *Staged Properties in Early Modern English Drama* attends to these movements to acquire a greater understanding of not just the Renaissance English stage's objects, but also the plays, theatrical institutions, and larger social arenas through which these objects passed. The volume also demonstrates that as early modern stage properties migrated, so did the very notions of property that they materialized. In attending to such migrations, we hope our readers will agree that (contrary to the misgivings voiced in the Victorian *Spirit of the Times*, with which we began) stage properties are indeed worth "spouting" about.

NOTES

We wish to thank the Folger Institute for the award of a research fellowship, without which it would have been impossible to complete this introduction. We are grateful also to Doug Bruster, Andrew Sofer, Leslie Thomson, Henry Turner, and Val Wayne for invaluable comments and questions about earlier drafts.
1. For general discussions of the materials, machinery, and effects employed in masque spectacle, see Lily B. Campbell, *Scenes and Machines on the English Stage During the Renaissance: A Classical Revival* (Cambridge: Cambridge University Press, 1923), esp. pp. 145–94; Allardyce Nicoll, *Stuart Masques and the*

Renaissance Stage (New York: Benjamin Bloom, Inc., 1963), esp. pp. 54–214; and Stephen Orgel, *The Illusion of Power: Political Theater in the English Renaissance* (Berkeley, CA: University of California Press, 1975), pp. 26–36. The staging of the children's company plays seems often to have been only slightly less visually spectacular than that of the court masques. William Percy's *The Faery Pastoral*, written for the children's company of St. Paul's, contains an elaborate list of stage properties: "The Properties: Highest, aloft, and on the Top of the Musick Tree the Title The Faery Pastorall, Beneath him pind on Post of the Tree The Scene Elvida Forrest. Lowest of all over the Canopie NAPAITBODAION or Faery Chappell. A kiln of Brick. A Fowen Cott. A Hollowe Oake with vice of wood to shutt to. A Lowe well with Roape and Pullye. A Fourme of Turves. A Greene Bank being Pillowe to the Hed but. Lastly A Hole to creepe in and out" (quoted in E. K. Chambers, *The Elizabethan Stage*, 4 vols. [Oxford: Clarendon Press, 1923], vol. III, p. 137).

2. Samuel Rowlands, *The Letting of Humor's Blood in the Head-Vaine* (London, 1600), sig. A2; Leonard Digges, "Upon Master WILLIAM SHAKESPEARE, the *Deceased Authour, and his* POEMS," prefixed to the 1640 edition of Shakespeare's *Poems*, sig. *4; Simon Forman, "The Bocke of Plaies and Notes therof per formane for Common Policie," Bodleian Ashmole MS 208, fols. 200–7v.

3. William Shakespeare, *Pericles*, ed. F. D. Hoeniger (London: Methuen, 1963), 1.Chorus.4; Thomas Middleton, *No Wit, No Help Like a Woman's*, in Middleton, *A Mad World My Masters and Other Plays*, ed. Michael Taylor (Oxford: Oxford University Press, 1995), Prologue.3–4.

4. Thomas Dekker, *The Gull's Hornbook* (London, 1609 [Bristol, 1812]), pp. 140–1. Henslowe lists several garments with gold lace in his inventory of missing goods; see *Henslowe's Diary*, ed. R. A. Foakes and R. T. Rickert (Cambridge: Cambridge University Press, 1961), pp. 319–21.

5. On the centrality of costumes in the public theatre, see Jean MacIntyre and Garrett P. J. Epp, " 'Cloathes worth all the rest': costumes and proper- ties," in John D. Cox and David Scott Kastan (eds.), *A New History of Early English Drama* (New York: Columbia University Press, 1997), pp. 269–85; Peter Stallybrass, "Worn worlds: clothes and identity on the Renaissance stage," in Margreta De Grazia, Maureen Quilligan, and Peter Stallybrass (eds.), *Subject and Object in Renaissance Culture* (Cambridge: Cambridge Univer- sity Press, 1996), pp. 289–320; Ann Rosalind Jones and Peter Stallybrass, "The circulation of clothes and the making of the Renaissance theater," chapter 7 of their *Renaissance Clothing and the Materials of Memory* (Cambridge: Cambridge University Press, 2001).

6. Quoted in *Henslowe's Diary*, pp. 319–21. For a very useful discussion of what these items imply about Elizabethan staging practices, see Carol Chillington Rutter (ed.), *Documents of the Rose Playhouse* (Manchester: Manchester Univer- sity Press, 1984), pp. 133–5.

7. See Alan C. Dessen and Leslie Thomson, *A Dictionary of Stage Directions in English Drama, 1580–1642* (Cambridge: Cambridge University Press, 1999).

8. George Peele, *The Battle of Alcazar*, 2.3.536, 4.Ind.980.4–5, 5.Ind.1168–81; in Frank S. Hook and John Yoklavich (eds.), *The Dramatic Works of George Peele*, 3 vols. (New Haven: Yale University Press, 1961), vol. II, p. 338.

9. Christopher Marlowe, *Tamburlaine Parts One and Two*, ed. Anthony B. Dawson (London: A. & C. Black, 1997), 2.3.2.0.4.

10. *The Second Maiden's Tragedy*, ed. Anne Lancashire (Manchester: Manchester University Press, 1978), 4.3.0.2–3. We have opted here to use the title favored by the editors of the forthcoming *Collected Works of Thomas Middleton*.

11. Thomas Heywood, *The Golden Age*, 5.1; *The Iron Age Part Two*, 2.1; and *The Silver Age*, 2.1, 5.1, 4.1, in *Heywood's Dramatic Works*, 6 vols. (London: John Pearson, 1874), vol. III, pp. 78, 372, 122, 159, 155.

12. Ben Jonson, *Every Man in his Humour*, ed. J. W. Lever (Lincoln, NE: University of Nebraska Press, 1971), prologue, line 16.

13. John Higgins, *The Nomenclator, or Remembrancer of Adrianus Iunius Physician, Diuided in Two Tomes, Conteining Proper Names and Apt Termes for All Thinges Vnder Their Conuenient Titles* (London, 1585), sig. N7v.

14. *Tamburlaine*, ed. Dawson, 2.5.1.63–4. For a translation of Johannes De Witt's diary entry concerning the theatre, see *Theatre Notebook* 20 (1965–6): 73.

15. Thomas Middleton and Thomas Dekker, *The Roaring Girl*, ed. Paul A. Mulholland (Manchester: Manchester University Press, 1987), 1.2.14–24.

16. Jonas Barish, *The Antitheatrical Prejudice* (Berkeley, CA: University of Californa Press, 1978), p. 164.

17. See the *OED*, definition 3a, which cites Rosaline's remark about Berowne in *Love's Labour's Lost*: "His eye begets occasion for his wit, / For euery obiect that the one doth catch, / The other turns to a mirth-mouing iest" (2.1.70–2).

18. Stephen Gosson, *Playes Confuted in Fiue Actions, Prouing That They Are Not To Be Suffred in a Christian Common Weale* (London, 1582 [?]), sig. E7v.

19. Gosson, *Playes Confuted in Fiue Actions*, sigs. C6, E7.

20. William Prynne, *Histrio-Mastix: The Players Scourge, or Actors Tragaedie* (London, 1633), p. 890.

21. For discussions of Jonson's antipathy to stage machinery, properties, and special effects, see William A. Armstrong, "Ben Jonson and Jacobean stage-craft," in John Russell Brown and Bernard Harris (eds.), *Jacobean Theatre* (London: Edward Arnold, 1960), pp. 43–61; and Jonas Barish, "Jonson and the loathèd stage," chapter 5 of *The Antitheatrical Prejudice*, pp. 132–54.

22. Thomas Dekker, *The Magnificent Entertainment*, lines 154–9; in Fredson Bowers (ed.), *Dramatic Works*, 5 vols. (Cambridge: Cambridge University Press, 1953), vol. II, p. 258.

23. Arjun Appadurai, "Introduction: commodities and the politics of value," in Appadurai (ed.), *The Social Life of Things: Commodities in Cultural Perspective* (Cambridge: Cambridge University Press, 1986), pp. 3–63.

24. Thomas Rymer, *A Short View of Tragedy; It's Original, Excellency, and Corruption. With Some Reflections on Shakespear, and other Practitioners for the Stage* (London, 1693), pp. 111, 112, 135.

25. Alexander Pope (ed.), *The Works of Mr William Shakespear*, 6 vols. (London, 1723), vol. I, pp. xiii, v, xvii–xviii.
26. Samuel Taylor Coleridge, *Coleridge's Shakespearean Criticism*, 2 vols., ed. Thomas Middleton Raysor (London: Constable & Co., 1930), vol. I, p. 199.
27. Charles Lamb, *Charles Lamb on Shakespeare*, ed. Joan Coldwell (New York: Barnes and Noble, 1978), p. 41.
28. Coleridge, *Shakespearean Criticism*, vol. II, p. 97.
29. Coleridge, *Shakespearean Criticism*, vol. II, p. 85.
30. Lamb, *Charles Lamb on Shakespeare*, pp. 41, 39–40, 36.
31. William Hazlitt, *A View of the English Stage; Or, A Series of Dramatic Criticisms* (London, 1818), pp. 220, 223.
32. On the modernist anxiety about the relationship between human and machine, see Harold B. Segel, *Pinocchio's Progeny: Puppets, Marionettes, Automatons, and Robots in Modernist and Avant-Garde Drama* (Baltimore and London: Johns Hopkins University Press, 1995).
33. In an influential essay from 1908 on the staging of *Macbeth*, for example, Gordon Craig elevates the play's ineffable spirit-world at the expense of its material and visible objects: "if we take as the main and primary point for our consideration Macbeth and his wife, Banquo and his horse, and the thrones and the tables," he argues, then we "let these things blind us to the real issues of the drama" (Edward Gordon Craig, *Craig On Theater*, ed. J. Michael Walton [London: Methuen, 1983], p. 176). Craig proposed not an abandonment of the theatre, of course, but a radical reconsideration of its production and staging values; in this respect, he reworked Lamb's hostility to performance into an aggressively anti-representational stagecraft for which the Coleridgean Romantic construction of Shakespeare's empty stage provided the obvious model. For a particularly useful discussion of Gordon Craig's debts to Romantic antitheatricality, see Simon Shepherd and Peter Womack, *English Drama: A Cultural History* (Oxford: Blackwell, 1996), pp. 100–1. In a sequence of productions from 1912–14, Harley Granville-Barker likewise employed Shakespeare and his supposedly "bare boards" as the basis for a stagecraft opposed to Victorian pictorialism; see the introduction to his *Prefaces to Shakespeare* (London: Sidgwick & Jackson, 1927).
34. Granville-Barker, *Prefaces to Shakespeare*, pp. xvii–xviii. The echoes of early modern Puritan antitheatricality are even more apparent in his *Study of Drama* (Cambridge: Cambridge University Press, 1934): "we do the English drama in general, and Shakespeare himself in particular, a mere disservice by separating him from the rest of it, treating him as a god and building temples to him in which he only is to be worshipped. That sort of worship soon degenerates into suspicion; and in these very theatres we may note the familiar signs of this degeneracy already appearing. What else is this extravagantly decorative ritual, which the high priests – the producers – have now begun to elaborate there? Do they fear their disciples may soon be bored by the simple worship of the god himself?" (pp. 39–40).

35. Granville-Barker's antipathy to "decadent" ostentation and machinery as the traps to be avoided by a theatre of dematerialized subjects proved remarkably persistent in twentieth-century criticism, as Peter Brook's influential *The Empty Space* (1968) makes clear. Describing his ideal theatrical practice in opposition to the visually flamboyant, expensive productions of Broadway (which he revealingly terms "The Decadent Space"), Brook invokes the example of the Elizabethan stage. The latter, he claims, "was a neutral open platform – just a place with some doors." What distinguishes this theatre, Brook claims, is that it "not only allowed the playwright to roam the world, it also allowed him free passage from the world of action to the world of inner impressions." Brook's Romantic preference for "the world of inner impressions" entails, not surprisingly, a stage stripped of objects and high-tech machinery: "the closer we move to the true nakedness of theater, the closer we approach a stage that has a lightness and a range far beyond film or television." The telling metaphor of nakedness resonates with Brook's discussion of *King Lear*, a play which he directed in now legendary productions for first the stage and then the screen in the late sixties. *Lear* the play and Lear the character together provide Brook with the exemplary instance of a drama of the mind that must literally be stripped of all external trappings: "the only way to see as much as Lear is to go through Lear's mill... If we are interested, that is what we will find. Fancy dress, then, will be left far behind." To follow the examples of blind Gloucester or naked Lear and to see "truly," Brook suggests, audiences have to be undistracted by the sight of *things*, especially the "fancy" costumes, props and mechanized effects that are the hallmark of the mainstream professional theatre and cinema. See Peter Brook, *The Empty Space* (New York: Atheneum, 1978), pp. 86–7, 93, 94.

36. Walter Benjamin, *Ursprung des Deutschen Trauerspiels* (Berlin, 1928), p. 175; *The Origin of German Tragic Drama*, transl. John Osborne (London: Verso, 1985), p. 133. For a fascinating discussion of the machine as allegory of industrial production in modernist appropriations of Shakespeare, see Richard Halpern, "Hamletmachines," *Shakespeare Among the Moderns* (Ithaca, NY: Cornell University Press, 1997), pp. 227–88.

37. Benjamin, *Origin of German Tragic Drama*, pp. 132, 133. See also Benjamin, *Understanding Brecht* (London: Verso, 1987).

38. Take, for example, the remarks of George F. Reynolds, the otherwise meticulous historian of the Red Bull theatre: "Some people want an elaborate display of costumes and scenery, for which certainly the [Shakespearean] plays offer extraordinary opportunities... But a good many auditors, an increasing number, I think, care less for carloads of scenery and more for emphasis on what the text itself provides... elaborate scenery competes with the actor instead of supporting him. As this idea undoubtedly fits the Elizabethan projecting stage better than heavy upholstery would, it is the principle I shall accept as the more desirable without further discussion"; George F. Reynolds, *On Shakespeare's Stage: Four Lectures at Stratford-upon-Avon*

before the Summer School of the Shakespeare Institute and the Department of Intermural Studies, University of Birmingham, July, 1954, ed. Richard K. Knaub (Boulder, CO: University of Colorado Press, 1962), p. 19. Even a critic as judicious and as attuned to the exigencies of Elizabethan staging as M. C. Bradbrook invokes its properties in order to suggest a teleology that leads away from them. Surveying the props of *A Midsummer Night's Dream*, she remarks that the flowery bank stage property on which Titania lies is "an odd relic of realism" – as if the ineluctable pull in the history of drama and in Shakespeare's own writing is away from things; M. C. Bradbrook, *Elizabethan Stage Conditions: A Study of Their Place in the Interpretation of Shakespeare's Plays* (Cambridge: Cambridge University Press, 1932), p. 42.

39. Frances Teague, *Shakespeare's Speaking Properties* (Lewisburg, PA: Bucknell University Press, 1991), p. 10. Felix Bossonet, *The Function of Stage Properties in Christopher Marlowe's Plays* (Berne: Francke Verlag, 1978), likewise views props as portals into the fictive world of the plays. For an extensive discussion of the twentieth-century critical literature on stage properties, see Andrew Sofer, *The Stage Life of Props* (Ann Arbor: University of Michigan Press, forthcoming 2003), introduction. We are immeasurably grateful to Professor Sofer for sharing a draft of his important study with us in advance of its publication.

40. James L. Calderwood, *Shakespearean Metadrama* (Minneapolis: University of Minnesota Press, 1971), pp. 12-13. See also his more recent work, *The Properties of Othello* (Amherst, MA: University of Massachusetts Press, 1989).

41. Sofer, *Stage Life of Props*, introduction.

42. There is no shortage of materialist studies of the ideological formation of the modern subject in the plays of Shakespeare and his contemporaries. See Jonathan Dollimore, *Radical Tragedy: Religion, Ideology, and Power in the Drama of Shakespeare and his Contemporaries* (Brighton: Harvester Press, 1984); Francis Barker, *The Private Tremulous Body: Essays on Subjection* (London: Methuen, 1984); Catherine Belsey, *The Subject of Tragedy: Identity and Difference in Renaissance Drama* (London: Methuen, 1985). For recent studies of early modern subjectivity in early modern drama that dialogue with materialist methodology without necessarily cleaving to it, see Linda Charnes, *Notorious Identity: Materializing the Subject in Shakespeare* (Harvard: Harvard University Press, 1993); and Elizabeth Hanson, *Discovering the Renaissance Subject* (Cambridge: Cambridge University Press, 1998). There have also been a number of attempts to reclaim for Shakespeare's drama an authentic proto-modern interiority; see Katharine Eisaman Maus, *Inwardness and Theater in the English Renaissance* (Chicago: University of Chicago Press, 1995); Peter Iver Kaufman, *Prayer, Despair, and Drama: Elizabethan Introspection* (Chicago: University of Illinois Press, 1996); and Harold Bloom, *Shakespeare: The Invention of the Human* (New York: Riverhead Books, 1998).

43. Recent studies of early modern material culture include Patricia Fumerton, *Cultural Aesthetics: Renaissance Literature and the Practice of Social Ornament* (Chicago: University of Chicago Press, 1991); Lena Cowen Orlin, *Private Matters and Public Culture in Post-Reformation England* (Ithaca, NY: Cornell

University Press, 1994); Margreta De Grazia, Maureen Quilligan, and Peter Stallybrass (eds.), *Subject and Object in Renaissance Culture* (Cambridge: Cambridge University Press, 1996); Lisa Jardine, *Worldly Goods: A New History of the Renaissance* (New York: Nan A. Talese, 1996); Patricia Fumerton and Simon Hunt (eds.), *Renaissance Culture and the Everyday* (Philadelphia: University of Pennsylvania Press, 1999); Lena Cowen Orlin (ed.), *Material London* (Philadelphia: University of Pennsylvania Press, 2000); Jones and Stallybrass, *Renaissance Clothing*; and Natasha Korda, *Shakespeare's Domestic Economies: Gender and Property in Early Modern England* (Philadelphia: University of Pennsylvania Press, 2002).

44. See Douglas Bruster, *Drama and the Market in the Age of Shakespeare* (Cambridge: Cambridge University Press, 1992), esp. chapters 5 and 6. See also Andrew Sofer, "The skull on the Renaissance stage: imagination and the erotic life of props," *English Literary Renaissance* 28:1 (1998): 47–77.

45. Margreta de Grazia, "The ideology of superfluous things: *King Lear* as period piece," in *Subject and Object in Renaissance Culture*, pp. 17–42, esp. p. 21.

46. For a useful survey of the various strands of materialist criticism of Shakespeare (which, significantly, does not extend to scholarship on stagecraft or props), see Ivo Kamps, "Introduction," in Kamps (ed.), *Materialist Shakespeare: A History* (London: Verso, 1995), pp. 1–17.

47. See Clifford Geertz, *The Interpretation of Cultures* (London: Hutchinson, 1975). For critiques of the new historicism's debts to Geertz and functionalist cultural anthropology, see Vincent P. Pecora, "The limits of local knowledge," in H. Aram Veeser (ed.), *The New Historicism* (New York: Routledge, 1989), pp. 243–76; Jonathan Gil Harris, *Foreign Bodies and the Body Politic: Discourses of Social Pathology in Early Modern England* (Cambridge: Cambridge University Press, 1998), chapter 1; and Harris, "Historicizing Greenblatt's containment: the cold war, functionalism, and the origins of social pathology," in Jürgen Pieters (ed.), *Critical Self-Fashioning: Stephen Greenblatt and the New Historicism* (Frankfurt: Peter Lang, 1999), pp. 150–73.

48. See Michel de Certeau, *The Practice of Everyday Life*, transl. Steven Rendall (Berkeley, CA: University of California Press, 1984).

49. Both of these objects are discussed in Fumerton and Hunt (eds.), *Renaissance Culture and the Everyday*. On the buck-basket, see Richard Helgerson, "The buck basket, the witch, and the Queen of fairies: the women's world of Shakespeare's Windsor," pp. 162–82, esp. pp. 169–71; on embroidered books, see Lena Cowen Orlin, "Three ways to be invisible in the Renaissance: sex, reputation, and stitchery," pp. 183–203, esp. pp. 187–8. For a critique of qualitative object studies, see Jonathan Gil Harris, "The new new historicism's *Wunderkammer* of objects," *European Journal of English Studies* 4:2 (2000), 111–24.

50. See Joan Thirsk, *Economic Policy and Projects: The Development of a Consumer Society in Early Modern England* (Oxford: Clarendon Press, 1978); Susan Staves, *Married Women's Separate Property in England, 1660–1833* (Cambridge: Harvard University Press, 1990); Carole Shammas, *The Pre-Industrial Consumer in*

England and America (Oxford: Clarendon Press, 1990); and Amy Erickson, *Women and Property in Early Modern England* (London: Routledge, 1993).

51. See Natasha Korda, "Household property/stage property: Henslowe as pawnbroker," *Theatre Journal* 48:2 (1996): 185–96; Lena Cowen Orlin, "The performance of things in *The Taming of the Shrew*," *Yearbook of English Studies* 23 (1993): 167–88; Stallybrass, "Worn worlds."

52. Aristotle, "De Anima," *The Basic Works of Aristotle*, transl. Richard McKeon (New York: Random House, 1941), vol. II, p. 555; Karl Marx, *Writings of the Young Karl Marx on Philosophy and Society*, transl. Lloyd D. Easton and Kurt H. Guddat (New York: Doubleday, 1967), p. 400. For a more extended analysis of this opposition, see Jonathan Gil Harris, "Shakespeare's hair: staging the object of material culture," *Shakespeare Quarterly* 53:1 (2002): 479–91.

53. See, for example, Ann Rosalind Jones and Peter Stallybrass, *Renaissance Clothing and the Materials of Memory* (Cambridge: Cambridge University Press, 2000); Dympna Callaghan, "Looking well to linens: women and cultural production in *Othello* and Shakespeare's England," in Jean E. Howard and Scott Cutler Shershow (eds.), *Marxist Shakespeares* (London and New York: Routledge, 2001); see also essays by Harris, Korda and Stallybrass in this volume.

54. See, for example, Foucault's discussion of punishment's changing "objects" in *Discipline and Punish: The Birth of the Prison*, transl. Alan Sheridan (New York: Pantheon, 1977), pp. 17–18.

55. Richard Halpern, *The Poetics of Primitive Accumulation: English Renaissance Culture and the Genealogy of Capital* (Ithaca, NY: Cornell University Press, 1991); see especially chapter 1. See also Henry S. Turner, "Nashe's red herring: epistemologies of the commodity in *Lenten Stuffe*," *ELH* 68 (2001): 529–61. Through extraordinarily insightful readings of Thomas Nashe, Marx, and Foucault, Turner teases out a strain of Aristotelian hylozoism in changing Western conceptions of the material. In its emphasis on the discursively constituted nature of objects, this strain contrasts with the more positivist tendencies of much recent work on "material culture."

56. Stephen Greenblatt, "Shakespeare and the exorcists," in *Shakespearean Negotiations* (Berkeley, CA: University of California Press, 1988), esp. pp. 112–13. See also Peter Stallybrass, "Worn worlds," which examines the transmigrations of costumes between the institutions of the church and the theatre in light of Greenblatt's essay. The mode of analysis we are sketching here is well illustrated by Stallybrass's observation that in clothes, "Memories are literally *worn* . . . clothes . . . both *are* material presences and they *encode* other material and immaterial presences" (p. 312).

57. Appadurai, "Introduction," in *The Social Life of Things*, pp. 34, 5.

58. Frances Teague, for example, chooses to employ another (and admittedly "highly subjective") set of categories: light properties, weapon or war gear, documents, riches or gifts, tokens of a character, and "other." See *Shakespeare's Talking Properties*, p. 157.

PART I

Histories

CHAPTER 2

Properties of skill: product placement in early English artisanal drama

Jonathan Gil Harris

> But lo, an horne spone that have I here,
> And it will herbar fourty pese,
> This will I giffe you with gud chere.
> Slike novelté may noght disease.
> *The Chandlers' Play of the Shepherds*, York
> Cycle, Play 15, lines 124–7[1]

> Here, take this pair of shoes cut out by Hodge,
> Stitched by my fellow Firk, seamed by myself,
> Made up and pinked with letters for thy name.
> Thomas Dekker, *The Shoemaker's Holiday*,
> 1.232–4[2]

> We specialize in the promotion & placement of products on PRIME
> TIME TV and in FEATURE FILMS giving you Big Time Exposure
> at extremely low costs . . . Hollywood International Placements, Inc.
> can *MAKE YOUR PRODUCT A STAR!* With H. I. P. you have the
> opportunity to have your product appear in scenes with famous
> stars, or signage, store display, or even get hands on usage with the
> Big Names in showbiz.
> Internet advertisement for product placement agency[3]

How might one read the props of the early English stage in accordance
with the root sense of the term – that is, as types of property? I offer
one such reading here. In this essay, I argue that the multiple, historically
shifting forms of property embodied by early English stage properties are
made visible through metatheatrical episodes that, in certain respects,
anticipate the modern practice of product placement.

It might seem anachronistic to speak of product placement – the deliberate insertion of brand-name products into screen entertainments
as a form of advertising – in early English drama. The practice is un-
mistakably a late twentieth-century development, involving institutions
that simply did not exist in Shakespeare's England: the television and

film entertainment industry, the brand-name manufacturer and retailer, and the advertising agency. Still, to regard product placement merely as the bastard offspring of showbiz and corporate capitalism also works to conceal its long, complicated pre-history. The above advertisement for Hollywood International Placements, Inc. highlights much of what often gets parenthesized in textually oriented criticism of drama – i.e. that multiple parties tend to have commercial interests at stake in the entertainment industry; that the products used in its entertainments play an important double role in promoting those interests, functioning not only as dramatic accessories for characters, but also as cost-effective advertisements for corporate suppliers; and that these products therefore have "social lives," to use Arjun Appadurai's resonant phrase,[4] which precede and outlast their acquisition by propmasters, scenic decorators, and costume designers. Indeed, the very practice of product placement depends on the spectacular foregrounding of this last process. For the practice to work, audiences need to recognize that the product has a life prior to the drama (i.e. that it exists in the real world, as does its corporate supplier), and to fantasize about the extension of that life after the show is over (i.e. about their purchase or consumption of the product, if not of the actual prop itself). This by no means amounts, of course, to a full awareness of either the material base of capitalist production or the social life of the prop. But the placed product does bring to at least partial visibility the otherwise hidden economic contexts of the entertainments in which it is deployed. Many early English stage properties, I shall argue, perform a similar function.

In what follows, I consider how certain props disrupt the fields of representation in which they appear by disclosing larger social lives that extend beyond the stage. Theatre historians have tended to read the props of early English theatre simply in terms of their phenomenological or symbolic dimensions within individual plays, neglecting their material pre- and post-stage histories.[5] Yet the props referred to in my first two epigraphs do more than serve their respective play-scripts as simply functional accessories to the dramatic illusion. The prop in each passage – a horn spoon that can fit forty peas, a pair of shoes customized to bear the name of its owner – is ceremoniously offered as a gift not only to a specific character, but also to a more generalized audience outside the play whose interest is pricked by such "novelté," in the words of the York Chandlers' play, that "may noght disease." Each passage thus has the force of an advertisement, a commercial break that gestures beyond the play to an extra-theatrical world of goods, producers, and consumers.

But if these passages are advertisements, what exactly do they advertise? The prop-product itself? Its manufacturers? Or something altogether different? Does it even make sense to lump together late medieval and early modern props, whose social as well as dramatic lives often trace quite different trajectories?

Such metatheatrical advertisements, I shall argue, entail primarily a problematic of property. What the passages from the York Chandlers' play and *The Shoemaker's Holiday* bring to visibility are two competing yet overlapping conceptions of property, the outlines of which are legible in the social and dramatic lives of artisanal stage properties from late medieval and Elizabethan theatre: the familiar notion of property as individuated commodity and/or capital *asset*; but also, just as importantly, the more elusive notion of property as *membership* within a corporate body.

PROPERTY AND IDENTITY

Any discussion of early English notions of property runs the risk of un-critically replicating the customary modern equation of property with privately owned things, summed up in John Locke's formula of "life, liberty and estate."[6] Notions of private property were articulated long before Locke, of course, and indeed loom large in the conceptual land-scape of Elizabethan and Jacobean drama as well as in the aspirations and career-paths of the theatre companies' investors and sharers. But there were other, quite different formulations of property also in circulation in Shakespeare's culture, some of which played a crucial role in the conceptualization of personal and social identity both on- and offstage.[7]

In contrast to those Gloucesters, Moroccos, and Navarres whose names and identities are determined by their kingdoms or private landed property, there is a small subset of Shakespearean characters whose titles are bound not to estate, but to trade. The names of Jack Cade's artisan supporters in *Henry VI Part Two*, Smith the Weaver and Dick the Butcher, find counterparts in the so-called rude mechanicals of *A Midsummer Night's Dream*. The latter sextet illustrates most clearly the interdependence of identity and vocation. Each character's name is not only con-joined with his craft; it is also to a large extent determined, as numerous commentators have pointed out, by its qualities, tools and products. So Snug the Joiner's name is suggested by his artisanal speciality ("snug" is a term from woodworking suggesting "tightly fitting"), as are the names of Snout the Tinker ("snout" was a common pronunciation of the "spout" of kettles or teapots, repaired by tinkers), Starveling the Tailor (tailors were proverbially skinny), Quince the Carpenter ("quoins" were wooden wedge tools), Flute the Bellows-Mender ("flutes" were the nozzles of bellows), and even Bottom the Weaver ("bottoms" were the cores around which skeins of wool were wound).[8]

What conceptions of property underwrite the identities of Shakespeare's artisanal characters? From our post-Lockean perspective, it is easy to read their names as evidence of early modern English identity's basis in yet another form of private property: an individual's labor, or to use the more customary early modern term, skill.[9] But the property of skill and the nomenclature that attached to it were not necessarily reliable indicators of one's occupation. Shakespeare's father, for example, was a glover, but seems to have rarely practiced the trade. Similarly, many of Shakespeare's fellow actors and playwrights professed a skill which they seldom, if ever, practiced. Robert Armin and John Lowin of the King's Men were officially goldsmiths; Ben Jonson acquired through patrimony his freedom as a bricklayer. In fact it was particularly common for London freemen of various livery companies to engage in trades other than their nominal ones: certain fishmongers were known to deal in textiles, and grocers in eye-glass manufacture. This was a longstanding phenomenon. Although artificers' ordinances technically restricted artisans to a single trade, there are many examples of medieval craftspeople practising a vocation other than the one they officially professed.[10]

The soubriquets "weaver," "baker," or "goldsmith" could possess as little descriptive accuracy concerning the nature of one's private labor, therefore, as the surnames that these trades have bequeathed Anglophone cultures. The identity that possession of skill conferred was of an altogether different order from the Lockean individuated identity commensurate with the private ownership of life, liberty, and estate – or labor. It was informed instead by a conception of property rooted in the craft-guild culture, and derived from public membership or association within a corporate body. As Margaret R. Somers explains, property in skill – or "mystery," as it was termed in the legal ordinances of the time – was "a *relational practice* rather than an individual attribute. Not the *capacity* to work a trade but the *right* to do so was endowed by virtue of membership in a skilled community."[11] To be known as Bottom the Weaver, therefore, Nick Bottom did not have to spend his days working with looms and textiles. Indeed, during the sixteenth century the Weavers of Coventry admitted to their fraternity many people who exclusively practiced other crafts, including a baker, a barber, a butcher, and the prior of the city.[12] Bottom's trade title announced simply that he possessed the *right* to practice the craft (an entitlement often obtained through a seven-year period of apprenticeship, but on many occasions also through inheritance, marriage to a master's widow, or purchase), and, more importantly, to associate with and be guaranteed the privileges, including the "freedom," of the other members of the Weavers' guild. In this respect, the notions of property and liberty implicit in the possession of skill were quite distinct from their classical Lockean formulations, inasmuch as they were not predicated on private autonomy from any larger public entity. Instead, as Anthony Black observes, in a guild "one achieved liberty *by belonging to* this kind of group."[13]

Thanks to the growth of merchant capital and amalgamated trading companies, the wider availability of imported goods, and the depletion of socio-religious corporate life throughout the country, the culture of the craft guilds was slowly unraveling in late sixteenth-century England, and with it the notion of property as public membership. This development is evident in the plays of Shakespeare, where the idea of the guild is striking for its virtual absence. When it does appear, it is almost always subjected to critical, even derisive treatment – witness, for example, the daft claims of decidedly anti-social characters such as Abhorson the Executioner in *Measure for Measure* and the Banditti of *Timon of Athens* that their occupations possess the status of a "mystery."[14] Such satiric opprobrium may well hint at the class prejudices of a playwright who, unlike many of his fellow actors, never publicly professed any artisanal skill or guild affiliation. In contrast to the wills of his fellow players, which often pair their names with their nominal skills, Shakespeare's will identifies him as William Shakespeare, Gent., highlighting the title he earned after his acquisition of a family coat of arms in 1597 (or, more accurately, after the death of his father, from whom he technically inherited the title in 1601). At the same time as the latter property indicates his purchased public membership within a class into which he was not born, the purchase itself (probably costing in excess of £100) signifies the social power afforded him by his private ownership of capital assets – shares, holdings, tax portions, estates – which testify in turn to the shifting notions of property that accompanied the transformation of England's political economy during the sixteenth century.

Will Shakespeare Gent.'s ambivalent social identity, poised at the cusp between public membership and private proprietorship, is perhaps not unconnected to the disjunctive social and economic organization of the joint-stock company to which he belonged for much of his adult life. On the one hand, the King's Men modelled certain aspects of their structure and activity on the guilds, as is made clear by the franchise they were awarded by King James in 1603 to "practice the Arte and faculty of playinge" – terms that recall the language of craft ordinances.[15] The company also adopted livery that resembled that of artisanal companies: the scarlet robes of the King's Men were reminiscent of the livery worn by the London Cordwainers' Company, for example. Yet the theatre companies also made a conscious break with guild practices, though less in their nominal neo-feudal subservience to a lord than in their attitudes to and use of property. The sizeable capital ventures and investments of the theatre companies' impresarios, such as Robert Keysar and Philip Henslowe, or of leading actor-sharers, such as Edward Alleyn and Shakespeare, mark a decisive shift in priorities from those of guild culture: exercising artisanal property in skill had become secondary to the accumulation of convertible private assets. Investment in private property did not always amount to a complete escape from the relational property of corporate membership, however. Actor-sharers often found it useful to retain their official artisanal affiliations, particularly as a means of legitimizing master/apprentice relations with boy-actors that would otherwise have been illegal.[16] The rival notions of property as membership and asset thus shed light not only on the contradictory structures of the theatre companies, but also on the frequently disjunctive activities and affiliations of the latter's principal figures.

This mutual implication of notions of property and the institution of the theatre finds particularly clear expression, I will argue, in the nature and use of early English stage properties. To help clarify the relations between props and property, I have deliberately confined my discussion to two seemingly disparate forms of drama: the artisanally performed Corpus Christi mystery play of the fifteenth and sixteenth centuries, and the so-called citizen comedy of the 1590s. In choosing this twin focus, I have sought also to problematize the conventional divisions, of geography as much as period, that organize and obscure the study of early English drama. The putatively "medieval" mystery play of the provinces is rarely if ever examined in conjunction with the "early modern" commercial drama of London.[17] The two types of entertainment are less straightforwardly unconnected than such tidy period designations might suggest, however, and not just because the mysteries were still annually performed in some parts of England when the first permanent playhouses were built in the nation's capital. Just as importantly, the Corpus Christi entertainments offer an indispensable set of dramatic and cultural codes with which to decipher the complex, conflicted practices of product placement and notions of property in an artisanally themed play such as Thomas Dekker's *The Shoemaker's Holiday*.

Corporate thought was deeply engrained in late medieval English culture.[18] Its religious roots are evident in the sacrament of the Eucharist, as well as St. Paul's letter to the Corinthians, which develops the conceit of the church as a harmonious body comprised of a rigid hierarchy of diverse members. But its manifestations weren't simply religious, as the longstanding tradition of the lay guild or fraternity testifies. Although the latter was appropriated by Christianity – ecclesiastical guilds were widespread throughout medieval England – the tradition was in many ways a secular one, providing one of the more effective means by which the increasingly powerful urban merchant and manufacturing classes declared their social exclusivity and safeguarded their economic interests. Nevertheless, even the trade guilds almost invariably had a religious character. Numerous craft fraternities were simultaneously constituted as religious guilds: in York, for example, the Carpenters' guild was known as the Holy Fraternity of the Resurrection, and that of the Weavers as the Guild of the Blessed Virgin Mary; in Coventry, the Fullers first came together as the Guild of the Nativity.[19]

Perhaps the clearest illustration of late medieval corporate thought and its yoking of religious and lay association is provided by the summer feast of Corpus Christi, instituted throughout England after 1317, and celebrated until the middle of the sixteenth century.[20] The festival's climactic ceremony, in which the Host was transported around the boundaries of the town accompanied by a substantial civic procession, entailed the cultural production of symbolic bodies within bodies, each linked to the others by a principle of cosmic similitude. Within the hierarchically ordered sacramental body of Christ, or the Church, was subsumed the body of the community, divided into ecclesiastical, civic dignitary, and artisanal sections. The latter was further subdivided into the smaller corporate units of distinct craft guilds, each of which marched (often in ascending order of status) as an identifiable group. Importantly, the procession sought also to accommodate within the synchronic body of Christ the diachronic body of sacred history: in many Corpus Christi celebrations, guild-operated pageant wagons depicting *tableaux vivants* of episodes from Creation to Doomsday were wheeled around the town as part of the procession. These pageant tableaux were related to but distinct from the extended dramas that have come to be known as the Corpus Christi cycle plays, which were likewise "put forth" – i.e. produced and acted – by the craft guilds, and which dramatized in considerably expanded detail the biblical episodes presented in the procession.

There has been considerable debate about the longer Corpus Christi guild plays and the details of their production. It is unclear whether the pageant wagons that featured in the civic processions were used also for the performance of the cycle plays; although many theatre historians have assumed this to be the case, some have suggested that a morass of staging complications would have arisen had the plays been performed on them. There has been disagreement also over whether the cycle plays were always performed in a variety of "stations" around a town, as was once customarily assumed, or on one stage.[21] Regardless of these disputes, however, a general claim may still be ventured about the various dramatic conventions of the Corpus Christi festival in its indubitably multiple local manifestations: the civic processions, the *tableaux vivants*, and the cycle dramas alike constituted public performances of the property of corporate membership – membership of guild, community, church, and sacred history.

The property of skill as a species of corporate membership was prominently on display during the Corpus Christi festival. In virtually every town, guilds adopted appropriate visual symbols to wear or carry in the civic procession to demonstrate the nature of their craft. Hence each guild sported its own distinctive livery and carried banners or signs proclaiming its identity or mystery.[22] But as theatre historians have increasingly come to recognize, the pageant tableau or cycle-play episode a guild performed could be just as if not more instrumental in displaying the property of its mystery. In a handful of cases, what Glynne Wickham has termed the "trade symbolism" of the pageant was quite transparent: for example, guilds associated with sailing, the sea, or water would commonly be assigned the story of Noah, Goldsmiths the episode of the Magi, and Bakers the Last Supper pageants. In each of these instances, Anne Higgins has surmised, ordinary artisanal life would be mapped onto the events of sacred history, and vice versa, to illustrate the cosmic continuum linking all facets of creation.[23]

The practice of assigning episodes to guilds based on links between the two was far more widespread than these few, and perhaps untypically clear-cut, instances might suggest: even the most seemingly arbitrary assignations often reveal upon closer inspection a significant link between episode and craft. In several cases, the point of connection was between the guild's religious identity and the episode in question. Hence in both York and Beverley, the Barbers' Guilds, traditionally associated with John the Baptist, presented the Baptism of Christ; the Worsted Weavers of Norwich, formerly known as the guild of the Holy Ghost, produced a pageant dramatizing that religious theme; and the Nativity Guild of the Coventry Fullers presented the Birth of Christ. In most instances, however, the connection linking an episode to a guild seems to have resided less in the latter's conventional religious associations than in the subtle features and foibles of its occupation. Thus in York, the Waterleaders presented a small scene of Christ washing the feet of the apostles; and in Chester, Wakefield, and York, guilds of Tanners and Barkers – who were notorious for the diabolically sulphurous odors generated by their treatment of leather and bark – presented the Fall of the Angels into Hell.[24] These various forms of connection between guild and episode hint at how the so-called mystery play was a production not only *by* a mystery, or guild, but also *of* a mystery, or property of skill and association. The performance of the latter, it has to be stressed, rarely amounted to a demystification of the mystery itself. There was little or no disclosure of the "secrets" of a craft; mystery plays were not inductions into how to spin wool, make nails, or treat leather. What tended to be divulged was not the craft's processes of *production*, but its *products*.[25]

Although theatre historians have begun to explain the connections between guilds and the episodes they performed, more work needs to be done on the privileged role the props of the pageant tableaux and cycle dramas played in establishing these connections – multiple connections between not just the guild and the historical episode, but also the guild and the community as well as the guild and the *corpus mysterium* of Christ or church. Any prop in the Corpus Christi cycle plays potentially had the status of a visual pun, functioning as a multivalent metonymy for a cluster of distinct but interrelated corporate structures. The bread of the Bakers' Last Supper pageants, for example, was at one and the same time the contemporary product of skilled labor by English artisans, the historical food shared by Christ with his disciples, and the eternal sacrament of the Eucharist; it thus materialized the Bakers' triple property in their mystery of baking, in sacred history, and in the body of Christ. When the Bakers of Chester flung their loaves into the audience at the end of their play, these three properties were supplemented by a fourth that was already implicit in the other Last Supper episodes: with what amounted to a secular recoding of the sacrament of the Eucharist – sharing their bread in communal solidarity with their fellow townspeople – the Chester Bakers asserted their guild's property of membership within the corporate body of their town.[26] In this pageant, therefore, the stage property was the fulcrum upon which the guild's corporate property of skill was interarticulated with the bodies of history, church and community.

As the example of the Bakers' pageants shows, a crucial precondition for this interarticulation was the cycle play spectators' awareness of the stage property's social life – that is, their recognition that the prop was not simply an object belonging to and defined by the dramatic illusion of the pageant or play, but also a real product with a distinctive offstage history, function, and owner. The possibility of such recognition was doubtless a spur to those people and institutions who, in arguably self-interested or self-advertising gestures that anticipate the modern practice of product placement, annually furnished the craft pageants with their unique properties. In the Lincoln civic processions, for example, the craft pageants were decked out in sumptuous ornaments temporarily loaned, with considerable *éclat*, by the local parish churches.[27] On rare occasions the town corporation itself assumed responsibility for the supply of a guild's props. In Beverley, one John Arras of the Hairers' guild was bonded to return upon his death sundry properties to the corporation from his craft's pageant of Paradise, including "j karre, viij hespis, xviij stapiloz, ij visers, ij wenges angli, j firsparr, j worme, ij paria caligarum linearum [linen stockings], ij paria camisarum [shirts], j gladius [sword]."[28] The document recording this bond implies not only that the Beverley town council regarded the Hairers' pageant and stage properties as valuable possessions to which it could forcefully lay claim, but – more importantly – that it believed their value to subsist less in their intrinsic worth than in their annual display as advertisements of the corporation's wealth and munificence. Indeed, municipal records from elsewhere in England often betray the assumption that high-quality stage properties, even if not owned or supplied by the corporation itself, served to glorify the town. When the Goldsmiths of York complained in 1432 about the heavy financial burden of presenting their two pageants, the city corporation acknowledged in its subsequent ordinance that the Goldsmiths had been under pressure to "produce . . . and play [the pageants] at their own expense . . . in the more lavish manner which is seemly for the praise of the city."[29]

The instance of the York Goldsmiths is in some ways typical, as most towns expected the crafts to "produce . . . and play at their own expense." This was a financially burdensome and often crippling charge. But it was not always an unwelcome one. The pageant wagon, which was in virtually all cases purchased, stocked, and maintained by the guild who exhibited it in the procession, often served as a convenient display case for that guild's skill, materialized in its own tools and products. For example, the Smiths of Coventry supplied various kinds of ironwork for their pageant of the Passion, including iron weapons for spear bearers; they also commissioned one of their fellows in the mid-sixteenth century to fashion "a new hoke to hange Judas," which, as Anne Higgins notes, constituted a spectacular if somewhat macabre way of displaying their products.[30] The stage properties of the York Mercers' pageant of Doomsday were even more eye-catching and costly: in addition to elaborate ironwork and mechanical flying angels, the inventory of their pageant stock taken in 1433 lists expensive mercer's goods ranging from shirts, stockings, wigs, and albs to colored cloth hangings for sunbeams, clouds, and stars – items for which their guild account books regularly document exorbitant annual payments to repair or replace.[31] Expensive guild-specific stage properties could also be supplied by individual benefactors. In 1446, for example, William Revetour willed a gilded crown as well as a gilded and enameled belt to the Girdlers of York for their pageant, the Slaughter of the Innocents.[32] Nothing about the pageant or the play-text itself suggests that the work or properties of girdlers were crucial to the performance. But Revetour's gift, typical of the products of the more well-to-do girdlers,[33] indicates that he – like his counterparts in the Coventry Smiths' and York Mercers' guilds – regarded his craft's pageant wagon less as the location for the performance of a specific biblical episode than as a repository for the display of the guild's property in skill.

To modern eyes, such forthright instances of commercial self-promotion in a nominally sacred context can possess an almost comic dimension. This might be especially the case with the York cycle, whose stage properties on a number of occasions advertise artisanal skill in ways that seem deliberately to disrupt or profane the biblical episode in which they appear, not to mention the characters who use them. The script of the Mariners' play of Noah, for example, calls anachronistically for a lead depth gauge so Noah can measure the depth of the flood; this prop, a relatively recent and sophisticated invention, could have drawn attention to itself as a newfangled device used exclusively by fifteenth-century English mariners and unknown to biblical sailors like Noah and his sons.[34] More infamously, the performance of Christ's Crucifixion, produced by the Pinners and Latteners (makers of pins and nails), featured hammer- and nail-wielding artisans playing the parts of soldiers who repeatedly congratulate themselves on their skill as they cheerily botch the job of nailing Christ to the cross – prompting from Jesus the memorable observation, "What they wirke wotte they noght."[35] A proto-Brechtian estrangement effect is generated in both plays, stemming from a calculated, momentary tension between contemporary artisanal actor and historical biblical episode. Such tension brings into clear focus the guild's property in skill, materialized in the stage property.

A similar estrangement effect was quite possibly deployed during the performance of the York Chandlers' play of the Shepherds. At play's end, one of the "shepherds" offers the baby Jesus an unusual version of the traditional christening spoon:

> Ye are a prince with-outen pere;
> I have no presentte that you may plees.
> But lo, an horne spone that have I here,
> And it will herbar fourty pese,
> This will I giffe you with gud chere.
> Slike novelté may noght disease.[36]

This gargantuan "horne spone," big enough to fit forty peas, hardly corresponds to any utensil that a shepherd would use in the course of his labor, let alone possess. But it might bear more than a passing resemblance to the ladle customarily used by a chandler in either of two activities – the basting of vertical wicks with wax, and the making of sauces, an activity with which candlemakers were associated.[37] Although the York Chandlers were distinguished from the Saucemakers, they certainly were accustomed to using ladles in the manufacture of candles: the widow Edonee Croxton was willed by her candlemaking husband the tools of his trade in 1480, including a waxboard, waxpan, moulds, and several ladles.[38] In the performance of the Chandlers' play, therefore, the shepherd who presents the christening gift to Jesus may have been – for a brief but significant moment – anamorphically reconstituted by spectators as a York candlemaker displaying a distinctive tool of his trade. The placed product on display, in other words, was not the candlemaker's produce *per se*, but his corporate property in skill.

Theatre historians have disagreed about whether such potentially disruptive displays of artisanal identity and property were indeed integral to the socio-religious corporate values that the Corpus Christi festival ostensibly celebrated, or whether they were simply instances of brazen self-promotion.[39] They were arguably both. The craft guilds may have used their pageant wagons as shop-window displays for their trades in ways that jarred with as well as complemented the biblical episodes they performed; but even their most seemingly irreligious displays of artisanal wares were already licensed by the festival's logic, which extolled the sacred properties of skill and corporate membership.[40] That is not to say, however, that the guilds' performances were dictated by this logic alone. The artisans had agency, as limited as it might have been, and their participation in the festival processions, pageants, and plays arguably served their interests as well as those of the town corporations or the church authorities. Whatever willingness they might have had to engage in conspicuous, often debilitatingly expensive displays of property – both the immaterial property of skill or membership and the material tools and merchandise of their crafts – was surely predicated on the expectation of *profit*: primarily cultural profit, in the guise of consolidated or boosted social status, but perhaps on occasion indirect financial profit as well, thanks to greater community awareness of their skills, tools, and related products.[41] Within the complex cultural and economic apparatus that surrounded the performance of the mystery pageants and plays, therefore, one may glimpse a potential for commercial gain arising from a guild's investment in stage properties as rudimentary capital – a potential which anticipates, even as it contrasts, both a later mode of economic production and a different conception of property.

FREEBOOTER PROPERTIES (BROUGHT TO YOU BY SHOES, MADE UP AND PINKED WITH LETTERS FOR THY NAME)

The exhibition of stage properties for the express purpose of commercial profit was in many ways one of the hallmarks of the professional Elizabethan theatre, and what distinguished it from the Corpus Christi civic spectacles. In the latter, financial gain was simply a potential consequence rather than a *raison d'être*; although a staggering amount of money could be spent on the stock and maintenance of a pageant, craft guilds probably never expected, and certainly never depended on, direct remuneration from paying audiences to defray their production costs.[42] By contrast, the entrepreneurs and player-sharers who sank money into the first permanent theatres did so in the hope that they would recoup their investments several-fold from the sale of entertainment as a desirable leisure commodity. Props played a crucial role in this sale. The prospect of viewing dazzlingly opulent properties – gilded crowns, lavish gowns, gaping hellmouths – doubtless helped lure many audience members and their money to the theatres, with the consequence that the professional companies' props and costumes became in a very real sense capital assets.[43] In some cases, stage properties were evidently regarded as more valuable assets than the play-scripts themselves. Much has been made of the fact that companies who paid £6 commissions for new works could also pay in excess of £20 for a single new costume. E. K. Chambers has estimated that Philip Henslowe spent a total of £1,317 on costumes and props between the years 1597 and 1603; Francis Langley, owner of the Swan Theatre, claimed to have spent in *one year* approximately £300 on playing stock.[44]

In the process, stage properties changed – although not so much in kind, for many types of prop or costume customarily used in the mystery plays (e.g. albs, beards, crowns, daggers, gloves) also appeared in the first professional playhouses. Rather, the change occurred in two more intangible yet no less significant dimensions: the nature of the prop's value, and the type of property it embodied. First, whereas the value of most Corpus Christi pageant stock resided largely in what Igor Kopytoff would term its "singular" status – that is, its exclusive use in a solitary annual play or pageant as the material manifestation of a craft's unique property in skill[45] – the stock of the professional theatre company or player frequently acquired value from not just its audience-drawing power, but also the multiple uses to which it could be put in a potentially limitless number of plays. Although many of the items listed in Henslowe's inventory of the Admiral's Men's playing stock are designated as properties pertaining to a character from a specific play (e.g. "owld Mahemetes head," "a cauderme for the Jewe," "Tamerlanes breches of crymson vellvet"), most additions to a company's or player's stock would surely have been purchased with the expectation that they would be employed in more than one production.[46]

Second, whereas the mystery play often presumed a direct link between the artisanal actor and the stage property – thereby evincing the *donné* of feudalism that petty producers own their tools of production – props in the professional playhouses tended to be alienated commodities, displayed not by their producers but by middlemen, professional actors. Hence the artisanal phase of props' pre-stage lives was far less likely to be an explicit feature of either play-scripts or performances in the professional theatre; the relational property of corporate association implicit in the display of craft-pageant props was for the most part eclipsed by the individuated property of private ownership – whether that of the stage-character, the company, the syndicate impresario, or, in rare cases, the player.[47]

These twin developments do not mean, however, that the props of the professional playhouses were *simply* capital assets within an emergent market economy or fledgling entertainment industry. Just as the props of the mystery plays potentially exceeded the bounds of the corporatist symbolic economy and the artisanal mode of production that they were nominally enlisted to serve and celebrate, so the props of the Elizabethan stage could participate within multiple systems of value, property and identity. This was particularly the case with props in productions of plays that involved artisanal characters and themes, thereby potentially pitting the emergent conception of property as privately owned capital asset against its residual relational formulation. I will turn now to one such play, Thomas Dekker's *The Shoemaker's Holiday*, in order to show how both its props and its related assumptions about property demonstrate this contest.

The Shoemaker's Holiday was the first of two artisan-themed citizen comedies produced by Philip Henslowe's syndicate in 1599–1600; the other was Thomas Heywood's *The Four Prentices of London*. Both plays can be viewed as shrewd attempts by the Admiral's Men to target and profit from London's large number of theatregoing craftsmen, especially prentices, although there is no reason why upper-class theatregoers might not have been attracted to these plays too.[48] On paper, there is much about Dekker's play that would appear to recommend itself to a diverse audience: in telling the story of Master Shoemaker Simon Eyre's acquisition of enormous wealth and the mayoralty of London, together with the tale of the artisanally disguised aristocrat Roland Lacy and his daring courtship of the bourgeois Rose, *The Shoemaker's Holiday* enacts a Dick Whittington-esque fantasy where craftsmen are rewarded with social advancement, and the nobility lend their approval to the virtues and accomplishments of an increasingly powerful yet ardently royalist manufacturing class. The play's seeming celebration of artisanal life has been noted and saluted by a number of commentators.[49] What hasn't been remarked upon, though, is how this celebration entails conceptions of property and presentations of props which in their bald outlines closely resemble those of the mystery plays. Such an overlap might be at first glance a little surprising: Thomas Dekker was born and bred in a London that had no Corpus Christi cycle-play tradition.[50] As I have argued, however, the latter was but one manifestation of the larger socio-religious corporate culture of late medieval England, in which the

notion of property as membership was fundamental. Although it was un-
dergoing considerable transformation, corporate culture was still strong
in Elizabethan London, where affiliated artisans constituted a sizeable
proportion of the free citizenry, and membership of merchant or livery
companies often conferred considerable social and political privileges.[51]

The property of skill is crucial to the play-world of *The Shoemaker's
Holiday*. Upon meeting Roland, who is disguised as a Dutch shoemaker,
Simon Eyre asks him whether he possesses "any skill in the mystery
of cordwainers" (4.87–8). Eyre's question is about more than simple
artisanal knowledge; in this scene and throughout the play, fellowship
or fraternity is repeatedly emphasized as the *sine qua non* of skill. Thus
Eyre's foreman Roger Hodge addresses lame Ralph, newly returned
from the wars in France, as "brother of our trade" (10.60); the journey-
man Firk, upon seeing the disguised Roland for the first time, calls him
"a brother of the Gentle Craft" (4.45–6) – a demonstration of his generous, if historically improbable, allegiance to the bonds of craft across
national boundaries;[52] and when Firk is offered a bribe by Oatley to disclose Roland's whereabouts, he exclaims: "No point. Shall I betray my
brother? No. Shall I prove Judas to Hans? No. Shall I cry treason to my
corporation? No" (16.95–97). These remarks align the property of mystery with a network of unbreakable fraternal relations, an alignment most
explicit in the shoemakers' concluding toast to Eyre and "incomprehensible good fellowship" (18.207) – a phrase that pointedly highlights the
secret, ineffable nature of the guild's "mystery."

Such displays of "incomprehensible good fellowship" are often
couched in corporate terms. Eyre addresses his workers as "you arms of
my trade, you pillars of my profession" (7.61–2); Hodge, leading a posse
of shoemakers who intercept the conniving Hammon as he attempts to
marry their fellow Ralph's "widow" Jane, identifies his men as "the brave
bloods of the shoemakers" (18.1–2), sworn to protect each other from all
outside threats. Indeed, organic analogy characterizes much of Eyre's
thinking: he several times refers to his wife Margery as his "midriff."
These corporate figures, while typical of late medieval artisanal culture
in general, might have been regarded as particularly appropriate for the
shoemakers. In his popular pamphlet about the history of English shoemakers, *The Pleasant and Princely History of the Gentle-Craft* (which provided
Dekker with much of his source material for the story of Simon Eyre),
Thomas Deloney relates the bizarre story of how the bones of the shoemakers' patron saint, the martyred St. Hugh, were transformed by his
fellows into the tools of their trade and signs of their mystery – hence

the customary reference, both in the play and in Tudor London, to the shoemakers' work utensils as "Saint Hugh's bones."[53]

The intertransfigurability of profane artisanal tools and sacred saint's body is redolent of the multivalence of artisanal props in the mystery plays, and like the latter provides the fulcrum for the articulation of corporate membership – membership of not only guild, but also the continuum of human history. Interestingly, the transfigurable quality of the shoemakers' tools applies also to the artisans themselves. Coining a barrage of fond nicknames for his fellows, Eyre frogmarches the shoemakers into a veritable karaoke bar of assumed classical identities: "mad Greeks" and "true Trojans" (4.115), "mad Hyperboreans" (4.123), "mad Mesopotamians" (7.78) "mad Cappadocians" (17.44–5) and "fine dapper Assyrian lads" (17.50). With this verbal pageantry, *The Shoemaker's Holiday* not only creates the double angle of vision characteristic of the cycle drama and its anamorphic juxtaposition of past and present, sacred and profane; it additionally drives home the fraternal, corporate nature of the shoemakers' identities.[54]

The Shoemaker's Holiday follows the Corpus Christi pageants and plays also by materializing property in skill in a plethora of artisanal stage properties. Stage directions at the beginning of several scenes require the shoemakers to be at work, wielding their "Saint Hugh's bones," and numerous other stage directions indicate the conspicuous display of shoemakers' products. Hammon's servingman turns up at Ralph's with one of Jane's shoes, requesting that a copy be made (14.8); a "neat leather" shoe is required when Roland courts Rose (15.30); and in the subsequent scene, Firk also enters with shoes for Rose (16.48). Perhaps the play's most remarkable display of artisanal products and property in skill occurs in the passage that I have quoted as the second of this essay's epigraphs. Before leaving for the wars, Ralph reveals the shoes he will give Jane as a going-away present:

> Here, take this pair of shoes cut out by Hodge,
> Stitched by my fellow Firk, seamed by myself,
> Made up and pinked with letters for thy name.
> Wear them, my dear Jane, for thy husband's sake.
> (1.232–5)

With this uncharacteristic foray into verse, Ralph ennobles the shoes as the skillful product of collective craftsmanship. In doing so, he invites the audience to view the shoes less as a love-token for Jane than as a homage to the artisans' property of fellowship and association; the placed product in this passage is just as much the relational property of skill, therefore, as the pair of shoes itself.[55]

As Ralph's tribute to the work of his fellows suggests, the relational property of skill in *The Shoemaker's Holiday* is repeatedly confined to male homosocial relations. Roland says that the "Gentle Craft is living for a man" (3.24); the women of the play are notably excluded from the property of skill. Instead, "living for a woman" entails either possession of or desire for a different species of property – fashionable luxury items, widely known in Elizabethan England as "cates."[56] When Rose bribes her maid Sybil, for example, she does so by tempting her with "my cambric apron, and my Romish gloves, my purple stockings, and a stomacher" (2.55–6). The female characters' allegedly typical desire for such commodities is inscribed most clearly in the derisive names Eyre devises for them. He brands first Jane and then his wife a "bombast cotton-candle quean" (1.211, 7.3), a term that editors gloss as "delicate wench," but which also refers to a popular cate (a costly, ornate candle) and hence, by association, the women who stereotypically own or covet it. In a related vein, Eyre taunts Margery by calling her "kitchen-stuff"; the latter epithet likewise suggests not only her "proper" place, or the grease of the kitchen, but also domestic accessories and her feminine desire for them. Revealingly, Margery replies, "I must be called rubbish, kitchen-stuff, for a sort of knaves" (7.49–50). As she recognizes all too well, her husband's slur against feminine kitchen-stuff is precisely what enables the articulation of *manly*, immaterial stuff – that is, the property which she here calls "sort," or fellowship.

After Simon Eyre's election to Mayor, however, the play presents cates in a decidedly different light. Instead of serving as vulgar feminine foils to the immaterial male property of skill, they are transformed into the laudable accessories of success and status. Once he has attained office, Eyre gives Margery free rein to act upon her desires for luxury goods. She gleefully exploits her new licence: "let me have a pair of shoes made: cork, good Roger – wooden heel too . . . Art thou acquainted with never a farthingale-maker, nor a French-hood maker? I must enlarge my bum – ha, ha!" (10.32–33, 35–36). Margery's acquisitive fantasies clearly illustrate the complexity of shoes as property in the play; they are at one and the same time the material embodiments of the collective male property in skill, feminine cates suitable for private gentlewomen, and badges of status for the gentlewomen's husbands. This disjunction is most apparent when Eyre upbraids Ralph and Hodge for devaluing their manly skill by making shoes for lower-class women: "Fie, defile not thy fine, workmanly fingers with the feet of kitchen-stuff and basting-ladles! Ladies of the Court, fine ladies, my lads – commit their feet to our apparelling" (7.86–9). Split along class lines, therefore, feminine cates stand in dual relation to male property: lowly "kitchen stuff and basting-ladles" are what the shoemakers must define their immaterial property of skill in opposition to; the custom of "fine ladies," however, ennobles both the men and the accessories they make.

Indeed, not only manufacture but also purchase of and dealership in feminine luxury goods profits the male artisans throughout *The Shoemaker's Holiday*. In what is perhaps the play's crucial development, Eyre engages in an act of entrepreneurial bravado: he buys a foreign ship's load of commodities, which consists exclusively of exotic cates such as "sugar, civet, almonds, cambric, end a tousand tousand things" (7.132–33). Selling them at a huge profit, he thereby creates the fund for his subsequent social and political advancement. Whereas this enterprise is depicted in Thomas Deloney's *History of the Gentle-Craft* as a morally dubious and even feminine one, performed at the urging of Eyre's covetous wife and prompting in the shoemaker a sustained attack of conscience, the play instead presents it as an example of a commendable, masculine acumen for derring-do and self-advancement.[57] By recoding luxury material goods as the appropriate products, accoutrements, and capital of the upwardly mobile private citizen, *The Shoemaker's Holiday* thus undermines its seeming glorification of the immaterial property of corporate membership.

In fact the more closely one looks at the play, the more conflicted its dramatic presentation of property in skill becomes. Most crucially, *The Shoemaker's Holiday* lacks the literally organic relationship between actor, character, and stage property that distinguishes the Corpus Christi entertainments. Nobody associated with the Admiral's Men – neither the principal investors nor the twelve sharers at the time the play was performed – had any explicit link with shoemaking, let alone professed the freedom of the London Company of Cordwainers.[58] It is thus highly improbable that the "Saint Hugh's Bones" and shoemaking products displayed in performances of *The Shoemaker's Holiday* would have been fashioned by the players who handled them. Some of the play's properties of skill, such as the scarlet satin livery hoods worn by Eyre's men during the final banquet, may have been loaned by shoemakers known to Henslowe or the players – although, as Chambers points out, the standard actors' livery was itself red cloth.[59] In all likelihood, the play's artisanal props were supplied by Henslowe himself, either by direct purchase from London cordwainers, or from his private inventory which, as both Peter Stallybrass and Natasha Korda have suggested, may have included unredeemed items from his pawnbroking business.[60] The shoemakers' properties exhibited in the play were signs not of its performers' property in skill, therefore, but of their impresario's as well as their own property in private stock.

The differences between property in *The Shoemaker's Holiday* and the Corpus Christi entertainments are made most visible by the play's use of the same proto-Brechtian estrangement of character that distinguished the performances of the York cycle. Dekker's play employs such a device to draw attention to the actor not as skilled artisan, however, but as *actor*. In the earliest performances of *The Shoemaker's Holiday*, audience members may have recognized that the scarlet livery of the "shoemakers" resembled – or even *was* – the livery of the actors. But another, crucial scene in the play more decisively foregrounds the work and property of the actor. To succeed in the enterprise that will make him rich, Eyre must first acquire and dress up in a damask cassock, alderman's gown, and sealing ring to fool the ship's skipper into thinking that he is someone respectable enough to sell commodities (7.104–6). His acquisition of this fine apparel is part of his successful capital investment. But it is more than that: Eyre's sumptuary pretence is also testimony to the entrepreneurial "skill" of acting, in which costly properties function not only as signs of social status, but also as collateral for its acquisition.[61] Upon seeing Eyre after his makeover, Firk gasps: "'Nails, my master looks like a threadbare cloak new turned / And dressed. Lord, Lord, to see what good raiment doth!" (7.117–18). In drawing attention to the transformative social power of Eyre's clothes, Firk's remark uncannily recalls Robert Greene's description of the *nouveau riche* actor:

What is your profession, sayd *Roberto*? Truely sir, said he, I am a player. A Player, quoth *Roberto*, I tooke you rather for a gentleman of great liuing; for if by outward habit men should be censured, I tell you, you would be taken for a substantiall man. So am I where I dwell (quoth the player) reputed able at my proper cost, to build a Windmill. What though the worlde once went hard with mee, when I was faine to carry my playing Fardle a footebacke; *Tempora mutantur*: I know you know the meaning of it better than I, but I thus conster it, it is otherwise now; for my share in playing apparell will not be solde for two hundred pounds.[62]

Like Robert Greene's player, like the sharers who performed *The Shoemaker's Holiday*, and like Philip Henslowe, both Firk and Simon Eyre recognize apparel's status as cultural and financial capital. Vestments and investments are synonymous in the play, as they were in the theatre business; clothes offered the means by which not simply poverty, but also the social immobility of the artisan could be escaped. Henslowe the ex-Dyer's successful garment-related careers in pawnbroking and theatrical management provide a notable case in point.[63]

By representing Eyre's theatrical disguise as a necessary and even commendable capital investment, *The Shoemaker's Holiday* declares its allegiance to a moral universe very different from that of medieval cycle drama. Satan's prologue to the N-Town Passion play lists amongst its catalog of sinners "A beggerys dowtere to make gret purvyauns / To cownterfete a jentylwoman, dysgeyesyd as she can"; significantly, Satan characterizes the daughter's stratagem of disguising herself in the hope of acquiring social mobility as a form of "chevesans," or usury.[64] In marked contrast, *The Shoemaker's Holiday*'s metatheatrical presentation of its props discloses a new mode of production in which the judicious "counterfeiting" of status by means of sumptuary display is not regarded as sinful or usurious, but as an enterprising route to actual private wealth and raised social standing – a route pioneered in no small part by the successful commercial theatre companies and their principals, thanks to their massive investments in clothes and props.

Indeed, the second half of the play gave Henslowe and his sharers a seemingly never-ending series of opportunities to flaunt their expensive, audience-attracting stock, much of which consisted of the very types of fashionable luxury garments denounced in the first few scenes as trivial feminine cates. The play's earliest audiences at the Rose would have been exposed to a dazzling parade of placed products that advertised less the skill of the artisan than the wealth of the theatre company and its impresario: Jane's shop goods, including calico, lawn, fine cambric shirts, bands, handkerchiefs, and ruffs (12.22, 23, 25); Lord Mayor Eyre's red petticoat and chain of gold, and Lady Margery's new farthingales, shoes and periwigs (17.18, 25); the expensive dresses and accessories Hammon buys for Jane (18.21). To this already flamboyant list there might also be added the regal garments of the King in the play's final scene, the shoemakers' scarlet livery hoods, and even Simon Eyre's luxuriant stage-beard, about which he boasts that "Tamar Cham's beard was a rubbing-brush to't" (21.24–25). This pointedly metatheatrical moment evokes not only a play previously performed by the Admiral's Men and its title role, for which Edward Alleyn was renowned,[65] but more specifically a striking stage property that may well have been used in both plays.

In its initial performances as much as in its plot, therefore, the moral of *The Shoemaker's Holiday* seems overwhelmingly to have been that profit is less the product of skill or membership than of investment in the capital assets of the theatre. I am thus arguing for a different reading of the play than the traditional one, which views Eyre's advancement simply as just reward for his honest profession and spirit of generous fellowship.[66] As much as the play *tries* to suggest that the success of Eyre and the shoemakers emerges from their exemplary fraternity in artisanal craft, an alternate perspective is glimpsed when Eyre addresses his men as "frolic freebooters," i.e. pirates (20.59). The term is wonderfully multivalent: punning off the fact that the shoemakers are a company of freemen who make boots, it nevertheless reveals how they – not to mention the actors playing them – are also swashbuckling profiteers in quest of booty. Eyre's term can be seen as an illuminating example of what Pierre Macherey and Etienne Balibar have termed the "linguistic compromise formation," by means of which social fractions accommodate within their ideological productions attractive aspects of competing fractions' practices or beliefs, but to defuse rather than empower the latter.[67] Hence onstage and off-, Elizabethan profiteers banded together as if they were guildsmen, but with the novel understanding that private financial gain as much as public membership is the natural end of fellowship. The term "freebooters" hints at how the residual relational property of artisanal skill was reconciled with and subordinated to the rival capitalist mode of production of the Elizabethan entrepreneur-players. The twenty-first-century fruits of this transformation may be witnessed in the institution of the capitalist corporation, which can be traced back to, yet differs so greatly from, late medieval structures of corporate identity.

The shift from guild to joint-stock company, and from pageant wagon to public playhouse, may be read as part of a larger, incomplete shift from a pre-capitalist conception of property as social membership to the modern conception of property as privately owned asset. Not all props in mystery plays are emblems of membership, of course, nor are all props in Elizabethan and Jacobean drama simply forms of capital; such global, monologic readings of stage properties in any one period or genre are manifestly untenable, as I hope the preceding analysis has shown. Nonetheless, the social and theatrical lives of early English stage properties were inevitably influenced by, and even helped reshape, larger cultural and economic processes. By paying attention to these lives, partially revealed through the metatheatrical disclosures of product placement that I have discussed here, we can learn a lot about not only the changing institution of the early English theatre, but also the different conceptions of property that accompanied the transition to early capitalism. Equally importantly, by paying heed to the relational property of skill we can also begin to think outside – and hence more comprehensively historicize – our common-sense, post-Lockean polarities of individual possessor and individuated possession, private and public, and subject and object.

NOTES

This essay was written with the assistance of a summer research fellowship at the Folger Shakespeare Library in Washington, DC. I am particularly grateful to Margaret Pappano and Michael Wright for sharing their thoughts with me and directing me to important archival resources while I was doing my research, for the comments of auditors at the University of Kansas, the University of Auckland, SUNY Buffalo, Columbia University, and the 34th Kalamazoo International Congress on Medieval Studies where I presented earlier drafts of this paper, and for the immeasurably helpful suggestions and criticisms of Madhavi Menon, Michael Neill, Shilpa Prasad, David Harris Sacks, Peter Stallybrass, and Wendy Wall.

1. All references to the York cycle dramas are from Lucy Toulmin Smith (ed.), *York Plays*, 2nd edn. (Oxford: Clarendon Press, 1963).

2. All references to the play are from Thomas Dekker, *The Shoemaker's Holiday*, ed. Anthony Parr, 2nd edn. (London: A. &. C. Black, 1990), citing the scene and line number.

3. Hollywood International Placements, Inc. web site, 11 September 1998.

4. Arjun Appadurai, "Introduction: commodities and the politics of value," in Appadurai (ed.), *The Social Life of Things: Commodities in Cultural Perspective* (Cambridge: Cambridge University Press, 1986), pp. 3–63.

5. This is the methodological orientation of the two book-length studies of Elizabethan stage properties; see Felix Bossonet, *The Function of Stage Properties in Christopher Marlowe's Plays* (Berne: Francke Verlag, 1978); and Frances Teague, *Shakespeare's Speaking Properties* (Lewisburg, PA: Bucknell University Press, 1991).

6. John Locke, *Two Treatises of Government*, 2nd edn. (Cambridge: Cambridge University Press, 1970), p. 368. For a fascinating critique of the Lockean legacy in modern definitions of property from the point of view of rival nineteenth-century Chartist definitions, see Margaret R. Somers, "The 'mysteries of property': relationality, rural-industrialization, and community in Chartist narratives of political rights," in John Brewer and Susan Staves (eds.), *Early Modern Conceptions of Property* (London: Routledge, 1995), pp. 62–92. My argument about property in early English drama is greatly indebted to Somers's important essay.

7. For a useful discussion of the relationships between property and identity in early modern English culture, see Margreta De Grazia, "The ideology

of superfluous things: *King Lear* as period piece," in De Grazia, Maureen Quilligan, and Peter Stallybrass (eds.), *Subject and Object in Renaissance Culture* (Cambridge: Cambridge University Press, 1996), pp. 17–42.

8. The names of *A Midsummer Night's Dream*'s artisanal characters are discussed by Wolfgang Franke, "The logic of double entendre in *A Midsummer Night's Dream*," *Philological Quarterly* 58 (1979): 282–97, and Patricia Parker, "'Rude mechanicals,'" in De Grazia, Quilligan, and Stallybrass (eds.), *Subject and Object*, pp. 43–82, esp. p. 55.

9. In his reading of the rhetoric of enclosure and the modes of property in *Richard II*, for example, James R. Siemon characterizes the Gardener's property as "neither capitalism's absolute property in land nor feudalism's conditional right to land but the capital of skill in his occupation"; see Siemon's essay, "Landlord not king: agrarian change and interarticulation," in Richard Burt and John Michael Archer (eds.), *Enclosure Acts: Sexuality, Property, and Culture in Early Modern England* (Ithaca: Cornell University Press, 1994), pp. 17–33, esp. p. 27.

10. On the artisanal backgrounds of Shakespeare's fellow actors, playwrights and theatrical entrepreneurs, see James H. Forse, *Art Imitates Business: Commercial and Political Influences in Elizabethan Theatre* (Bowling Green: Bowling Green State University Popular Press, 1993), pp. 7–15; and Paul S. Seaver, "Thomas Dekker's *The Shoemaker's Holiday*: the artisanal world," in David L. Smith, Richard Strier and David Bevington (eds.), *The Theatrical City: Culture, Theatre and Politics in London 1576–1649* (Cambridge: Cambridge University Press, 1995), pp. 87–100, esp. p. 93. For an important discussion of how artisans during the fourteenth to sixteenth centuries often practiced many crafts other than the nominal one to which they were restricted by law, see Heather Swanson, *Medieval Artisans: An Urban Class in Late Medieval England* (London: Basil Blackwell, 1989), esp. chapter 1.

11. Somers, "The 'misteries of property,'" p. 69.

12. See *Records of Early English Drama: Coventry*, ed. R. W. Ingram (Toronto: University of Toronto Press, 1981), p. 563; henceforth referred to as *REED: Coventry*.

13. Anthony Black, *Guilds and Civil Society in European Political Thought from the Twelfth Century to the Present* (Ithaca: Cornell University Press, 1984), p. 65.

14. *Measure for Measure*, 4.2.27, 33; *Timon of Athens*, 4.3.506, in David Bevington (ed.), *The Complete Works of William Shakespeare*, 4th edn. (New York: Harper Collins, 1996). For an analysis of the decline of guild culture in the sixteenth century, see John E. Martin, *Feudalism to Capitalism: Peasant and Landlord in English Agrarian Development* (Atlantic Highlands, NJ: Humanities Press, 1983), pp. 117–27. For a slightly different view that suggests trade guilds in some parts of England prospered rather than declined during the sixteenth century, see D. M. Palliser, "The trade gilds of Tudor York," in Peter Clark and Paul Slack (eds.), *Crisis and Order in English Towns, 1500–1700* (Toronto: University of Toronto Press, 1972), pp. 86–116.

15. See Michael D. Bristol, *Big-Time Shakespeare* (London: Routledge, 1996), p. 40. For other suggestive discussions of Elizabethan theatre companies' transitionality as economic institutions, poised between guild structures and the newer arrangements of venture capital, see William Ingram, *The Business of Playing: The Beginnings of the Adult Professional Theatre in Elizabethan London* (Ithaca: Cornell University Press, 1992); Peter Stallybrass, "Worn worlds: clothes and identity on the Renaissance stage," in De Grazia, Quilligan, and Stallybrass (eds.), *Subject and Object*, pp. 289–320, esp. pp. 293–5; and Stephen Orgel, *Impersonations: The Performance of Gender in Shakespeare's England* (Cambridge: Cambridge University Press, 1996), pp. 65–70, esp. p. 67.

16. On the capital ventures of Keysar, see William Ingram, "Robert Keysar, playhouse speculator," *Shakespeare Quarterly* 37 (1986): 476–85; for the theory that actors retained guild affiliations so that they could apprentice boy-actors, see Orgel, *Impersonations*.

17. There are encouraging signs that the traditional separation of "medieval" and "early modern" dramatic studies is, if not coming to an end, then at least being subjected to increasing critical scrutiny. The publication of the *Records of Early English Drama* series has been largely responsible for the growing popularity of "early drama" as a more generalized rubric within which to plot the continuities and discontinuities between medieval entertainments and the public commercial theatre of early modern London, a development evidenced by John D. Cox and David Scott Kastan's important edited collection, *A New History of Early English Drama* (New York: Columbia University Press, 1997). On the specific relations between cycle drama and Shakespeare's theatre, see Michael O'Connell, "Vital cultural practices: Shakespeare and the mysteries," *Journal of Medieval and Early Modern Studies* 29 (1999): 149–68.

18. Important studies of socio-religious corporate imagery in late medieval England include Sarah Beckwith, "Ritual, church and theatre: medieval dramas of the sacramental body," in David Aers (ed.), *Culture and History 1350–1600: Essays on English Communities, Identities, and Writing* (Detroit: Wayne State University Press, 1992), pp. 65–90; Mervyn James, "Ritual, drama and social body," *Past and Present* 98 (1983): 3–29; Sarah Kay and Miri Rubin (eds.), *Framing Medieval Bodies* (Manchester: Manchester University Press, 1994); Miri Rubin, *Corpus Christi: the Eucharist in Late Medieval Culture* (Cambridge: Cambridge University Press, 1991).

19. See Alan D. Justice, "Trade symbolism in the York cycle," *Theatre Journal* 31 (1979): 49; James, "Ritual, drama and social body," 20. For discussions of the history of craft guilds in medieval and early modern England, see Black, *Guilds and Civil Society in European Political Thought*; Stella Kramer, *The English Craft Gilds and the Government* (New York: Columbia University Press, 1905); and Heather Swanson, "The illusion of economic structure: craft guilds in late medieval English towns," *Past and Present* 121 (1988): 29–48. Eamon Duffy provides an invaluable account of the role played by religious guilds in late medieval civic culture in *The Stripping of the Altars: Traditional*

Religion in England c. 1400–c. 1580 (New Haven: Yale University Press, 1992), esp. pp. 43–5.

20. In the old Christian calendar, the festival was scheduled to fall on the Thursday following Trinity Sunday, five weeks after Easter; it could take place any time between May and July. As Alan H. Nelson has shown, however, anomalies in the Julian calendar would have meant that Corpus Christi day usually fell closer to the summer solstice than the feast of Midsummer itself; see his *The Medieval English Stage: Corpus Christi Pageants and Plays* (Chicago: Chicago University Press, 1974), pp. 13–14. In some towns, the corporate rituals that are elsewhere associated with Corpus Christi were displaced to other festivals: in Lincoln, the guilds displayed their pageants on St. Anne's day; Coventry, while having its own Corpus Christi celebrations, also had a craft guild procession on Midsummer's Eve; and in Chester, the craft pageants took place at Whitsun. See Nelson, pp. 104, 140–1, 155.

21. For a thorough overview of different theories about staging in the Corpus Christi festivals, see Nelson, *The Medieval English Stage*, esp. chapter 2. William Tydeman critically summarizes the positions in the debate over staging at York in *The Theatre in the Middle Ages* (Cambridge: Cambridge University Press, 1978), pp. 114–20.

22. Glynne Wickham, *Early English Stages, 1300–1600*, 3 vols. (London and New York, 1959–72), vol. 1, p. 123.

23. Anne Higgins, "Work and plays: guild casting in the Corpus Christi drama," *Medieval and Renaissance Drama in England* 7 (1995 [for 1992]): 76–97, esp. 78. Although theatre historians from E. K. Chambers on have noted the "appropriateness" of many guild attributions in the Corpus Christi cycle plays (see *The Medieval Stage*, 2 vols. [Oxford: Clarendon Press, 1903], vol. 11, pp. 117–18), few have attempted to explain the logic behind the attributions; notable exceptions include Anne Higgins and Alan D. Justice (see the latter's "Trade symbolism in the York cycle"). Glynne Wickham coined the term "trade symbolism" in his discussion of the phenomenon (*Early English Stages*, vol. 1, p. 54).

24. On the Barbers of York, see Justice, "Trade symbolism in the York cycle," 48; on the Barbers of Beverley and the Norwich Worsted Weavers, see Nelson, *The Medieval English Stage*, pp. 94, 130; on the York Carpenters and Coventry Fullers, see James, "Ritual, drama and social body," 20; on the Tanners and Barkers, see Higgins, "Work and plays," 79; on the York Waterleaders, see *Records of Early English Drama: York*, ed. Alexandra F. Johnston and Margaret Rogerson (Toronto: University of Toronto Press, 1978), 11, p. 671; henceforth referred to as *REED: York*.

25. A notable exception is the Noah play in the York cycle, performed by the Shipwrights, in which an ark is constructed on stage. For a discussion of the "mystery" of shipbuilding disclosed by the play, see Richard Beadle, "The York Cycle," in Beadle (ed.), *The Cambridge Companion to Medieval English Theatre* (Cambridge: Cambridge University Press, 1994), pp. 85–108, esp. p. 87.

26. On the multiple meanings of the Baker pageants and plays, see Higgins, "Work and plays," 79; for details about the Chester Bakers' pageant and the throwing of loaves into the audience, see *Records of Early English Drama: Chester*, ed. Lawrence M. Clopper (Toronto: University of Toronto Press, 1979), p. 245; henceforth referred to as *REED: Chester*.

27. See Nelson, *The Medieval English Stage*, pp. 104–6.

28. See *Beverley Town Documents*, ed. A. F. Leach (Selden Society 14: London, 1900), p. 37; also cited in Nelson, *The Medieval English Stage*, p. 92.

29. *REED: York*, ii, pp. 732–3.

30. *REED: Coventry*, pp. 25, 289. For a very useful discussion of the Coventry Smiths' pageant wagon and the guild-specific technologies on display in it, see Clifford Davidson, *Technology, Guilds, and Early English Drama* (Kalamazoo, Michigan: Medieval Institute Publications, 1997), pp. 34–47.

31. The details I have cited from the Mercers' pageant inventory are taken from the transcription presented in "The doomsday pageant of the York Mercers, 1433," *Leeds Studies in English* n.s. 5 (1971): 29–30. For a discussion of the guild-specific contents of the pageant, see Davidson, *Technology, Guilds, and Early English Drama*, pp. 29–31.

32. *REED: York*, i, p. 68.

33. Swanson, *Medieval Artisans*, p. 63.

34. "I sall caste leede and loke the space, / Howe depe the watir is ilke a dele" (*York Plays*, play 9, lines 199–200). Alan D. Justice discusses these lines in "Trade symbolism," 49–50. On the self-conscious anachronisms of the mystery plays, see Robert Weimann, *Shakespeare and the Popular Tradition in the Theatre: Studies in the Social Dimension of Dramatic Form and Function*, ed. Robert Schwartz (Baltimore: Johns Hopkins University Press, 1978), pp. 80–4.

35. *York Plays*, play 35, line 261. For a useful discussion of the guild-appropriate properties and thematization of work in the Pinners' and Latteners' play, see Beadle, "The York cycle," pp. 85–108, esp. pp. 101–3. Other guilds may have used their pageants to engage in deliberately grotesque advertisements of their produce. Martin Stevens suggests that the "Sausagemakers," whose pageant of the hanging of Judas was discontinued for financial reasons in the mid-fifteenth century, may have represented Judas's guts as a string of sausages: see *Four Middle English Mystery Cycles* (Princeton: Princeton University Press, 1987), p. 21. Sarah Beckwith reiterates the assertion in her essay, "Making the world in York and the York cycle," in Kay and Rubin (eds.), *Framing Medieval Bodies*, pp. 254–76, esp. p. 273, n. 53. However, both Stevens and Beckwith may be wrong in assuming that the "Salsarii," as they were called in the Latin ordinances of the time, were known as the Sausagemakers. The term translates simply as the Saucemakers; it is quite possible, therefore, that the pageant would have used sauces instead of sausages to represent Judas's exploding viscera, though certainly to equally grotesque effect. I'm grateful to Margaret Pappano for drawing this pageant and the problems of its craft attribution to my attention.

36. *York Plays*, play 15, lines 122–8.

37. On the skills of different types of chandlers, see Randall Monier-Williams, *The Tallow Chandlers of London: The Mystery in the Making* (London: Kaye and Ward, 1970), pp. 19, 35–7.

38. Swanson, *Medieval Artisans*, p. 100. The ladle was not the only trade-related stage property that the Chandlers may have supplied for their play. The *Ordo Paginarum*, a document drawn up in 1415 by the York City clerk which lists the order of guilds in the civic procession and describes the pageants they exhibited, includes in its description of the Chandlers' pageant the striking detail "stella in oriente," suggesting that the chandlers had constructed either a large candle or waxwork apparatus to represent the star that guided the shepherds to the baby Jesus. See *REED: York*, 1, p. 18.

39. See Higgins, "Work and plays," 77.

40. Peter Womack notes how in the performance of the mystery play, "the actor moves easily between the world of the story and that of the audience, not because the authors are historically naïve, but because it is only when the figures of the Christian story become the common property of the crowd that the crowd realizes its common membership of the body of Christ." Womack's remarks suggestively illuminate the corporate logic that informed the late medieval cultural production of the property of membership, whether that of the guilds or the spectators, in the Corpus Christi festival. See his "Imagining communities: theatres and the English nation in the sixteenth century," in Aers (ed.), *Culture and History*, pp. 91–146, esp. p. 103.

41. This is not to deny, however, that for many guilds participation in the Corpus Christi festivals was a bitterly resented, financially destructive obligation. Heather Swanson is especially skeptical of any suggestion that the guilds had agency in their everyday as well as ritual activities; see her *Medieval Artisans, passim*. Still, to see the guilds as simply instruments or victims of oppressive power runs the risk of eliding the ways in which they could lend expression to rather than smother artisanal interests. In *Shakespeare and the Popular Tradition in the Theatre*, Robert Weimann argues that "the mystery plays reflected the impact of various changes in society and social consciousness, most conspicuously the increased need for plebeian instruction and entertainment (which was granted by the church itself) and the growing awareness (which varied from place to place) of the social aspirations and cultural traditions of the rural and artisan populace" (p. 58). Here he discusses the artisanal class's accumulation of *cultural* capital through the performance of the mystery plays; but the "social aspirations" to which he refers might also be extended to include the more immediate prospect of financial gain from the display of skill.

42. Indeed, the Banns read before the last performance of the Chester play in 1575 insisted that the guilds had no pecuniary motive in putting forth their pageants: "By Craftes men and meane men these Pageanntes are playde . . . / Oure playeinge is not to gett fame or treasure" (*REED: Chester*, p. 247). Still, we should be wary about taking the Chester Banns' claim

entirely at its word. The Corpus Christi pageants from a very early date provided townspeople with opportunities for making money from audiences: take, for example, the 1417 ordinance of the York city corporation, which mandated that "all those who receive money for scaffolds which they may build [for spectators at pageant stations] shall pay the third penny of the money so received to the chamberlains of the city" (*REED: York*, II, pp. 713–14). We cannot know for sure whether the scaffolders, and those who commissioned them, acted as private citizens or on behalf of crafts looking to recoup their production costs. What is perhaps more noteworthy about the 1417 ordinance, though, is that rather than outlawing the practice of charging spectators, the corporation itself sought to share in the scaffolders' profits. Money-making, in other words, was very much on many Corpus Christi festival participants' minds. For an important discussion of the York stations and the parties that profited from them, see Meg Twycross, " 'Places to hear the play': pageant stations at York, 1398–1572," *REED Newsletter* 2 (1978): 10–33.

43. Michael D. Bristol discusses the Elizabethan theatre as an emergent entertainment industry in *Big-Time Shakespeare*. For other important discussions of the theatre as a laboratory for early market capitalism, see Jean-Christophe Agnew, *Worlds Apart: The Market and the Theatre in Anglo-American Thought* (Cambridge: Cambridge University Press, 1986); Douglas Bruster, *Drama and the Market in the Age of Shakespeare* (Cambridge: Cambridge University Press, 1992); Forse, *Art Imitates Business*; William Ingram, *The Business of Playing: The Beginnings of the Adult Professional Theatre in Elizabethan London* (Ithaca, NY: Cornell University Press, 1992); and Kathleen McLuskie, *Dekker and Heywood: Professional Dramatists* (London: St. Martin's Press, 1994). The extent to which props, and particularly costumes, proved instrumental in luring audiences to the theatre is discussed by Ann Rosalind Jones and Peter Stallybrass in "The circulation of clothes and the making of the Renaissance theatre," chapter 7 of their *Renaissance Clothing and the Materials of Memory* (Cambridge: Cambridge University Press, 2000).

44. E. K. Chambers, *The Elizabethan Stage* (Oxford: Clarendon Press, 1923), I, p. 211. On costumes and properties as capital assets, see Jean MacIntyre and Garrett P. J. Epp, " 'Cloathes worth all the rest': costumes and properties," in Cox and Kastan (eds.), *A New History of Early English Drama*, pp. 269–85, and Stallybrass, "Worn worlds"; on Francis Langley's expenditures at the Swan, see Andrew Gurr, *The Shakespearean Stage 1574–1642* (Cambridge: Cambridge University Press, 1970), pp. 29–30.

45. Igor Kopytoff, "The cultural biography of things: commoditization as process," in Appadurai (ed.) *The Social Life of Things*, pp. 64–91, esp. pp. 68–70.

46. Henslowe's inventory of the Admiral's Men's stock is included in R. A. Foakes and R. T. Rickert (eds.), *Henslowe's Diary* (Cambridge: Cambridge University Press, 1961), pp. 319–21. On the multi-use value of costumes and properties, see Macintyre and Epp, "'Cloathes worth all the rest,'" pp. 278–80.

47. Acting companies were not always the sole owners of the properties employed in a production. On occasion, actors privately owned playing apparel; Edward Alleyn of the Admiral's Men inventoried an extensive stage wardrobe in 1598, and Henslowe loaned actors money to purchase stage garments for their private stock. See Macintyre and Epp, "'Cloathes worth all the rest,'" p. 278.

48. For a useful discussion of the theatrical predilections of apprentices and the theatre companies' attempts to accommodate them, see Andrew Gurr, *Playgoing in Shakespeare's London*, 2nd edn. (Cambridge: Cambridge University Press, 1996), esp. pp. 151–8, 165–9. It is important not to succumb to a reflectionist assumption, however, and conclude that the plays targeted artisanal audiences alone. King James's son Henry wore the livery of the Merchant Taylors; James himself donned the livery of the Clothmakers in 1607. And a play like *Henry V*, which famously invokes one of the shoemakers' patron saints, Crispin, fantasizes a model of monarchy based on the ethic of fraternity underwriting guild culture. For an illuminating discussion of English nobility's nostalgic fantasies about guild life, see Jones and Stallybrass, "The circulation of clothes."

49. See David Bevington, "Theatre as holiday," in Smith, Strier and Bevington (eds.), *The Theatrical City*, pp. 101–16; Seaver, "Thomas Dekker's *The Shoemaker's Holiday*"; and Laura Caroline Stevenson, *Praise and Paradox: Merchants and Craftsmen in Elizabethan Popular Literature* (Cambridge: Cambridge University Press, 1984), pp. 202–4.

50. London had no cycle play, but it did have a Corpus Christi procession until the mid-sixteenth century; craft guild involvement was minimal, however, limited to the Skinners. See Nelson, *The Medieval Stage*, chapter 10.

51. On the composition and power of London guilds, see Joseph P. Ward, *Metropolitan Communities: Trade Guilds, Identity, and Change in Early Modern London* (Stanford, CA: Stanford University Press, 1997).

52. Nevertheless, guilds made rigid distinctions between local and "foreign" craftsmen, i.e. artisans born outside the city, who were in turn distinguished from "alien," i.e. immigrant, workers. The latter were repeatedly subjected to violence: perhaps the most notorious instance is the Evil May Day riots of 1517, when London artisans took to the streets to protest the growing numbers of alien workers. For a discussion of the utopian fantasy of "Hans"'s treatment in the play and the social tensions it masks, see David Scott Kastan, "Workshop and/as playhouse: *The Shoemaker's Holiday* (1599)," in David Scott Kastan and Peter Stallybrass (eds.), *Staging the Renaissance: Reinterpretations of Elizabethan and Jacobean Drama* (New York: Routledge, 1992), pp. 151–63, esp. p. 152.

53. On the myth of St. Hugh's bones, see Thomas Deloney, *The Pleasant and Princely History of the Gentle-Craft* (London, 1696), sigs. c3–c4.

54. This oscillation works at several levels in *The Shoemaker's Holiday*. The story takes place in the fifteenth century, during the French wars of Henry V. When the King grants permission to the shoemakers at play's end to ply their trade

at Leadenhall, however (21.132, 159), an anamorphic turn from fifteenth to late sixteenth centuries is effected: audiences would have recognized both the landmark and the London Cordwainers' connection to it in the present.

55. For similar conclusions about this passage, see Bruster, *Drama and the Market in the Age of Shakespeare*, pp. 78–9, and Peter Stallybrass, "Footnotes," in David Hillman and Carla Mazzio (eds.), *The Body in Parts: Fantasies of Corporeality in Early Modern Europe* (New York: Routledge, 1997), p. 317.

56. The most extensive discussion of "cates" on the Elizabethan stage, to which I am much indebted, is Natasha Korda's "Household Kates: domesticating commodities in *The Taming of the Shrew*," *Shakespeare Quarterly* 47 (1996): 109–31.

57. See Deloney, *The Pleasant and Princely History of the Gentle-Craft*, sig. E4v.

58. Philip Henslowe was apprenticed as a Dyer and Edward Alleyn might have been an Innkeeper by patrimony; only one of the twelve sharers of the Admiral's Men at the time of *The Shoemaker's Holiday*'s first performance, Anthony Jeffes, seems to have professed a skill (Brewing) in any public documents. See Edwin Nungezer, *A Dictionary of Actors, and of Other Persons Associated with the Public Representation of Plays in England before 1642* (New Haven: Yale University Press, 1929).

59. Chambers, *The Elizabethan Stage*, I, p. 312.

60. See Natasha Korda, "Household property/stage property: Henslowe as pawnbroker," *Theatre Journal* 48 (1996): 185–96; Stallybrass, "Worn worlds," pp. 315–16. At approximately 8s. in worth, shoemakers' tools were relatively inexpensive compared to those of other artisans; see Swanson, *Medieval Artisans*, p. 129.

61. This acumen is even more explicit in Deloney's retelling of the story, although it is displaced onto Eyre's nakedly covetous wife, who primes her husband for his performance. Deloney's account suggests Eyre worries about the immorality of his deception; Dekker's Eyre notably lacks any such compunction. See Deloney, *The Pleasant and Princely History of the Gentle-Craft*, sigs. F I – F I V.

62. Robert Greene, *The Life and Complete Works in Prose and Verse of Robert Greene*, ed. Alexander B. Grosart (New York: Russell and Russell, 1944), xiii.131.

63. Neil Carson, *A Companion to Henslowe's Diary* (Cambridge: Cambridge University Press, 1988), pp. 1–5. For a discussion of Blackfriars' investor Robert Keysar's prior apprenticeship and occupation as a goldsmith, see William Ingram, "Robert Keysar, playhouse speculator."

64. Stephen Spector (ed.), *The N-Town Play: Cotton MS Vespasian D. 8*, 2 vols. (Oxford: Oxford University Press, 1991), play 26, lines 101–3. I am grateful to Paula von Loewenfeldt for drawing my attention to this reference.

65. Carson, *A Companion to Henslowe's Diary*, p. 122. The prop is referred to also by Benedick in *Much Ado About Nothing*, 2.1.233–4. For a general discussion of stage-beards, see Will Fisher's essay in this volume.

66. See, for example, Anthony Parry's introduction to the New Mermaids' edition of *The Shoemaker's Holiday*: "as Alexander Leggatt puts it, 'Simon Eyre

became Lord Mayor of London because he was a jolly and energetic shoe-maker.' In preserving this legend, with its overtones of Dick Whittington, the play suggests that Eyre's attainment of high office is a proper outcome of his skill and pride in his craft" (xxii). Seaver similarly interprets the play as "an assertion of a new gentility to be gained not by birth, but by honest labour" ("Thomas Dekker's *The Shoemaker's Holiday*", p. 100). Bevington, by contrast, sees Eyre's entrepreneurial acumen as evincing "the spirit of many a multinational corporation" ("Theatre as holiday," p. 107).

67. Pierre Macherey and Etienne Balibar, "Literature as an ideological form: some Marxist hypotheses," *Praxis* 5 (1980): 43–58, esp. 48. For an illuminating application of Macherey and Balibar's notion to Shakespeare's presentation of artisanal labor in *A Midsummer Night's Dream*, see James H. Kavanagh, "Shakespeare in ideology," in John Drakakis (ed.), *Alternative Shakespeares* (London: Methuen, 1985), pp. 144–65.

CHAPTER 3

The dramatic life of objects in the early modern theatre

Douglas Bruster

καὶ γὰρ πρὸς ἄψυχα καὶ τὰ τυχόντα ἔστιν ὡς ὅπερ εἴρηται
συμβαίνει, καὶ εἰ πέπραγέ τις ἢ μὴ πέπραγεν ἔστιν ἀναγνωρί-
σαι.

. . . for indeed, [recognition] may take place in this manner through
lifeless things or chance events, and one may recognize whether
someone has or has not done something.

Aristotle, Poetics 1452a34–37

Sometime you shall see nothing but the adventures of an amorous
knight, passing from country to country for the love of his lady,
encountering many a terrible monster made of brown paper, and
at his return, is so wonderfully changed, that he cannot be known
but by some posie in his tablet, or by a broken ring, or a handkircher
or a piece of a cockle shell, what learn you by that? When the soul
of your plays is either mere trifles, or Italian bawdry, or cussing of
gentlewomen, what are we taught?

Stephen Gosson, Playes Confuted in Five Actions

The early modern playhouse in England was a theatre of easily held
things. Handheld objects figured centrally in plays of all genres there,
not just the dramatic adventures of "amorous knight[s]" which Gosson
derides. Indeed, one of the clearest departures that early modern playwrights made from Aristotle's precepts came in the ready employment
of those "lifeless things" which the *Poetics* goes on to criticize when used
as a means of recognition, for dramatic works of this era routinely called
upon hand properties, or "props," to qualify and further their plots.[1] So
common was this practice, in fact, that our memories of many early modern plays involve images of characters holding things. With Shakespeare,
for example, *Hamlet* can suggest a man contemplating a skull; *Antony and
Cleopatra*, a woman with an asp; *Romeo and Juliet*, a young woman with
a dagger. Sometimes this link between character and prop is so strong
that certain objects can gesture toward a drama, character, and scene:

a severed finger might call to mind De Flores in the third act of *The Changeling*; a skewered heart, Giovanni in the final scene of *'Tis Pity She's a Whore*. The endurance of such images – often aided by contemporary and subsequent printed illustrations – helps us to understand why Gosson would claim that, from a spectator's point of view, the "soul" of many plays resided in their objects.

Criticism devoted to these objects has usually come in a few established modes. One approach, influenced by the study of iconography, has built on the visual status of familiar hand props. Thus the skulls of *Hamlet* and *The Revenger's Tragedy* are explained in relation to the memento mori tradition, the severed hands of *Titus Andronicus* as icons of political agency, and the heart and dagger of *'Tis Pity* alongside baroque and neo-Platonic imagery.[2] Another critical vein springs from the study of metaphor and signification; this approach examines what one critic has called "the language of props," seeing handheld objects as "the realization of the verbal image in dramatic terms."[3] Because such objects are often related to the body, and may be the focus of characters' desires, they are sometimes described in psychoanalytic ways – the handkerchief of Othello being the *locus classicus* of this approach.[4] Still another critical genre explores the manner in which such props reveal social relations in the dramatic worlds they help define, or resonate with other issues of their texts' historical moments. Criticism in this mode might take up, for example, the viol of *The Roaring Girl* for what it can tell us about the operation of gender in this play, or the severed head of *Macbeth* as an object rich in cultural symbolism.[5]

Yet while these approaches have often shed light on important aspects of early modern plays, their helpfulness has just as frequently been limited by several factors. The first involves the matter of focus: in many instances of the critical traditions outlined above, insights are restricted by the particular objects under discussion. That is, where such analyses can teach readers a great deal about specific objects in specific plays, the insight they lend is often confined to the prop in question. Because hand props were prevalent in all dramatic genres of the era, and because the "same" prop appears in many plays, over time, a critical approach that focuses on single props, in single plays, can unnecessarily limit our understanding of such props' significance; this seems especially true in relation to audiences and playwrights who were familiar with numerous plays.[6] These critical traditions can also be hampered by their success. Thus while a strongly iconographic, or strongly semiotic, or strongly cultural materialist inquiry may illuminate hand props in the early modern theatre, and give the appearance of explaining them, the roles which such objects assumed were multiple, and routinely elude those who press forceful claims about theatrical objects in relation to select domains of experience.

What criticism of hand props in the early modern theatre most attests is our lack of a general account of such objects, an account in relation to which more specific claims might be measured. This essay aims to provide such an account. Offering a general description of hand props in early modern plays, it necessarily passes over the "thick description" which has characterized so much criticism of theatrical objects to date. Yet by describing hand props in a broader way, it seeks to lend this critical detail a context which will deepen our understanding of the materiality of the early modern playhouse. The following paragraphs begin, therefore, by locating hand props in relation to the array of physical objects appearing on the early modern stage, and survey a variety of contemporary records that mention hand properties. This essay then goes on to explore the relations among these properties, the dramatic genres of the era, and the playwrights who employed them. Among the questions it addresses: What general truths can we offer about the number, kinds, and roles of hand props in early modern plays? What influence might genre, author, venue, and historical moment have had upon these? How did contemporaries describe and account for these props? And how might the answers to such questions affect our understanding of the plays and playhouses of early modern England?

A variety of things appeared on the otherwise bare stages of early modern England, from actors and costumes to scenic decorations, signs, and hand props. Their "thing-ness" may be more or less apparent, depending on both the production in question, and our definition of a thing. We might qualify the immediately preceding questions, then, with still others: How should we define a theatrical object? What do hand props have in common with bodies, costumes, and larger properties, and how do they differ? Objects in the theatre can be defined in many ways, of course. As Shoshana Avigal and Shlomith Rimmon-Kenan have suggested, a theatrical object can become so by being:
— either inanimate or capable of becoming inanimate;
— transportable or placed so as to enable the actors to move around it;
— deprived of intentionality: the object is manipulated but cannot itself initiate discourse;

- either multifunctional, or different from its everyday use, or completely non-utilitarian except in its technical theatrical function;
- capable of "furnishing" the "stage-space" and acting as mediator between the actor's body and this space;
- seemingly mimetic and referential;
- artificial, "fabricated," unnatural;
- artifact, capable of being evaluated with the help of such aesthetic criteria as are used in the plastic arts.[7]

Most of these aspects relate objects closely to the human. Actors transport objects, and objects are placed in relation to actors. Objects imitate and refer for humans, and are fabricated, used, and evaluated by them. It is also true, however, that such objects help to define human subjects through their felt difference: if an object is that which is for a subject, we are subjects because we are not – perhaps not only – objects. Thus do the above descriptions, which set out to define theatrical objects, wind up telling us about theatrical subjectivity: in particular, that it is often established in relation to objects.[8] It was perhaps partly in response to such dependency that the *Poetics* criticized dramatic recognition deriving from trivial properties. By defining human relations through the inanimate, such recognition worked to blur the distinction between person and thing. It therefore threatened to challenge the sharp boundaries that Aristotle sought to establish in describing tokens as *apsuka*, or "lifeless."[9]

Granting the thoroughly material nature of the early modern stage, and the fact that objects can seem quite vital, how might we justify a focus on hand props? How do they differ from other things in the theatre? Hand props of course share with costumes, bodies, and scenic devices the condition of being "materially realizable on stage in three dimensions." And all these things possess a certain "mobility," a capacity to acquire various states, shapes, and meanings within the context of the theatrical production.[10] On stage a living body may seem to become an inanimate one; a shoe can signify a personal relation; a lone tree, a garden. And, like hand props, costumes and items of apparel can be acquired, exchanged, altered, and discarded, frequently changing in significance as this occurs. Yet if hand props – what we might define as "unanchored physical objects, light enough for a person to carry on stage for manual use there"[11] – shared the essential nature of these other objects, they differed in an important way. Hand props in early modern drama had more mobility than costumes, bodies, and larger properties. Because they are detached, and easily held, they are more easily transferred from one character, play, and genre to another. Much like coins and other units of currency, hand props testify by their size and portability to an open potential. They can be variously possessed, traded, lost, found, concealed, and evaluated. This allows them to relate characters to each other, and to larger elements in their dramatic worlds, as well as to qualify those relations, more fluidly than can such larger properties as costumes and scenic devices.

Yet it is precisely this fluidity that ensured that hand props would steadily disappear from discourse concerning the stage. If we imagine a sequence beginning with the plays themselves, then including bills and inventories, descriptions of productions, and, finally, formal criticism of these plays, what becomes apparent is that the number of hand props diminishes as one moves from plays and theatrical records to criticism. Where a play might easily contain thirty or more hand properties, a playhouse inventory will list only a fraction of these, an account or illustration of a production fewer still, and critical essays (when they mention properties at all) commonly only one.[12] As the introduction to this essay maintained, close focus on certain resonant properties has, ironically, worked to limit our understanding of these and other objects. We need to read against this tendency to recover the range of props in, and their importance to, early modern drama. To place such a way of reading, however, we should examine the ways in which properties have disappeared from view, and determine why they have done so.

We might begin with contemporary bills and other lists of expenses connected with theatrical productions. A record detailing the most basic theatrical materials appears in the "emptions and provisions" for the Christmas entertainments at court in 1572, which lists expenses incurred by a "propertymaker" named John Carow in relation to such objects as "A nett for the ffishers maskers," "wooll to stuf the fishes," "speares for the play of Cariclia," "A tree of Holly for the Duttons play," "13 Arrowes," "A palmers staf," "A desk for farrantes playe," "A vyzarde for an apes face," "A keye for Janus," "A Monster," "Dishes," and "Egges counterfet vii doozen."[13] Such a list is as close as we may come to a document which acknowledges, as fully as the plays themselves, the drama's use of and dependence on various materials. Of course, in some ways a list like this is likely to be even more thorough than a dramatic text in that it catalogues physical objects whose use the play's fiction may not make explicit. Thus, besides the wool used to stuff fishes, the bill submitted by the property-maker Carow includes such items as "syxpeny nayles," "three peny nayles," "twopeny nayles," "Tackes," and "hoopes for the monster" – things not only unannounced in dramatic texts, but which a playwright or show organizer might never have considered when writing or producing a drama.[14]

Objects typically make their way onto the page in direct relation to their value to the one who writes that page. Because it is probable that Carow first purchased the materials for the above items himself (and most likely submitted the bill within a short time of fashioning them), he had reason fully to detail his expenses. Nails were well worth itemizing, as were visors, staves, and arrows. We gain the benefit of this detail because they were important expenses to Carow. On the other hand, some documents pass over such detail because they contain items of a much greater value, with the expensive forcing out the less valuable. Here we might consider a transcript of Philip Henslowe's list of stage properties – reproduced as an appendix to this volume. Henslowe originally recorded this list in his "diary" under the heading: "Enventary tacken of all the properties for my *Lord Admeralles men*, the 10 of Marche 1598."[15] The first thing to point out about this list is that it comes in the context of other inventories, and of payments throughout Henslowe's diary, related to costumes. The early modern theatre was, of course, thoroughly invested in the display of clothing.[16] The Elizabethan eye was attracted to sumptuous dress to a degree that can be hard for us to imagine, and early modern playhouses were careful to satisfy the many playgoers who wished to see sumptuous costumes. Thus Henslowe's inventory of physical "properties" from 1598 should be seen in relation to the most important property in Henslowe's theatrical business: not actors, playwrights, play-texts, or hand props, but clothing. More valuable than other properties, clothing largely supplants notice of other theatrical objects throughout Henslowe's diary.

Even as mention of "harder" properties pales in comparison with the attention paid to costumes, however, so are the more ordinary properties – and especially the smaller ones – given little notice in Henslowe's inventory. This list mentions approximately eighty-four objects and groups of objects; a precise count is made difficult by Henslowe's tendency to record a type of object – say "iij tymbrells" – alongside a less generic property: "j dragon in fostes."[17] As even a brief sampling of the inventory shows, Henslowe stresses special things, objects related to particular characters and plays. Within a few lines of the inventory, for instance, one finds references to Mahomet, Phaeton, Argus, Neptune – even, in light of "gowlden flece," Jason and Medea (and, perhaps, Hercules); and the inventory may also list properties from Dekker's *Phaeton*, the anonymous *Mahomet, Jupiter and Io*, and Heywood's *Golden*

Age, among other dramas. And while over half the objects that Henslowe records (forty-four of eighty-four) might be defined as hand properties, it is worth noting that very few of them are ordinary or unremarkable.

On the contrary, Henslowe's inventory primarily records objects that, if lost, stolen, or damaged, would require special fabrication to replace. Of such smaller and everyday objects as purses, documents, jewels, toothpicks, or coins it makes no mention. In his extended analysis of Henslowe's diary, Neil Carson relates that "Almost as surprising as the presence of so many large properties [in Henslowe's accounts] is the inexplicable absence of some small ones." He continues:

> There are, for example, no chairs or benches in the inventory, nor any tables, trenchers, or mugs for the numerous banquet and tavern scenes in Elizabethan drama. The seventeen foils (while certainly more than the four or five mentioned by the chorus in *Henry V*), seem an absolute minimum to present believable battle scenes. There are none of the letters and purses regularly required in plays of the period, nor is any mention made of books, writing materials, and other objects needed for "study" scenes. It would seem that the inventory is only a partial list of the Company's resources. Many of these smaller items were probably kept backstage or supplied by the actors.[18]

It might be argued, following Carson, that the small size of such objects entailed they be kept in a separate place – for instance, a locked chest or chests in the playhouse's wardrobe. And that their existence, if recorded at all, is noted in a list that has not survived. Recently, however, a more intriguing suggestion has been advanced by Natasha Korda, who, exploring the relations between Henslowe's pawnbroking and his theatrical investments, proposes that the absent properties which Carson details may have been supplemented by unredeemed items in the pawn accounts.[19] The pawnbroker Henslowe might be expected to have had a surplus of the ordinary objects missing from the diary's lists. As a company would not need a property-maker to fashion them, these objects would likely be absent from any bill. The acting company would merely have borrowed from another of Henslowe's businesses. Whatever the explanation for their absence, one truth remains. However important they were to the function of all the plays his company put on, these more ordinary objects were not included in what Henslowe's list calls "all the properties for my Lord Admeralles men."

Their absence might be less noteworthy here were it not part of a larger pattern. We hear even less about hand props, for instance, in contemporary descriptions of dramatic performances, although the exceptions are familiar. The account of *Twelfth Night* that John Manningham recorded in his diary in 1602 mentions the letter which Maria counterfeits to fool Malvolio, and likewise Simon Forman's memories of *Cymbeline* include Iachimo's theft of Imogen's bracelet.[20] Significantly, each of these instances involves some kind of transgression. We could take it as a given, in fact, that objects customarily appear in such accounts when they are involved in some breach of decorum or audience expectation. The Induction to *A Warning for Fair Women*, for example, complains of those plays which feature "two or three like to drovers, / With taylers bodkins, stabbing one another."[21] Here the difficulty is over the triviality of the entire production, from actor to property and, in the famous lines just prior to these, diction: "skreaming like a pigge half stickt, / And cries Vindicta, revenge, revenge." Instead of swords – appropriate to a dramatic spectacle – the actors are said to bear weapons small enough to be mistaken for "bodkins."[22] Other instances where a breach of decorum appears to have made props more remarkable include Thomas Platter's description of a play in which a "servant proceeded to hurl his shoe at his master's head"; Ben Jonson's sneer at spectacles in which "egges are broken" (apparently when thrown at others); and Sir John Chamberlain's gossipy hearsay to the effect that the King's Men had obtained Gondomar's cast suit and litter for their scandalous production of *A Game at Chess* in 1624 (these representing objects larger, of course, than the hand properties of our other examples).[23] An allusion to a stage fool who will "twirle his Bawble" in Thomas Goffe's *The Careless Shepherdess* may nod to the potential indecorum associated with fools' bawdy actions, for baubles (fools' clubs or instruments) were often material for indecent jests.[24] Of course, fools were expected to have baubles, which often served as an extension, if not mark, of their characters. And this near identification of character and thing was typically solidified in the many visual representations of dramatic performance, and of characters and situations associated with the theatre.

If objects found their way into the gossip of social records when they were involved in indecorous actions, they were most often portrayed in visual representations when they upheld decorum of character. In early modern illustrations, hand properties seem not the exception but the rule. Perhaps this was because such properties helped identify a character and scene, and more fully embodied a play. Perhaps it was owing also to a certain *horror vacui* when it came to figures' hands: illustrators preferred that hands be used for gestures, or rest on something, or grasp an object, rather than remaining empty. Whether we explain this tendency through content (through what a hand held) or process (through the fact that a hand was doing something), illustrations connected with the early modern stage routinely feature characters holding things.[25] The visual representations that R. A. Foakes gathers in *Illustrations of the English Stage 1580–1642* feature approximately seventy props in figures' hands (there are more properties, of course, when one counts worn weapons, hats, and other items worn on the body, or objects on tables accessible to these figures).[26] Most of these held props are weapons and objects of authority. The weapons include swords, daggers, halberds, lances, pikes, staves, mauls, and crossbows. Although many of these weapons convey authority, there are also scepters and orbs (particularly in representations of Elizabeth) which remain authoritative without the direct threat of violence. Besides such props, dramatic illustrations also feature objects more firmly grounded in the routines of everyday life. Among these are food, utensils (goblets and knives), books, papers, letters, pipes, snuff boxes, lights, fans, canes, crutches, and hats.

In some illustrations, hand props work to identify the figure. For instance, the book and staff on the title page of the second quarto of Marlowe's *Doctor Faustus* join with a doctor's gown and hat, a magic circle, and an impish devil to tell us that this is the title character. Likewise a cane or walking stick in the 1658 quarto of *The Witch of Edmonton* helps identify old "Mother" Sawyer. And hand props similarly confirm the identities of characters on the title page of Henry Marsh's collection of drolls, *The Wits, or, Sport upon Sport* (1662, 1673), where such figures as Falstaff and Antonio (the latter from *The Changeling*) are identified both by their names and by such physical accouterments as costume and prop: the "Changling" wears a fool's cap and has a horn-book dangling from his wrist; Falstaff is dressed in clothing redolent of Shakespeare's time, and his identity is fleshed out not only by a protruding stomach, but by the cup he holds aloft – a confirming symbol of his epicurean character.[27] Perhaps no illustrated prop is more clearly a token of a character's identity, however, than the bracelet that an almost nude Bateman displays in a woodcut published with William Sampson's *The Vow Breaker* (1636).[28] The object in question is a kind of "charm-bracelet" from which hangs one half of a piece of gold that he and Anne, his beloved, had divided between them as a love token. Bateman, having been away as a soldier, returns from the wars on the very day when Anne has married another man. In the woodcut, Bateman is pointing to the bracelet, and saying "Thinke on thy promise alive or dead I must and will injoy thee."

The marking of this bracelet as the living symbol of Anne's "promise" also marks Bateman as her intended; the bracelet contains within itself their history together, and the grounds of his present and future actions. One could say that the bracelet is a miniature "plot" or summary of the play's action. Much like the tokens which Gosson derided in the epigraph to this essay ("he cannot be known but by some posie in his tablet, or by a broken ring"), it does more than trivial objects are commonly thought capable of doing. And it is in this function that we see a reason for the intensive commentary that such objects have drawn. What Aristotle, Gosson, and Thomas Rymer after them responded to is, in part, the indecorum of recognition deriving from the trivial, and, in part, the irrationality of fictions which define human relations through small properties. As Rymer complained, in his well-known description of *Othello*, "So much ado, so much stress, so much passion and repetition about an Handkerchief!"[29] To critics of this orientation, reducing social relations to the level of trivial, "external" things makes no sense.[30]

Yet where these commentators could appear the exception (in that their emphasis on decorum and reason may seem too strict), they established the pattern that most later criticism has followed. In writing about Desdemona's handkerchief, or Hamlet's skull, that is, critics follow in the footsteps of Rymer, Gosson, and Aristotle, who responded to the exaggerated importance given to certain objects in plays. It is difficult to avoid repeating these commentators' rationalism because analysis often finds itself drawn to moments of the irrational – to sequences in plays, for instance, that cross the boundaries of reason, and so call for dispassionate analysis. Thus a concentration of social or psychological energy on a seemingly trivial object appears to be "fetishism" (the sustained exaggeration of an object's value or importance), which in turn begs for critical rationalization. We are drawn to the handkerchief, and to the skull, not only because the characters in these plays are drawn to them, but in part because we feel they should not be.

Significantly, this moralistic evaluation of objects begins not with critics but with the plays themselves. One might compare Hamlet's incredulous "This?" in response to hearing that a skull belonged to someone he once knew – upon which he addresses it, asking

Where be your gibes now, your gambols, your songs, your flashes of merriment, that were wont to set the table on a roar? (5.1.182, 189–91)

– with Vindice's famous apostrophe to the skull of Gloriana, his beloved:

> Does the silkworm expend her yellow labors
> For thee? For thee does she undo herself?
> . . .
> Does every proud and self-affecting dame

Camphire her face for this? and grieve her maker
In sinful baths of milk, when many an infant starves,
For her superfluous outside – all for this?

$$(3.5.71-2, 83-6)^{31}$$

What we hear in these well-known passages are variations on a single rhetorical question concerning the lack of fit between the object at hand and a complex set of memories and truths separate from, if related to, the object. There is an edgy surprise behind the utterances: How could such a vital, irrepressible body be reduced to so unremarkable an object? Why do Nature, society, and individuals waste resources on such hollow vanities?

It is this kind of dramatic moment that sees hand props at their most resonant. Time slows as the speaker, like Bateman pointing toward his bracelet, directs our attention toward the object. Not coincidentally, it is precisely such moments that draw the most critical attention. In fact, one could offer no better example of a "reading effect": the process by which a structure in a literary text uncannily shapes, in its own image, critical accounts of that structure or text. As Shoshana Felman defines this phenomenon:

The scene of the critical debate is thus a repetition of the scene dramatized in the text. The critical interpretation, in other words, not only elucidates the text but also reproduces it dramatically, unwittingly participates in it. Through its very reading, the text, so to speak, acts itself out. As a reading effect, this inadvertent "acting out" is indeed uncanny: whichever way the reader turns, he can but be turned by the text, he can but perform it by repeating it.[32]

We can learn about our relation to object criticism from this description. Insofar as we "read" the same objects that dramatic characters read, and read them in similar ways, the criticism we produce runs the risk of being more an effect than an analysis of such texts. In our continual concern with a select few properties in early modern drama, we might be seen as performing these texts, participating, like the plays' characters, in their scenes of wonder. Therefore if we are to avoid asking the same kinds of questions that a play's characters ask (and possibly getting the same answers that they do), we need to work against the selective focus displayed by the speeches examined above. For plays are full of objects, and while many of these objects fail to draw extended notice from the plays themselves, they remain integral to their dramatic worlds – not despite but because of their ordinariness.

To return to the primary question which began this essay: What general truths can we offer about the number, kinds, and roles of hand

props in early modern plays? We might begin by establishing what is
known about hand props. Most of our objective knowledge about the
broad range of hand props in early modern drama derives from Frances
Teague's *Shakespeare's Speaking Properties*. (Prior to this collection, Teague's
study was one of only two books devoted to the subject, the other being
Felix Bosonnet's *The Function of Stage Properties in Christopher Marlowe's Plays*.)
A major virtue of Teague's study is that it includes, in its appendices,
figures relating to properties in plays written by Shakespeare (excepting
The Two Noble Kinsmen). Her first appendix offers a detailed property list
for each drama. The second divides these properties into categories, and
calculates the distribution of properties across the plays. And though the
chapters of Teague's book offer many insights about the function of stage
properties in Shakespeare's plays, the figures in these appendices are for
the most part underutilized by the study they close. Because these figures
are the first hard data concerning hand properties in any body of early
modern plays, it will be useful here to listen to what they tell us.

We might begin with numbers. How many hand props appeared in
Shakespeare's plays? Teague counts the props in the thirty-six Folio plays,
and in *Pericles*. She records them on their first appearance only, and omits
references to costumes, unless they come to function as a property – such
as, for example, Osric's hat, and Troilus's sleeve. Teague's figures suggest
an average of thirty-four properties per play.[33] What these numbers show
at once is that Shakespeare's plays used more props than actors.[34] If we
still needed a reason to take the function of props in early modern drama
seriously, the fact that the typical play in such a grouping employed more
inanimate things than actors as their "performing objects" would seem
to give us our warrant.[35] This was not true for every play, of course.
Some plays, especially shorter ones, had fewer props than actors. To
make comparisons with plays of various lengths, therefore, it will be
helpful to find out how many properties might occur in units both shorter
and longer than Shakespeare's average play. The calculations might be
made as follows: if we average the through line numbers of Shakespeare's
plays, we come up with a composite play of around 3,018 lines, or a text
approximately the length of *All's Well That Ends Well*. Given the typical
frequency of properties across all of Shakespeare's plays, one could expect
approximately 11.26 properties for every 1,000 lines.

What kinds of props made up these numbers? Teague offers six categories or kinds: lights; weapons or war gear; documents; riches or gifts; tokens of characters; and "other." Were a typical Shakespeare play to exist,
it might contain at least one light (e.g. a torch, a candle), three rewards

(money bags, coins), six documents (letters, proclamations), five tokens of identity (crowns, gloves, rings, scepters), six weapons, and nine "other" or miscellaneous objects. (The numbers here total less than thirty-four because of rounding.) Of course, no play is typical in this way, because genre strongly influences both the number and kind of props which a play uses.[36] In relation to genre, it might be pointed out that tragedies tend to have the most props, histories the second greatest number, and comedies the least. The numbers, on average: tragedies, 11.48 props per 1,000 lines; histories, 10.6 props per 1,000 lines; comedies, 8.43 props per 1,000 lines.

The romances pose a special problem. Although romances have a higher frequency of props than the comedies, *Pericles* remains something of an anomaly, with almost double the number of props as its companion romances. Figures for the romances are as follows: *Pericles*, 19.14 per 1,000 lines; *Cymbeline*, 10.21 per 1,000 lines; *The Winter's Tale*, 8 per 1,000 lines; *The Tempest*, 11.53 per 1,000 lines. Acts 1 and 2 of *Pericles*, usually thought non-Shakespearean, have a frequency of 23 props per 1,000 lines, whereas if we inspect acts 3, 4, and 5 of the play, most of which is traditionally ascribed to Shakespeare, we find a lower frequency, of 16 props per 1,000 lines. Some, though not all, of this density of props in the first two acts of *Pericles* involves the parade of knights in 2.2, each of whom bears a device upon his shield. As we will see, this procession recalls the practices of an earlier moment in the early modern theatre, when, in histories and romances alike, spectacular displays of arms and colors were common.[37]

Genre affects not only the number but the kinds of props which appear on stage. It is apparent, for instance, that certain kinds of properties serve as generic signals: a lute or a hobby horse might signal a comedy, a skull or a dagger a tragedy. And knowing the genre of a play can lead one to expect it to feature certain properties. We can see this in table 3.1, which draws on Teague's figures to show both the composite and generic distribution of properties across her six categories. The figures in bold face show percentages higher than the mean.

Some of the figures in table 3.1 confirm what we could have surmised about the plays from an ordinary acquaintance: that Shakespeare's comedies, for example, feature more "rewards" than do his histories and tragedies. However, several facts might surprise us. For instance, we might be surprised to see that the comedies employ more documents than do the other genres, for critics usually emphasize writing and writings in the tragedies and histories.[38] A typical comedy, however, will feature more

Table 3.1. *Distribution of props in Shakespeare: composite and by genre*
(by percentage)

	Lights	Rewards	Documents	Identity tokens	Weapons	Other
Composite	3.2	10.33	19.79	16.1	21.55	29
13 Comedies	2.7	**18.61**	**27.62**	10.81	16.21	24
10 Histories	1.6	5.67	16.48	**25.1**	**22.7**	28.37
10 Tragedies	**5.4**	7.37	18.18	12.53	**25.06**	**31.44**
4 Romances	2.17	**11.59**	14.49	15.21	21	**35.5**

Based on figures from Frances Teague, *Shakespeare's Speaking Properties*

documents than a tragedy and history play combined. Comedy's emphasis on interpersonal relations, and the tendency of comedic characters to express their desires in letters and poems, helps to explain this feature. We might notice the four male lovers and their individual "papers" in 4.3 of *Love's Labour's Lost*, or the various letters which the lovers exchange in *The Two Gentlemen of Verona*.

Similarly, we may not be surprised to find that Shakespeare's histories use more identity tokens (usually objects of authority and rank) and weapons than the average; or to find that his tragedies rely even more heavily still on weapons. On the whole, it is the tragedies' use of weapons – daggers, swords, rapiers, and cudgels – that accounts for their greater frequency of props. But we might be taken by the tragedies' heavy employment of lights, something that reminds us how many of these plays unfold mainly at night. In contrast, the history plays transpire largely during the day, and have the fewest lights of any genre.

Like his comedies, Shakespeare's romances employ a higher than average percentage of rewards, yet differ from the comedies in their comparative paucity of documents. In fact, the romances use fewer documents than any of the other three genres. We might understand this, first, as a function of how the romances present desire (that is, in a chaster way than do the passionate poems and letters that characterized Shakespeare's comedies in the 1590s) and, secondly, as a function of alienation in the romances: the emotional reconciliations at the ends of *Pericles, Cymbeline, The Winter's Tale*, and *The Tempest* depend in part on the fact that characters have been profoundly divided from each other, not communicating through letters to the same extent as characters in the comedies. *The Tempest*, which has no letters, epitomizes this tendency. Stranded on an island, Prospero seems unable to send letters; after the storm has delivered his enemies and friends to him, he does not need to send any.

Because Shakespeare changed his generic emphasis during his career, pronouncements about the effect of chronology on the frequency of properties in his plays can be dangerous. Nonetheless, we can offer certain observations. If we were to graph the frequency of properties in Shakespeare's plays, we would see something like a shallow "V" over the course of his career. That is, beginning with many props in the early 1590s, we witness a gradual diminishing through the following decade. Early plays like *Titus Andronicus* (21 props per 1,000 lines) and *Henry VI Part Two* (15.5 props per 1,000 lines) have comparatively many props when examined in the context of similar tragedies from later in the 1590s and early 1600s. *Hamlet*, for instance, has 10.24 props per 1,000 lines, and *Henry V* has 7.7 props per 1,000 lines – a much lower frequency than the history plays and the tragedy from earlier in Shakespeare's career. After this decline in frequency, we see a significant increase beginning about 1605, when such tragedies as *King Lear* (16 props per 1,000 lines), *Macbeth* (17.4 props per 1,000 lines), and *Timon* (17.64 props per 1,000 lines) approach and exceed the frequency for tragedies of the 1590s, and when a collaborative history play, *Henry VIII*, exceeds the frequency for all history plays, with 17.61 props per 1,000 lines. *Henry VIII* recalls the heavy use of things in the "drum and trumpet" shows of the late 1580s and early 1590s, and nostalgically recreates that environment – perhaps even with a surplus of things.

We might pause to ask what may have caused Shakespeare to vary the frequency of props over the course of his career. Genre alone cannot account for the variation, as plays written between 1598 and 1605 tend to have fewer props than plays of the same genre written before and after this period. We have already seen that *Hamlet* and *Henry V* have fewer properties than, respectively, *Romeo and Juliet* and *Titus Andronicus*, and seven earlier history plays. And significant here is the fact that the middle comedies also have fewer properties than earlier comedies. For instance, one might compare such plays as *Much Ado About Nothing* (6.33 props per 1,000 lines), *As You Like It* (5.36 props per 1,000 lines), and *Measure for Measure* (5.1 props per 1,000 lines) with earlier works like *The Merchant of Venice* (13.5 props per 1,000 lines), *The Merry Wives of Windsor* (13.55 props per 1,000 lines), and *A Midsummer Night's Dream* (9 props per 1,000 lines). Clearly the decline in numbers during this time was apparent across various dramatic kinds, and did not occur because of changes in Shakespeare's generic preferences.

How, then, to explain it? Venue might seem to offer a solution. For
the first "Globe" plays so considered – *Henry V*, and *Julius Caesar* (9.9
props per 1,000 lines) – have fewer properties than earlier instances of
their genres. And, as we have seen, *As You Like It* has noticeably fewer
than either *The Merchant of Venice* or *The Merry Wives of Windsor*. Did the
move to a "new" playhouse cause a reduction of the props called for
in Shakespeare's plays? Even if we answered this in the affirmative, we
would have to recognize that it would not be the entire story. For the move
from Theatre to Globe occurred during 1599, and a noticeable decline in
property use appears in *Much Ado About Nothing* – commonly, though not
universally, dated 1598/99. Moreover, the King's Men leased the Blackfriars for indoor performances in 1608 – again, after Shakespeare's use of
properties had begun to increase. It might be, then, that this variation is
evidence of a response to alterations in audience tastes, and in the company's taste in audiences, which the change in venues signaled. That is,
that rather than being the cause of such variation, these changes of place
were, at least in part, an effect of the same cultural and aesthetic forces
which produced changes in property use. Causality was overdetermined:
properties were thus not only a signal of larger theatrical changes, but
were themselves changed by those transformations.

Such an interpretation would also remain consonant with thematic
changes in Shakespeare's plays. Broadly stated, during the late 1590s and
early 1600s his plays focus increasingly on individuals, psychology, and
character, and less on the surface stories of nations and factions. With
Prince Hal, Brutus, and Hamlet, a shift toward the interiority of the later
tragedies has occurred. This emphasis meant that more of a play's time is
spent with fewer characters – in short, that sieges give way to soliloquies.
If we compare the props in the first acts of *Titus Andronicus* and *Hamlet*,
for example, we find that the early tragedy includes: "colors," "swords
for Saturninus's party," "swords for Bassanius's party," "crown," "coffin
covered in black," "laurel wreath," "Titus's sword," "four sons' swords,"
"Titus's palliament – white cloak," "patrician swords," "chariot," and
"Titus's crest." *Hamlet*, in contrast, offers us exactly half this number of
properties: "seats," "ghost's armor," "Marcellus' partisan," "Claudius'
letter to Norway," "Hamlet's tablet," "Hamlet's sword."[39] These lists
are a study in contrast. The props of *Titus Andronicus* seem those of a
playwright utilizing display to its maximum advantage, and perhaps for
its own sake. A coffin competes with a chariot, and a laurel wreath with
a crown for the audience's eye. *Hamlet*, on the other hand, is quite spare.
Its properties seem to follow the action, arising out of it, rather than

providing the action's reason for being. The same is apparent if we contrast the two props in *Henry V*'s first act – a throne, and tennis balls – with the various swords, letters, armor, petitions, colors, robes, and halberds in the first acts of earlier history plays. With their respective assertion and denial of his authority, the throne and the tennis balls help to establish the play's focus on Henry's character, whereas the assortment of props in earlier history plays indicates nothing if not the dispersion of dramatic interest across various characters and factions.

If during the last years of the Elizabethan era Shakespeare increasingly stressed the tragedic individual, and in so doing departed from the early plays' larger groupings of characters and the objects which identified them, another kind of shift may have been responsible for the eventual increase in his plays' use of properties after 1604. Where the first half of his career witnessed a shift from spectacle to speech, the second half saw a return to spectacle, as his generic emphasis moved from history plays and comedies to tragedies and romances. All plays, of course, use more properties when they show instead of tell. Dumb shows, for example, rely heavily on props to convey their information. One has to look no further than the prop-intensive dumb show in *Hamlet* for a silent language that speaks through properties:

Enter a King and a Queen very lovingly, the Queen embracing him and he her. She kneels and makes show of protestation unto him. He takes her up and declines his head upon her neck. He lies him down upon a bank of flowers. She, seeing him asleep, leaves him. Anon come in another man, takes off his crown, kisses it, pours poison in the sleeper's ears, and leaves him. The Queen returns, finds the King dead, makes passionate action. The pois'ner with some three or four mutes come in again, seem to condole with her. The dead body is carried away. The pois'ner woos the Queen with gifts; she seems harsh and unwilling awhile, but in the end accepts love. (3.2.135 s.d.)

Crowns, a bank of flowers, poison, gifts. Increasingly after the accession of James, such silent language came to influence Shakespeare's dramatic practice, as the spectacular nature of courtly shows displaced some of the intensively verbal copia that had been his trademark during the late 1590s and early 1600s.[40] Similarly, we know that during this period the way Shakespeare described playgoers changed. As Andrew Gurr points out, "From 1600 onwards, Shakespeare abandoned the idea of an auditory in favour of spectators."[41] What we may be witnessing in the decline, and rise, of Shakespeare's use of props, then, are larger changes in the nature of his plays, and in the desires of the audiences for whom he wrote. An intensively visual theatre of the late 1580s and early

Table 3.2. *Frequency of props in non-Shakespearean plays, 1587–1636*

Play	Approx. year	Total lines	Total props	Props per 1,000 lines
The Spanish Tragedy	1587	2,625	42	16
The Battle of Alcazar	1589	1,591	35	22
The Jew of Malta	1589	2,385	28	11.74
Woodstock	1592	3,218	56	17.4
Edmund Ironside	1595	2,063	21	10.18
Every Man in His Humour	1598	3,074	30	9.76
All Fools	1601	1,858	15	8.07
Sejanus	1603	3,146	19	6.04
A Trick to Catch the Old One	1605	2,139	17	7.94
The Revenger's Tragedy	1606	2,534	24	9.47
A King and No King	1611	2,665	17	6.37
The Devil is an Ass	1616	3,235	20	6.18
Women Beware Women	1621	3,311	25	7.55
The Roman Actor	1626	2,282	17	7.45
The Picture	1629	2,672	20	7.48
Perkin Warbeck	1633	2,539	20	7.87
The Royal Slave	1636	1,665	7	4.2

1590s was temporarily affected by verbal preferences in the late 1590s and early 1600s, which in turn gave way to practices influenced by the spectacles of the Jacobean court, and by audiences oriented toward those spectacles.

While within Shakespeare's career we see a double movement in the frequency of hand props, in early modern drama as a whole the narrative is more straightforward. Using the same principles underlying the preceding examination of Shakespeare's plays, an original survey of twenty non-Shakespearean dramas from approximately 1587 to 1636 helps contextualize the Shakespeare figures even as they show a discernible pattern in the use of hand properties across early modern plays.[42] We can begin with the figures shown in table 3.2 for seventeen plays by various authors, and in various genres.

We might notice a number of things about the figures from this table. First, it reveals that, regarding numbers, playwrights' use of hand props was close to that of their contemporaries. Those plays written during the period in which Shakespeare was active approximate his practice in relation to hand props. And his contemporaries' practices are also equivalent to one another: Middleton's practice in *Women Beware Women* is close to that of Massinger's in *The Roman Actor*, which in turn is much like that of Ford in *Perkin Warbeck*. Indeed, the second important thing this table tells us is that the practice of such writers appears to have moved steadily in one direction: these numbers show a general decline in the number of hand props used. Before 1603, no play here has a frequency of fewer than 8 props per 1,000 lines; after 1606, there is no play here with a frequency greater than 8 props per 1,000 lines. George Peele's *The Battle of Alcazar* features the greatest frequency of props, a number which includes, like *Titus Andronicus*, a potentially embarrassing array of such props as swords, chariots, whips, knives, drums, and brands. And although the frequency here might seem inflated because of the comparative brevity of the play (1,591 lines), it is not clear that, writing a play on this subject of twice the length, Peele would not have employed even more props to illustrate his dramatic tableau.

Plays written in the late 1580s and early 1590s employed the most hand properties – a truth confirmed by similarly high frequencies in Shakespeare's early plays. Thus even a late history such as *Perkin Warbeck* has a frequency closer to other plays from the 1620s and 1630s than to a history play from the late 1580s or early 1590s. A comedy such as *The Jew of Malta*, from 1589, features more properties than comedies written ten, fifteen, and forty years later. And *The Spanish Tragedy* likewise has a greater frequency of properties than all the tragedies written after it on the above table. Seen over nearly half a century like this, the frequency of hand props appears to have been more greatly influenced by historical moment than by genre. And, despite the temporary increase we have seen in Shakespeare's practice after the accession of James, with the shift from Tudor to Stuart we are witnessing an overall decline in the frequency of hand properties in plays.

One of the causes of this decline may have been a constriction of the numbers of actors and roles in early modern plays. The expansive tableaux of all genres in the 1580s and 1590s (one might recall, for instance, the parade of characters even in the comedy of *Love's Labour's Lost*) entailed numerous figures entering and exiting the audience's view; many of these figures carried hand properties as part of their play-world activity. Such would dovetail with scholars' accounts of the "large" plays and repertories established in London during the 1580s and early 1590s, a phenomenon explored by Andrew Gurr, David Bradley, T. J. King, and Scott McMillin, among others.[43] Gurr points to the establishment of the first "large" acting company in 1583 (twelve sharers rather than eight in the Queen's Men), a fashion which had become the norm by the early 1590s and which influenced the writing of "large" plays (mainly chronicle histories) until 1593–4. After this, the ambitions of these "large-capacity" companies – and, accordingly, the number of roles in the plays they staged – declined as the plague, travel, and economic truths brought home to the companies the difficult realities of their augmented size.[44] By the time Cartwright pens *The Royal Slave*, the sprawling organization of the Elizabethan repertories had given way to smaller acting repertories accustomed not to the expansive plebeian amphitheaters but to the more restricted spaces of the hall playhouses.[45] Fewer actors generally meant fewer roles, which in turn reduced the quantity of hand props in dramatic productions. In itself, though, the reduction of roles explains a decline in number but not in frequency. The latter may have come from a diminished need to differentiate characters from one another: with fewer "group" scenes, there is less need to mark characters by means of such an identifying property as, for instance, a banner or shield.

Three plays examined fell out of the above range, and make up something like a distinct "genre" of drama in their infrequent use of – and, in one case, reference to – hand props. The plays in question are Daniel's *Philotas* (1600–4), Jonson's *Catiline* (1611), and Elizabeth Carey's *The Tragedy of Mariam* (1602–8). Daniel's play fell under the auspices of the Queen's Revels, and Jonson's play was acted by the King's Men. Carey's text is a "closet" drama, of course, never meant to be acted, and is included here for precisely that reason: to suggest how frequently a dramatic text not connected to the theatre might be expected to call on hand properties in imagining a dramatic world. Using the same criteria employed in the previous tabulation, we see that *Mariam* has a frequency of 2.76 props per 1,000 lines, which is almost exactly like *Philotas*, which has 2.81 props per 1,000 lines, and only slightly below *Catiline*, which has 3.11 props per 1,000 lines. Taken as a group, these plays are remarkably spare in their use of properties, calling on fewer than half the props of any play in the preceding table. In doing so, they might be said to constitute a non-theatrical dramatic genre, one devoted more to political philosophy than to popular entertainment.

There are of course several possible reasons why *Catiline* was "damned" when first staged in 1611, but surely first among these is its essentially untheatrical nature.[46] *Catiline* gradually metamorphoses from a drama into a collection of speeches. No one better realized this than Jonson, who, in his letter "To the Reader in Ordinairie" prefaced to the first quarto in

1611, remarked that "you commend the two first Actes, with the people, because they are the worst; and dislike the Oration of Cicero."[47] The division Jonson draws here is significant, for the first two acts of *Catiline* contain most of its props, seven of eleven, with a frequency of just over 7 props per 1,000 lines – very close to the other non-Shakespearean plays on the table above. However, after act 3, properties disappear entirely from the play, and it turns into a series of long speeches without the familiar attraction of objects to engage the audience's eyes. This is not to say that *Catiline* failed because it had no properties after its third act. Yet it is clear that, at the same time he turned his back on the world of things, Jonson forgot what helped to make plays successful on the early modern stage.

We might take Jonson's reluctance over properties in *Catiline* as indicative of a larger trend in his thinking about the stage and society. Jonson's tension with the stage is, of course, a staple of criticism. However, we are often reluctant to say what, specifically, about the stage led to this tension. As Jonas Barish has argued, Jonson retained a special animosity toward theatrical stuff, the stage objects and material practices that made the early modern theatre what it was:

When it came to stagecraft, [Jonson] rejected with equal vehemence all the varieties of theatrical claptrap most cherished by Elizabethan audiences: fireworks, thunder, and ordnance, the raising of ghosts from the cellarage and lowering of gods from the hut. In the course of his feud with Inigo Jones, Jonson also ridiculed such newer and more esoteric wonders as the *machina versatilitas*, or turning device, and the *machina ductilis*, or tractable scene, both of them among the admired playthings of the court theatre. One common factor in all these dislikes, as W. A. Armstrong has pointed out, is that "they were all directed against scenes, lights and machines which moved before the spectators' eyes" and were hence "most likely to distract attention from the spoken word."[48]

Barish's observation perhaps asks us to consider *Catiline*'s second half less in relation to the theatre than the pulpit, where few if any props would have distracted the audience from the speech in question. It is just such a reluctance over the objects of theatre that one can sense in Shakespeare's middle period, when a larger antitheatrical sentiment shaped by both satirical verse and the poetomachia of the late 1590s and early 1600s may well have affected the employment of props in his plays. When Hamlet remarks, for instance, that he has "that within which passes show," we need to remember the theatrical context of his statement, which completes a sentence that begins: "These indeed seem, / For they are actions that a man might play," and likewise ends with a nod to the costumes of grief in mentioning "the trappings and the suits of woe" (1.2.83–6).

The preceding remarks have attempted to ascertain some basic truths about hand props in the early modern playhouse: how many were used, of what kind they were, and in which genres they appeared. In trying to establish such information, this essay has engaged in what we might call "thin description," eschewing the intensive focus on a particular text and textual moment and the rhetorical amplification common to recent modes of cultural and historicist interpretation. It has therefore not aspired to the kind of qualitative analysis of selected props that more narrowly focused essays perform. But its emphasis on evidence drawn from a variety of plays, over an expanse of five decades, has foregrounded one of the notorious shortcomings of new historicism: its inability to describe or account for historical change. The "thin" description of this essay perhaps resembles less a still-life painting than a larger historical canvas; with its scale, however, comes not only a variety of evidence, but an insight about the nature of evidence itself. It reminds us that evidence does not speak for itself – that it has an evidentiary as well as cultural context. Before we draw a conclusion from a single piece of evidence, that is, we owe it to our subject matter to determine the genre of the evidence and the place of our evidence within this genre. In so doing, we may come to realize that such may be less representative than we had believed. At the very least we will have performed more responsible research, and have avoided being "written" by the documents we study.

With this said, it is worth asking here a different kind of question, one concerning not the numbers and kinds of stage properties, but the roles of objects in plays of the sixteenth and seventeenth centuries. We might start by observing that plays of the later 1590s and early 1600s often show an intensive interest in particular properties. This interest seems similar to the process of the poetic blazon so popular during the 1590s, and may itself borrow from the blazon. We might compare Hamlet and Vindice's meditations on the skulls they hold with any of a number of aggressive treatments of faces and bodies in late Elizabethan poetry, and even with such a passage as Marlowe's "Was this the face that launched a thousand ships / And burnt the topless towers of Ilium?"[49] In such passages the Elizabethans' inquisitiveness is at its most apparent, as is their almost childlike habit of restlessly pushing against things, both animate and inanimate, to define themselves.

Elsewhere, I have argued for a historical shift in the function of hand properties, tracing a marked liveliness to these objects during the late Elizabethan and Jacobean eras:

> Mimetically glossing a growing cultural preoccupation with commodity and materiality... the role assumed by movable objects in the drama from (roughly) 1590 to 1620 progresses to the point where stage "properties" not only serve as floating signifiers between individuals – signs, for example, of chastity, marriage, and social position – but become a focus of interest in themselves. Whereas through most of the Elizabethan drama, in plays such as *Gammer Gurton's Needle* (1553), *The Comedy of Errors* (1592), and *The Two Gentlemen of Verona* (1593), for instance, dramatic commodities like needles, chains, and rings were important for what could be called their locative signification – that is, where the stage property implied certain things in relation to theme, character, and characters' personal or social relationships – in the late Elizabethan and early Jacobean drama commodities would come to be a source of interest in their own right, as the center of a purity discourse which worked to equate subject and object on the material plane. Shifting its attention from semiosis to subjectivity, the drama began to explore the reified basis of personal relations even as it tended, with more and more frequency, to personify commodities, according them a life of their own. Identity thus came to be inscribed in, instead of by, these objects.[50]

What this essay's analysis of the frequency of props has shown is that the moment of this shift – best represented in Shakespeare's works by such plays, for example, as *Hamlet*, *Troilus and Cressida*, *Twelfth Night*, or *Othello* – saw the playwright exploring the "life" of objects even as he reduced their number in his plays. It is as though the price of focusing on a central object or objects (a sleeve, a handkerchief, a skull) were presenting the audience, his actors, and himself, with fewer objects to consider.

By way of conclusion, it may be useful here to gather some of the observations this essay has made about props in early modern plays. I began by pointing out that criticism of hand props has traditionally confined itself to selected modes, and has in turn been limited by this selective focus. After discussing various definitions of dramatic properties, the preceding paragraphs identified a fluidity between person and thing on the early modern stage, and cited this fluidity as one spur to the moralizing criticism of objects which has long been part of both dramatic texts themselves and commentary on those texts. Objects seem to "stand out" from their surroundings when they are involved in some breach of decorum, and usually receive attention when they contravene expectation. It was maintained, however, that to pay attention to objects only in these circumstances, and on the plays' terms, is to repeat rather than analyze these texts.

An examination of props in Shakespeare's plays showed that, like the dramas of his contemporaries, they call for more props than actors. It also indicated that Shakespeare's use of hand props changed significantly: plays written at the beginning of his career have more props than plays written between 1598 and 1604; plays written after 1604 – most probably under the influence of Jacobean taste for spectacle – resume the pattern established early in his career. The fifteen non-Shakespearean plays scrutinized tell a larger story. Although genre is an important determinant of the kinds (and, to a lesser extent, the quantity) of props a play will employ, historical moment most affected the number of props in a dramatic text. From the late 1580s through the 1630s, the number of props in early modern plays decreased at a steady rate. As for numbers, playwrights were quite like their contemporaries in their deployment of hand props. Correspondingly, their practice changed as a group over the early seventeenth century: plays used fewer and fewer props, but at the same time increased their pressure on these props, and on the putative difference between the animate and the inanimate.

This seems to speak to a cultural shift in what the theatre was, and in what, and how, plays acted there meant to their audiences. A theatre which had established itself as a commercial entity through the display of objects found its voice, and gradually put some of those objects behind it as the next century unfolded. When its actors were themselves put aside with the closing of the playhouse doors, however, the early modern theatres came to see that they, as well as their actors, had more in common with those objects than had once been imagined.

NOTES

Approximate dates for the composition of plays mentioned in this essay come from *Annals of English Drama 975–1700*, 3rd edn., ed. Alfred Harbage, rev. S. Schoenbaum and Sylvia Stoler Wagonheim (London and New York: Routledge, 1989). All quotations from Shakespeare are taken from G. Blakemore Evans et al. (eds.), *The Riverside Shakespeare*, 2nd edn. (Boston: Houghton Mifflin, 1997). I am grateful to Jonathan Gil Harris and Natasha Korda for offering insightful comments on earlier versions of this essay.

1. Aristotle ranks recognition by means of external tokens, τὰ δὲ ἐκτός, as the least artistic method of anagnorisis. See the *Poetics*, 1454b24–30.
2. See, for examples of criticism which relates stage objects to the traditions of iconography, Bridget Gellert, "The iconography of melancholy in the graveyard scene in *Hamlet*," *Studies in Philology* 67 (1970): 57–66; Katherine A. Rowe, "Dismembering and forgetting in *Titus Andronicus*," *Shakespeare*

Quarterly 45 (1994): 279–303; Michael Neill, " 'What strange riddle's this?' Deciphering *'Tis Pity She's A Whore*," in Neill (ed.), *John Ford: Critical Re-Visions* (Cambridge: Cambridge University Press, 1988), pp. 153–81; Houston Diehl, "Inversion, parody, and irony: the visual rhetoric of Renaissance English tragedy," *Studies in English Literature 1500–1900* 22 (1982): 197–209; Samuel Schuman, *'The Theatre of Fine Devices': The Visual Drama of John Webster* (Salzburg: Inst. fur Anglistik & Amerikanistik, Univ. Salzburg, 1982); and Brownell Salomon, "Visual and aural signs in the performed English Renaissance play," *Renaissance Drama* n.s. 5 (1972): 143–69. Stating that "certain hand properties have a metaphoric value matching that used in Renaissance iconography," Salomon goes on to discuss the bleeding heart in *'Tis Pity*, and describes the human skull in revenge tragedy as a memento mori emblem (161).

3. Alan S. Downer, "The life of our design: the function of imagery in the poetic drama," *The Hudson Review* 2 (1949): 242–60; reprinted in Leonard F. Dean (ed.), *Shakespeare: Modern Essays in Criticism* (New York: Oxford University Press, 1975), pp. 19–36; p. 28. Downer's lone example of this "language of props" involves Macbeth and his borrowed robes, which he relates to the imagery studies of Caroline Spurgeon and Cleanth Brooks, respectively. Downer's connection of props to language has since found expression, of course, in semiotic analysis of the theatre. See, for example, Jiří Veltruský, "Man and object in the theater," in Paul L. Garvin (transl. and ed.), *A Prague School Reader on Esthetics, Literary Structure, and Style* (Washington: Georgetown University Press, 1964), pp. 83–91; and Ruth Amossy's relation of stage objects to verbal systems in "Toward a rhetoric of the stage: the scenic realization of verbal clichés," *Poetics Today* 2:3 (1981): 49–63.

4. Psychoanalytic readings of stage props include Lynda E. Boose, "Othello's handkerchief: 'the recognizance and pledge of love,'" *English Literary Renaissance* 5 (1975): 360–74; Barbara Freedman, "Errors in comedy: a psychoanalytic theory of farce," in Maurice Charney (ed.), *Shakespearean Comedy* (New York: New York Literary Forum, 1980), pp. 233–43; and Edmund Wilson, "Morose Ben Jonson," in *The Triple Thinkers* (New York: Oxford University Press, 1948), pp. 213–32, who remarks on the significance of the *absence* of a certain property in a Jonson play: "in *Volpone*, where real gold is involved, we are never allowed to see it" (p. 227). It might be observed that Wilson's insistence on the reality of this unseen stage gold speaks to the power of theatrical properties, even in their absence.

5. See, for example, Linda Austern, " 'Sing againe syren': the female musician and sexual enchantment in Elizabethan life and literature," *Renaissance Quarterly* 42 (1989): 420–48; Jean E. Howard, "Sex and social conflict: the erotics of *The Roaring Girl*," in Susan Zimmerman (ed.), *Erotic Politics: Desire on the Renaissance Stage* (New York: Routledge, 1992), pp. 170–90; Douglas Bruster, chapters 5 ("The objects of farce: identity and commodity, Elizabethan to Jacobean") and 6 ("The farce of objects: *Othello* to *Bartholomew Fair*") in *Drama and the Market in the Age of Shakespeare* (Cambridge: Cambridge University Press,

1992), pp. 63–80, 81–96; and Steven Mullaney, *The Place of the Stage: License, Play, and Power in Renaissance England* (Chicago: University of Chicago Press, 1988), pp. 128–9. Mullaney suggests that Macbeth's severed head "doubles the stage it bloodies" by reminding the viewer of the similarities between the platform stage and the scaffolding which authorities would erect for a public execution (p. 129).

6. One of the most extensive studies of hand props in the early modern era focuses on Shakespeare. Frances Teague's *Shakespeare's Speaking Properties* (Lewisburg: Bucknell University Press, 1991), to which this essay will later make reference, provides valuable information on Shakespeare's use of hand props, but does so without placing his use of these objects in the context of others' uses of hand props. See also Felix Bosonnet, *The Function of Stage Properties in Christopher Marlowe's Plays*, The Cooper Monographs on English and American Language and Literature, "Theatrical Physiognomy Series," vol. 27 (Bern: Francke, 1978).

7. Shoshana Avigal and Shlomith Rimmon-Kenan, "What do Brook's bricks mean? Toward a theory of the 'mobility' of objects in theatrical discourse," *Poetics Today* 2:3 (1981): 11–34; 12–13. Avigal and Rimmon-Kenan acknowledge this list's debt to the approach of Anne Ubersfeld. See her *Lire le Théâtre*, 4th edn. (Paris: Messidor, 1982), especially the appendix to chapter 4, "L'objet théâtral," pp. 177–85.

8. For the role of objects in certain dramatic constructions of the "human" in early modern England, see Margreta De Grazia, "The ideology of superfluous things: *King Lear* as period piece," in De Grazia, Maureen Quilligan, and Peter Stallybrass (eds.), *Subject and Object in Renaissance Culture* (Cambridge: Cambridge University Press, 1996), pp. 17–42.

9. See note 1, above.

10. Avigal and Rimmon-Kenan, "What do Brook's bricks mean?" 13ff.

11. Brownell Salomon, "Visual and aural signs," 160. Teague cites alternate definitions of *property* as well: "appurtenances worn or carried by actors" (David Bevington, *Action is Eloquence* [Cambridge, MA: Harvard University Press, 1984], p. 35); "Any portable article of costume or furniture, used in acting a play" (Bosonnet, *Function of Stage Properties*, p. 10). See Teague, *Shakespeare's Speaking Objects*, p. 15.

12. For exceptions to this, see Lena Cowen Orlin, "The performance of things in *The Taming of the Shrew*," *YES* 23 (1993): 167–88; and Natasha Korda, "Household Kates: domesticating commodities in *The Taming of the Shrew*," *Shakespeare Quarterly* 47 (1996): 109–31.

13. "SUMMA of all the Wages in December, January, and February *anno Regni Reginæ Elizabeth prædictæ* Xv^{to}," in *Documents Relating to the Office of the Revels in the Time of Queen Elizabeth*, ed. Albert Feuillerat (Louvain: A. Uystpruyst, 1908), p. 175. The plays involved in the Christmas Revels that year are no longer extant, but those associated with the objects described here have been tentatively identified as *Chariclea* (*Theagenes and Chariclea*), and *A Double Mask* [*of Fisherman and Fruit-wives*?]. See Harbage (ed.), *Annals of English Drama*.

14. Feuillerat (ed.), *Documents Relating to the Office of the Revels*, p. 175.
15. *Henslowe's Diary*, ed. R. A. Foakes and R. T. Rickert (Cambridge: Cambridge University Press, 1961), pp. 319–21. On Henslowe's inventory, see Lena Cowen Orlin's essay in this collection, "Things with little social life."
16. See, for example, Ann Rosalind Jones and Peter Stallybrass, *Renaissance Clothes and the Materials of Memory* (Cambridge: Cambridge University Press, 2001); Stallybrass's "Worn worlds: clothes and identity on the Renaissance stage," in *Subject and Object*, pp. 289–320; and Stallybrass's "Properties in clothes" in the present collection.
17. Foakes and Rickert (eds.), *Henslowe's Diary*, p. 320, line 84.
18. Neil Carson, *A Companion to Henslowe's Diary* (Cambridge: Cambridge University Press, 1988), p. 53. I am indebted, for this reference, to Natasha Korda's "Household property/stage property: Henslowe as pawnbroker," *Theatre Journal* 48 (1996): 185–95.
19. Korda, "Household property/stage property," 194. See also Harris and Korda's introduction to the present volume, and Korda's essay, "Women's theatrical properties."
20. These references are quoted in Teague, *Shakespeare's Speaking Properties*, p. 9.
21. *A Warning for Fair Women* (London: 1598). Quoted in Andrew Gurr, *Playgoing in Shakespeare's London* (Cambridge: Cambridge University Press, 1987), Appendix 2, "References to playgoing," p. 213.
22. Bodkins were short, pointed instruments used, variously, as weapons, to pierce cloth, and to curl and fasten up women's hair. Perhaps in relation to the latter usages, and to their diminutive status as weapons, bodkins were commonly represented as "feminine" objects. In the *New Arcadia*, for example, Sidney has Pamphilius attacked by a group of nine women, all of whom "held bodkins in their hands wherewith they continually pricked him." Sidney, *The Countess of Pembroke's Arcadia*, ed. Maurice Evans (Harmondsworth: Penguin Books, 1977), p. 334. Jonathan Gil Harris relates to me (in private communication) the relevance here of Arden's rebuke to Mosby in *Arden of Faversham*, 1.310–14. Depriving Mosby of his sword, Arden remarks "So, sirrah, you may not wear a sword. / The statute makes against artificers, / I warrant that I do. Now use your bodkin, / Your Spanish needle, and your pressing iron, / For this shall go with me." *Arden of Faversham*, ed. Martin White (New York: Norton, 1982).
23. Quoted in Gurr, *Playgoing*, pp. 213, 218, 235.
24. Quoted in Gurr, *Playgoing*, p. 246. For sexual play on a fool's "bauble," see *Romeo and Juliet* 2.4.91–3, and *All's Well That Ends Well* 4.5.30–31.
25. For an extended study of the social and psychological valences of hands and manual agency in literature, see Katherine Rowe, *Dead Hands: Fictions of Agency, Renaissance to Modern* (Stanford: Stanford University Press, 1999).
26. R. A. Foakes, *Illustrations of the English Stage 1580–1642* (Stanford: Stanford University Press, 1985). As Foakes reminds us, we need to exercise considerable caution in evaluating visual records of the early modern stage (p. xvi). Illustrations published with dramatic texts do not necessarily represent the

plays in question or any actual performance. Printers often used "stock" pictures to illustrate dramatic texts. So while the woodcut on the title page of Robert Wilson's *The Three Lords and Three Ladies of London* (1590), for instance, appears to represent a dramatic performance of some kind, the fact that it had appeared in a text published over two decades prior to Wilson's play, and comes from an earlier illustration still, should give us pause (p. 164). But such representations can nonetheless provide evidence relating to "stage practices, costumes and properties" which might otherwise escape us (p. xvi). Even illustrations of a non-theatrical origin, once selected to accompany a play text when printed, speak to contemporary notions of the appropriate. What does it mean, we might ask, that those responsible for bringing out Wilson's play chose *this* illustration rather than another? And that readers of *The Three Lords and Three Ladies of London* had an illustration (in which one figure holds a pointing stick, apparently lecturing or directing another figure) which they might associate with the play? It is certainly not the case, as Foakes alleges, that the illustration "has no reference to Wilson's play," for the prominent position of the woodcut on the title page makes it something like the primary visual reference to and of Wilson's play as originally published. There is thus a literalism about "the" theatre in Foakes's collection which detracts from his analysis of the illustrations.

27. On the historical era of Falstaff's costume in this illustration, see T. J. King, "The first known picture of Falstaff (1662). A suggested date for his costume," *Theatre Research International* 3 (1977–8): 20–3.

28. Reproduced in Foakes, *Illustrations*, p. 141.

29. Thomas Rymer, "A short view of tragedy," in *The Critical Works of Thomas Rymer*, ed. Curt A. Zimansky (New Haven: Yale University Press, 1956), p. 160.

30. Compare Aristotle's τὰ δὲ ἐκτός cited in note 1, above.

31. Cyril Tourneur, *The Revenger's Tragedy*, ed. Lawrence J. Ross (Lincoln: University of Nebraska Press, 1966).

32. Shoshana Felman, "Turning the screw of interpretation," *Yale French Studies* 55/56 (1977): 94–207; p. 101 (emphasis in the original).

33. Teague, *Shakespeare's Speaking Properties*, Table B: "Frequency of properties in the Folio," p. 197. The data in Teague's appendices come as a welcome revision of more subjective estimations of hand props, such as that of Mary Crapo Hyde – who, in *Playwriting for Elizabethans, 1600–1605* (New York: Columbia University Press, 1949), calls "love tokens" (i.e. rings, etc.) "the most common dramatic properties" (p. 147). Hyde discusses properties on pp. 146–9. Teague's tabulations in *Speaking Properties* have been the subject of critical remarks in a review by C. E. McGee; see *Shakespeare Quarterly* 48 (1997): 353.

34. We can see this by gauging, first, the number of actors which T. J. King estimates could perform the principal parts in most plays of the late Elizabethan and early Stuart eras. King suggests that fourteen actors, ten men and four boys, would have been required for most of the lines, with other personnel

hired to fill in the few remaining lines and roles. Even if we grant a fair number of these extra personnel, there would still have been fewer people than hand props in most of Shakespeare's plays. See King, *Casting Shakespeare's Plays: London Actors and Their Roles* (Cambridge: Cambridge University Press, 1992), chapter 2, "Eight Playhouse Documents," pp. 27–49.

35. I borrow this phrase from the work of Scott Cutler Shershow. See, especially, his essay "'The mouth of 'hem all:' Ben Jonson, authorship, and the performing object," *Theatre Journal* 46 (1994): 187–212.

36. The most "typical" play in regard to distribution and number is *Richard III*, which has close to this distribution of props, but over more lines (3,887) than is usual for a Shakespeare play.

37. In addition to Peele's *The Battle of Alcazar* – discussed later in this essay – one might look to Nashe's *The Unfortunate Traveller* for a parodic salute to the ostentation of neo-chivalric display. See his extended and loving mockery of the "lists" before the Duke of Florence. Thomas Nashe, *The Unfortunate Traveller and Other Works*, ed. J. B. Steane (London: Penguin, 1985), pp. 316–23.

38. See, for example, Jonathan Goldberg, "Rebel letters: postal effects from *Richard II* to *Henry V*," *Renaissance Drama* 19 (1988): 3–28, and "Hamlet's Hand," *Shakespeare Quarterly* 39 (1988): 307–27. Even Teague's index to *Shakespeare's Speaking Properties* replicates this tendency, indexing pages dealing with documents in history plays and in tragedies, but not in the comedies.

39. Lists of properties here are taken from Teague, *Shakespeare's Speaking Properties*, appendix A, "Property lists for Shakespeare's plays," pp. 157–93.

40. Daniel called these masques "Punctillos of Dreams and shows." Samuel Daniel, Epistle prefaced to *The Vision of the Twelve Goddesses*, l. 269, in Alexander B. Grosart (ed.), *The Complete Works in Verse and Prose of Samuel Daniel* 5 vols. (1885; New York: Russell & Russell, 1963), vol. III, p. 196. I have made a similar observation about this shift, from verbal to visual, in "Local *Tempest*: Shakespeare and the work of the early modern playhouse," *Journal of Medieval and Renaissance Studies* 25 (1995): 33–53.

41. Gurr, *Playgoing*, p. 93.

42. Because it is a widely available text, Fraser and Rabkin's two-volume anthology – *Drama of the English Renaissance (Vol. I: The Tudor Period; Vol. II: The Stuart Period)* – was employed for the following plays in this survey: *The Spanish Tragedy*, *The Jew of Malta*, *A King and No King*, *The Roman Actor*, and *Perkin Warbeck*. For the Jonson plays (*Every Man in His Humour* [Quarto], *Sejanus*, *Catiline*, and *The Devil is an Ass*), the texts employed were those in *Ben Jonson*, 11 vols., ed. C. H. Herford, Percy Simpson, and Evelyn Simpson (Oxford: Clarendon Press, 1925–50). For the Middleton plays (*A Trick to Catch the Old One*, *The Revenger's Tragedy*, and *Women Beware Women*), the texts used were those in *Thomas Middleton: Five Plays*, ed. Bryan Loughrey and Neil Taylor (London: Penguin Books, 1988). Peele's *The Battle of Alcazar* was edited by John Yoklavich in *The Dramatic Works of George Peele* (New Haven: Yale University Press, 1961). *Woodstock* comes from the edition of

A. P. Rossiter (London: Chatto and Windus, 1946). George Chapman's *All Fools* was edited by Frank Manley in the Regents Renaissance Drama series (Lincoln: University of Nebraska Press, 1968). The anonymous *Edmund Ironside* was edited by Eric Sams (Aldershot, Hants.: Wildwood House, 1986). Massinger's *The Picture* comes from *The Plays and Poems of Philip Massinger*, ed. Philip Edwards and Colin Gibson, 5 vols. (Oxford: Clarendon Press, 1976), vol. III. G. Blakemore Evans' edition of Cartwright's works (*The Plays and Poems of William Cartwright* [Madison: University of Wisconsin Press, 1951]) was used for *The Royal Slave*. Carey's *The Tragedy of Mariam* was edited by Barry Weller and Margaret Ferguson (Berkeley: University of California Press, 1994). And *Philotas* comes from Alexander Grosart's edition of *The Complete Works in Verse and Prose of Samuel Daniel*, 5 vols., vol. III (1885; New York: Russell and Russell, 1963). The tabulation of total lines for each play here includes stage directions, as it is in such stage directions that many references to props occur. For a compelling treatment of the differences among three early modern playwrights, see Paul Yachnin, *Stage-Wrights: Shakespeare, Jonson, Middleton, and the Making of Theatrical Value* (Philadelphia: University of Pennsylvania Press, 1997).

43. See Andrew Gurr, *The Shakespearian Playing Companies* (Oxford: Clarendon Press, 1996), pp. 40, 43, 47, 48, 59–60; David Bradley, *From Text to Performance in the Elizabethan Theatre: Preparing the Play for the Stage* (Cambridge: Cambridge University Press, 1992); T. J. King, *Casting Shakespeare's Plays: London Actors and Their Roles, 1590–1642* (Cambridge: Cambridge University Press, 1992); and Scott McMillin, *The Elizabethan Theatre and the "Book of Sir Thomas More"* (Ithaca: Cornell University Press, 1987).

44. See Gurr, *The Shakespearian Playing Companies*, pp. 59–60.

45. Gurr, *The Shakespearian Playing Companies*, pp. 131, 150.

46. Quotation from *Ben Jonson*, vol. 9, p. 240. Ian Donaldson aptly characterizes the drama's reception when he refers to *Catiline* as "disastrously unsuccessful." Donaldson, *Jonson's Magic Houses: Essays in Interpretation* (Oxford: Clarendon Press, 1997), p. 42.

47. *Ben Jonson*, vol. V, p. 432.

48. Jonas Barish, *The Antitheatrical Prejudice* (Berkeley: University of California Press, 1981), p. 135.

49. *Doctor Faustus* from the A-text in David Bevington and Eric Rasmussen (eds.), *Doctor Faustus* (Manchester: Manchester University Press, 1992), 5.1.91–2. On the politics of the poetic blazon, see Nancy J. Vickers, "Diana described: scattered woman and scattered rhyme," *Critical Inquiry* 8 (1981): 265–79, who explores Petrarch's "legacy of fragmentation" and its relation to "the development of a code of beauty, a code that causes us to view the fetishized body as a norm" (277).

50. Bruster, *Drama and the Market in the Age of Shakespeare*, pp. 64–5.

PART II

Furniture

CHAPTER 4

Things with little social life (Henslowe's theatrical properties and Elizabethan household fittings)

Lena Cowen Orlin

The presence among Philip Henslowe's papers of an "Enventary tacken of all the properties for my *Lord Admeralles men*" has been more a source of puzzlement than enlightenment.[1] Notoriously, the inventory, along with several lists of costumes, is itself lost. The catalogues survive only as transcribed by Edmond Malone in 1790, and, while it is generally agreed (in the words of R. A. Foakes and R. T. Rickert) that "There is no reason to doubt that the lists were genuine, and were probably, if the spelling is a guide, in Henslowe's hand,"[2] their disappearance underscores the fragility and fungibility of the textual records on which we build our histories of the past. Further, the property list has been of limited value for theatre historians; so many of its items are of restricted use. Tied to specific plays as are the "tome of Dido" and "j payer of stayers for Fayeton," Henslowe's properties seem largely unrevealing of more general stage practices. In their *Dictionary of Stage Directions*, Alan C. Dessen and Leslie Thomson meticulously point up such correlations as can be effected between Henslowe's inventory and surviving plays of the period. As they review the number of extant stage directions making reference to onstage trees, for example, Dessen and Thomson note that Henslowe inventoried three: "j baye tree," "j tree of gowlden apelles," and "Tantelouse tre."[3] But immediate connections such as these are few enough. In his *Companion to Henslowe's Diary*, Neil Carson reaches what may be the most important general conclusion about the inventory: "The Company was equipped with not one but two mossy banks, no less than three trees, as many tombs, and one Hell mouth. All this suggests a stage more cluttered than is sometimes imagined." Carson also identifies a chief source of perplexity: "Almost as surprising as the presence of so many large properties is the inexplicable absence of some small ones."[4]

Both of Carson's observations are germane to our understanding of the original staging of Christopher Marlowe's *Tamburlaine, Parts One and Two*, his *Dr. Faustus*, and perhaps also Thomas Heywood's *The Silver Age*.

These are but four of the plays that seem to be implicated in Henslowe's inventory. Henslowe makes specific reference to "Tamberlyne's brydell," presumably the sort of muzzle employed in the last act of *Tamburlaine, Part Two*, when Amyras advises Tamburlaine that the Kings of Natolia and Jerusalem "will talk still my lord, if you do not bridle them," and Tamburlaine confirms the order to "Bridle them." Also on Henslowe's list are a "cage" that might have been used for Bajazeth in *Part One*; a "bedsteade" and then one of two "coffenes" perhaps occupied by Zenocrate in *Part Two*; and a "golden scepter," "iij Imperial crownes," and "j playne crowne" of the sorts presumably called for especially in *Part Two*. Similarly, Henslowe lists "j dragon in fostes," probably referring to the disguise specified for Mephistopheles in the B-text of *Dr. Faustus*, before the over-reaching academic commands the devil to appear in the guise of a friar. The play could also make good use of Henslowe's crowns, as well as the trees, "j crosers stafe" (which Marlowe's Bishops are indicated to have carried), "j poopes miter" (for the Pope's appearance in the play), "Cupeds bowe & quiver" (inasmuch as the B-text has Helen appearing between two Cupids), "the sittie of Rome" (or so argued F. G. Fleay),[5] and, perhaps most likely of all, both "j Hell mought" (to which Faustus might address his closing cry to "Ugly hell" to "gape not") and "the limes dead" (for the final scene in which the scholars discover "Faustus' limbs, All torn asunder"). For *The Silver Age*, Henslowe makes no reference as concrete as that of "Tamberlyne's brydell" or "j dragon in fostes," and it has been argued that Henslowe's references elsewhere in the *Diary* to two plays of *Hercules* indicate not the *Silver Age* but an earlier rendition of the Hercules myth.[6] Judging from the properties alone, though, the connections between the play that has come down in Heywood's name and a putative earlier version would seem to have been close. Henslowe lists "iij clobes," "j lyon skin," "ij lyon heades," "j snake," "Serberosse [Cerberus's] iij heades," "Ierosses [Iris's] head," "Cadeseus," "Mercures wings," and the "raynbowe," all of which would have been useful for the Hercules story as *The Silver Age* tells it. In addition, *The Silver Age* employed a Hell mouth, a bedstead, royal crowns, and a scepter.

Together, these properties of Henslowe's go a long way toward establishing Carson's "more cluttered" stage. But if it is indeed the case that they were intended for the four plays specified, then Carson's "inexplicable absences" come immediately to the foreground, as well. Each of the identified plays includes a "banquet" scene, and, while *Tamburlaine* is vague about what properties its banquet might employ, *The Silver Age* specifies that such staging demands "stools, cups, and bowls." *Dr. Faustus* calls for books, a wine vessel, a container for holy water, a chafer, and a cup, in addition to its banqueting stools and dishes. Banqueting items constitute the most obvious additions to the properties required for these plays, but there are many more. The principle holds for all the plays to which Henslowe's inventory seems to refer. For Marlowe's *The Jew of Malta*, for example, Henslowe records "j cauderm for the Jewe," undoubtedly used in Barabas's spectacular death scene. But there is no mention of the pot and ladle for the rice with which he poisons a convent full of nuns (and his own daughter).

Assuming, again, that the identifications between Henslowe's properties and these Admiral's Men's plays are accurate, then we must confront the question of why Henslowe's inventory lists some of the properties required for them but not all. Carson concludes that "It would seem that the inventory is only a partial list of the Company's resources," and he conjectures somewhat vaguely that "Most of these smaller items were probably kept backstage or supplied by the actors."[7] More recently, Natasha Korda has suggested that the smaller properties existed in a separate category for Henslowe because they circulated among the goods he held in pawn.[8] This theory would certainly redress at least some of the presumed deficiencies of the inventory, for, while Henslowe's pawnbroking records are best known for the clothing he traded in, they also itemize an extravagant number of household linens – sheets, pillowberes, towels, napkins, blankets, quilt, cupboard cloths – as well as curtains, wall hangings, bed hangings, carpets, a featherbed, a bolster, a rug, a cushion, goblets, cups, salts, a jug, platters, dishes, porringers, a basin, spoons, candlesticks, pots, a skillet, a mortar and pestle, fire tongs, a fireshovel, andirons, a looking glass, a child's seat, and a Bible.[9]

Korda has crucially recognized that Henslowe's inventory is resistant to interpretation conducted strictly from within the world of stage practice and, thus, that it requires another frame of reference to be made intelligible to us in any useful way. In large part because the inventory is unique as a stage document, we lack the analytical tools to decode its theatrical purposes and strategies. For Korda, the revelatory frame of reference is commercial: she relates the inventory to other papers in Henslowe's hand and to the varied entrepreneurial endeavors they depict. In a complementary spirit, this chapter seeks to develop an alternative model for approaching the inventory, from a frame of reference best described as archival. Henslowe's list may be *sui generis* among theatrical documents, but there are other classes of document that offer useful analogues and explanatory protocols. These are documents of personal

property, specifically household property. To analyze postmortem household inventories is to discover a range of "absences" that have seemed
"inexplicable" to us only because we have not fully understood the nature of these documents. But there were other kinds of inventories that
filled in some of the household gaps, and to take these on board is also
to discover that the domestic environment was "more cluttered" than
we have appreciated. In this, early modern household documents and
Henslowe's stage inventory for the Rose playhouse run parallel.

HOUSEHOLD INVENTORIES

For the most part, literary historians think of personal property in binary terms. We distinguish between "real" property and chattels, and
we understand that each was represented in its own class of documents,
respectively deeds and postmortem inventories. The latter class has received the most attention from historians of all stripes. Beginning in 1529,
English law required that for any person dying in possession of goods
worth more than £5, an inventory of those goods had to be registered by
a group of "indifferent" (objective) men. All listed goods were notionally
withheld from a dying person's heirs until his or her debts had been rec-
ompensed by his or her executor(s). As objects to answer debts, goods had
also to be appraised. For poorer men and women, and especially those
unmarried and in service, an inventory might list only clothing and ready
money. For others, though, household furnishings were itemized room
by room, often in pictorial detail. Such postmortem inventories seem to
provide snapshots of a dying person's household. Deposited as part of
the probate process, they survive in such quantity, cut across so many
lines of wealth, occupation, and region, and preserve so much interesting information, that they have been taken to constitute an essential data
base for social and economic history of the early modern period. They
are, however, treacherous. Elsewhere, I have outlined some of the omis-
sions and obfuscations of these documents.[10] Here I consider the other
inventories that filled in some of the blind spots in their pictures of early
modern households. In fact, there were many kinds of inventories. Most
were far more ephemeral than the postmortem inventories preserved in
local record offices. Many are lost, and those that have survived are not
always well known to us.

For example, wealthy persons might commission inventories during
their lifetimes, on an occasional basis, as a means of monitoring and
controlling their possessions. The Copthall papers contain a series of

inventories dealing with possessions moving between a family's country estate in Middlesex and their city home in Chelsea. There survive "A note of such Plate as is sent to London out of the charge of Thomas Carter of Copt-hall this 29 January 1629," and "A note of such Plate as is yet remaining in the charge of the said Thomas Carter at Copt-hall 29 January 1629."[11] Carter was presumably a family retainer at the country house, Copthall, and these checklists distinguish between those items for which he continued to be responsible and those which had moved into the domain of another, unnamed family agent in London. They thus served the interests of the principal family, which aimed to deter property loss, theft, or misplacement by fixing accountability, and they also served the interests of their man Carter, who revised and reduced the list of goods for which he was answerable.

Such inventories as that of Copthall have come down to us from the garrets or muniment rooms of great families. Many other sorts of inventories, though, survive only referentially. As probate documents, wills were also lastingly deposited in record offices, and they make mention of many inventories not preserved with them. This is one reason why, in the complex history of the gendering of personal property, much remains to be disentangled about the extent to which women retained title to goods that were usually described as those they "brought" to marriage. Generally, it seems that women understood that they forfeited ownership to their spouses, as *The Lawes Resolution of Womens Rights* insists upon.[12] And when a woman predeceased her husband, her former property was so thoroughly absorbed into his estate that only by his permission did she have the testamentary right to distribute any piece of it. But the husband's legal entitlement could also be either reversed by pre-nuptial negotiations or nullified by extra-legal, moral claims, factors often established in special inventories. Dying husbands frequently reinstated "all the household stuff she brought me." This was a simple matter when what was involved was, as for Thomas Palliser, "one press which she did bring with her," or, as for William Cooke, "a standing bedstead and a trundle bedstead in as good a manner as she brought them to me." Often, however, the list was lengthier. Agnes Gine, for example, brought "two mattresses, two blankets, two bolsters, two coverings, three pillows, four pairs of sheets, two hutches, a little coffer, a stool, an old kettle, three tables, a sieve, half the painted cloths about the house, a banker [a covering for a chair or bench], a tablecloth, and both bedsteads." Especially in such cases, detailed and binding documentation might be called for. Thus, James Roger bequeathed his wife "all such goods as she brought with her as in an inventory." Yeoman John Jackson indicated in his will that his wife was to receive two chairs in addition to the "moveables" she had brought, as specified in "an inventory written with my own hand."[13]

Sometimes couples were careful to maintain separate property records. Sir George Freville of Durham died childless in the first year of his marriage, in 1619. Four years later his widow recorded that "I have made an Inventory...signed with my own hand and subscribed with my hand at the several pages thereof, containing all such household stuff as was then remaining in my hands" which had once belonged to him. Ten years after that, her will recorded that "my late husband did by his last will commit the disposing of his household stuff to my discretion after my death." Although all the goods were in her control, she scrupulously maintained records preserving distinctions of ownership. Meanwhile, Andrew Sutton ordered that when his son came of age, he was "not [to] meddle with anything that was [his mother's] before I married her"; those things were returned to her. The son was to receive only such goods as were Sutton's own before marriage, "as appeareth by an inventory."[14]

Any testator, contemplating a fairly lengthy list of objects, could avoid iterating them in his will by preparing and citing a partial inventory. As stated before, postmortem inventories were incomplete documents, but they were more akin to full playscripts than were these special inventories, which might be analogized to "parts" written for individual actors. Joan Busshe, for instance, remembered one kinsman with three sheep, another with a pewter dish and a saucer, and a third with two lambs and a chest. Bequests to her daughter and heir, however, she "caused to be comprised in an inventory." William Sanderson compiled a similar "schedule" of "implements of household" for his daughter, and for safety's sake he placed that inventory in the "custody" of a trusted friend. John Page, a blacksmith, left household goods to family and kin but prepared a separate inventory of his tools and equipment, all of which went to his manservant to use for ten years. Joan Petitte had loaned her son household goods which she subsequently bequeathed to him outright. She referred to them as "all the stuff which he hath of mine, whereof I have an inventory written with his own hand."[15] Had any of these partial inventories survived without the wills that contextualized them and suggested their principles of selection, they would have given us highly misleading information about Joan Busshe, William Sanderson, John Page, and Joan Petitte.

Thomas Jenynges died in 1558, while his son was still underage. His will directed: "Such stuff as I have bequeathed to [my son William] shall be bestowed in the loft over the hall: the door shall be locked by my executors, they to keep the key for four years, and every quarter they shall peruse that no part of the stuff do perish, and beforehand they shall make an inventory indented, the two parts to them and the overseer; the stuff delivered to William at the end of four years."[16] Thomas Jenynges' locked loft was, in effect, a materialization of the inventory, or at the least its logical extension. The overriding interest of all these occasional inventories was to fix, locate, and secure personal property. Such documents were composed in an attempt to withstand the known nature of goods, a nature best revealed by that other early modern name for them, moveables.

Even postmortem inventories worked primarily to ensure that goods stood still to answer the charges that could be brought against them – that is, to satisfy a testator's debts. Among other things, they aimed to prevent heirs from claiming their bequests until executors had settled an estate and determined the extent to which a testator's obligations permitted his last wishes to be honored. In his *Brief Treatise of Testaments and Last Wills*, Henry Swinburne lists "What things are to be put into the [postmortem] Inventory" as answerable items.[17] He confirms that such real properties as "lands, tenements, hereditaments" are to be omitted for the purposes of debt resolution (sig. Ff6r). But from here our presumed binary index of "real" property and "chattels" is inadequate to the more complex codifications of the *Brief Treatise of Testaments and Last Wills*.

Swinburne establishes three categories of things distinct in nature from "real" property. These are, first, "immoveables," and, second and third, two types of "moveables." Immoveables, or (a) "leases for years," and also (b) trees and plants, and (c) the fruits of trees and plants, are not to be included in a postmortem inventory as resources against which debts can be lodged. "Moventia," which Swinburne defines as (a) money and (b) goods that "actively and by their own accord do move themselves," such as horses, oxen, sheep, and cattle, must be itemized in the postmortem inventory. "Mobilia," what Swinburne calls the "passively... moveable or removeable," with its subcategories of (a) clothing and (b) household stuff, must also be listed in the postmortem inventory (pp. 132–3). ("Household stuff," Swinburne specifies, consists of "Tables, Stools, Forms, Chairs, Carpets, Hangings, Beds, Bedding, Basons with Ewers, Candlesticks, all sorts of vessel serving for meat and drink, being either of earth, wood, glass, brass, or pewter, Pots, Pans, Spits"

[p. 144] – many of the items we most miss from Henslowe's inventory.)
The two types of moveables comprise things that naturally resist stasis,
that materially threaten the desired order of ownership and transfer, and
that particularly require textual regulation.

Because the text of any type of inventory seems conspicuously to be
motivated by this regulatory impulse, it is difficult to resist the inevitable,
a priori notion that all goods represented in inventories are circulatory
in nature. The very fact that an object is listed in an inventory implies
that it has an active social life.[18] To the contrary, however, there were
goods with very little social life, and for them there were yet other sorts of
inventories with other motivations. To acknowledge this fact is to reach
the third of three conclusions that need to be emphasized at this stage of
our search for analogues to Henslowe's inventory.

First, the archival dominance of postmortem inventories has overshadowed the existence and relevance of other household inventories.
Occasional and ephemeral as these documents often were, their survival
rate was apparently low, as presumably was that for theatrical inventories. There may well have been other stage records like Henslowe's,
even among Henslowe's own papers, which would have shed interpretive light on this one, had they come down to us. Henslowe's inventory
provokes us to acknowledge the vastness of the world of lost records and
the eccentricities of documentary preservation.

Second, the variety of inventories might seem too self-evident to remark were it not that different types had different rules of inclusion. Even
with respect to postmortem inventories, in the presumed completeness
of which we have powerfully invested, we are mistaken in our guiding
assumption that these documents were comprehensive records of goods
in one person's ownership, one household's containment, or one room's
space. This was not their nature. Critically, however, our conviction that
their catalogues were exhaustive has led to a kind of unthinking corol-
lary that those of all inventories were. And we have formed our own,
often erroneous assumptions about what it is that a given inventory must
exhaustively represent. In fact, any inventory can be complete in its way,
but we must work to discover the specific and sometimes quite narrow
way in which it sought to be complete. For our purposes as historians,
every inventory may well be more partial than we would have wished it
to be, and, by juxtaposing Henslowe's inventory with the play-texts to
which it seems to refer, we can be certain that this is true in the case of
Henslowe's inventory, as well.

Third, our task is to understand its partialities, as this chapter seeks
next to do. Because postmortem inventories are in essence monitory and

goods seem by their nature to circulate, we have automatically understood Henslowe's inventory to partake of a certain set of anthropological axioms. But it is possible to identify and describe goods with less unstable natures that may well have been more analogous to those listed in Henslowe's inventory than were moveables. There is no single contemporary term for these analogues, but I will call them household "fittings."

HOUSEHOLD FITTINGS

The vocabulary of household fixtures was not yet fully formed in the Tudor years. In preceding centuries, the emphasis had been on flexibility and transportability in furnishings, so that the members of a family with more than one house might have had only one set of goods and implements. These travelled with them between properties. Notoriously, as late as 1567 glass windows were installed whenever the earl of Northumberland visited his castle at Alnwick and, as soon as he departed, were "taken down and laid up in safety" from damaging winds. Some men travelled with their casements as well as their beds, tables, and chests. When Henry VIII went on progress the royal convoy transported his tapestries in addition to his courtiers and retainers. As such nomadic practices changed, however, those associated with the court began to refer to "standing palaces," which were distinguished for being permanently equipped for habitation. Over the course of the century, the list of things that were required to make a house "perfect" grew: glass windows, fixed floorboards, oak wainscoting, and more.[19] As was consistent with the language of the court, objects that we might term "fixtures" were more often referred to as "standards." They could also be called "implements." In wills, nouns were frequently avoided. Things were often described as "belonging" to a house or were designated to "remain" in it. In fact, there was no general agreement on the terminology; Henry Swinburne, writing in 1590, did not seem to have a proper name for what he called "such things as are affixed" in households.

The subject of "affixed things" arises in the *Brief Treatise of Testaments and Last Wills* when Swinburne provides his readers with a summary of the main talking points for the production of postmortem inventories:

1. All goods, chattels, wares, merchandises, moveable and immoveable, are to be put into the Inventory.
2. Leases are to be put into the Inventory.
3. Corne on the ground is to be put into the Inventory.

4. Grass or trees growing, are not to be put into the Inventory.
5. Whether such things as are affixed to the freehold, ought to be inventoried.
6. Whether debts are to be put into the Inventory.
7. Whether money due for land, is to be put into the Inventory. (sig. Ff6r)

It is assumed that the postmortem representation of household goods, shop wares, building leases, and plants and their products (numbers 1, 2, 3, and 4) is easily agreed upon; all but plants have an essential liquidity and are therefore to be inventoried. Swinburne may have to remind his readers of the legal status of these properties, but he does not need to argue or justify their disposition. A similar clarity does not obtain, however, with respect to debts, rents, and "such things as are affixed to the freehold."

In a signal both of how problematic the category of "affixed things" was and also of the growing importance of these things in the domestic environment, definitions and possible sources of confusion were addressed in later editions of the *Brief Treatise of Testaments and Last Wills*:

...the glass annexed to the windows of the house, because they are parcel of the house, they shall descend as parcel of the inheritance to the heir, and the executors shall not have them [thus, their withholding from the postmortem inventory]. And although the lessee himself, at his own cost, do cause the glass to be put into the windows, yet the same being one [sic for once?] parcel of the house, he cannot take the same away afterwards, without danger of punishment for waste. Neither is there any material difference in law, whether the glass were annexed to the window with nails, or in other manner, either by the lord or by the tenant, for being once affixed to the freehold, the same cannot be removed by the lessee, but shall belong to the heir, and not to the executors as is aforesaid, and therefore the same is not to be put into the Inventory, as part or parcel of the goods of the deceased. The like may be concluded of wainscot, that it ought not to be put into the Inventory, as parcel of the goods of the deceased, for being annexed unto the house, either by the lessor or by the lessee, it is parcel of the house. And there is no difference whether it be affixed with great nails, or little nails, or by screws, or irons thrust through the posts, or walls of the house, for howsoever it be affixed either in manner aforesaid, or in any other manner, it is parcel of the freehold, and if the executors should remove them, they are punishable for the same. And not only glass and wainscot, but any other such like thing, affixed to the freehold, or to the ground, with mortar and stone, as Tables dormant [i.e., fixed to the wall or floor], Leads [roofs], Bays, Mangers [feeding troughs], etc., for these belong to the heir and not to the executor: and therefore they are not to be put into the Inventory of the goods of the deceased. (pp. 51–2)

Although Swinburne tries to suggest that the matter of "affixed things" was a clear one, the *Brief Treatise of Testaments and Last Wills* itself gives evidence of prevailing uncertainties. Throughout the sixteenth century and well into the seventeenth, wills were written bequeathing fixtures as if they were as "moveable" as tables and chairs. Testators who had made improvements to their properties – and who wished to be certain that the improvements remained in place for the use of their heirs – preferred not to take any chances with an incompletely regularized practice. Edward Goodsonne, for example, in 1590 left "the messuage, with the glass, lead, wainscot, portals, doors, locks, staples, windows, bench and benchboards, shelves, iron, ironwork, studs, posts, and other things thereunto fixed or appertaining." Anxieties on this subject were most often displayed by male testators, who, consigning their houses to their widows for fixed terms or for life, insisted that women were to leave important household implements behind for the sons who would eventually inherit. Among the most common language of testamentary documents is the stringent demand that women not "remove" the many items that could fall within the category of fittings. Long and oppressive rosters detailing the implements were often included: "all the glass in the windows of my house, the windows, doors, locks, bolts, benches, shelves, all the boards and planks in the garrets and upper chambers and floors beneath, nailed and unnailed, the gates and pales of my yard and iron work, as they now stand, to remain to the house." As late as 1647, a testator was still directing that "any thing which is fixed to the freehold or by removal will practically deface the house be not removed, sold or dispersed, but may remain to the use and benefit of my son."[20] Despite Swinburne's explanation that the law directed otherwise, "affixed things" were occasionally inventoried, as well.[21]

For all these individual deviations from his recommended probate practices, however, Swinburne correctly represented one broad historical movement of his time, which was to recognize that any house or tenement was incomplete, not "perfect," or "defaced" without a growing list of amenities and conveniences. In the late fifteenth century, London tailor William Smith sued in Chancery for the "glass windows, lattices, doors, locks" he had installed in a rental property. He claimed that these objects were neither "principals nor fastened to any principles" of the tenement; "after the custom of the City," he said, they were "removeable," but he had been prevented from removing them.[22] By the mid-sixteenth century, the London Viewers, a group of four men commissioned by the Mayor and Aldermen to adjudicate property disputes, were terming it "the ancient custom of the city of London" that such items as "seats, benches, doors, locks and keys, glass, lattice, and windows that be there fixed and fastened... *ought of right to remain*" in a tenement as its "implements and standards" (emphasis added). In other decisions the Viewers ruled similarly for wainscoting, floorboards, and shelves nailed to the frame of the building.[23]

In one important respect, however, Swinburne is an inadequate guide to the history of personal property, its categories, and its definitions. As mandated by his highly technical focus on postmortem inventories and legally valid probates, Swinburne was a strict constructionist about the nature of "affixed things." For all his discussion of great nails, little nails, screws, and irons, the "fixing" of things that belonged to a house grew increasingly metaphorical in the sixteenth century, at least for individual testators. That is why the term "fittings" is more useful than "fixtures." By designating some objects to "remain" in their house, testators could prevent these items from being listed in their postmortem inventories. All other goods and resources would be exhausted to answer debts before the implements could be attached. Testators could and did nominate many kinds of possessions to be fittings. Often these were things important to a household's workings and provisions, like brewing vessels. Sometimes they were essential furnishings without which a home would feel incomplete; hall tables, forms, and stools were among the most common of standards. Occasionally, wills created "heirlooms" of the sort that we are more likely to recognize, referring to important pieces of plate.

For some idea of how variable a list of a household's fittings could be, one of the best documentary sources is the parish church record book. Most churches held residential properties, including those occupied by their clergy. Because improvements to these properties belonged to the parishioners rather than to any tenant, churchwardens kept careful accounts of them. Over the years, their lists of fittings might diminish through normal wear and attrition, lengthen as the parish was obliged to accommodate at least some of the elements of rising standards of living, or lengthen further when clergy willed their own goods to the parish after their deaths. For example, the churchwardens' account book for St. Lawrence Pountney in London includes a 1580s "Inventory of all such Implements as appertain unto the parishioners of St. Lawrence Pountney being in the house where Mr. John Halton now inhabiteth, all which Implements they have paid for and owe to be left in the house at his departure." The list includes window glass, doors with their locks and keys, shelves, and an iron pothanger in the hall chimney – affixed things all – but also painted cloths and hangings in the hall and chamber, kitchen grates, two bedsteads, two settles, an old chest, and a cupboard.

Halton duly signed the inventory to relinquish any personal entitlement to these items, adding "Minister" after his name; a later interlineation records that "The bedstead Mr. Halton is accountable for." Presumably he owed the parish the value of the bed – nearly two shillings, it was noted – rather than the bed itself.[24]

In 1594, the parish paid 26s. 8d. for improvements to the property. Another "Inventory" was prepared with the observation that the implements were "to be left whensoever the said Mr. Richard Lightfoot minister shall depart from thence." There were more glazed windows, another door, a "face of wainscot" over the chimney mantle, and a table and shelves fitting out the study, among other things. At St. Stephen Walbrook in London, a 1639 record of fittings in the parsonage house included such fixtures as wainscoting, benches, an interior porch,[25] and a lead cistern, but also such furnishings as tables, stools, a court cupboard, dressers, painted cloths, a tablet inscribed with the Ten Commandments, and "a great old map." At London's St. Bartholomew Exchange, in 1619, Dr. Robert Hill added amenities for his own comfort and then left them "for the use of the parsons succeeding." He contributed thirty-four window casements, several rooms' worth of wainscoting, shelves, built-in cupboards, an interior porch, overmantles, a cistern, locks and keys, and window shutters. Dr. Hill also hung some rooms with painted cloths, had one chamber's walls "fair painted" (either with images or with text), and left "a fair marble stone with a writing upon it in gold letters."[26]

The history of household fittings can also usefully be reconstructed in connection with documents recording the transfer of property. "Schedules" of fittings were sometimes attached to deeds of sale or lease. The appendix to this chapter transcribes one such schedule: in 1595, the fittings of two London messuages, one tenanted by Bevis Bulmer and one by Bartholomew Chapple, were inventoried for a single act of transfer, and the schedule demonstrates how extensive a list of things "belonging" could be. There are, admittedly, many "affixed things" of the sort Swinburne would have recognized: glass windows, a bay window, clerestory windows, wainscoting, benches, interior porches, doors, locks, hinges, shelves, curtain rods, work surfaces, a cistern, a pump, pipes, ovens, a furnace. But there are also things that we would have assumed to be "moveables": tables, beds, a settle, cupboards, forms, stools, a ladder, painted cloths, room hangings. In addition, the inventory lists curious and interesting items, like a wall rack on which to mount weapons, artificial "horses" on which to store saddles, and roof racks for poles on which to dry clothing. There was a "lead to piss in" in the yard, chicken coops in both the kitchen and the garden, and one set of hangings that told the story of "King Pharoah."[27]

"Affixed things" constitute a principal class of unspoken absences in postmortem inventories. And because they were not generally represented in postmortem inventories – with all those documents' advantages of preservation and accessibility – household "fittings" have a fairly hidden history. It is a profoundly important one, however, for our sense of the early modern domestic environment and its level of clutter. To imaginatively reconstruct any given household space, one would have at the very least to pair a schedule of fittings with its postmortem inventory of moveable goods. But I have evoked this history here in order to elaborate on the notion that, while his "house" was the Rose playhouse, the objects in Henslowe's inventory were nonetheless more closely related to domestic fittings than to any other category of personal property. Presumably, this hypothesis is credible enough for objects that would appear to have been large and unwieldy, among them "j payer of stayers for Fayeton," "j wooden canepie," and "Belendon stable," inventory entries that Carol Chillington Rutter suggests "sound like modern sets."[28] Accepting the same for Henslowe's "limes dead," "rowghte [wrought or embroidered] gloves," and "gilt speare," however, requires a greater leap of interpretation. To advance the case that all the items inventoried by Henslowe may be characterized by analogy as theatrical "fittings," three points should now be emphasized.

First, the categories of things that made a house "perfect" in the sixteenth century were in the process of definition, even as was London stage practice in the 1590s. Some things, such as roofing lead and doors with their hardware, were intrinsically necessary to a house's functions of shelter and personal security. Others, such as the hall table and stools, were generally understood to be indispensable furnishings, especially for that other important function of the house as a site for provision and sustenance. Still others, such as window glass, were increasingly common as rising standards of living elevated levels of expectation. And then there were amenities such as wainscoting that, once invested in, performed stability. Because the process of fixing things was progressive and highly individualized, requirements and desires varied from house to house and from room to room within a house. This is shown even in the two schedules transcribed in the appendix, where the emphasis for Bevis Bulmer's house is on things literally fastened to the property, like windows and doors, while the accent for Bartholomew Chapple's house is on goods

metaphorically attached, like bedsteads and tables. The functions ful-
filled by Henslowe's stage "fittings" would have been similarly variable.
Different plays made different property demands.

Second, no household objects, even if they actually were "affixed"
things, were "immoveables," as is preeminently true of stage properties,
as well. Lead could be and was stripped off one household roof to be
employed on another, wainscoting could be and was pulled down to
be reattached elsewhere, floorboards could be and were pulled up and
recycled in other construction, staircases could be and were relocated to
rooms or houses different from those for which they had been built. It is
because they were removeable that there was a need for their specialized
inventories. In Henslowe's theatre, stage properties would similarly have
had to be "removeables." A change of scene would have mandated a
change of property. Whether the objects in Henslowe's inventory were
large or small, they could still have been understood to be stable holdings
for the company. In households, for example, fixity was often an illusion
created around moveable goods by social consensus or by the will of their
owner. The common understanding was that fittings should be permitted
(in the case of "affixed things") or encouraged (in the case of designated
implements) to remain at rest and in place; the latter was presumably
intended for the Rose playhouse properties.

Thus, third, the boundary between moveables and fittings was less
secure than Swinburne, for one, was in a position to reveal to us. His was
only a very partial list of what might have been considered the essential
fittings of an early modern home. Identical goods could be placed in op-
posing categories depending upon individual situations; bedsteads were
notoriously promiscuous travelers among the different types of household inventory.[29] Henslowe's inventories seem to have had a similar
situational ethic. The fact that a particular item of clothing – "rowghte"
gloves, for example – might appear in his property inventory, his costume inventory, or his pawn records can make his catalogues appear
indiscriminate or disorganized. What it really reveals is that genre was
not the ruling determinant of categorization. Either Henslowe or the
men of the Admiral's company presumably knew the history and use
of each of the properties, and this knowledge would most likely have
informed the sites of their registration. Even as household moveables
could be imported into the category of fittings simply by the will, sentiment, calculation, or whimsy of a testator, so Henslowe's lists allowed
the company to enact its own definitions. Such flexibility left space for
any owner or occupant to determine just what made his or her house or

any room within it "perfect." Henslowe's inventory of stage properties leaves space for us to conjecture about his rules of representation.

HENSLOWE'S INVENTORY

Distinctions between household fittings and moveables cannot always be made on generic grounds: a bed, a table, even a casement might be inventoried in either category. In any early modern household, the difference between the two obeyed an internal and often unrecoverable logic which might, on the one hand, reflect the house's own history and might, on the other, indicate its owners' desires for its future. If we hypothesize that "all the properties for my *Lord Admeralles* men" amounts to being a list of theatrical fittings and that there were other, now lost, accountings for moveables, it still remains to inquire into Henslowe's principles of categorization for the two. These principles may also be unrecoverable. But even to speculate about them is to formulate new possibilities for understanding early modern stage properties, both in terms of a history that encompasses structures of spatial organization, value, ownership, and accountability, and also in terms of the future that may have been imagined for them.

It is possible that for Henslowe there was a locational principle at work for such distinctions as he seems to have made. This is the implication of the shortest of Henslowe's costume inventories. One list gives clothing "Gone and loste"; another, "dievers...sewtes"; and a third, "all the aparell...taken the 13th of March 1598." But a fourth is an "Enventory of all the apparell for my *Lord Admiralles* men, taken the 10 of marche 1598. — Leaft above in the tier-house in the cheast."[30] Even as this last inventory catalogued the contents of one chest, so the property inventory may have catalogued the contents of one room or one area in the playhouse. The third and fourth clothing inventories both claim to list "all the apparell," but only the fourth reveals its principle of completeness, listing "all the apparell" of a single chest. The property inventory may simply have neglected to specify that it lists "all the properties" of a separate space. Unfortunately, this reading of the inventory does not explain why some properties were first housed apart from others. With items like the "eleme bowl" and the "rowghte gloves" in the surviving inventory, size cannot have been the sole determinant for assignment to the space for stage "fittings." This may be to assume a level of chance involved in the distinction between "fittings" and "moveables," with all objects that happened to have been placed in one area essentially taking on a characterization reified by the preponderant nature of the objects in that area.

Location may also have been at issue for Henslowe in a larger sense. Fittings made a house or room "perfect" in entirely subjective ways. A laborer might term his hall perfect, undefaced, if it contained its table and stools, while a gentleman would have required many more furnishings and amenities to make the term applicable. To apply this household concept to playhouse practice is to return to the issue of the "more cluttered" stage. Our interpretive emphasis on the bare stage derives to some extent from our knowledge that traveling companies needed to be able to get up a play in any space and without many properties. But even as there were status differences in household fittings, so there were undoubtedly regional differences in playhouse fittings. London, in short, had higher standards for its performances. Just as its resident cast was larger than that of travelling companies, so what made plays "perfect" in London may have been a more extensive set of goods and implements than were elsewhere obligatory. If the law of property in the sixteenth century increasingly held that a house was no house without its fittings, so the custom of the London stage may have come to mean that a play was no play without its properties. The properties listed in Henslowe's inventory may have been those that were "standards" for London performances (and that were not permitted to "move" with travelling players).

If location is one possible categorical variable, another may have been value. Douglas Bruster argues that the properties listed in Henslowe's inventory were of particular concern to the Admiral's Men as, essentially, bespoke objects, and thus difficult and costly to replace (see page 73). This would presume, as is entirely possible, that the "bedsteade," the "eleme bowle," the "sack-bute," the "paire of rowghte gloves," and other implements were of a more specialized fabrication than the inventory itself immediately conveys, somehow akin to the idiosyncratic "tome of Guido" and "sittie of Rome." It is worth noting, however, that properties of this special significance to the company would not necessarily have had much market value. By contrast to Henslowe's other accounts with monies given out and taken in for both theatrical and pawnbroking activities, the list of properties is not in any way correlated to costs or appraisals, a fact which has gone unremarked by F. G. Fleay, W. W. Greg, Glynne Wickham, and those who have characterized Henslowe almost exclusively in terms of his mercenary instincts.[31]

Perhaps the inventory of properties includes no appraisals because the market value of these properties was in fact negligible. How much call might there have been for "j Hell mought," "j tome of Dido," the mysterious "hecfor for the playe of Faeton," or "Serberosse iij heades"? And even those things which would seem to have had a more general usage, such as "j bedsteade," "j payer of stayers for Fayeton," and "j wooden canepie" might have had no more functional integrity than, one could assume, "j frame for the heading in Black Jone." The "golden scepter" was probably not gold, the "greve armer" may not have been battleworthy, and Henslowe's three trees were presumably no more alive than the "snake" and the "great horse with his leages." With the possible exception, again, of the "rowghte gloves," the properties presumably had little hope of a social or economic life beyond the movement they enjoyed when brought on stage for the specific play for which they had been purchased or fabricated. In this, these "fittings" would have been distinguished from "moveables" for which value inhered in their easy ability to enter a commodity phase of their existence.

Yet another critical factor in the logic of the inventory may have been ownership. By one reading, the properties would have belonged to the Admiral's Men, with Henslowe acting primarily as their cataloger. Thus, R. A. Foakes has emphasized the significance of the inventory date of 10 March 1598. Only a few months earlier, Pembroke's Men had joined the Admiral's Men at the Rose, and the Admiral's Men may therefore have required a formal record of their own standing property and apparel. Also in late 1597 Edward Alleyn, lead actor of the Admiral's Men and, by virtue of his marriage to Joan Woodward, Henslowe's stepson, made a temporary "retirement" from acting at the Rose. That this had some impact on Henslowe's bookkeeping is indicated elsewhere in the *Diary* by his "not[e] of all suche goods as I haue Bowghte for playnge sence my sonne edward allen leafte [p]laynge."[32] If ownership was at issue in Henslowe's property list, then those objects that Carson characterizes as "inexplicably absent" and that I have analogized to "moveables" were either inventoried in another list now lost or were not owned by the Admiral's Men at all. In the latter case, the Admiral's Men may have relied on Henslowe's pawnbroking business to supplement their stock, as Natasha Korda has suggested.

At the same time, what may be at issue in the compilation of the inventory is less ownership than accountability. Like Thomas Carter, who listed the plate "remaining in [his] charge" at Copthall, Henslowe may have been responsible for objects he had not purchased and did not own but that were left in his charge. In other words, these were items that were stored in his playhouse, on his property, and in which he was therefore expected to take a protective interest. This does not tell us much about why these objects were assigned to him and others were not, but it does turn our focus to Henslowe's role as landlord, and this may suggest yet another hypothetical paradigm for the use and administration of these stage fittings. If Henslowe had himself invested in the properties, then analogy might usefully be drawn not to the lists of the Copthall family agent but instead to the churchwardens' accounts of St. Lawrence Pountney.

This analogy would play itself out in the following ways: the parish was dependent on its resident minister to perform significant spiritual and ecclesiastical functions. So, Henslowe was reliant on his resident company, although for him the players produced the entertainment that generated income from his real estate. One of the elements of exchange in the relationship of community and curate was that the community acted as landlord and provided a house to fill the curate's human needs. One of the terms of association for Henslowe and the Admiral's Men was that he provided a building for their use. In a single notable respect, the house used by the parish minister was specifically adapted to his purposes; it more often had a study than did other, similar London housing, and the study was fitted out with shelves for books. Similarly, the Rose playhouse had a specialized structure in its platform stage, its tiring house, its galleries, and its "gates"; it was purpose-built for performance. Perhaps it contained other amenities, as well, in the properties inventoried by and, thus, provided by landlord Henslowe – in contradistinction from the "moveables" provided by the tenants, the Lord Admiral's Men. In both parsonage house and playhouse, ownership and use may have been reciprocal functions.

But even to think of ownership in such unilateral terms may be inappropriate to the corporate operations of the Rose playhouse, as an analogy to the domestic sphere can again help instruct us. Household moveables belonged fully to individuals; household fittings did not. A moveable was one person's to use, to store, to lend, to sell, to pawn, to surrender in marriage, to discard, to bequeath. But fittings were dislodged from private ownership. In a fundamental sense, as Swinburne indicates, they belonged to their location. The house to which they were attached – whether physically or metaphorically – might stand in for the multiple descendants of a family, as a testator devised his fittings in perpetuity, for all his heirs rather than just the most immediate one. Or the house might represent an entire community's ownership, as was the case for the parsonage houses maintained by parish churches. If this analogy is applicable, neither Henslowe nor any member of the Admiral's Men had the right to remove, sell, or "deface" the Rose playhouse of its theatrical properties.

Thus, Swinburne indicates that "immoveables" "do not immediately belong to the person, but to some other thing, by way of dependency; as, trees growing on the ground, or fruit growing on the trees" (p. 133). Fittings, however, had a liminality he could not completely acknowledge; their dependency was not "natural" but, literally, constructed. It was the nature of goods to move, and fittings had a contrary inertia, but this was not an inertia that could not be overcome. While "The Enventary tacken of all the properties for my *Lord Admeralles men*, the 10 of Marche 1598" may serve to indicate all the objects that Henslowe and the Admiral's Men sought to hold out of circulation, we of course do not know the extent to which these goods obeyed their designated function. The ominous "Gone and loste" heading on one short list of costumes suggests that there may have been unlicensed traffic in the company's fittings, after all.

More importantly, the implication of the inventory is that the enterprise of the Rose was or would have been in an important sense damaged or "defaced" by such losses. Even those costumes known to be "Gone and loste" go unappraised in Henslowe's catalogue. The silence of these inventories on the subject of their commodity value suggests some appreciation that the damage of loss was more than monetary. Inventories yield up their full significance in revealing human aspirations for goods. They represent acts of will imposed upon objects. In contrast to those inventories that assigned ownership, responsibility, and tangible value, schedules of fittings imposed stability. In this, they had more magical meanings than most inventories. They commanded goods to stay in place for as long a future as was foreseeable. Henslowe's list of "all the properties" may thus project a long view of his theatre's life. The inventory expresses a commitment to these plays, these players, and this theatrical enterprise. Perhaps, in fact, the "mercenary" Henslowe also collaborated in the corporate project to make *Tamburlaine, Dr. Faustus, The Jew of Malta, Hercules,* and various other plays in the Rose repertory "perfect."

NOTES

I am grateful to R. A. Foakes for his comments on an earlier version of this paper; to the staff of the London Guildhall Library and the Centre for Kentish Studies, where some of its research was conducted; to Bernice Kliman and the Columbia University Shakespeare Seminar, where the work was first presented; and to editors Jonathan Gil Harris and Natasha Korda.

1. See the appendix to this volume. My source is *Henslowe's Diary*, ed. R. A. Foakes and R. T. Rickert (Cambridge: Cambridge University Press, 1961), appendix 2, "Playhouse inventories now lost," pp. 319–21. Although my general practice below is to modernize spelling and punctuation, I transcribe Henslowe's references directly rather than offer interpretive interventions that, given the eccentricity of his spelling, are necessarily speculative.

2. Foakes and Rickert (eds.), *Henslowe's Diary*, p. 316.

3. Alan C. Dessen and Leslie Thomson, *A Dictionary of Stage Directions in English Drama, 1580–1642* (Cambridge: Cambridge University Press, 1999). See, for example, *tree*, p. 236.

4. Neil Carson, *A Companion to Henslowe's Diary* (Cambridge: Cambridge University Press, 1988), pp. 52–3. Carol Chillington Rutter preceded Carson in observing that, judging from Henslowe's inventories, "the Elizabethan stage was not as bare as has sometimes been argued." She transcribes the inventories and provides useful background information in her edition, *Documents of the Rose Playhouse*, The Revels Plays Companion Library (Manchester: Manchester University Press, 1984); see pp. 133–7.

5. Fleay cited by Foakes and Rickert (eds.), *Henslowe's Diary*, p. 319.

6. See for example Ernest Schanzer, "Heywood's *Ages* and Shakespeare," *Review of English Studies*, n.s. 11 (1961): 18–28.

7. Carson, *A Companion to Henslowe's Diary*, p. 53.

8. Natasha Korda, "Household property/stage property: Henslowe as pawnbroker," *Theatre Journal*, 48:2 (1996): 185–95.

9. This list is culled from Henslowe's pawn accounts, transcribed on pages 55–61, 73–81, and 133–6 of Foakes and Rickert's edition of *Henslowe's Diary*. Some of the linens came into Henslowe's accounts wrapped around bundles of other linens or clothing.

10. See my "Fictions of the early modern probate inventory," in *The Culture of Capital: Property, Cities, and Knowledge in Early Modern England*, ed. Henry S. Turner (New York: Routledge, 2002).

11. Centre for Kentish Studies MS U269 E198/2.

12. According to T. E., "If before Marriage the Woman were possessed of Horses, Meat, Sheep, Corn, Wool, Money, Plate and Jewels, all manner of moveable substance is presently by conjunction the husbands, to sell, keep or bequeath if he die: And though he bequeath them not, yet are they the Husband's Executors and not the wife's which brought them to her Husband." See *The Lawes Resolutions of Womens Rights* (London, 1632; STC

7437), p. 130. In his will of 1572, for example, Edward Harvy used the first-person possessive pronoun in referring to goods that had been his wife's, even while giving back "half of my household stuff which she brought me, being divided by two or more honest men, she being at choice which part she will have." See *Essex Wills (England), Volume 3: 1571–1577*, ed. F. G. Emmison (Boston: New England Historic Genealogical Society, 1986; hereafter, *Essex Wills, Volume 3*), no. 674 (pp. 287–8).

13. For Palliser (1606), see *Wills and Administrations from the Knaresborough Court Rolls, Volume 2*, ed. Francis Collins, *Publications of the Surtees Society*, 110 (1904), pp. 2–3. For Cooke (1581), see *Essex Wills: The Bishop of London's Commissary Court, 1578–1588*, ed. F. G. Emmison (Chelmsford: Essex Record Office, 1995; hereafter, *Essex Wills, Volume 10*), no. 198 (p. 46); Cooke bequeathed these objects to his wife for her use during her life only, meaning that she had no testamentary rights to them herself. For George Gine (1578), see *Essex Wills, Volume 10*, no. 362 (p. 80). For Roger (1573), see *Essex Wills, Volume 3*, no. 209 (p. 81). For Jackson (1575), see *Essex Wills, Volume 3*, no. 365 (p. 149).

14. For Freville (1630), see *Wills and Inventories from the Registry at Durham, Volume 4*, ed. Herbert Maxwell Wood, *Publications of the Surtees Society*, 142 (1929), pp. 223–9. For Sutton (1562), see *Essex Wills: The Bishop of London's Commissary Court, 1558–1569*, ed. F. G. Emmison (Chelmsford: Essex Record Office, 1993; hereafter, *Essex Wills, Volume 8*), no. 669 (p. 141).

15. For Busshe (1569), see *Essex Wills: The Bishop of London's Commissary Court, 1569–1578*, ed. F. G. Emmison (Chelmsford: Essex Record Office, 1994), no. 38 (p. 8). For Sanderson (1609), see *Wills and Inventories from the Registry at Durham, Volume 4*, pp. 39–41. For Page (1583), see *Essex Wills, Volume 10*, no. 741 (pp. 162–3). For Petitte (1585), see *Essex Wills: The Archdeaconry Courts, 1583–1592*, ed. F. G. Emmison (Chelmsford: Essex Record Office, 1989; hereafter, *Essex Wills, Volume 5*), no. 109 (pp. 31–2).

16. For Jenynges (1558), see *Essex Wills, Volume 8*, no. 468 (p. 102).

17. Henry Swinburne's *A Brief Treatise of Testaments and Last Wills* was originally published in London in 1590 (STC 23537), was first "augmented" in 1611 (STC 23548), and was reprinted in 1635 (STC 23550; STC 23549 is a ghost). Topics introduced in 1590 were sometimes treated more expansively later. I quote from 1590 where possible, and so indicate by giving signature numbers. When quoting from added material, I use the 1635 edition and so indicate by giving page numbers. Throughout, I consult the sixth and seventh "parts" of the volume; in the 1635 edition, there was repagination from the fifth part on, meaning that "p. 50" here refers to the second page 50 in the volume. The following discussion oversimplifies Swinburne, who presents divergent legal opinions on such subjects as whether money can be considered a chattel.

18. I owe the term to Arjun Appadurai, ed., *The Social Life of Things: Commodities in Cultural Perspective* (Cambridge: Cambridge University Press, 1986).

19. For Northumberland, see *The Earl of Northumberland's Household Book* excerpted by M. Jourdain, *English Interior Decoration, 1500–1830* (London:

B. T. Batsford, 1950), p. 127. For "standing palaces," see *The History of the King's Works, Volume IV: 1485–1660 (Part II)*, ed. H. M. Colvin et al. (London: HMSO, 1982), pp. 28–9. See also Nancy and Jeff Cox, "Probate inventories: the legal background – Part I," *The Local Historian*, 16:3 (1984), especially 139–40.

20. For Goodsonne, see *Essex Wills, Volume 5*, no. 804 (p. 213). In the course of a useful discussion of "fixtures," F. G. Emmison also cites the 1597 will of Gilbert Isaac in *Elizabethan Life: Home, Work, and Land* (Chelmsford: Essex Record Office, 1991), p. 9. For the quoted will of Henry Simpson from 1647, see *Wills and Inventories from the Registry at Durham, Volume 4*, pp. 309–14.

21. For the 1593 inventory of yeoman Nicholas Hore, which lists glass and wainscoting in the hall and parlor, see Derek Portman, "Vernacular building in the Oxford region in the sixteenth and seventeenth centuries," in C. W. Chalklin and M. A. Havinden (eds.), *Rural Change and Urban Growth, 1500–1800* (London: Longman, 1974), pp. 154–5. For a 1570 inventory that includes wainscoting, see *Wills and Inventories Illustrative of the History, Manners, Language, Statistics etc. of the Northern Counties of England, Part I*, ed. James Raine, *Publications of the Surtees Society*, 2 (1835), pp. 335–42. For a 1596 inventory listing many fixtures, including glass and wainscoting, see that of Bishop Hugh Bellot, *Remains Historical and Literary Connected with the Palatine Counties of Lancaster and Chester*, ed. Rev. G. J. Piccope, *The Chetham Society*, 54 (1861), pp. 1–8.

22. Case cited by L. F. Salzman, *Building in England down to 1540: A Documentary History* (Oxford: Clarendon Press, 1967), p. 185. Salzman also reports that in 1493 the churchwardens of St. Mary-at-Hill paid a tenant for the window lattice and also the glass windows "that he left behind him."

23. See *London Viewers and their Certificates, 1508–1558*, ed. Janet Senderowitz Loengard (London: London Record Society, 1989), no. 226 (p. 92). In 1542, the Viewers ruled that wainscoting and shelves not fastened or nailed to the frame of the house were removable, while those fastened or nailed "may not be removed nor taken away without special license" (no. 172). See also no. 380 (1557).

24. London Guildhall Library [hereafter, Guildhall] MS 3907/1.

25. Interior porches, usually highly decorative, cut down on drafts in the principal rooms of houses. For a further description of these and other fittings, see the notes to the appendix to this chapter.

26. For St. Stephen Walbrook, see Guildhall MS 593/2. For St. Bartholomew Exchange, see Guildhall MS 4384/1.

27. Guildhall MS 10,334. See also the extraordinary 1607 inventory of fittings for the house renovated by London mayor Robert Lee in the late sixteenth century, transcribed by John Schofield in *Medieval London Houses* (New Haven and London: Yale University Press, 1995), appendix, pp. 233–5; for more on this property, see also his "Selective gazetteer of sites," no. 115 (pp. 194–5).

28. Rutter (ed.), *Documents of the Rose Playhouse*, p. 134.

29. See Guildhall MS 13029, property documents relating to the gift of Richard Casteler to Christ's Hospital, for duplicate schedules of implements in a messuage sold by Dame Winifryde, Lady Marchioness of Winchester to Roger Maners and Robert Adkinson. The schedules vary in only one detail: one includes beds and bed furnishings, while the other does not.
30. See Foakes and Rickert (eds.), *Henslowe's Diary*, pp. 317–19.
31. For a review of Henslowe's hostile treatment by early scholars, see Rutter (ed.), *Documents of the Rose Playhouse*, pp. 1–5. That Henslowe does not list the value of these properties does not mean that he made no investment in them. See also his "Note of all suche bookes as belong to the Stocke, and such as I have bought since the 3d of March 1598," which also includes no costs or charges. However, elsewhere in the *Diary* payments for these playscripts are confirmed, as is not the case with the properties.
32. I am grateful for the suggestions of R. A. Folkes, made in private correspondence. For Alleyn's retirement, see S. P. Cerasano, "Edward Alleyn, 1566–1626," in Aileen Reid and Robert Maniura (eds.), *Edward Alleyn, Elizabethan Actor, Jacobean Gentleman* (London: Dulwich Picture Gallery, 1994), pp. 17–18. For Henslowe's "Note," see Foakes and Rickert (eds.), *Henslowe's Diary*, pp. 83–4.

APPENDIX

London Guildhall Library MS 10,334: Documents of 5 May 1595 relating to the sale by John Martyn and Margerie his wife to William Burcher of two messuages in Little Wood Street in the parish of St. Albans in London, one in the tenure of Bevis Bulmer, esquire, and one in the tenure of Bartholomew Chapple, gentleman. Deed of sale accompanied by the following "schedule."

The Schedule Indented of all and singular those parcels of goods, chattles, wainscot, and implements which are remaining, fixed, or being within and about the several messuages or tenements now in the tenures or occupations of Bevis Bulmer, esquire, and Bartholomew Chapple, gentleman. And which are granted, bargained, and sold by the indenture whereunto this Schedule is annexed. That is to say.

*First in the messuage or tenement now in the occupation
of the said bevis bulmer, viz*

In the hall of the said messuage.
 Imprimis, a long table of wainscot with a frame to it.[1]
 Item, two benches fixed[2] therein.
 Item, a joined[3] settle with a back of wainscot.[4]
 Item, a little cupboard of fir boards with a lock.
 Item, two racks to lay harquebusses and pikes upon.[5]
 Item twenty-four panes of glass in the windows.

In the parlor of the same messuage.

Item, the wainscot round about painted yellow and red.

Item, two portals[6] painted, with latches and bolts upon them.

Item, two painted heads (a man and a woman) standing on the said portals.[7]

Item, one drawing wainscot table[8] with four joined stools.

Item, a form of wainscot with turned pillars.[9]

Item, one carving board of wainscot fixed with hinges.[10]

Item, the glass windows with five casements.[11]

Item, three cupboards with locks and keys, joined, with the wainscot by the chimney.

Item, two little green shelves.

In the buttery of the same messuage.

Item, two tiers or rows of shelves round about and a broad bin.

In the kitchen of the same messuage.

Item, three dressing planks[12] with feet fixed.

Item, five shelves with one capon[13] coop.

Item, a cistern of lead under the stairs with a cock[14] into the kitchen for conduit water.

Item, a great cistern of lead for rain water.[15]

Item, five racks for spits.[16]

Item, nine glass windows with two casements.

In the dry larder of the same messuage.

Item, one door with hinges and a latch.

In the bolting house.[17]

Item, a fair bolting pipe to bolt in.

Item, a door with hinges and a latch.

In the pastry.

Item, two fair ovens with one iron cover.

Item, three pastry planks fixed fast.

Item, one shelf and a hanging shelf.

Item, the one side glazed.

Item, a door with lock and key, latch and hinges.

In the washing house.

Item, an oven, one pair of pothangers in the chimney, one glass window with a casement, a door with lock and a latch.

Item, a door to the privy[18] in the entry with a lock.

In the three rooms over the washing house.

Item, two horses to set saddles upon with pins to hang bridles on, two forms, one dresser plank to scour upon, one settle, three glass windows with two casements, two doors with bolts, and a foot ladder.

In the yard.

Item, a pump, one great cistern of lead, with a waste pipe of lead and a cock for rain water, one long cistern of lead with three partitions to wash in. And a lead to piss in with a pipe.

In the garden.

Item, privy hedges being foursquare railed with turned posts, one coop for chickens. And one door with lock and two bolts.

In the dining chamber.

Item, the wainscot round about with a portal and a joined door to it with a latch and one bolt.

Item, one other joined door with a latch and a bolt.

Item, a great door of wainscot, with a plate, lock, and key.

Item, a long drawing table of walnut tree, and a frame with six pillars, eight joined stools of walnut tree, one bench of wainscot fixed to the wainscot, one joined form of wainscot, three glass windows with eight casements, one iron back[19] fixed to the chimney, one carving board with hinges and framed, two curtain rods.

In the counting house.[20]

Item, the glass windows with a casement.

Item, a counting board[21] covered with cloth, the shelves, and a set with twelve boxes to put writings[22] in.

In another counting house.

Item, the shelves about it.

In the entry next the dining chamber.

Item, a glass window with a casement and a press[23] with four doors, four locks, and two keys.

In the chamber next.

Item, the wainscot round about.

Item, a portal of wainscot with a joined door of wainscot with a latch and a bolt.

Item, a door with a plate, lock, and key, and one bolt.

Item, two glass windows with four casements.

Item, a joined door of wainscot by the chimney with a bolt.

In the chamber over the dining chamber.

Item, the painted cloths.[24]

Item, two glass windows with two casements and two doors with locks and keys and bolts.

In one of the maids' chamber.

Item, a little painted cloth of nine yards and one foot ladder to the garret.

In the chamber next the hothouse, and in the hothouse.

Item, a glass window, a furnace for water with two cocks, a glass window [sic], one pipe of lead to convey water, and two doors of fir board, with lock, key, and bolt.

In the gallery.

Item, the most part hanged with fine stained cloth, the other part with painted cloth of flower and arras.[25]

Item, a portal to the privy of wainscot with a bolt, and four glass windows with six casements.

In the flockwork[26] chamber.

Item, all hanged with painted flockwork cloth. Two glass windows with five casements.

Item, half a screen[27] of wainscot.

Item, a door of wainscot with a plate, lock, and key, and one flat bolt.

Item, a door to the privy.

Item, two curtain rods.

In the middle chamber.

Item, the same all hanged with painted cloth of King Pharoah.[28]

Item, one bay glass window with a casement and one clerestory.

Item, a portal with a door, lock, and key. And one door, lock, and key to go into the flockwork chamber.

In the chamber with dornix.[29]

Item, the third part hanged with dornix and the fourth part wainscotted with a cupboard in the wainscot,[30] lock and key.

Item, a bay glass window with three casements and two clerestories glazed, one with a casement.

In the two little garret chambers.

Item, two glass windows with two casements and two doors to them with locks and keys.

Item, in the same gallery two clerestories glazed, and one door with hinges, lock, and key.

In the garret upon the leads.[31]

Item, one glass window and one door with lock and key.

Adjoining to the leads.

Item, five bars of iron to stay the battlements, five racks of iron for poles to hang clothes on.

Item, the casement of the stairs glazed with ten lights.

Item, at the stair foot one great wainscot door with plate, lock, and key, and two flat bolts.

Item, in the wine cellar, two joists to lay wine or beer upon.[32]

Item, three hanging shelves with boards.

Item, in the outward cellar two joists for beer, one long hanging shelf, one bin, and a hogshead[33] with a cover for salt.

In the messuage or tenement now in the occupation
of the foresaid bartholomew chapple

First in the kitchen of the same messuage.

Item, a bar and an hook of iron.

Item, a jack[34] for a spit.

Item, a cistern of lead.

Item, a stool.

Item, a dresser board and shelves.

In the hall of the same messuage.

Item, a table and six stools of wainscot.

Item, a long form of wainscot.

Item, two andirons.

Item, thirty yards of painted cloth.

Item, thirty-seven yards and a half of wainscot.

In the chamber over the kitchen.

Item, a field bed[35] with a tester of blue cloth, and a mat.[36]

Item, a table with a stool.

Item, forty yards of painted cloth.

In the chamber over the hall.

Item, a joined bedstead.

Item, sixty-five yards painted cloth.

In the chamber over the entry.

Item, a joined bedstead.

Item, a joined press with two cupboards.

Item, fifty-four yards of painted cloth.

In the chamber over the warehouse.

Item, a field bedstead standing with a tester.

Item, fifty-five yards of painted cloth.

Item, a little table.

In the garret.

Item, a little bedstead.

Item, two shelves and an old table.

In the entry.

Item, a cock of brass in the cistern.

In the cellars.

Item, a beer joist and a little form.

NOTES

1. Here, *table* means "table board," *wainscot* most likely means "oak" (the wood so often used in wall panelling that the two became roughly synonymous), and the *frame* is the support or trestle for the board.
2. I.e., two *benches* were *"fixed"* or attached to the walls of the hall.
3. *Joined* work was more expensive and of higher status than "carpenter's" nailed work.
4. Here, *wainscot* probably refers to the appearance of the back of the settle, with carved panels resembling the wainscoting affixed to walls.
5. A *harquebus* was a large portable gun; a *pike*, a long wooden shaft with a pointed metal tip. *Racks* to store and display these weapons were affixed to the walls; an example of a rack for bows survives over the hall fireplace at Wilderhope Manor in Shropshire.
6. *Portals* were interior porches, intended to cut down drafts from frequently opened doors (the person entering a room would first open its main door, step into the small enclosed box of the porch, then close the main door behind him before opening the portal door into the room). These were often highly decorative, with carved wainscoting, finials, and, as described here, ornamental painting.
7. These *painted heads* were presumably portraits set into the wainscot panels of the portal.
8. A *drawing table* had leaves or extensions to make its length adjustable.
9. As opposed to a *bench* fixed to the wall, a *form* was a freestanding bench or long seat. The legs of this bench were *turned* on a lathe.
10. The *carving board* indicates that this parlor was used as a dining room; the hinges suggest that the board was affixed to the wall and could be lowered against it when not in use.
11. Only some of the glass of early modern windows was in *casements*, meaning that the windows could be opened. Others were glazed shut.
12. *Dressing planks* were work surfaces either for dressing meat or, as in the washing house, below, for scouring. These planks were fixed to the floor (rather than the wall).
13. A *capon* was a castrated cock or rooster.
14. A *cock* was a tap or implement to regulate the flow of water from a pipe.
15. This house had two sources of water: rain water gathered in a cistern and conduit water piped into the house. London had an early conduit system for the delivery of water, to supplement well water.
16. A *rack* was a bar or set of bars, often of iron, used to support *spits* or broaches for roasting meat.

17. This room or building was reserved for *bolting*, which involved sifting grain or meal.

18. The sanitary arrangements of this house become clear: this ground-floor privy near the washing house; a second-floor privy off the gallery and the flockwork chamber (see below); and a cistern for urinating in, in the yard (see below).

19. The *back* was a slab of iron, often molded with decorative images and/or a date, which protected the brick at the lower rear of the chimney.

20. The *counting house* was a room in which accounts were kept and papers stored.

21. The *counting board* was a table for counting money and working accounts.

22. *Writings* referred specifically to property documents or other "evidences" of ownership or property negotiations.

23. A *press* was a kind of cupboard, generally with shelves, and sometimes set into a wall. It was primarily associated with the storage of clothing and linens.

24. *Painted cloths* were hung on walls in imitation of more expensive tapestries, and, unlike tapestries, purely for decorative purposes. (Tapestries also served to warm a room.)

25. *Stained cloths* were like painted cloths, but produced by a different technique. *Arras* was a sort of tapestry noted for its rich colors.

26. *Flockwork* was a kind of cloth with thick tufts of cotton or wool.

27. A *screen* was a partition or partial wall, most often associated with a hall but here, unusually, with a bedchamber.

28. Many painted cloths showed general outdoor scenes, but this one of "King Pharoah" probably illustrated a Biblical story, perhaps of Joseph or of Exodus.

29. *Dornix* was a cloth named for a Flemish town in which it was worked. It might be silk, wool, and/or linen.

30. This *cupboard* was evidently built into the wall or nailed to the wainscoting on the wall.

31. *The leads* refer to the roof of the house, so called for the strips or sheets of lead laid there to protect the building from water damage.

32. *Joists* were supporting beams, generally standing on edge, often associated with subflooring, but in this case used with barrels or casks to keep them from rolling.

33. A *hogshead* was a large barrel or cask often used for storing wine or beer but also, as the cover for salt in this instance suggests, for storing salted meat.

34. A *jack* was an implement for turning the spit on which meat was roasted.

35. A *field bed* was a portable bed, originally designed for use as a camp bed outdoors, but popular in late sixteenth- and early seventeenth-century interiors, as well. That this field bed had a fairly permanent status as a standing bed is indicated by its *tester* or canopy.

36. A *mat* was a thick piece of coarse or woven fabric which could support a chair seat or, equally, as here, such bedding as a feather or flock bed.

CHAPTER 5

Properties of domestic life: the table in Heywood's A Woman Killed With Kindness

Catherine Richardson

The domestic tragedy, which emerges in the last decade of the sixteenth century, is innovative in its representation of the private lives of private individuals. Domestic tragedies concentrate on crime within the family, specifically on greed, adultery, and murder. Consequently, their purpose has often been seen as a morally didactic one: they display the results of transgression in order to alert their audiences to the consequences of immoral actions within the home.[1]

These plays frequently draw attention to their status as almost sensationalist peddlers of private actions and emotions. Modes of defining, and then representing, the personal are crucial to their success because only a significant level of mimesis will achieve their desired effect. This essay investigates the ways in which the subjects of such plays are presented through objects: its focus is on the operation of the domestic as a context for tragedy, the way in which the personal and social implications of crime are given meaning by their environment of household things.[2]

During the period when domestic tragedy was popular (the end of the sixteenth and start of the seventeenth century) the contents of the majority of households was changing in substance and hence in meaning. The physical composition of the domestic was becoming more complex, and the range of goods which it contained was increasing and altering in quality, substance and provenance, denoting a new relationship with goods which can be seen as a nascent consumerism.[3] Partly in response to the social location of the most visible of such changes, the indisputable "core texts" of the genre present a socially specific, particularized view of domestic aberration, one which situates it within the houses of an often provincial bourgeoisie.[4]

The probable heterogeneity of the audiences for such plays,[5] though, presents the paradox of a didactic drama, necessarily of wide application, which deals with the socially particular. Domestic tragedies play subtle

games with the traditional relationship at the heart of moral theatre
between the general and the specific, between the macro- and the
microcosmic, between the community and the individual. Rather than
rejecting the idea of a didactic purpose for the plays, however, I want to
argue for stage properties as a focus for the mechanics of the relationship
between the narrative and the individual spectator. I do so with reference
to a specific example, that of scene 8 of Thomas Heywood's *A Woman
Killed With Kindness*, a domestic tragedy in which props are chosen and
used with the utmost care. This scene has been chosen because of the
specific way in which it makes use of domestic properties: a table and its
associated paraphernalia are employed as a crucial symbol which gives
meaning to the actions of the play as a whole.[6]

My argument here concentrates on two sets of meanings that are
attached to the theatrical property in domestic drama. First, it has a situation within the play: this is constructed through the dramatic narrative,
which creates a context for the object on the stage. The identification
of the status of the characters is a part of this process. Second, there is
the accepted usage of such an object outside the theatre: its employment
in everyday social practice. Knowledge of these meanings is brought to
the theatre by the audience in shades of explicitness which the play itself can stimulate. The connections between the "stage history" of the
domestic object and the social significance of such a piece of furniture
construct meanings for an early modern audience which, I will argue,
are not immediately obvious to the modern reader.

This argument is based on the capacity of household objects on the
stage to invite audience members to make connections between what
they see in the theatre and their own domestic practice.[7] In this way
the essay is similar in approach to Juana Green's analysis of Jonson's
Epicoene in this volume. The essays share an interest in the ability of
props to materialize extratheatrical issues concerning material goods,
ownership, and status.

Because domestic tragedy is so strikingly grounded in the cultural
practices, and in some cases, even the actual events, of early modern
England (several plays are based on contemporary murder cases), it has
lent itself to a variety of interdisciplinary approaches. Recent work on
the plays has shed valuable light on their relationship to a range of other
kinds of text including conduct books of gentlemanly behavior, political
theories of patriarchal control, and murder pamphlets.[8] This essay takes
a rather different historicist approach. It endeavors to reconstruct the
contemporary meanings of the objects used as props in Heywood's play

through an understanding of their particular function within the early modern house.

Inventories have been studied in relation to these plays before,[9] but they have only been analyzed qualitatively, mainly in order to establish the essential realism being aimed at in the works. My methodology with regard to these documents relates most directly to the second trend in materialist analysis outlined in the introduction to this volume, in that it is primarily quantitative. I seek to establish a generalized meaning for the objects represented in relation to the rooms in which they were used. I contend that it is only by setting the qualitative evidence for the use of individual props within a wider conception of their general social meaning that we will understand their true significance.

This contention puts my argument in direct conflict with Calderwood's claim, quoted in the introduction to this volume, about the closed meanings of the stool in the banquet scene of *Macbeth*. He sees the introduction of props into narrative as causing a process of transformation: "Now Macbeth owns [the stool] uniquely; it has been wholly interiorized by the fictive world and no longer bears any likeness to its original form" (see page 14). However, as its form patently *does not* change, neither does its mnemonic facility, and Calderwood has picked the one object of which every single person in early modern England would unquestionably have had personal experience. The argument presented here has implications beyond *A Woman Killed With Kindness* because it suggests that unless connection can be made between the stool on which Banquo's ghost is (not) sitting, and the ones the audience sat upon at home, the dislocation of the senses which Macbeth is experiencing will offer a considerably less "realistic illusion." I see props as stimulating the imagination, and I do not see this as a threat to "illusion," but rather as a way of strengthening it through the employment of the knowledge and emotions of the audience.

This essay begins by considering domestic properties in relation to household routines, seeing them as supremely useful and yet simultaneously highly symbolic objects. The central section of the essay uses the evidence of inventories to situate those objects precisely within the home. It describes their relationship to the room space that they habitually occupy, and in so doing it attempts to reconstruct the implicit knowledge of object and space which the audience bring with them to the theatre. Finally, the essay returns to the issues raised here about how properties work: the *type* of connections they might make between the text and the audience's imagination. This last section sets out to clarify dramatic purpose by suggesting a range of potential relationships between the play and its consumers.

A Woman Killed With Kindness opens with the celebration of the marriage of Frankford and Anne, and the opening scenes explore the newly formed household, which has been created by their wedding. This mood of celebration is broken when a fight over hawking leads to the death of two servants, setting in motion a subplot that traces the fall of their otherwise morally admirable murderer Sir Charles and his sister Susan from gentle status to poverty. Contrasting with their changed estate is the social advancement of Wendoll, a gentleman "somewhat pressed by want" (4.33), whom Frankford takes into his house and offers "Your man, your gelding, and your table" (4.71). Wendoll, however, goes one step further and also takes Frankford's wife in an affair whose discovery explains the title of the play: Frankford spares Anne's life to give her time to repent her adultery in isolation from her family, and the story ends when she dies having received his forgiveness. As a play it is tense in its concentration on social competition and transformations, and differences in social status are frequently elucidated through divergent household routines and their associated properties.

The scene on which this essay focuses occurs at the point where Nick, the servant whom Frankford has given to Wendoll, tells his old master about his suspicions regarding the adulterous pair. The importance of this scene lies in its significance as the point in the dramatic narrative at which the husband retakes control of his household, generating the events which constitute the rest of the play.

Enter three or four servingmen (including Nick and Spiggot the Butler), one with a voider and a wooden knife to take away all, another the salt and bread, another the table-cloth and napkins, another the carpet. Jenkin with two lights after them.

JENKIN: So, march in order and retire in battle 'ray. My master and the guests have supped already, all's taken away. Here now spread for the servingmen in the hall. Butler, it belongs to your office.[10] (8.1–4)

These are the opening lines of the scene, following on from the fairly lengthy stage business. In his short speech Jenkin sets the space that the stage is asked to represent in the context of Frankford's house as a whole. At first reading, it appears that the servants lay a table on the stage itself in dumb show, as servant and master discuss betrayal further downstage. But Frankford questions Nick later on in the scene:

FRANKFORD: Nicklas, what make you here? Why are not you at supper in the
hall there with your fellows? (8.123–4)

It seems, then, that the line of servants enters holding the material
necessities for dining in such a household, and then exits having displayed their wares to the audience. Nick has one soliloquy in which
he agonizes over the knowledge that he possesses about Wendoll and
Anne, and by the end of which he has decided to reveal his suspicions to
Frankford. When the latter subsequently enters Nick begins to broach
the subject. After some misunderstandings created by the subtlety of his
approach to such a sensitive issue, Frankford finally comprehends what
is being suggested. Unable to take the information in, the latter strikes
Nick, and then asks him for his proof. Weighing the evidence, he decides
that he must engineer a situation whereby he can observe the couple in
bed together with his own eyes. Having formed a plan, Frankford turns
his attentions back to the evening's entertainment, asserting his authority
over the domestic environment by directing the stuff of the house:

FRANKFORD: Lights and a table there! Wife, Master Wendoll and Gentle
Master Cranwell –

Enter Anne, Wendoll, Cranwell, Nick and Jenkin with cards, carpet, stools and
other necessaries. (8.116–17)

Jenkin underlines the function of the items that are brought onto the
stage at this point by talking through the servants' actions as they put
them to use:

JENKIN: A pair of cards, Nicklas, and a carpet to cover the table. Where's Sisly
with her counters and her box? Candles and candlesticks there! Fie, we
have such a household of serving creatures! Unless it be Nick and I, there's
not one amongst them all can say boo to a goose. (8.121–5)

It is these two sets of stage directions upon which I want to concentrate;
investigating how they function in relation to one another, and the ways
in which they direct and enhance the meanings of the narrative which
is played out between them.

Both directions make reference to the laying of tables, the first for
dining and the second for recreation and leisure purposes. What I want
to argue initially is that the introduction of a table and the objects associated with it into a domestic drama offers particular resonances with
extratheatrical routines. The table functions to alert the audience to the
imminence of a domestic ritual, making reference to the habitual function of such objects within the house. The form in which the properties

are brought onto the stage is also ritualized, and the construction of this scene makes clear and determined reference to such self-consciously mannered aspects of household routine. It is worth playing out some of the contemporary resonances of such a scene at this point.

When the servants enter at the beginning of the scene, they come on one after the other in a progression, and the objects that they hold are suggestive of this sequence too. First come those who will remove what is already there, those who will tidy up what is left of the previous meal, and in so doing prepare the table for the next event. Next come those who provide for the present, for the ritual that is to be participated in now. The objects that they hold are divided along the lines of a contemporary inventory. In such records these items are revealed to be different categories of things that commonly occur in clusters. Table cloths and napkins, for instance, are kept together in the same chests, often elided into the same items in inventories for which a total price is given, and bequeathed as sets from one generation to the next in wills. Coming under the generic term of "linen" they are related to carpets, both of which are "fabric" items, the latter also kept in chests for protection when they are not in use.

The objects are also coverings, items that can be seen either as clothing, protecting, or concealing the furniture of the house. They are adjuncts to the table, the things that it needs to define it in the context of dining. When one puts a carpet, cloth, and napkins upon the table and then the salt and bread, one determines, delimits, and fixes the event that is about to occur there. The table for which these items are destined will not be used for cards, it will be used for a meal, and the parade of props signals this like a prior warning, an advertisement for the future.

Also of importance is the fact that the things come on in reverse order, apart from the lights. Presumably one has to lay the carpet first, then the cloth, then the food. So it might be that they come on in reverse order of value, with the pageant of goods becoming a progression of statements of wealth. This also works visually – the carpet will be the most eye-catching of the props, it could be colorful and complex in design, and it may refer to exotic countries and the wealth and status to be gained from trade connections with them.[11] And both servants carry very important possessions, those things which are, after the plate collection of the house, amongst the most valuable of its moveable assets. The wealth of the house, its reserves of splendor, are played out before the eyes of the audience in what one presumes is silence. The first actor to speak is at the end of the line, ensuring that the goods have been fully appreciated visually before he characterizes their situation discursively.

These are the extradramatic resonances of these actions. But the purely theatrical meanings of the scene are important as well. In terms of its dramatic form, this is a pageant or procession, an organization of space and actors more usually associated with displays of military might, where the props carried are weapons and standards. This is, of course, an impression which is reinforced by Jenkin's first speech about "marching in order" and "retiring in battle 'ray." It is old-fashioned in its static presentation, as opposed to explication, of dramatic evidence, but it is visually exciting and redolent of solemnity, gravity and dignity. The dramatic convention of the pageant is also associated with royal progress, with church processions, and with displays of civic unity – all of which are implemented in the hierarchical organization of space. As an image, it emphasizes the respect inspired by the correct display of status. But here status is not indicated by the parade of the insignia of office, by emblems of power such as a crown, which have efficacy because they relate to the historical role rather than its present representative. Instead, it is suggested by the trappings of an emerging bourgeois culture, by the acquisitions made imperative by consumerism, and without which the definition of status has, by the time of this play, become hard to achieve.

At this juncture in the play the dramatic convention of the pageant is used to set up echoes with "real life" ritual moments associated with household activities. When the servants bring on their goods and walk across the stage with them, the action alludes both to the forms of display of power and control which are available within contemporary society, and to the daily routines of the household. At this point, the play takes advantage of both its mimetic capacities and the opportunity for extratheatrical gesturings through the form that its presentation of properties takes. All these different interpretations of the use of properties in this scene, the ritual, the routine, and the dramaturgical, merge at this point into the many meanings of the Frankford house, which it is the function of the props to characterize. It is now necessary to understand the significance of their very conspicuous appearance at this particular point in the play.

The domestic rituals that the table projects into this play have the effect of stressing the regular, the predictable, and the routine. But the initial parade of goods, having indicated a projected narrative for the audience, and suggested dining with the broad but expressive brushstroke of equipment, proceeds to frustrate those anticipations and to reveal them to be a dramatic "blind alley" as it leaves the stage by the other door. Because these properties are capable of representing their own uses simply by being on the stage, because they symbolize those uses instantly through the audience's familiarity with them as domestic items, *A Woman Killed With Kindness* is able to work against these inherent meanings, setting them up only to knock them down again.

In terms of public display, the domestic ritual is interrupted, and such an interruption signals the importance of the dialogue that is to follow. Similarly, the dining in the parlor is itself interrupted, as Frankford's suggestive gesture makes clear:

Enter FRANKFORD as it were brushing the crumbs from his clothes with a napkin, and newly risen from supper.

Both characters in this part of the scene are *en route* to social events that are put on hold for their presence. The servants have gone off through one door to lay the table in the hall, and Frankford has entered through the other, having come from the parlor where he has been dining. In both parlor and hall a household event has been interrupted; time has been paused for the conversation that they are about to have.

Indirectly, the properties used in this scene are used at this point to characterize the kind of space in which master and servant stand. Nick and Frankford's exchange, situated between the parlor and the hall and occurring between two meals, nestles within a domestic space not designed to be a space; it is pragmatic and inventive with its surroundings. At this point the stage affords them a kind of privacy, one that is constructed by its lack of a social audience, rather than being enclosed spatially. The space is within the house, paradoxically given meaning by those rooms that it is not (neither parlor nor hall), and yet it has no physical anchor. We see the house at this point from the underside, behind its scenes, from a place that is traversed rather than inhabited, much as the stage itself is, without the illusory permanence of the prop. The very absence of the properties, fresh in the mind from their recent exit, sharpens the audience's perception of the space as an unlocated one.

This definition of privacy is in contrast to that of the chamber to which the adulterous Anne and Wendoll retreat in scene 11 to enjoy a forbidden intimacy. The latter is shut off with the use of lock and key, but the servants are nevertheless aware of the actions that are being performed within. The stage on which master and servant stand in scene 8 provides a space for speech which is unheard because it has no formal situation: no one but the audience knows that anything at all has happened, let alone the nature of what has occurred. This is a space constructed in relation to the absence of properties in conjunction with the mere mention of the names of the rooms to which they have been sent. Whilst the audience is aware of a paradigm shift in domestic relations, as far as the other characters are concerned, this part of the scene is a "non-event."

Implicit in the positioning of Frankford in such a liminal space without property is the unsettling feeling that his social standing is compromised. While even his wife and her lover can command the public areas of the house in scene 11, he is reduced to inhabiting its comfortless passageways. Even the servants are ensconced in the hall, that lower status public space against which the play sets the parlor where his guests dine.[12] Such ultimate privacy, a desocialized invisibility within the household, is contrasted uncomfortably with the surrounding action. Describing space necessarily characterizes those actions that take place within it, and the individuals who are involved in them. There is an intricate web of meaning in this play that connects properties, stage space, action and characterization.

We are reminded that a drama that allows access to the private house necessarily deals with two kinds of audience, those on and those off the stage. The invited guests of the household, those not a part of its everyday nuclear operations, provide a further complication of the divide between social actor and audience. Frankford's action in brushing the crumbs from his clothing seems to underline this confusion perfectly: his behavior not only insists upon interruption, the arresting of one set of actions in order to make space for another, it is also a gesture which suggests the private man.[13]

Whereas the parade of goods was about self-conscious, prepared, con- structed definition, this is about the imperfections of reality. Frankford's clothes, which are the supremely self-defining exterior expression of a person in interaction with society, are here sullied. The implication is that we are seeing behind his mannered social identity to the man himself, and polished domestic show is followed on stage by the representation of confused domestic experience. The audience must compare his physical presence on the stage to the representation of his status offered by the parade of properties, and the juxtaposition points up the possible dis- junctions between goods as signifiers of status, of situation, and of present reality.

The parade of goods has a further function in this scene, and that is to provide a ground against which the sin that Anne and Wendoll are to commit can achieve its fullest significance. The goods do not only suggest domestic routine and its hiatus, they also bring into play a whole range of meanings associated with meals and communal dining, simultaneously offering supremely materialist and richly symbolic meanings. Dining has connotations of bounty and of Christian charity through such imperatives as the corporal acts of mercy, and is related to Christ's actions at the Last Supper. It therefore functions within the household to cement the bonds between individuals and to aid their formation into a community. The form of the table itself underlines this function by joining all those participating in the meal around its sides; it stresses interconnection and responsibility. Protestantism had strengthened and drawn attention to these meanings through the altered form of the Eucharist with its "table" and "cup" in place of altar and chalice. Christian teaching, filtered through domestic practice into a moralized discourse of involvement, sets up a fleeting typological association between Frankford's impending sufferings and those of Christ.

Seen in terms of these connections to other culturally significant discourses, the table focuses attention upon ideologies of the provision by the householder of sustenance for those who are dependent upon him, and the consequent, expected return of allegiance from those who receive at his hands: a feudal reciprocity with a Protestant twist.[14] The meanings of the image presented by the properties can then be seen to resonate with the discursive identifications of dependency which occur soon after the departure of the parade of goods: Wendoll is said to be "a daily guest" (8.8), in contrast to Cranwell's position as "the gentleman who came but this afternoon" (8.9).

In the context of the unselfish provisioning of the domestic environment, and against the bounty of cloths and candlesticks, the play sets the revelation of betrayal. This has the effect of figuring unfaithfulness not only in personal, emotional terms, but also as a sin against the very house itself. Problematized here is the richer concept of "household" as a very intimate connection between property and people, in which both sides give meaning and context to each other. The two sides begin to pull away from one another as a result of Anne and Wendoll's sin, and the presence of properties associated with household rituals comments ironically upon a disjunction much more fundamental than the interruption of a meal.[15]

This section has suggested the rich range of contemporary meanings that might be generated by the properties in scene 8 of *A Woman Killed With Kindness*. It has done so by demonstrating the significance of the domestic routines with which they would have been associated by an early modern audience. The intention here has been to see how Heywood manipulates audience familiarity with household situations through his deployment of their material apparatus. In the following section I want to locate these objects within specific rooms in the early modern house in order to understand more fully the importance of the relationship between action, space, and object in the domestic experience that the audience bring with them to the theatre.

It will have become obvious by now that the differences between rooms are very important in *A Woman Killed With Kindness*. Scene 8, of course, sees the family dining in the parlor and the servants in the hall. In addition, the opening marriage celebrations are divided along lines of status between parlor and yard, and the decisive moment in Wendoll's seduction of Anne comes when he invites her to move their impending meal from the public room they share with their guests to her "private chamber" (11.92).

The relationship between the properties and the rooms of Frankford's house is also an important one. The specific distinction between parlor and hall in scene 8 invites further contextualization if we are to understand the resonances of these words for the audience at this key moment in the play. I would also argue, though, that the use of domestic properties in general demands such a sensitivity to context on the part of the critic.

We should see the stage table, for instance, as possessing its own coherent spatial context for the audience: acting as a metonym for the kind of room in which it would typically be used for the purpose suggested by the narrative. The prop must indicate the room as a whole to the audience; the distinct meanings, for instance, of parlor as opposed to hall. The audience bring to the representation their memory of an organization of space, a conjunction of objects, the missing details of the room that houses the prop in their memory or their imagination.

As the procession of objects which initially suggests this particular table in scene 8 of *A Woman Killed With Kindness* enters then, it does so like the edge of a curtain, necessarily pulling with it its domestic situation: the original position of goods in the chests and cupboards of the house; the likely position of furniture in the hall or parlor for which it is destined; the most likely type of events in such a room; their probable nature in such a house. What *actually* happens will be set against these notions of probability.

In order to reconstruct such spaces it is necessary to consider the empirical evidence for these rooms, the fullest accounts of whose constituent parts are to be found in probate inventories. These documents list all the goods owned by the householder at the time of his or her decease, and give them a current value on the secondhand market.[16] Such an analysis is valuable because it makes it possible to reconstruct the spaces with which the prop is associated, and therefore to fully comprehend the significance and function of that prop. When the action is explicitly divided between hall and parlor, we need to be alive to the cultural resonances of such a distinction if we are to realize the full importance of the organization of space within the play. In addition, an understanding of the nature of the historical parlor makes it possible to see the *level* of representation the play affords: the kind of properties which are chosen from those which the room originally contained in order to represent it on stage. By understanding such differences between representation and reality it is possible to see why particular items are chosen as stage properties.

I have analyzed the inventories of the inhabitants of Canterbury, Sandwich and Faversham, three of the largest towns in Kent in this period, with additional documents from their satellite villages. This provides information from just over 1,200 inventories registered in the Consistory and Archdeaconry courts of the diocese of Canterbury, all those which survive between the 1560s, when the practice of recording such information began, and the early 1590s, when the genre of domestic tragedy began to flourish.[17] The social status of those whose property they record ranges from artisans and petty traders to master craftsmen, wealthy merchants, landowners and the minor gentry. There are clear comparisons here with the majority of the putative audience for these plays, and with the majority of those whose lives provide a focus for domestic plays. Indeed the historical Thomas Arden, whose murder by his wife is shown in *Arden of Faversham*, would almost certainly have been among them had he lived out his natural life.

Over one hundred distinct objects, whether fittings, furniture, or furnishings, are to be found in both halls and parlors, taking the sample as a whole. But there are significant differences between the kinds of items that the two rooms contain. These variations can be roughly divided into categories: bedding; seating; storage; working tools and valuables, each of which I shall address separately.

There are fewer bedsteads, featherbeds, flockbeds, trucklebeds, valances, coverlets, and testers in halls than there are in parlors. To give just two numerical examples, 11 percent of halls contain bedsteads, as opposed to 69 percent of parlors; 8 percent of the former contain featherbeds and 48.5 percent of the latter. Indeed, the hall is the only room in the house in which very few people seem habitually to have slept. Whilst the hall has about one third of the number of trucklebeds (those which slide under other beds) as it does of the more elaborate 'standing' variety, the parlor has many more, suggesting that if necessary it could sleep many more people. So, generally speaking, the hall is quiet at night, a more public room suited to daytime use, while the parlor is used for sleeping, but holds mainly high-status, good-quality bedding. This is an impression that is reinforced by the large percentage of parlors containing costly featherbeds.

During the day, however, the objects that are housed in the hall suggest that it, more than any other room, played host to the various activities of domestic cloth production. Five percent of halls contain trendles as opposed to an odd 0.5 percent of parlors, 7 percent have spinning wheels (as opposed to 1.6 percent), and 0.6 percent of halls even have expensive and specialized weavers' looms. Halls also possess more chairs (132:110), more forms (98:80), and almost the same number of settles (25:27) as parlors, although they do have fewer stools (228:308).[18] This suggests that whereas the parlor could provide a suitably reserved space for sleeping, the hall could seat many more, and was hence the place in which large social occasions might take place. Stools being the most moveable type of seating, parlors appear to draw a distinction between the capacity to provide a certain type of space and the permanent provision of such an area at all times and for all situations.

Halls were used to a limited degree for storage, having a larger number of cupboards than parlors (93:78), but chests, in which things that were not being used on a daily basis were kept, were to be found in 83 percent of parlors as against only 24 percent of halls. Cupboards suggest the keeping of goods to hand, perhaps set out on shelves where they can be clearly seen, possibly the frequently mentioned "garnish" or set of pewter vessels. Halls are also the place where weapons are kept in greater numbers (30:17), items to which it was always necessary to have easy access.

Within the chests which fill the parlors, expensive items such as silver and gold plate are kept (18:3), and fine linens, perhaps from women's dowries, the household stock which is kept for special occasions and important visitors (52:3). Similarly prevalent are quantities of cloth that are ready to be made up into either garments or furnishings (10:2), and silver spoons, the single most important and widely bequeathed portable asset of the early modern bourgeois household (51:12). The cloths that are laid on the table in scene 8 may well have been kept within this room.

The final category of goods that I want to consider is in some ways the most telling. Although the hall has a greater number of cupboards than the parlor, it has nothing like the same number of cupboard cloths, those coverings which were laid on top of the piece of furniture, using it as a further surface on which to display rich fabric, embroidery, trimmings: wealth. It is in their storage and possession of textiles that the two rooms differ the most, acknowledging an inventive diversity in terms of the particular cloths selected and their positioning. The parlor contains more carpets (44:17), more curtains (94:9), more cushions (329:261), and more wall hangings (22:13). Of every type of clothing there is less to be found in the hall, especially those items which were used for special occasions. This primarily suggests that a great deal of the parlor's goods were kept in chests, reserved in a safe space (with implications of "private" and "secluded"). When an item of furniture is listed in the parlor, however, it is invariably priced as a unit with a covering of some sort, and frequently with the items that are placed on top of that covering, such as a ewer and bowl, or a candlestick. The parlor both contains and displays splendor in a way that the hall does not.

A brief look at the different kinds of fabric that are identified as constituting the properties of the parlor gives a visual depth to the mental image of the room. The cushions are made of carpet, of "church work," of velvet and even of cloth of gold. The linen is of diaper, the coverlets of "boughton" and cruel work, different types of embroidery applied to the cloth. The hangings of the bedsteads provide a huge visual impact in red, green, yellow and blue say, often all on the same bed, or, higher up the social scale, of similarly brightly colored silks. In small amounts, cloths that are identified as foreign and exotic are entering the parlor – satin of Bruges and fustian from Milan are not to be found in the hall. And techniques of applied work from other countries are present in the parlor in larger numbers: Venice work, and "turkey," or Turkish work.

To draw out the qualitative threads of this quantitative evidence then: the parlor plays host to a smaller number of people in much more comfortable surroundings. Its space is more flexible because the seating that it contains is more likely to be moveable. The goods within it are more valuable, of better quality, and less likely to be produced within the home, sometimes even within the country. It provides a storeroom for the reserved goods of the household, with which extraordinary domestic rituals are provisioned. It is not often the site for domestic production itself, but rather reaps the benefits of it either directly or indirectly. It offers comfort to a very high degree, and a level of visual stimulation (there are more pictures in parlors [33:16], as well as the colorful and textured cloths which it contains). In other words the parlor, in contradistinction to the hall, both stores and displays wealth. This combination of known reserves and exhibited splendor is receptive to and provides a foundation for intimacy. To dine in such a room is to be made aware of all that your host has to offer, and to enjoy its sensory appeals; special provision has to be made for such an event, furniture has to be rearranged. Finally, fewer tables are kept in parlors than in halls (120:134), which makes being seated at one in the former a clear indication of relative status within the household.

This section has demonstrated the selectivity involved in the choice of props for this and, by implication, for other domestic plays. Whilst the early modern interior is crowded with goods, Heywood chooses carefully from those available. In doing so he introduces a group of properties that are capable of carrying the symbolic and metaphorical resonances outlined in the first section of this paper.

The section has also argued for the specificity of meanings that are likely to have attached to, for instance, the word "parlor," and the range of sensory memories that it is likely to have evoked. This must be particularly true in a period when meanings were becoming more complex because domestic possessions were increasing and altering in nature across the social scale. Such changes are likely to have produced a heightened sensitivity to the distinctions between different kinds of domestic space. Seeing a table on stage then, and being told that it is in a parlor, permits an early modern audience to complete the representation from memory in ways that it has been possible to begin to reconstruct here.

What I want to argue in this final section is that domestic objects in domestic tragedies operate in two very specific and at least partly contradictory ways. First I want to suggest that the contemporary changes in domestic arrangement, and their links with the pressures and impulses of consumerism, give the props in plays like *A Woman Killed With Kindness* a particular kind of provocative appeal. But I will also argue that household objects fundamentally provide a sense of permanence and stability that is invaluable to the narrative of domestic tragedies.

There are analogies to be drawn between the theatrical economy and the early modern world of commodities, and therefore between the way in which the stage functions as a context for properties, and what Appadurai terms the commodity context. This he defines as the "variety of *social* arenas...that help link the commodity candidacy of a thing to the commodity phase of its career."[19] Such places or events focus attention upon objects and hence demand that their cultural value be assessed. Objects on the stage become foci for enquiry and emotion in a similar way: sites for the working through of complicated issues. The audience is forced to engage with their meanings; attention is drawn to their relevance to narrative situations, and their implication in the representation and resolution of narrative problems.

Display of the table in *A Woman Killed With Kindness* advertises its worth, not in terms that are primarily economic as it would in the marketplace, but with an emphasis upon social and cultural values. This display sets up questions about the possible owners of such an object, questions which deal with the complexities of the relative economics that lie behind cultural choices: the object has an economic value that is either inside or outside of the range of goods that the audience are able to purchase.

Yet the table operates differently than a non-domestic object because it is placed within a specific household environment. In Frankford's house its singularity and its potential for commoditization are stressed simultaneously. The situation of such props draws attention to their status as private property, out of reach as the possession of another. It is this dual call that the domestic property makes – its invitation to give it value, and yet to accept it as singularized within the household – that I want to explore here.

The most important issue that arose from the reading of probate inventories in the previous section was the selectivity of the stage properties that represent the Frankford household and position it socially. The most readily identifiable feature of the change in the domestic environment in the late sixteenth and early seventeenth centuries was the downward diffusion of better quality materials. Even when he was writing in the 1570s, William Harrison claims that materials such as "Turkey work, pewter, [and] brass" were within the reach of "the inferior artificers and many farmers," and my work on Kentish inventories has demonstrated that such objects were being owned in much larger numbers by the end of the century.[20]

As there are far more goods from which to choose at the time when this play was written than there were in the first half of the sixteenth century, the job of selecting a representative prop had perhaps become more complex in terms of sheer numbers. But in another way, and one that has important ramifications for the relationship between the play and its audience, the metonymic exercise is simplified. Knowledge of such items was becoming increasingly detailed, partly because of their greater prevalence within the marketplace, and partly because of the larger numbers of the population involved in their manufacture.[21] A greater range of the audience was now more familiar with the look and feel of a wider variety of objects.

However, whereas larger numbers of people might have owned a carpet in the 1590s than in the 1560s, it is nevertheless not the case that the whole audience would respond to it as an object that formed a part of their domestic routines. Appadurai defines the diversity of understandings of the central object in commodity exchange thus: "the commodity context, as a social matter, may bring together actors from quite different systems who share only the most minimal understandings (from the conceptual point of view) about the objects in question."[22] This definition is useful here because it makes it possible to see the wider significance of the domestic object as dramatic property at this historical juncture. The emergence of a consumer society necessitates a heightened degree of sensitization to the meanings and importance of commodities. The property can therefore be made to mean in many different ways and with a wide range of resonances, from the direct identification of what is seen on stage with the domestic environment of the wealthier audience members, to the provision of a personal and particular context for domestic goods that one does not own. In the latter case, familiarity comes from production within the home, or from the kinds of stuff that one sees for sale in the wider marketplace, which one hears report of in tracts about conspicuous consumption and in the conversations of others.[23]

The breadth of this array of possible interpretations of the same object may provide a useful analogue to the heterogeneity of London audiences in this period. But, as stated at the outset of this essay, it nevertheless presents a problem for a moral narrative that demands that viewers should be able to apply the message of its closure to their own lives and experiences. It is precisely this cultural specificity that leads to a view of domestic tragedy as a genre that slides fairly lurid sensationalism of contemporary events under the superior attire of the cloak of morality drama. I want to suggest a relationship between the audience and the property, however, which I think mitigates the problem sufficiently to allow *A Woman Killed With Kindness* to occupy a middle ground between sensational excess and didactic social control.

What I want to stress is a scale of functions for the props that I have been discussing, suggestive of a variety of relationships with an audience. At one end of this scale the domestic rituals discussed above, at whose heart the table is situated, work as a generalizing reference to household routine that has universal significance and meaning. Because such rituals as dining are common in one form or another, they offer the audience a point of connection with the play, and in the most literal sense, the message is "brought home." What cuts across this fundamental mnemonic are the nice social and economic distinctions to which the carpet, for instance, makes reference. These suggest new and exciting *kinds* of ritual that are becoming more common, perhaps within reach for the first time for a large section of the audience. Both similarities to and differences from domestic experience are, I would argue, signaled by the particular properties chosen in this play.

Those properties that cover the table close down meanings and narrow significances by tying them to cultural specifics. They characterize the particular household that Frankford runs, and therefore the particular type of man he is. His is clearly a socially specific house, with the logic of such an interior (in terms of practice, ritual and meaning) that this implies. Each audience member is then invited to compare these objects to the possessions and social situations with which they themselves are familiar. Servants may recognize such items as ones that they lay on tables for others; labourers may never have touched them before; gentlemen may be more used to seeing their tables set with silverware. In a period of social movement, other people's houses become interesting in different ways, as frissons of desire are triggered by the possibility of possession.

An early modern household table is peculiarly "singular" in Kopytoff's terms: it is unique and "unexchangeable" because it is not just any table but one whose provenance in relation to family history and lineage will have been carefully remembered.[24] This singularity provides a particular type of context for the events of the plot. It is against the *normality* of the domestic environment that Anne and Wendoll's crime is so shocking, so "unnatural."

Those things that are familiar in everyday life, that make space personal by being constant, go unnoticed because they fulfill their function so effectively. Their surfaces, whose marks of wear and tear fade into the subconscious and come to mean only "hall," or "parlor," are culturally silent until violated. The construction of a sense of what is normal on stage is difficult, then, because it depends upon creating the illusion of something that has become invisible through familiarity and stability. Domestic properties make it possible to realize the culturally invisible as representation, in order to set up a contrast with the unusual, the bizarre: to give the latter a sense of being "out of place."

The property achieves this effect through a kind of "production" of the history of the household. An audience's individual experiences of the domestic object attest to a meaning enriched by time depth, by the function of a table to reflect in its physical nature the emotional dynamics of the household as these are inscribed in the special occasions to which it has played host and its links to the past of the family. Household goods are essentially stabilizing entities because they have a past, they bear the marks of changing circumstance, they relate to marriage, birth, and death through the ways in which they enter the house and the rituals surrounding these rites of passage to which they are party. The floor of the hall to which the opening scene of the play refers, pockmarked by the boots of the wedding guests, is just such a physical reminder of the past.[25]

The value that becomes attached to the early modern domestic object outside the theatre is one of constancy, where a way of moving into the past by tracing back the thread of memory is provided, one that is organized around the object itself. Identity is formed through these objects, as the sum of what has been passed on and what has been personally acquired. Similarly, the domestic prop has a temporal function in making reference to domestic ritual. Ritual, as a form that connects past, present, and future through the repetition of particular actions, brings with it the suggestion of customary practice and reiteration when it is produced on the stage. It forces the present to be seen in terms of a putative past and a projected future, and it becomes a way of suggesting a posterity for the characters that is then cut short by crime.[26]

This temporal function of the object is seen most clearly by comparing the "biographies" of domestic items and stage properties; demonstrating the position of particular items in relation to the construction of family and household identity. Off stage, meaning is given to the table by its location within a certain domestic context. Depending upon the room in which it is placed, and the time of day at which it is required, it will fulfill different functions, and its significance in relation to other household objects will be either increased or diminished. There is, of course, a general cultural meaning that a table brings with it wherever it might be situated. What it gathers in addition within the house is a more sharply defined set of actual, as opposed to potential, uses, ones that are particular to that household.

Before the property table is brought onto the stage it has a set of meanings attached to it as a part of the assets of the company of actors who make use of it in their productions. Once the play begins, however, it becomes particularized. In addition to the connections that the audience make between the current representation and their domestic reality, this particular table's significance is determined by its position within a specific narrative, where it is used for a specific set of purposes. When it enters its dramatic context it is abruptly cut off from its particular history. The methods, means and motivations for its production, the production of this specific table, are purposefully redirected by what we are told about its new context.

If the play is to succeed in portraying a coherent narrative, then on one level the audience must think of the table as a piece of furniture in Frankford's house. This severing of the past from the present moment of representation happens through the provision of an alternative, fictional context for it, constructed out of the narrative of that day's performance. This narrative context has, then, to act as a shorthand for the particularizing process that domestic objects usually undergo: their layering with specific cultural meanings.

It is a shorthand mediated through socially specific properties such as cloths and candlesticks. These trappings, like the gendered clothing that covers the body, define the way in which the object functions in its social setting. They make the connection between the narrative construct of household and the domestic object on stage. As each cloth and each article is laid down upon the table, its social significance becomes further and further differentiated, meanings accumulate in luxurious complexity, in the thickness of layer upon layer of properties.

The properties used in *A Woman Killed With Kindness* enable the audience to read all the events of the play up to scene 8 back into the domestic environment, to imbue that environment with a time depth that is achieved in a matter of minutes. In place of the truncated biography of the stage property, the audience substitutes the suggested past of the Frankford family, with its celebrations and rites of passage, its networks of kin and inheritance. The subsequent actions of the play, especially perhaps the discovery scene in the chamber and the banishment of Anne from the family home with a small number of possessions, can then be seen against this background, starker and more meaningful as a result.

The final section of this essay has argued that the properties in *A Woman Killed With Kindness* communicate both competitive social distinctions and stabilizing normality to an audience. This is a combination freighted with contemporary concerns about the changing meaning of the household, and one that suggests, I hope, the complexities of the moral relationship between stage properties and narratives of domestic crime.

NOTES

1. H. H. Adams, *English Domestic or Homiletic Tragedy, 1575–1642* (New York: Columbia University Press, 1943), still one of the most comprehensive and illuminating studies of the genre, initiated this reading of the texts.
2. In doing so, it follows the emphasis of Douglas Bruster's essay in this volume on an early modern theatre driven by the object as opposed to the subject. On the more general relationship between objects and subjectivity, see Margreta De Grazia, Maureen Quilligan, and Peter Stallybrass (eds.), *Subject and Object in Renaissance Culture* (Cambridge: Cambridge University Press, 1996), and Ann Rosalind Jones and Peter Stallybrass, *Renaissance Clothes and the Materials of Memory* (Cambridge: Cambridge University Press, 2001).
3. Chandra Mukerji, *From Graven Images: Patterns of Modern Materialism* (New York: Columbia University Press, 1983), p. 5. The "birth of consumerism" has been located anywhere from the fifteenth to the twentieth centuries, depending upon the specific definition of the term used. I am taking consumerism to mean the production and consumption of manufactured and "luxury" goods in a society placing increasing emphasis upon the quality of the domestic environment, and significantly among the middling ranks. See also, on this subject, Jean-Christophe Agnew, "Coming up for air: consumer culture in historical perspective," in John Brewer and Roy Porter (eds.), *Consumption and the World of Goods* (London: Routledge, 1993), pp. 19–39; Natasha Korda, "Household Kates: domesticating commodities in *The Taming of the Shrew*," *Shakespeare Quarterly* 47 (1996): 109–31. Full-scale assessments of evidence for the sixteenth century are still needed, but see Catherine Richardson, "The meanings of space in society and drama: perceptions of domestic life and domestic tragedy c.1550–1600," unpublished Ph.D. thesis, University of Kent, 1999.
4. The majority of studies define domestic tragedy in different terms, constructing their arguments around different plays. Consensus rests mainly upon the portrayal of domestic life of those below the nobility. See Sturgess for his interest in "journalistic treatment"; Dolan for the importance of links to historical events; Orlin for the importance of property ownership; and Comensoli for the focus on household. Keith Sturgess, *Three Elizabethan Domestic Tragedies* (Harmondsworth: Penguin, 1969); Frances E. Dolan, *Dangerous Familiars: Representations of Domestic Crime in England 1550–1700* (Ithaca: Cornell University Press, 1994); Lena Cowen Orlin, *Private Matters and Public Culture in Post-Reformation England* (Ithaca: Cornell University Press, 1994); Viviana Comensoli, *Household Business: Domestic Plays of Early Modern England* (Toronto: University of Toronto Press, 1996).
5. Andrew Gurr, *Playgoing in Shakespeare's London* (Cambridge: Cambridge University Press, 1987), *passim*.

6. In a sense this essay represents a microhistorical investigation of a dramatic genre. Its intention is to use this scene, which it must be stressed is unique within the genre as a whole, to broaden the perceived implications of the domestic property to their widest horizon. The same exercise could be undertaken for, for instance, the bed in *A Yorkshire Tragedy* or the chair in *Arden of Faversham*: similarly important properties with complex moral and social meanings.

7. In its interest in the relationship between objects and their social contexts this essay follows the methodological interest of the volume as a whole in the anthropological approach offered by Arjun Appadurai (ed.), *The Social Life of Things: Commodities in Cultural Perspective* (Cambridge: Cambridge University Press, 1986).

8. See Laura G. Bromley, "Domestic conduct in *A Woman Killed With Kindness*," *Studies in English Literature 1500–1900* 26:3 (1986): 259–76; Lena Cowen Orlin, *Private Matters and Public Culture*; and Frances E. Dolan, *Dangerous Familiars*, respectively.

9. Most notably by Lena Cowen Orlin; see for instance Orlin, *Private Matters and Public Culture*, pp. 182–9.

10. All references are to the New Mermaid edition of the play, edited by Brian Scobie (London: A. & C. Black, 1985).

11. Lisa Jardine, *Worldly Goods* (London: Macmillan, 1996), pp. 83, 123, 429; for the rich significance of the oriental object within Western culture see Brian Spooner, "Weavers and dealers: the authenticity of an oriental carpet", in Appadurai (ed.), *The Social Life of Things*, pp. 195–235.

12. For the relative status of parlors and halls in the sixteenth century, see Sarah Pearson, *The Medieval Houses of Kent: An Historical Analysis* (London: HMSO, 1994), pp. 96, 114–15; John Schofield, *Medieval London Houses* (London: Yale University Press, 1994), pp. 66–7, 93; Frank E. Brown, "Continuity and change in the urban house: developments in domestic space organisation in seventeenth-century London", *Comparative Studies in Society and History* 28 (1986): 583, 588; but see also the following section for the relative physical composition of both rooms.

13. A private moment with its own symbolic ritual is what is being signalled here, as opposed to the dramatic presentation of interiority of character. See Alan Dessen, *Elizabethan Stage Conventions and Modern Interpreters* (Cambridge: Cambridge University Press, 1984), p. 3, where he points out that the "as from dinner" convention often included a napkin and the brushing of crumbs. Its conventional nature need not, of course, negate its mimetic qualities.

14. For a detailed discussion of this phenomenon over the early modern period, see Felicity Heal, *Hospitality in Early Modern England* (Oxford: Oxford University Press, 1990). Although "shame traditionally attached to those who failed to personate themselves as men of generosity," this image of "an elite given in honour to open hospitality" was, interestingly, diminishing by the later sixteenth century; p. 390.

15. The consequences of sin are frequently manifested in the disruption of normal procedure in domestic plays. See, in addition to scene 13 of *A Woman Killed*, *Two Lamentable Tragedies*, in which the community's sleep is interrupted by the murder of Beech's boy, and neighbors converge on his shop from their beds; and *Arden of Faversham*, where Alice's loss of control leads her servants to ask who should wait on whom, and culminates in the image of her kneeling to scrub the blood with her maid – an image which gains dramatic weight, as it does in *Two Lamentable Tragedies*, from its similarity to a perfectly normal domestic routine.

16. For the informed use of probate inventories, and the pitfalls involved (comprehensiveness; omission of information useful for assessing the total wealth of the deceased; under-representation of those with few possessions) see A. M. van der Woude and Anton Schuurman (eds.), *Probate Inventories: A New Source for the Historical Study of Wealth, Material Culture and Agricultural Development. Papers Presented at the Leeuwenborch Conference* (Utrecht: HES Publishers, 1980), and subsequent work by Mark Overton; see Lena Cowen Orlin's chapter in this volume on the issue of comprehensiveness.

17. The following information from those documents, where given, has been recorded in a relational database: the name and description of each item (its color, the stuff from which it is made, and the methods used in its construction); its location within the room; the location of the room within the house; the price for the individual item or the group of items with which it is valued.

18. Numbers of parlors vs. halls containing one instance of the item under consideration.

19. The examples which he gives are the bazaar and the marriage transaction, which "might constitute the context in which women are most intensely, and most appropriately, regarded as exchange values," Appadurai (ed.), *The Social Life of Things*, p. 15. Other works discuss the relationship between the theatre and the marketplace and draw analogies between their discourses, most obviously, Jean-Christophe Agnew, *Worlds Apart: The Market and the Theatre in Anglo-American Thought, 1550–1750* (Cambridge: Cambridge University Press, 1986); but also Kathleen E. McLuskie and Felicity Dunworth, "Patronage and the economics of theater," in John D. Cox and David Scott Kastan (eds.), *A New History of Early English Drama* (New York: Columbia University Press, 1997), pp. 423–40.

20. William Harrison, *The Description of England*, ed. Georges Edelen (Ithaca: Cornell University Press, 1968), p. 200. Work undertaken on the latter half of the century for my doctoral thesis has tended to substantiate Harrison's remarks. Almost all categories of domestic goods listed in inventories were more prevalent by 1600 than they had been in the 1560s, and they were to be found in increasing numbers of inventories. All domestic spaces elucidated by these inventories were more crowded by 1600, and their rooms were more specialised, with sleeping in particular developing a space of its own; Catherine Richardson, "The meanings of space in society and drama."

21. See Joan Thirsk, *Economic Policy and Projects: The Development of a Consumer Society in Early Modern England* (Oxford: Clarendon, 1988), for the numbers of people involved in the hundreds of new manufacturing projects in progress in this period.

22. Appadurai (ed.), *The Social Life of Things*, p. 15.

23. In addition, the social composition of London was changing, and the increased social diversity must have led to growing familiarity amongst audience members with the ways of life of those whose status was different to their own. See F. J. Fisher, "The development of London as a center of conspicuous consumption in the sixteenth and seventeenth centuries," in P. Corfield and N. B. Harte (eds.), *London and the English Economy, 1500–1700* (London: Hambledon Press, 1990); and C. G. A. Clay, *Economic Expansion and Social Change: England 1500–1700*, vol. 1 (Cambridge: Cambridge University Press, 1984). It seems very significant that these internal migrations were taking place at the time when domestic tragedy was flourishing.

24. Igor Kopytoff, "The cultural biography of things: commoditization as process," in Appadurai (ed.), *The Social Life of Things*, p. 69.

25. Sir Francis: "You shall see tomorrow / The hall floor pecked and dinted like a millstone" (I. 88–9).

26. Other plays use small tropes of domesticity in a similar way. The scene in *A Warning For Fair Women* where Anne sits at the door with her small son and discusses the new suit he may have at Easter pathetically presents a future for Browne to truncate. *Two Lamentable Tragedies* has Beech crossing the stage with a piece of cheese which he has cut to eat with his drink, ironic because the social event for which he has thoughtfully prepared is his own murder.

CHAPTER 6

"Let me the curtains draw": the dramatic and symbolic properties of the bed in Shakespearean tragedy

Sasha Roberts

If "commodities, like persons, have social lives," then stage properties have especially malleable, shifting, complex, and multifaceted social lives.[1] In different theatrical contexts a stage property will evoke different meanings, be put to different uses, and play different roles. This makes recovering the uses and meanings of stage properties in the early modern theatre all the more problematic: records detailing how stage properties were used on the different stages of early modern London and beyond are notoriously scarce, while surviving documents that allude to stage properties (particularly inventories, but also play-texts) are far from transparent. Analysis of the "career" of early modern stage properties is thus to some extent an exercise in conjecture. Yet despite the limitations of the archives, there still remains much to be learned about stage properties in different theatres, plays, and transactions.

This chapter explores the dramatic uses and symbolic meanings of the bed in Shakespearean tragedy – one of the most significant of household artifacts alluded to and made theatrical use of in the Shakespearean canon. There are, astonishingly, over 350 allusions to beds in Shakespeare's works, including a cluster of phrases coined by Shakespeare (bed-presser, bed-right, bed-swerver, bed-vow, bed-work). Evidently the bed was an especially rich source of image-making, particularly around sex, marriage, sickness and death, and was a key stage property in a handful of plays.[2] What associations did the bed evoke on stage, and why was it such a powerful signifier of marital sexuality? How were beds used in the early modern theatre, and in what ways might the stage property of the bed operate as a means of characterization? My focus in this chapter is upon the "work" of the bed in two Shakespearean tragedies that examine domestic and sexual relations, *Romeo and Juliet* and *Othello*. In these plays the stage property of the bed becomes like a stage-within-a-stage, an intense and compelling visual and symbolic arena for acting out powerful passions and transgressions, and for mapping the disruptions

safeguarding – addresses ambiguity

and collisions of private and public space. To better understand the symbolism and function of the bed in these plays it is necessary to engage with the material history of the bed in early modern culture, for as Jonathan Gil Harris and Natasha Korda argue in the introduction to this volume, "theatrical objects have a habit of drawing attention to themselves as things with material lives surplus to the 'fictive worlds' into which they have been enlisted" (p. 14). But I also want to attend to the "materialities" of theatrical texts, for when it comes to assessing the possible uses Shakespeare made of the bed on the early modern stage, the so-called "bad" quartos of *Romeo and Juliet* and *Othello* offer unique insights into early modern stage practice and the function of the bed as a stage property.[3] It remains, of course, imperative to distinguish between different modes of "materiality" – historical and textual "materialities" are different in kind – and to acknowledge that literary representation cannot simply be equated with "material" or historical practice. Recovering the history of early modern material culture, and more particularly the history of stage properties, thus requires that we pay careful attention to the specificities of and distinctions between different types, texts, and contexts of "evidence." We overlook the contingencies of genre, form, rhetoric, characterization, and dramaturgy at our peril.

The symbolic power of the bed on the early modern stage is rooted in, though not equivalent to, cultural practice. The bed was among the most significant of personal and household possessions in the period; one of the most valuable forms of so-called "moveable" property in the home.[4] The joined bedsteads, field beds (readily dismantled for traveling), and trucklebeds (low beds that could be slotted under joined bedsteads) that furnished the homes of the middling sort, much of the gentry, and the less prestigious rooms of noble households, were often simple in construction, and were simply recorded in household inventories as, for instance, "a joined bedstead," "a little bedstead."[5] But what especially interests me here are the lavish "state" beds that belonged to the elite (richly ornamented "four-poster" or, more properly, "tester" beds with a canopy) that were often more expensive than any other single item of household furniture, since they required the labor of a wide range of skilled craftsmen, many of whom were drawn from the communities of immigrant artisans from the Low Countries centered in London.[6] The inventory of Charles I's domestic goods of 1651 is a case in point of the huge sums invested in the state bed: while his set of Raphael cartoons was valued at £300, his bed with richly embroidered green satin furnishings was worth £1000.[7] Similarly, the "crimson velvet bed and furniture" bought, for instance, in

1604 for Lady Frances Egerton, cost over £300 and included payments to the joiner and gilder, upholsterer and draper.[8] State beds were dressed with luxurious bed-curtains while valances running along the top of bedsteads were the site of elaborate needlework devices, emblems, and figurative pictures, often drawn from the Old Testament or from classical legend and mythology.[9] It is a measure of the bed's prominence within noble households that detailed descriptions of these profusely carved and sumptuously dressed beds often run to greater length in inventories than entries for any other category of household good; the "Bedstead of wallnutte, topp fashion" listed at Kenilworth Castle in 1583, for instance, takes up a whole paragraph of the inventory.[10]

For the elite, a state bed was a sign of social status: built to last beyond the generation that commissioned it, the bed embodied economic power and fashionable taste, conferring prestige upon its owner and his (or more rarely her) heirs. Thus Sir Thomas Hungerford drew special attention in his will to his "beddes and their appurtenances," stipulating that "for all wayes as long as the said beddes will endure they remayne from heire to heire in worship and memory of my lord, my father, Walter, Lord Hungerford, that first ordeyned them and paid for them."[11] For Hungerford, the bed evokes the relationship between father and son; it becomes symbolic of the Hungerford patrimony. Hence many state beds bore crests and coats of arms, locating them within the family dynasty.[12] But the bed was also a uniquely important possession within the early modern household for its role in the major rites of passage in men's and women's lives; rites that are crucial to the formation of patrimony: marriage, birth, and death. Thus, rites of passage were used by men and women to discriminate between actual beds and bedchambers: Lady Anne Clifford, for instance, picked out specific beds for their associations with birth or death, as on 15 April 1617 when she wrote in her diary that "I left *Judith's* chamber and came to lie in the chamber where I lay when my Lord was in *France*, in the green cloth of gold bed where the Child was born."[13] Special preparations were made to the élite bedchamber for childbirth and for the lying-in period that followed, when mothers kept to their bed for up to a month to receive (above all) women guests. The extraordinary sum of £52,000 was spent on the lying-in of Anne of Denmark in 1605, while in 1612 John Chamberlain reported that "the Countess of Salisbury was brought a bed of a daughter, and lyes in very richly, for the hangings of her chamber being white satin embroidered with silver and pearl, is valued at fourteen thousand pounds."[14] Even greater care might be taken over the deathbed, for to die with dignity was of such paramount importance. In their final hours, the dying were comforted in bed by close friends and relatives; after death the body was laid out upon the bed so that people might pay their last respects, and bed, bedchamber, and sometimes spouses' beds, were draped in black mourning cloth.[15]

The rite of passage which most interests me here is that of marriage. Not until Hardwick's Marriage Act of 1753 was the marriage ceremony fully formalized; in addition to and sometimes in place of the church service, a range of secular rituals "registered" a marriage. The culmination of wedding day celebrations was the bedding ceremony which, in cases of dispute, was used as evidence of marriage: performing the ritual of the bedding ceremony was akin to signing a marriage contract – hence the contractual "bed-trick" in Shakespearean comedy.[16] The example of Thomas Thynne's marriage is a case in point: Thomas eloped with Lady Audley's daughter Maria in 1595 and Lady Audley, anxious to secure her daughter's marriage out of the elopement, "caused a pair of sheets to be laid on a bed" where the young couple "butted and sported for a little while, that it might be said they were abed together." The "policy and cunning" that Lady Audley used on this occasion, writes Thomas's mother Joan Thynne to her husband, were enough "to make it so sure that you nor I shall not break" the marriage – and sure enough the marriage was upheld in 1601 by the Court of Arches.[17] The bedding ceremony proper might encompass a variety of rituals: the bedchamber was often decorated and the bridal bed dressed with wedding sheets and blessed; the bride and groom might be sewn into their wedding sheets (as at Sir Philip Herbert's wedding in 1604); wedding guests were invited to enter the bedchamber and share a celebratory drink; the bride and groom, perhaps accompanied by the bridesmaid and best man in bed, might play "flinging the stocking" in which the bride's hose was flung out of the bed; finally, the wedding guests wished the bride and groom well, drew the bed-curtains, and left the couple to consummate their marriage in private, possibly to the accompaniment of "bedding ballads" outside the bedchamber. Above all, the bedding ceremony was, apart from its final consummation, *publicly* witnessed – such that even at a wedding unusual for its "modesty and gravity" in 1665, Samuel Pepys reports that he "got into the bridegroom's chamber while he undressed himself, and there was very merry – till he was called to the bride's chamber and into bed they went. I kissed the bride in bed, and so the curtaines drawne... and so good-night."[18] Precisely because the bridal bed was the focal point of the wedding ceremony it gained considerable symbolic power, and after the ceremonies were over the "marriage bed" became a potent emblem of a couple's marriage; a marker of the fact of marital sexuality.

The bed marked out rites and relationships in men's and women's lives – between husband and wife, father and son, mother and child – and so accrued a ritual and symbolic significance for their owners that no other household object could share. And because the bed was generally the largest single item of household furniture, carving out with its posts, ceiling and curtains an intimate space *within* the bedchamber, it afforded a level of privacy that set it apart from other pieces of domestic furniture.[19] It is not surprising, therefore, that beds and bedchamber scenes should figure prominently in Elizabethan and Jacobean drama, particularly in scenes dealing with marriage, sexuality, childbirth, and death.[20] As E. K. Chambers notes in his analysis of seventy-three plays of the period, more interior scenes are set in the bedchamber than in any other room, while George Fullmer Reynolds records that beds were among the most commonly used of large stage properties in plays performed at the Red Bull theatre in the period 1605–25.[21] But how were beds used on the early modern stage? Given the size and bulk of a bed with curtains – even one prepared for ease of movement, perhaps upon a rolling stage – it might be assumed that beds were generally positioned on the rear stage or within the discovery space (or tiring-house). *Tamburlaine (Part Two)* for instance, attributed to Marlowe and performed "vpon Stages in the Citie of London" (the Theatre, Rose, and Red Bull) by the Lord Admiral's Men, includes the stage direction "The Arras is drawen and Zenocrate lies in her bed of state, Tamburlaine sitting by her"[22] – a direction which points to the use of a curtained discovery space, revealed by drawing aside the "Arras" or tapestry.[23] Similarly, stage directions instructing that a bed is "discovered" on stage may suggest the use of the discovery space – as in the stage direction "A bed discovered, on it Lazarello" from Middleton and Rowley's *All's Lost By Lust* (1617–19), performed by Queen Anne's men at the Red Bull and the Phoenix. On the other hand, instructions for characters to "enter" on a bed – as in the stage direction "Enter Mistress Frankford in her bed" (5.5) from Heywood's *A Woman Killed With Kindness* (1603), performed by Worcester's Men at the Rose – might suggest that the bed was placed or pushed out onto the rear stage.[24] However, the terminology of early modern stage directions is often ambiguous and imprecise: "enter" and "discover" may mean different things in different contexts.[25] Moreover, we cannot rule out the use of the bed either on the front stage or prominently "thrust out" onto center-stage. This is suggested, for instance, by the stage direction "A bed

thrust out upon the stage, ALLWIT'S WIFE in it" (3.2) in Middleton's
A Chaste Maid in Cheapside (performed by Lady Elizabeth's Company at
the Swan in 1613), and by stage directions in other plays calling for a bed
to be "thrust" or "drawn" out and then "pulled" or "drawn" in again.[26]
As Glynne Wickham and Richard Hosley point out, thrusting a bed
forward into center- or even front-stage makes dramatic sense in scenes
which centered around a bed and provided leading actors with some of
their best speeches.[27] Furthermore, new staging possibilities were made
available with the construction of new theatres: thus E. K. Chambers
suggests that a "new feature" of the Globe (completed in 1599) was the use
of properties in bedchamber scenes which "during the sixteenth century
[would] have been placed in the alcove, but now appear to have been
brought forward and to occupy, like hall scenes, the main stage."[28] In
short, bed-scenes in early modern drama may have been staged in the
discovery space, rear-, central-, or even front-stage; different theatres and
stage properties presented different staging opportunities, while regional
theatres, stages, and touring companies complicate still further the range
of possible uses of the bed on stage. In the final analysis, the variety of
theatrical stages in early modern England – coupled with the lack of evidence about how they were used – must sound a note of caution against
arriving at hard-and-fast generalizations about the deployment of stage
properties in the period.

What, then, might the beds actually used by theatre companies as
stage properties have looked like? The illustrated woodcut to the title
page of William Sampson's play *The Vow Breaker* (1636) shows a heavy
tester bed with curtains.[29] As R. A. Foakes points out, title-page illustrations do not necessarily represent the play in question or an actual
performance: printers often made use of "stock" illustrations when pub-
lishing play-texts.[30] Nevertheless, such illustrations can reveal what might
be considered an *appropriate* representation or evocation of contemporary
stage practices, costumes, and properties. In the case of *The Vow Breaker*,
the title-page woodcut seems to refer directly to that play in that it alludes precisely to the breaking of vows: in addition to a full tester bed,
the woodcut depicts a man pointing to a bracelet saying "Thinke on thy
promise alive or dead I must and will injoy thee" – words which recall
those of the play's hero, Bateman, to his adulterous wife. The tester bed
depicted on the title page of *The Vow Breaker* is fully reminiscent of an élite
state bed, complete with intricate carving and wreaths of fabric: as such
it operates as a sign both of marital sexuality (the bed vow) and of class
(élite status). As such, the use of a sumptuous bed on stage may speak,

as Catherine Richardson argues in this volume, of "a heightened degree of sensitization" to the conspicuous consumption of commodities in the context of an emerging consumer society (p. 145); the opulent domestic object on stage functions as a spectacle of wealth.

Even if the beds used by theatrical companies were constructed on a much simpler basis than the bed depicted in *The Vow Breaker*'s title page, those stage-beds might still have produced the *impression* or *effect* of a state bed, especially through the display of sumptuous fabrics. Clearly some, if not all, stage-beds were curtained and were used as such to their full dramatic potential on stage: bed-curtains allowed for secrecy, surprise, revelation, and dramatic irony. Stage directions specifically point to the use of bed-curtains for their dramatic impact, such as when Sextus Tarquinus remarks upon Lucrece lying "beneath these curtaines" when Lucrece is "discovered in her bed" in Heywood's *The Rape of Lucrece* (ll. 221–5), performed by Queen Anne's Men at the Red Bull, or *The Iron Age Part Two* (1612–13), where Egisthus enters with his sword drawn and "hideth himselfe in the chamber behind the Bed-curtaines" (ll. 411–14).[31] But there remain few references to beds or bed-curtains in surviving theatrical documents. A single "bedsteade" is listed in the 1598 "Enventary tacken of all the properties for my *Lord Admeralles men*"; the bedstead is one of several large items of stage furniture – including tombs of Dido and Guido, a rock, a cage, a chain of dragons, a wooden canopy, a pair of stairs, a bay tree, and two coffins – that, as Neil Carson argues, "suggests a stage more cluttered than is sometimes imagined."[32] In Henslowe's *Diary* a note "of what m*r*s alen hath payd sence her husband went into th*e* contrey" for 1593 includes an "Item pd vnto th*e* Joyner for th*e* bedstead xvs" alongside an "Item pd for coshenes vs," possibly to furnish the bedstead.[33] It is not clear whether this payment was made in relation to a particular production or indeed whether the bed was intended for the stage, but *if* the bedstead was used as a stage property then we can note that at fifteen shillings it cost a fraction of the price of a state bed and almost certainly would have been of simple construction.[34] This is the only mention of a bedstead in Henslowe's *Diary*, perhaps indicating that bedsteads were not stage properties that commonly changed hands or had much ready value within the pawn trade. Indeed, there are remarkably few payments listed in Henslowe's *Diary* for stage properties, and on the whole those payments rarely exceed £5 – a marked contrast to the precise and extensive accounting of clothing (a much more costly commodity than stage properties) in Henslowe's *Diary*.[35] The Lord Admiral's Men's "Enventary" and Henslowe's *Diary* remain, however, opaque documents;

as Lena Cowen Orlin suggests, the "Enventary" is marked like so many household inventories of the period by its occlusions, while Juana Green and Natasha Korda note that the modest sums spent on stage properties in Henslowe's *Diary* do not give a complete picture, since the stock of properties may have been supplemented with secondhand or pawned goods.[36]

If the staged property of the bed could be put to different theatrical uses, then the symbolic properties of the bed in early modern drama are multifaceted; for the bed is invested with different, sometimes conflicting, associations. Shakespeare alludes to beds in all of his works (with the exception of *Love's Labour's Lost*, *A Lover's Complaint* and *The Passionate Pilgrim*), and the range of terms he uses to characterize the bed are extensive – especially around chastity (such as maiden bed, honor's lofty bed, wholesome bed), marriage (nuptial bed, bridal bed, the bed of blessed marriage, Hymen's purest bed, master of the bed, husbanded her bed; a dull, stale, tired bed), and adultery (luxurious bed; to truant with your bed; the abused, blameful, contaminated, defiled, disloyal, lust-stain'd bed; the rank sweat of an enseamed bed). Beds are only required as stage properties, however, in perhaps six Shakespeare plays: *The Taming of the Shrew* (1.2), *Henry IV Part Two* (4.5), *Henry VI Part Two* (3.2), *Cymbeline* (2.2), *Romeo and Juliet* (4.3) and *Othello* (5.2) – variously performed at the Globe (*Shrew*, *Romeo*, *Othello*, *Cymbeline*), Blackfriars (*Shrew*, *Othello*) and possibly the Theatre (*Shrew*, *Henry IV Part Two*, *Romeo*).[37] Notice that a bed is *not* required in the "closet scene" of *Hamlet* (3.4): the convention of playing the scene in Gertrude's bedchamber – in which the stage property of the bed enables the portrayal of sexualized relations between Hamlet and Gertrude – is a later interpellation, first promulgated, perhaps, in the early eighteenth century in an illustration of the scene in Tonson's 1714 reissue of Rowe's edition of Shakespeare's *Complete Works*.[38]

It is the work of the bed in Shakespearean tragedy that specifically interests me here. In *Romeo and Juliet* the bed is used both as a literary trope and as stage property. Traditionally the play's repeated references to the bridal bed and deathbed have been viewed in terms of theme: the Death-as-Bridegroom motif, expressed in lines such as "My grave is like to be my wedding bed" (1.5.133–4) and "I'll to my wedding bed, / And death, not Romeo, take my maidenhead" (3.2.136–7).[39] Elizabethan staging practice may have visually emphasized the Death-as-Bridegroom motif by using the same stage space (perhaps the discovery space) for Juliet's bed and tomb.[40] But the bed plays more than a thematic function in *Romeo and Juliet*: as Margreta De Grazia has argued, "personal effects" were intimately linked with "subjectivity effects" or, as Felix Bosonnet puts it, stage properties "operate as a means of characterisation."[41] Crucially, the "characterization" of Romeo and Juliet's wedding bed impacts upon the characterization of Romeo and Juliet, and thus upon the play's construction of romantic love as a whole. Dympna Callaghan has recently argued that *Romeo and Juliet* presents Juliet's desire as "benign and unthreatening"; the play idealizes Romeo and Juliet's relationship and validates their marriage, thereby promoting the interests of a Protestant bourgeois construction of companionate marriage.[42] But in my view the play works rather to complicate, question, and problematize Romeo and Juliet's marriage. As I have argued elsewhere, Juliet's exceptionally young age (thirteen), the rashness of the couple's contract and marriage within two days – "too rash, too unadvised, too sudden" (2.2.118) – and their depiction as melancholic, immature, and "hot" Italians (3.1.4) cast doubt upon the appropriateness and advisability of the couple's actions, even as their plight and romance evokes sympathy.[43] The use of the bed as stage property compounds these issues. Juliet's "wedding bed" (3.2.136), far from being the focus for a range of publicly witnessed rituals, is clandestine; kept hidden from view. Instead of being accompanied to Juliet's bedchamber by the wedding guests, Romeo has to make a surreptitious entry through Juliet's bedchamber window by rope ladder, and their "amorous rites" must remain "untalked of and unseen" (3.2.7). Read against the context of contemporary rituals surrounding the bridal bed, the very secrecy surrounding Juliet's wedding bed denotes the troubled and transgressive nature of her marriage – rather as "the absence of customary signs" in Morose's wedding in *Epicoene* "marks the marriage as invalid," as Juana Green argues (p. 227). As Douglas Bruster points out, "objects seem to 'stand out' from their surroundings when they are involved in some breach of decorum, and usually receive attention only when they contravene expectation" (p. 89). This is precisely what we see at work in the staging of Juliet's wedding bed.

Furthermore, the disruption of contemporary wedding rituals in *Romeo and Juliet* is anticipated in the recital of Juliet's epithalamion or wedding poem (3.2.1–31). As George Puttenham explained in *The Arte of English Poesie* (1589), the epithalamion or "bedding ballad" was sung "at the chamber dore of the Bridegroome and Bride...at the bedding of the bride" to mask "the shreeking & outcry of the young damosell feeling the first forces of her stiffe & rigorous young man" and to encourage "the bride so lustely to satisfie her husbandes love...to animate new appetites with cherefull wordes."[44] Juliet's epithalamion shares many of

the characteristics of contemporary epithalamia: the use of classical allusion (Phoebus' lodging, Phaeton); the appeal to a benevolent external
force to aid the bride ("Come civil Night, and learn me how to lose a
winning match, / Played for a pair of stainless maidenhoods"); the allusion to the bride's sexual desire ("Hood my unmanned blood, bating
in my cheeks"); the anticipation of sexual consummation ("and when I
shall die..."). But Juliet's epithalamion crucially differs from Elizabethan
convention in that it is spoken by herself, alone. She appropriates a role
usually reserved for men (generally the composers and performers of
"bedding ballads"), and she performs that role in private. Juliet's epithalamion, laden with sexual innuendo, is not present in Shakespeare's
primary source for the play, Arthur Brooke's *Tragicall Historye of Romeus
and Juliet* (1562). Its addition to the Second Quarto (1599) of *Romeo and
Juliet*, whilst demonstrating Shakespeare's command of the epithalamion form, also testifies to his interest in the forceful, erotic nature of
Juliet's passion and the clandestine nature of her wedding; indeed, Mary
Bly argues that its excision from the First Quarto (1597) points "to the
fact that Juliet's expression of erotic desire represented a breach of cultural expectation."[45] In effect, Juliet assumes proprietary control over
her marriage bed; she bypasses the investment her parents, family, and
community might have had in her marriage bed as a means to legitimize
her marriage and secure the Capulet patrimony, and instead treats her
marriage bed – and her marriage – as if it were her own.

Public rituals and rites of passage that surround the bed are again dis-
rupted with Romeo and Juliet's deathbeds: Romeo and Juliet die alone,
without the comfort of family and friends, and out of their beds (contrast
this with the dignity and publicity of King Henry IV's deathbed in *Henry
IV Part Two*, 4.5). Against this context, the closing gestures of the play can
be regarded as an attempt to reinstate ritual order. Montague's promise
to "raise [Juliet's] statue in pure gold" and Capulet's response to erect
a statue of Romeo (5.3.299–304) has been regarded as a trite commem-
orative gesture: thus Susan Snyder has argued that it "suggests vulgar
show...an inauspicious beginning for a new era of peace."[46] But the
fathers' gesture also suggests the enactment of contemporary practices
of honoring the dead – funeral monuments and statues, many painted
in garish colors and gold leaf, proliferated in the late sixteenth century
and can still be seen today in English parish churches and cathedrals.[47]
Indeed, this is precisely the context evoked in the concluding lines of
Brooke's *Romeus*: "There is no monument more worthy of the sight: /
Then is the tombe of Juliet, and Romeus her knight" (3019–20). Situating

Capulet's gesture in the social context of Elizabethan funerary customs – a context that tends to get overlooked in criticism of the final scene of *Romeo and Juliet* – works to diminish the cynicism of Montague and Capulet's gesture.

The Elizabethan play-texts of *Romeo and Juliet* do not indicate that Romeo and Juliet were ever shown in bed together on the Elizabethan stage – unlike modern productions of the play where the use of the bed as a stage property repeatedly works to emphasize the intimacy and passion between the newlywed couple, and in so doing heightens audience sympathy for their plight. According to the First and Second Quartos a bed is not required on stage until 4.3, when Juliet takes the Friar's potion. Here the Q1 stage directions are revealingly specific: first, after drinking the potion Juliet "fals upon her bed *within the Curtaines*" (my italics).[48] This allows for an element of surprise when the Nurse, after chatting to "slug-a-bed" Juliet lying within the bedcurtains (4.5.2), withdraws the curtains to discover the "dead" Juliet; here the physical properties of the curtained bed enable dramatic irony. Secondly, on hearing the news of Juliet's "death" Lady Capulet, Capulet, Paris and the Nurse "All at once cry out and wring their hands," as if in a chorus of grief; finally, "They all but the Nurse goe foorth, casting Rosemary on her and shutting the Curtens" (4.5). The allusion to rosemary recalls the practice of strewing the bridal bedchamber with flowers and herbs (echoed in Capulet's lament that "Our bridal flowers serve for a buried corse," 4.5.89), while the closing of the bed-curtains around Juliet's body serves as a dramatic emblem of the closure of Juliet's life (and anticipates her enclosure within the Capulet tomb).

The First Quarto of *An Excellent Conceited Tragedie of Romeo and Juliet* has traditionally been regarded as a "bad" quarto, corrupt in origin and a lesser play than Q2 – *The Most Excellent and Lamentable Tragedie of Romeo and Juliet. Newly corrected, augmented, and / amended*. But, as Cedric Watts points out, Q1's precise stage directions suggest that it "bears a close relationship to what was actually performed; at times, indeed, Q1 gives a clearer insight into the stage practice than does Q2," indicating its status as a performance text.[49] Now that the ranking of quartos as "good" or "bad" has increasingly come under scrutiny, their differences – and particularly in this context the fuller details about the use of stage properties that early quartos yield – should become a point of critical departure, not closure.[50]

The metaphorical trope of Death-as-Bridegroom in *Romeo and Juliet* is dramatically realized in *Othello*: Desdemona's "death-bed" (5.2.51) is dressed in her "wedding sheets" (4.2.103) – sheets which Desdemona also intends for her "shroud" (4.3.23), recalling the practice popular among élite Jacobean women of using their wedding sheets for shrouds.[51] There are some striking parallels between the two tragedies: both center on a newlywed couple and in this respect are "domestic" in focus; both feature an Italian heroine involved in a clandestine marriage; and in both plays, the public wedding and bedding ceremonies that should ordinarily belong to a gentlewoman's marriage are carried out in secret. Like Juliet, Desdemona exceeds her prerogative by assuming proprietary control over her marriage bed; she gives herself away in marriage. In *Othello*, however, this act prompts anxiety about the future integrity of Desdemona's marriage bed; the bed not fully possessed by the husband but appropriated by the wife who may use it – or give it away like her handkerchief – as her desire dictates. Thus in *Othello* the marital bed becomes an intensely potent and conflicted symbol of sexuality, and the focus for the play's climactic final act: "Look on the tragic loading of this bed" (5.2.359). While the wedding sheets which Desdemona instructs Emilia to "lay on my bed" (4.2.103) evoke the vows and "rites" (1.3.253) of her marriage and serve for her – and the audience – as an emblem of her marital fidelity, for Iago the marital bed becomes a site of adultery, even prostitution: "it is thought abroad that 'twixt my sheets / [Othello's] done my office" (1.3.369–70); women, he resolves, "go to bed to work" (2.1.113). Othello, tragically, submits to Iago's narrative of the "contaminated" and "lust-stain'd" bed (4.1.196 and 5.1.36) as a sign of marital infidelity in the play. As Michael Neill argues in his subtle and persuasive analysis of the bed, race, and adultery in *Othello*, the bed emerges as "the imaginative center of the play – the focus of Iago's corrupt fantasy, of Othello's tormented speculation, and always of the audience's intensely voyeuristic compulsions."[52] Further, the play enacts a structural reversal of the bedding ceremony, whereby the offstage elopement of act 1 turns the public wedding into "a furtive and private thing," while in act 5 the private scene of the marital bed is exposed to "a shockingly public gaze."[53] Desdemona's handkerchief is notoriously the most strategic of stage properties in the first four acts of *Othello*, but in the final act it is the marital bed that becomes the most significant physical and symbolic property of the play.

The staging of Desdemona's murder in bed at the Globe and Blackfriars remains unknown, but given that this is the climactic scene of the play – and that Desdemona speaks from her bed in an exchange with Othello of some sixty lines – it seems reasonable to assume that the main action took place center- or even front-stage with the bed playing a prominent visual role.[54] The use of bed-curtains to create an element of surprise and enable dramatic irony is certainly indicated by Othello's line "Let me the curtains draw" on hearing Emilia's voice (5.2.105): Emilia then discovers the murdered Desdemona in bed (5.2.121).[55] The stage directions to the scene supplied by the First Quarto of *The Tragedy of Othello... As it hath beene diuerse times acted at the Globe, and at the Black Friers, by his Maiesties Seruants* (1622) once again give the most clues as to the original staging of the scene. Q1 stage directions instruct that Othello enters "with a light," "kisses her" while she lies asleep, "stifles her," and "fals on the bed" after Emilia denounces Iago's accusation of Desdemona's infidelity as a lie.[56] Like Q1 *Romeo and Juliet*, Q1 *Othello* has traditionally been regarded as an inferior text, but with its specific and elaborate stage directions it is, as Andrew Murphy points out, "theatrically, a much more fully imagined text" than that of the First Folio.[57]

For audience response towards the early staging of *Othello* we have to look beyond London. When *Othello* was performed by the King's Men touring at Oxford in 1610, the bed was close enough to the audience for them to be moved by the facial "countenance" of the boy actor playing Desdemona. One member of the audience, Henry Jackson, reported:

> not only by their speech but also by their deeds [the actors] drew tears. – But indeed Desdemona, killed by her husband, although she always acted the matter very well, in her death moved us still more greatly; when lying in bed she implored the pity of those watching with her countenance alone.[58]

Jackson's comment is revealing on several counts. It registers the significance of the "bed" as a stage property in the play and the impact it made on the audience, and it shows that on tour the King's Men not only made use of large stage properties like beds, but that it was situated close enough to the audience for the actor's facial expressions to be seen – indeed, the bed operates here rather like an intimate stage-within-a-stage, framing the actor. Further, Jackson's comment points to how audiences were, as Andrew Gurr suggests, sometimes "highly responsive in sentiment," moved to tears by performances.[59] Intriguingly, Jackson makes no reference to Othello's race, though it is hard to gauge what his "silence" on Othello's color might mean. However, Jackson's use of pronouns indicates how the illusion of the boy actor as woman could be so convincing that Jackson treats the boy actor as though he were female (or alternatively, that the practice of boy actors playing women was so conventional as not to be worthy of comment in the context of a play which makes no explicit allusion to cross-dressing): "*she* always acted the matter very well...*she* implored the pity of those watching with *her* countenance" (my italics).

In *Romeo and Juliet* and *Othello* Shakespeare makes full use of the bed's potent dramatic potential, witnessed especially in the stage directions of the plays' early quartos. But while I have been arguing in this chapter for the continuities between social practice and dramatic representation, it is, finally, important to register the contingencies of genre. In *Romeo and Juliet* and *Othello* Shakespeare works within the remits of tragedy, more particularly tragedy that centers on newly and clandestinely married couples: the "tragic loading" of the bed in these plays is distinct from the symbolism and use of the bed in the comedies and histories. The bed may be a site of marital conflict in the middle acts of comedies – particularly in the so-called "problem" plays making use of the "bed-trick" – but in the comic resolutions of the final act the bed is generally anticipated as the pleasurable, chaste domain of marital consummation: "To the best bride-bed will we" (*Midsummer Night's Dream* 5.1.393); "go to bed now" (*Merchant of Venice* 5.1.303); "O blessed bond of board and bed!... [go] to a long and well-deserved bed" (*As You Like It*, 136 and 184); "Come, Kate, we'll to bed" (*Taming of the Shrew* 5.2.184); "bless the bed of majesty again" (*Winter's Tale* 5.1.33); "We'll to bed then" (*Two Noble Kinsmen* 5.2.86). The only occasion on which a bed is possibly required as a stage property in the comedies is the induction to *Taming of the Shrew*, in which the bed is an untroubled place of pleasure and plenty – and a marker of élite status. Where attention is focused on domestic and sexual relations in the histories the bed may be a site of marital conflict or union (see for instance *Richard III* 3.7.190 and *Henry V* 5.2.364), but the bed is also, more prosaically, a place of sleep (as in *Henry IV Part One* 2.1.43) or sickness (as in *Richard II* 2.1.137). The only occasions on which a bed is required as a stage property in the histories is in the context of sickness and death: King Henry's deathbed in *Henry IV Part Two* (4.5) and Beaufort's deathbed in *Henry VI Part Two* (3.2). The Shakespeare play that perhaps comes closest to the use of the bed as a stage property in *Romeo and Juliet* and *Othello* is *Cymbeline* where, in an intensely voyeuristic scene, Imogen is discovered asleep in bed by Iachimo as he compiles an incriminating inventory: "I will write all down: / Such and such pictures; there the window; such / Th'adornment of her bed..." (2.2.23–6). Like *Othello*, *Cymbeline* centers on a clandestinely married couple and Imogen's marriage bed becomes implicated in a tragic narrative of male sexual jealousy; unlike *Othello*, however, *Cymbeline* moves from tragedy to comedy, and faith in Imogen's fidelity is fully restored.

Thus Shakespeare makes different use of the bed according to generic demands. This generic differentiation should alert us to the ways in which early modern drama *mediates* social practice, and stage properties are part of that process of mediation: they serve multiple functions and tell diverse stories in different dramatic and theatrical contexts. A materialist analysis of stage properties must not, then, lose sight of the contingencies of drama or the imperatives of fiction. Nor should it overlook the varieties of stages in early modern England. Henry Jackson's vivid account of the pitiful Desdemona "lying in bed" when the King's Men performed *Othello* at Oxford serves as a useful reminder of theatrical activity beyond the capital city. Yet the history of stage properties in the early modern period is, inevitably, centered on London: the records of metropolitan theatres and companies, and the plays that were written for them, dominate our history of early modern drama. The challenge for future research in this field is, then, to reconstruct the histories of stage properties in early modern England not only in generic and dramatic, symbolic and iconographic, material and economic terms, or with a view to historical change – but in relation to *local* contexts and regional difference. In short, there remains much work to be done.

NOTES

1. Arjun Appadurai, "Introduction: commodities and the politics of value," in Appadurai (ed.), *The Social Life of Things: Commodities in Cultural Perspective* (Cambridge: Cambridge University Press, 1986), pp. 3–63; p. 3. See Igor Kopytoff's account of the "biography" of an object as a "culturally constructed entity, endowed with culturally specific meanings, and classified and reclassified into culturally constituted categories" ("The cultural biography of things," in Appadurai [ed.], *The Social Life of Things*, pp. 64–91; p. 68). Stage properties work in similar ways, classified and reclassified into cultural codes and categories with each dramatic context in which they appear.
2. *Oxford English Dictionary*, Bed. 19.
3. See Peter Stallybrass and Margreta De Grazia, "The materiality of the Shakespearean text," in *Shakespeare Quarterly*, 44:3 (1993): 255–83.
4. I examine the role and decoration of the early modern bed, particularly in relation to notions of marital sexuality and chastity, in "Lying among the classics: ritual and motif on an Elizabethan bed," in Lucy Gent (ed.), *Albion's Classicism: The Visual Arts in Britain, 1550–1660* (*Studies In British Art* 2; London and New Haven: Yale University Press, 1995), pp. 325–57. For general studies on Elizabethan and Jacobean beds see Ivan G. Sparke, *Four-Poster and Tester Beds* (Hereford West: Shire Publications, 1990); H. Clifford Smith, *Catalogue of English Furniture and Woodwork: Volume II, Late Tudor and Early Stuart* (London: Victoria and Albert Museum, 1930); Victor Chinnery,

Oak Furniture: the British Tradition (Woodbridge: Antique Collectors' Club, 1986); Peter Thornton, *Seventeenth Century Interior Decoration in England, France, and Holland* (New Haven and London: Yale University Press, 1978), esp. pp. 149–79, and *Authentic Decor: The Domestic Interior* (London: Weidenfield and Nicolson, 1984), pp. 18–27; and Philippe Ariès and Georges Duby (eds.), *A History of the Private Life: Volume III, Passions of the Renaissance* (Cambridge, MA, and London: Harvard University Press [Belknapp Press], 1987).

5. See, for instance, the Schedule of Goods relating to the sale by John and Margerie Martyn to William Burcher of two messuages in 1595, cited by Lena Cowen Orlin in this volume; on the distribution of beds in households belonging to the provincial gentry see Catherine Richardson's essay in this volume. The price of beds varied enormously according to social scale and function: a modest "large bedstead" for Jane, Lady Townshend, cost £32 6s (Bacon Papers, Folger Shakespeare Library MS L.d.796), while Elizabeth Sly of Banbury, of the "lower sort," owned "a bedsted and 2 boordes" valued at 1s 8d (cited by Bernard Denvir, *From the Middle Ages to the Stuarts: Art, Design, and Society before 1689* [London: Longman, 1988], p. 136).

6. The Great Bed of Ware, for instance, was probably ornamented by a Flemish craftsman (Peter Thornton, *The Great Bed of Ware* [London: Victoria and Albert Museum, 1976], pp. ii–iii).

7. See Eileen Harris, *Going to Bed* (London: Victoria and Albert Museum, 1981), p. 13.

8. Bridgewater and Ellesmere Domestic Papers, Huntington Library: EL 149.

9. On Elizabethan and Jacobean bedhangings see for instance George Wingfield Digby, *Elizabethan Embroidery* (London: Victoria and Albert Museum [Faber and Faber], 1963); Margaret Jourdain, *A History of English Secular Embroidery* (London: Kegan Paul & Co., 1910); A. F. Kendrick, *English Needlework* (London: A. & C. Black, 1933); and Roszika Parker, *The Subversive Stitch: Embroidery and the Making of the Feminine* (London: Women's Press, 1984). I discuss a valance of Philomel now in the Irwin Untermeyer Collection at the Metropolitan Museum of Art (New York) in "Historicizing ekphrasis: gender, textiles, and Shakespeare's *Lucrece*," in Valerie Robillard (ed.), *Pictures Into Words: The Tradition of Ekphrasis, Renaissance to Postmodernism* (Amsterdam: Amsterdam Free University Press, 1998), pp. 103–23.

10. *Manuscripts of Lord de L'Isle and Dudley: Volume I, Historical Manuscripts Commission*, Bart.1.77, pp. 278–86. For an example of a more condensed description of a bed in a noble household see, for instance, the Inventory of Household Stuff belonging to the Earl of Essex at Wanstead (1597), where "a Bedsted guilte w[i]th Tester vallances, curtaines and counterpointe of purple Sattine Imbroydred w[i]th gold & siluer" is listed "In the chamber next the w[i]thdrawing chamber" (Folger MS G.b.4).

11. Cited by Harris, *Going to Bed*, p. 13.

12. A painted Jacobean bedstead (c. 1610) originally from Chewton House, for instance, shows the crests and arms of both the owner's family and his

two successive wives: see Clifford Smith, "A Painted Jacobean Bedstead," *Burlington Magazine*, 45 (July–Dec. 1924): 66–72; 71; and Chinnery, *Oak Furniture*, p. 205, fig. 2:231.

13. *The Diary of Lady Anne Clifford, 1590–1676*, ed. Vita Sackville-West (London: William Heinemann, 1923), p. 30. Likewise when people were shown around great houses, particular beds and their personal histories were carefully pointed out. At Hampton Court Paul Hentzner, for instance, was shown "the bed in which Edward VI is said to have been born, and where his mother Jane Seymour died in childbed" (cited by Denvir, *From the Middle Ages to the Early Stuarts*, p. 147).

14. Letter to Alice Carlton, cited by Percy Macquoid, in *Shakespeare's England: Volume II*, ed. Lionel Cust (Oxford: Clarendon, 1916), p. 144; on Anne of Denmark's lying-in see Reginald Reynolds, *Beds: With Many Noteworthy Instances Upon Them* (London: Andre Deutsch, 1952), p. 56. On the custom of lying-in see Richard W. and Dorothy C. Wertz, *Lying-In: A History of Childbirth in America* (London: Yale University Press, 1989), and Jacques Gelis, *A History of Childbirth: Fertility, Pregnancy and Birth in Early Modern Europe* (Oxford: Polity Press, 1991).

15. See Nigel Llewellyn, *The Art of Death: Visual Culture in the English Death Ritual, c.1500–c.1800* (London Reaktion [Victoria and Albert Musesum], 1991); and Clare Gittings, *Death, Burial and the Individual in Early Modern England* (London and Sydney: Croom Helm, 1984).

16. For the importance of the bedding ceremony to the confirmation of marriage see, for instance, Henry Swinburne's *A Treatise of Spousal, or Matrimonial Contracts* (London, 1711), article 12, pp. 224–5; Ralph A. Houlbrooke, *The English Family, 1450–1700* (London: Longman, 1984), p. 87; and John Gillis, *For Better For Worse: British Marriages, 1600 to the Present* (Oxford: Oxford University Press, 1985), pp. 68–9 and 72. The elaborate and often prescribed nature of the bedding ceremony indicates its importance: the *Second Northumberland Household Book* (c.1511–15), for instance, devotes six articles exclusively to the bedding ceremony at the marriage of Northumberland's daughter – with precise instructions for guests to witness the "hallowing of the bed" (cited by Suzanne Westfall, "Public privacy: early Tudor wedding revels" [unpublished paper given at the Shakespeare Association of America Annual Meeting, 1994], p. 14). On the bed-trick in Shakespeare see Marliss C. Desens, *The Bed-Trick in English Renaissance Drama: Explorations in Gender, Sexuality, and Power* (Newark and London: University of Delaware Press, 1994), and Julia Briggs, "Shakespeare's Bed-Tricks," *Essays in Criticism* 44:4 (1994): 293–314.

17. Alison Wall (ed.), *Two Elizabethan Women: Correspondence of Joan and Maria Thynne 1575–1611* (Devizes: Wiltshire Record Society, 1983), p. 8.

18. *Diary of Samuel Pepys*, ed. Robert Latham and William Matthews (London: Bel, 1972), vol. VI, p. 176. Pepys reports here on the wedding of William Procter's daughter; for his account of the more boisterous bedding ceremony at Frances Stuart's wedding see *Diary*, vol. IV, p. 38. For Sir Philip

Herbert's bedding ceremony see Alan MacFarlane, *Marriage and Love in England: Modes of Reproduction, 1300–1840* (Oxford: Blackwell, 1986), p. 313. The raucous nature of wedding and bedding ceremonies – particularly among the élite – was repeatedly commented upon by contemporaries: see Roberts, "Lying Among the Classics," pp. 328–9 and 340–1.

19. On the bed as a private refuge, see Orest Ranum in Aries and Duby (eds.), *A History of the Private Life*, pp. 217–21; and Gaston Bachelard, *The Poetics of Space* (New York: Orion Press, 1964), pp. 136–7.

20. In addition to Shakespearean bed-scenes see, for instance, Marlowe, *Edward II* (c.1592) and *Tamburlaine Part Two* (1590); Peele, *The Battle of Alcazar* (c.1589) and *Edward I* (1593); Heywood, *A Woman Killed With Kindness* (1603), *If You Know Not Me (Part 1)* (1604–5), *The Rape of Lucrece* (c.1608), *The Golden Age* (c.1610), *Silver Age* (1610–12), *Iron Age (Part 2)* (1612–13), and *A Maidenhead Well Lost* (1634); [Middleton and Tourneur], *The Revenger's Tragedy* (1606–7); Middleton and Rowley, *All's Lost By Lust* (1617–19); Beaumont and Fletcher, *The Maid's Tragedy* (c.1610); Fletcher, *Monsieur Thomas* (c.1615); Webster, *The White Devil* (1612) and *The Devil's Law Case* (c.1620); Dekker, *If It Be Not Good, the Devil Is In It* (1611–12) and *The Wonder of a Kingdom* (1623); Dekker and Massinger, *The Virgin Martyr* (1620); Ford, *'Tis Pity She's A Whore* (c.1630) and *Love's Sacrifice* (c.1631); W. Smith, *The Hector of Germany* (1615); I. C., *The Two Merry Milkmaids* (1619–20); William Sampson, *The Vow Breaker* (1636); Shirley, *The Traitor* (1635) and *Love's Cruelty* (1640); Davenport, *A New Trick to Cheat the Devil* (1639). These plays were variously performed at the Red Bull, the Cockpit, the Globe, Blackfriars, and possibly the Theatre.

21. E. K. Chambers, *The Elizabethan Stage*, Vol. III (1923; Oxford: Clarendon, 1974), p. 65; George Fullmer Reynolds, *The Staging of Elizabethan Plays at the Red Bull Theater, 1605–1625* (New York: Modern Language Association of America, 1940; reprinted by Kraus Reprint Corporation, New York, 1966), p. 65.

22. Christopher Marlowe, *Tamburlaine the Great*, (London, 1590), sig. G6.

23. Ibid., title page; see also Chambers, *The Elizabethan Stage*, p. 69, and Peter Thomson, *Shakespeare's Theatre* (London and New York: Routledge, 1983), p. 52. I have followed Andrew Gurr's account of the playhouses in which *Tamburlaine 1 and 2* were staged from his *The Shakespearean Stage 1574–1642* (Cambridge: Cambridge University Press, 1992), p. 241. A "bedsteade" is listed among properties belonging to the Lord Admiral's Men in 1598 (see below).

24. For the performance of *All's Lost by Lust* see Gurr, *Shakespearean Stage*, p. 233; Reynolds, *Staging of Elizabethan Plays*, p. 22; The play's title page claims, possibly erroneously, that it was "divers times Acted by the Lady Elizabeth's Servants"; Gurr notes that the play was also performed by Beeston's Boys at the Cockpit in 1639. Stage directions instructing a bed "discovered" on stage include Heywood's *The Rape of Lucrece* (c.1608, performed at the Red Bull) and Dekker's *The Wonder of a Kingdom* (1623, performed at the Cockpit); stage directions instructing characters to "enter" on a bed include Heywood's *If*

You Know Not Me, You Know Nobody (Part 1) (1604–5; Red Bull), Webster's
The White Devil (1612; Red Bull), and Ford's *'Tis Pity She's A Whore* (c.1630;
Cockpit). On the discovery of beds in the discovery-space or on the rear
stage see also Reynolds, *Staging of Elizabethan Plays*, pp. 68–9; Chambers,
Elizabethan Stage, p. 65, note 2; Gurr, *Shakespearean Stage*, p. 146.

25. See Reynolds, *Staging of Elizabethan Plays*, pp. 68–9; Gurr, *Shakespearean Stage*,
p. 188; and Richard Hosley, "The discovery-space in Shakespeare's Globe,"
Shakespeare Survey 12 (1959): 35–46; 37.

26. See for instance stage directions instructing "Enter the foure old Beldams,
drawing out Danae's bed: she in it," and "The bed drawne in" (ll. 67–70)
in Heywood's *The Golden Age* (c.1610, Red Bull); "Enter Anne in Bed" and
"The bed pull'd in" in Davenport's *A New Trick to Cheat the Devil*; and "A Bed
thrust out, the Palsgrave lying sicke in it" and "The Bedde drawne in" (sc. 1)
in W. Smith's *The Hector of Germany* (1615, Red Bull). Reynolds argues that
such instructions "definitely sound as if they meant the bed to be put out on
the front stage" (*Staging of Elizabethan Plays*, p. 69); see also King, "Staging
of plays at the Phoenix," pp. 156 and 158–9.

27. Glynne Wickham, *Early English Stages, 1300–1600*, 3 vols. (London and
New York, 1959–72), vol. II, p. 316; Richard Hosley, "The Staging
of Desdemona's Bed," *Shakespeare Quarterly* 14 (1963): 57–65. G. K. Hunter
argues that "it is clear that beds, thrones, desks, etc. were pushed out on to
the main stage after their 'discovery' and there claimed their relationship
to the world around them" ("Flatcaps and bluecoats: visual signals on the
Elizabethan stage," *Essays and Studies* 33 [1980]: 16–47; 21).

28. Chambers, *The Elizabethan Stage*, p. 111.

29. See also Reynolds, *Staging of Elizabethan Plays*, p. 65.

30. R. A. Foakes, *Illustrations of the English Stage 1580–1640* (Stanford: Stanford
University Press, 1985), p. xvi. See also the discussion by Douglas Bruster
of the illustration to Sampson's *The Vow Breaker* in this volume.

31. Other plays which make use of bed-curtains include Heywood's *The Golden
Age* (1610?); the *Contention* plays attributed to Shakespeare (*The First Part of
the Contention of York and Lancaster* and *The True Tragedy of Richard III*, 1594–5);
Peele's *The Battle of Alcazar* (c.1589); anon., *The Famous Victories of Henry V*
(1588?). See also Reynolds, *Staging of Elizabethan Plays*, pp. 66–7; and Chambers, *Elizabethan Stage*, vol. II, pp. 65–6. Heywood's use of the bed-curtains
in *The Rape of Lucrece* is strongly reminiscent of Shakespeare's poem *Lucrece*,
where Tarquin stalks into Lucrece's bedchamber and "gazeth on her yet
unstained bed. / The curtains being close, about he walks ... the curtain
drawn, his eyes begun / To wink" (366–74). Shakespeare's *Lucrece*, which
makes extensive use of domestic detail particularly around the bed and
bedchamber, was one of Shakespeare's most frequently reprinted texts
in the early seventeenth century (see Sasha Roberts, "Editing narrative,
sexuality, and authorship: the altered texts of *Lucrece*," in Cedric Brown
and Arthur Marotti (eds.), *Texts and Cultural Change in Early Modern England*,
[Harmondsworth: Macmillan, 1997] 124–52).

32. Transcribed in *Documents of the Rose Playhouse*, ed. Carol Chillington Rutter (Manchester: Manchester University Press, 1984), pp. 136–7; Neil Carson, *A Companion to Henslowe's Diary* (Cambridge: Cambridge University Press, 1988), pp. 52–3; see also Rutter (ed.), *Documents of the Rose Playhouse*, p. 134.

33. *Henslowe's Diary*, ed. R. A. Foakes and R. T. Rickert (Cambridge: Cambridge University Press, 1961), p. 5. On Joan Allen see Carson, *A Companion to Henslowe's Diary*, pp. 4–5, and Reynolds, *Staging of Elizabethan Plays*, p. 65.

34. The plays listed in Henslowe's diary in repertory during 1593 were *The Jealous Comedy*, *Guise*, *Christmas Week* (Strange's Men) and *Titus Andronicus* (Sussex's Men); there were sixteen plays listed in repertory during 1594 under the auspices of Sussex and Queen's, Admiral's and Chamberlain's Men (see Carson, *A Companion to Henslowe's Diary*, pp. 118–20).

35. Properties cost £2 4s. while costume material alone cost £3 12s. 6d. (*Henslowe's Diary*, p. 49; see also Carson, *A Companion to Henslowe's Diary*, pp. 103 and 113). Other references to stage properties in Henslowe's *Diary* include 25 shillings "to paye vnto hime wch made ther propertyes for Jeffa [*Jeptha*]" in May 1602 (p. 203); £5 "for carpenters worke & mackinge the throne In the heuenes" in June 1595 (p. 7); two payments of £6 and £4 to Thomas Dowton "to bye divers thinges" for *The First Civil Wars of France* in October 1598 (p. 99); 5 shillings for a painted picture for *Earl Goodwin Part Two* (p. 93); £5 to Thomas Dowton's boy "to bye dyvers thinges for the playe of the spencers [*The Spencers*]" on 16 April 1599 (p. 107); one shilling for the "crowne & other thing" for *Mahomet* in August 1601 (p. 178); 8 shillings for four lances possibly for *Albere Galles* (p. 215); two payments of 20 shillings for targets from the armourer in September 1602, possibly for *Cutting Dick* (pp. 216–17); 18 shillings paid to the carpenter for a 'scafowld & bare' for the play *Biron* in September 1602 (p. 217); 14s. 3d. for "a tabell & a coffen" for *The Three Brothers* (p. 218); 10 shillings for two "cvrenet[s]" [coronets] (p. 221), and 22 shillings for lamb skins, a canvas suit and skins for *The Black Dog of Newgate* (p. 222).

36. See the essays by Lena Cowen Orlin and Juana Green in this volume, and Natasha Korda, "Household property/stage property: Henslowe as pawnbroker," *Theatre Journal* 48 (1996): 185–95.

37. Performance details are taken from Gurr, *Shakespearean Stage*, pp. 236–41.

38. See Bernice W. Kliman, "The bed in *Hamlet*'s closet scene," *The Shakespeare Newsletter* 43:1 (1993): 8–9.

39. See also *Romeo and Juliet* 3.5.140 and 200–1, 4.5.38–9, and 5.3.102–5. On the Death-as-Bridegroom motif see for instance Molly Mahood, *Shakespeare's Wordplay* (London: Methuen, 1957); Graham Holderness, " 'My grave is like to be my wedding bed': stage, text and performance," in Linda Cookson and Brian Loughrey (eds.), *Critical Essays on "Romeo and Juliet"* (Harlow, Essex: Longman, 1991), pp. 19–28; Peter Holding, *Romeo and Juliet: Text and Performance* (London: Macmillan, 1992); and James Black, "The visual artistry of *Romeo and Juliet*," *Studies in English Literature 1500–1900* 15 (1975): 245–56.

40. See Leslie Thomson, " 'With patient ears attend': *Romeo and Juliet* on the Elizabethan Stage," *Studies in Philology* 92:2 (1995): 230–47; esp. 234, 241–4 and 246–7.

41. Margreta De Grazia, "The ideology of superfluous things: *King Lear* as period piece," in Margreta De Grazia, Maureen Quilligan, and Peter Stallybrass (eds.), *Subject and Object in Renaissance Culture* (Cambridge: Cambridge University Press, 1996), pp. 17–42; p. 21; Felix Bosonnet, *The Function of Stage Properties in Christopher Marlowe's Plays* (Biel: Francke Verlag Bern, 1978), p. 195. Douglas Bruster argues that stage properties can "take on a higher importance for subjectivity" in *Drama and the Market in the Age of Shakespeare* (Cambridge: Cambridge University Press, 1992), p. 86. Similarly, Brownell Salomon argues that the "language" of props is a crucial component of a "theatrical semiology" in which "nonverbal elements are often quite as significant as verbal ones" ("Visual and aural signs in the performed English Renaissance play," *Renaissance Drama* 5 [1972]: 143–69; 143 and 168; see also 160–3 on hand and large properties), while G. K. Hunter argues that "the Elizabethan language of visual effects" is "an essential part" of Elizabethan drama ("Flatcaps and bluecoats," p. 17).

42. "The ideology of romantic love: the case of *Romeo and Juliet*," in Dympna C. Callaghan, Lorraine Helms and Jyotsna Singh (eds.), *The Weyward Sisters: Shakespeare and Feminist Politics* (Oxford: Blackwell, 1994), pp. 59–101; p. 84; see also pp. 62, 65 and 88.

43. Sasha Roberts, *Writers and their Work: Romeo and Juliet* (Plymouth: Northcote House [British Council], 1998), esp. chapters 2 and 3.

44. Puttenham, *The Arte of English Poesie* (1589), ed. Gladys Doidge Willcock and Alice Walker (Cambridge: Cambridge University Press, 1970), pp. 50–3. Bishop Miles Coverdale condemned the practice of reciting bedding ballads: newlyweds, he argued, are allowed "no quietness. For a man shall finde unmanerly & restless people. that wyll first go to their chamber-doore, and ther syng vicious and naughty balates [ballads]" (*The Christen State of Matrimonye* [London, 1575], fols. 58v–60v). On the Stuart epithalmic tradition see Heather Dubrow, *A Happier Eden: The Politics of Marriage in the Stuart Epithalamium* (London: Cornell University Press, 1990).

45. Mary Bly, "Bawdy puns and lustful virgins: the legacy of Juliet's desire in comedies of the early 1600s," *Shakespeare Survey* 49 (1996): 97–109; 105; see also Gary M. McCown, " 'Runnawares Eyes' and Juliet's epithalamium," *Shakespeare Quarterly* 27 (1976): 150–70. Bly assumes here that Q1 represents an excised text rather than Q2 representing an expanded text; in fact the relationship between Q1 and Q2 of *Romeo and Juliet* is not entirely clear.

46. Susan Snyder, "Ideology and the feud in *Romeo and Juliet*," *Shakespeare Survey* 49 (1996): 87–96; 96.

47. On funeral monuments see for instance Nigel Llewellyn, *The Art of Death*, and "The royal body: monuments to the dead, for the living," in Lucy Gent and Nigel Llewellyn (eds.), *Renaissance Bodies: The Human Figure in English Culture c.1540–1660* (London: Reaktion Books, 1990), pp. 218–40.

48. *An Excellent Conceited Tragedie of Romeo and Juliet* (1597) ed. Cedric Watts (Shakespearean Originals; Hemel Hempstead: Prentice Hall/Harvester Wheatsheaf, 1995), p. 85.

49. Introduction, *An Excellent Conceited Tragedie of Romeo and Juliet* (Q1), p. 15. In addition, the variant readings of Q1 *Romeo and Juliet* merit further attention for the alternative interpretations of character and action in the play they offer (see Roberts, *Writers and their Work: Romeo and Juliet*, esp. pp. 7–9).

50. As Leah Marcus argues, "bad" quartos should be regarded "as different rather than debased" ("Levelling Shakespeare: local customs and local texts," in *Shakespeare Quarterly* 42:2 [1991]: 169–78; 169).

51. See Gittings, *Death, Burial and the Individual*, pp. 111–12.

52. Michael Neill, "Unproper beds: race, adultery and the hideous in *Othello*," *Shakespeare Quarterly* 40:4 (Winter 1989): 383–412; 412.

53. Ibid., 411.

54. See Richard Hosley, "The staging of Desdemona's bed," *Shakespeare Quarterly* 14 (1963): 57–65; Norman Sanders also discusses possible stagings of the scene on the Jacobean stage in his edition of *Othello* (Cambridge: Cambridge University Press, 1984), pp. 36 and 191; for later staging see James R. Siemon, " 'Nay, that's not next': *Othello*, V.ii in performance, 1760–1900," *Shakespeare Quarterly* 37 (1986): 38–51. Neill notes that in illustrations of *Othello* 5.2 "the bed is invariably the center of attention and often occupies the entire space" ("Unproper beds," p. 385, n. 9); see also Paul H. D. Kaplan, "The earliest images of *Othello*," *Shakespeare Quarterly* 39 (1988): 171–86.

55. Lodovico's line "Let it be hid" (5.2.361) possibly indicates that the bed-curtains were then redrawn around the bodies of Othello and Desdemona, rather as the Nurse is seen "shutting the Curtens" around the apparently dead Juliet (*An Excellent Conceited Tragedie of Romeo and Juliet*, ed. Watts, p. 87).

56. *The Tragedie of Othello, the Moore of Venice* (1622), ed. Andrew Murphy (Shakespearean Originals; London: Prentice Hall, 1995), pp. 122–8.

57. Ibid., p. 21.

58. Quoted by Andrew Gurr, *The Shakespearean Stage*, p. 226. Jackson's comment was written in Latin and is variously translated; see for instance the translation included in Julie Hankey (ed.), *Othello*, (Plays in Performance Series; Bristol: Bristol Classical Press, 1987), p. 18.

59. Ibid., p. 226.

PART III

Costumes

CHAPTER 7

Properties in clothes: the materials of the Renaissance theatre

Peter Stallybrass

Before the advent of the modern bank, men and women of every class stored up wealth in clothes.[1] Modern scholars have usually failed to understand the crucial economic significance of clothes because they have failed to imagine what people without bank accounts did with the money they had. Even the rich were often strapped for ready cash. Since there were no deposit banks in early modern England, those who accumulated money had to store it themselves, like the Duchess of Somerset who, when she died in 1587, had £5,200 in gold in her closet, or like Sir John Oglander, who, in the early seventeenth century, kept £2,400 in gold hidden in a hole in his parlor and another £220 in gold in a box in his study.[2] Before the full development of the accumulative processes of capitalism, such hoarding appeared both miserly and pointless. What good did gold do lying around when it could be transformed into clothes or food or land or buildings or any other useful and sociable material form? If and when ready cash was necessary, clothes, jewels, and other moveable goods could be pawned or sold. Of course, the rich had more, and more expensive, garments and accessories, but even the poorest had clothes that could be pawned. And it made more sense to hoard clothes than money, since clothes had use-value.

The theatre had a particular investment in clothes-hoarding, since clothes were a crucial part of Renaissance theatrical display. In the late 1520s, John Rastell prosecuted his former friend, Henry Walton, for the decay of the theatrical garments that Walton had looked after for Rastell. Rastell, who owned a stage at Finsbury, claimed that the clothes were worth twenty marks; they included "a player's garment of green sarcenet lined with red tuke and with roman letters stitched upon it of blue and red sarcenet lined with red buckram," a garment "for a priest to play in," and "a garment of red and green Say, paned and guarded with gold skins, and fustians of Naples black, and sleeved with red, green, yellow, and blue sarcenet." Rastell left these clothes with Walton when he traveled to Europe. When he returned, Rastell discovered that Walton had "let out the same garments to hire to stage-plays and interludes sundry times" ("above three or four score times") and had made considerable money from them. Moreover, according to Rastell, the clothes had been damaged in the process. Walton responded that the clothes were already "worn and torn players' garments." The details of each and every garment were presented in court, and the witnesses called included a tailor, a merchant tailor, a stationer, and a latten founder. Whatever the rights and wrongs of the case, the fundamental economic significance of clothes to Rastell's theatre is striking. Such clothes were worth a legal battle.[3]

Clothes had a particular importance for actors in the Renaissance, who were noted, both off and on the stage, for the splendor of their apparel. That is the point of the prologue to Henry Medwall's *Fulgens and Lucres*, which John Rastell published c. 1515. "A" thinks that "B" is "oon / Of them that shall play" by his "apparell." He is wrong only because now gallants wear as "nyce aray" as actors.[4] Rastell had practical knowledge of the economic relations between the writing of plays and the materials of their performance. In 1527, he was employed (together with Holbein) to devise a pageant for the French ambassadors. He was paid a modest 3s. 4d. for writing the interlude of *Love and Riches* and Mercury's Latin address to the king, but he was paid the substantial fee of £26 9s. 11 d. for his designs for the pageant.[5]

In calculating profit and loss, the professional theatre companies had to work out how much they could afford to spend for magnificent apparel. If they didn't spend enough on costumes, they were in danger of undermining one form of the magic upon which theatrical profits depended. By all accounts, Fletcher's *The Faithful Shepherdess* was a flop when it was first staged. But when it was put on over twenty years later at Somerset House before Charles and Henrietta Maria, its success seems partly attributable to "the clothes the Queen had given Taylor the year before of her own pastoral."[6] Costumes that had been seen too often, on the other hand, could bring a masque, where novelty and surprise were at a premium, into disfavor. The Office of the Revels made an inventory of masquing costumes and of materials that had already been "often translated" into different costumes. Many were finally retired from service because they were "forworne" or "to[o] much knowen."[7] The masque that Francis Bacon arranged for Gray's Inn and the Inner Temple to stage for James on 18 February 1613 was, Chamberlain thought, likely to be a flop when it was restaged. The first performance had been cancelled shortly after it had begun because the king was tired, "[b]ut the grace of their masque is quite gone when their apparel hath been already showed and their devices vented."[8]

After the Restoration, John Downes's records suggest that splendor of costumes might take precedence over a company's acting skills: *The Adventures of Five Hours* was "Cloath'd so Excellently Fine in proper Habits," and only secondarily "Acted so justly well." Companies, though, had to work out a balance between staging new costumes to draw spectators and saving expenses by drawing upon stock. And Downes suggests how delicate that balance was. *Ulysses*, being "all new Cloath'd, and Excellently well perform'd," had "a Successful run" and thus presumably recouped the investment in the costumes. On the other hand, *Iphigenia*, "a good Tragedy and well Acted," "answer'd not the Expences they were at in Cloathing it." Similarly, *The Fairy Queen*, for which new clothes, scenes and music cost the staggering sum of £3,000, was well received "but the Expences in setting it out being so great, the Company got very little by it."[9] Theatre companies throughout the seventeenth century invested, wisely or not, in clothes, and they contributed to the remarkable growth of the Merchant Taylors' Company and to the development of the fashion industry. They did so both as capitalist investors and through hoarding and circulating garments.

If the theatrical companies spent large sums of money on "nyce aray," their expenditure was preserved in the clothing in a way that is unimaginable today. Money was turned into clothing. But clothing could be turned back into money. And the companies participated not only in the rapidly expanding market in new clothing but also in the circulation of secondhand clothing. Indeed, since there were no ready-made clothes until the later seventeenth century, every record of the buying of a gown or a petticoat or a doublet or breeches must be presumed to refer to the purchase of secondhand clothing unless there is evidence to the contrary. New clothing is recorded by payments for cloth, for ribbon, for lace and points, and for the transformation of these into a garment by a tailor.

One can get a sense of the distinction between new and secondhand clothes from Henslowe's accounts. Henslowe lent money to the theatre companies both for materials to make costumes (and to pay tailors) and for specific items of clothing. Here are two consecutive records from his accounts:

Lent vnto Thomas dowton the 31 of Janewary 1598 to bye tafetie for ij womones gownes for the ij angrey wemen of abengton the some of ix li

Layd owt for the company the 1 of febreyare 1598 to bye A blacke velluet gercken layd thicke wth blacke sylke lace & A payer of Rownd hosse of paynes of sylke layd wth sylver lace and caneyanes of clothe of sylver at the Requeste of Robart shawe the some of...[10]

The distinction is clear between lending money for textiles (taffeta) and for buying clothes (a black velvet jerkin with black silver lace etc.). Named pieces of clothing like the jerkin and the canions above are almost certainly secondhand clothes.

It's just possible that the company went to great lengths to describe a garment to Henslowe that they wanted to make up or had already made up. But that seems unlikely, particularly in view of the repeated emphasis in plays, pamphlets, and satires on the theatres' use of secondhand clothing. Henslowe was lending money not only for new fabrics but also for a wide variety of made-up, i.e. secondhand, clothes: an embroidered waistcoat; "a flame coler satten dublett"; a long, tawny cloak made of wool; a white satin doublet; a damask cassock with a decorative border of velvet; a pair of hose, decorated with bugles and cloth of silver; a rich cloak from "mr. langley."[11] These clothes could scarcely be described so specifically unless they were already made up and this means that they were secondhand. Indeed, the companies usually could not afford to buy new clothes for new plays except on a small scale. So they depended on, and participated in, the circulation in secondhand clothes, buying the cast-offs of the court, reusing ecclesiastical vestments, buying from frippers.

PAWNBROKERS

At the center of the circulation of secondhand clothing in Renaissance England were pawnbrokers. The word "pawn" itself probably derives from the Latin root *pannus*, meaning cloth or rag. (The French "*pan*" which can mean a skirt derives from the word that also used to mean a pledge.) Clothes were indeed the main form of pledge, exchanged for money at the pawnbroker.

Henslowe's pawnbroking accounts, preserved somewhat sporadically for 1593 to 1596,[12] reveal that, although his business accepted ear-picks and pewter pots, the vast majority of his pledges were in the form of clothes.[13] There is nothing surprising in this. European pawnbroking records from the fourteenth to the nineteenth century show that, for the average business, clothing was by far the commonest pledge. Here, for instance, are the kinds of object pledged over five days in 1417 in Pistoia, listed as percentages:

Clothing and apparel: 57.5%

Jewelry: 11.2%

Tools, agricultural implements: 11.2%

Arms and armor: 8.8%

Bedding: 7.5%

Kitchenware and household utensils: 2.5%

Calf skins: 1.3%[14]

More than 70 percent of these pledges are objects worn upon the body (including jewelry and armor as well as clothes). Comparing these accounts with Henslowe's pawnbroking accounts, it's clear that Henslowe's business was fairly typical for a commercial pawnbroker. Clothes (and a small quantity of cloth) account for 62.2 percent of his pledges; another 13 percent is for clothes and household goods, clothes and plate, or clothes, household goods and plate; household goods (mainly linen) account for 12.2 percent; and "plate" (mainly in the form of rings) accounts for 11.5 percent.[15] Despite changes in fabrics (above all the massive increase in cotton), industrialization, and the consequent reduction in the value of clothes, clothing still accounted for more than 75 percent of the total pledges in an 1836 survey of English pawnbrokers, with metal goods (including watches, rings and medals) a mere 7.4 percent, and bibles 1.6 percent.[16]

As the surviving records throughout Europe show, every social class pawned goods. This is surely the most notable shift between the Renaissance and today, when it is mainly the poor who turn to pawnbrokers. In Renaissance Florence, borrowers included patricians, notaries, bakers, weavers, and secondhand dealers; in Bruges, the count of Flanders pawned the crown jewels and the countess of Bar a gold coronet to the same pawnbroking business that had rules about what they would and would not accept from weavers; in Nivelles, the clientele included barons, knights, burghers, the lower clergy, craftsmen, and tenants; in Siena between 1483 and 1511, the clientele included a tailor, a book publisher, a stationer, priests, doctors, lawyers, members of the patriciate, and eleven women, including a nun and the daughter of a dyer. One also gets a sense of who was trying to use pawnbrokers by noting what could *not* be pledged. In Bruges, it was forbidden to lend money on church ornaments and vestments (this seems to have been a widespread prohibition). Despite the prohibition, a dalmatic from St. Walburge was in fact used as a pledge. In Louvain, students were forbidden to pawn their school texts. In Troyes, one could not pawn agricultural instruments.[17] But the important point to note is the wide variety of the pawnbrokers' clientele, and the fact that it included the élite, who were often cash-poor. When William Lord Vaux came to London in 1593 to attend the House of Lords, he was unable to do so because he had pawned his parliamentary robes and the broker refused to lend them back unless the principal was paid as well as the interest.[18]

But clothes could only be pawned if there was a market for unredeemed pledges. Henslowe sent Goody Watson clothes that he now called "my owne" and required that she sell them at the prices he set.[19] Just how sure Henslowe was of a market in secondhand clothes is demonstrated by the sums he was prepared to pay for them. If we recall that the cost of admission to the public playhouses was 1 d., we get some idea of the value of even the smallest item of clothing: Henslowe lent 10s. "vpon a payer of blacke sylke stockenes of goody streates"; 10s. "vpon a velluatte cappe"; 6s. "vpon a lynynge of shage for A clocke"; 6s. "vpon A dublet & A payer of breches ffor A chylld."[20] The pawn value of a pair of silk stockings was enough to pay for 72 visits to the theatre (which means that the stockings themselves might cost as much as 216 cheap theatre tickets, since pledges were usually worth two to three times what they could fetch at the pawnbroker). At the other end of the market, Henslowe lent £3 10s. to Mr Crowche "vpon his wiffes gowne"; £5 for "A womones gowne of branched damaske & lyned throwghe wth pincked tafetie & layd wth a lace of sylke and gowld"; £3 10s. "vpon A sylke grogren gowne garded wth veluett & lyned wth saye of mr. Burde."[21]

Henslowe created a banking system in clothes in a variety of ways. Most obviously, he lent money to the sharers of the professional theatre companies so that they could buy clothes. But he also pawned and sold clothes either directly himself or through agents. Henslowe's use of women agents as the collectors of pawns appears to be entirely typical. The middlemen who bring the clothes of women to the pawnbroker in Middleton's *Your Five Gallants* are men but this is surely only for theatrical effect in a play that emphasizes the "handling" of women by men.[22] In reality, the day-to-day circulation of household goods was, as Natasha Korda has argued, the work of women. As Korda points out, we need to rethink our concept of an all-male theatre in relation to the number of women involved in the making of linen undergarments, the stitching and repairing of clothes, the pawning and selling of secondhand clothes.[23]

Henslowe employed at least three women as agents (Goody Watson, Mrs. Grant, and Ann Nockes, his nephew being the only man he

employed), and he conducted his pawnbroking business by my calculations with fifty-nine named women as compared to thirty-five named
men. The preponderance of women in the business of pawnbroking
is suggested by other evidence as well. In Salisbury, Edith Pines was
owed £15 upon pawns in 1625 and Agnes Masters, a butcher's widow,
was described in 1631 as "a coman carrier of cloathes and other things
about the towne to sell and to pawn."[24] A century and a half later, in
Paris, we find a clear division of labor between the richer pawnbrokers
and frippers, usually men, and the poorer street pawners, buyers and
sellers of secondhand clothes, usually women. In 1767, after they had
organized the *revendeurs* and *revendeuses* into a "free craft," the police
recorded 1,263 women as against 486 men. Of these traders in secondhand goods, 800 women and 250 men sold old clothes and secondhand
linen.[25] Henslowe's records also show that pledges were more often of
women's than of men's apparel. Of his pledges in 1593 that one can
identify as male or female clothing (some of them undoubtedly repeats),
thirty are men's and eighty-three are women's.[26]

Women, then, played a particularly important role in the circulation of
clothes. For all the ideological conflation of women with domestic space,
in reality their wealth was in the form of portable property that moved
across the imaginary boundaries separating "public" from "private"
space.[27] As women's clothes circulated, so too did women as frippers
and as pawnbrokers' clients. Ironically, despite ideologies of women's
"domestic sphere," in Henslowe's business it was women who travelled
the streets of London, collecting pledges and buying secondhand goods.
The circulation of these women presumably allowed Henslowe himself
to stay at home, doing his accounts and controlling the shop. There
was another group besides women that was peculiarly associated with
portable property: actors. Like women, they were engaged in the accumulation and circulation of wealth in the form of moveable property and,
like women, they had a close relation to the trade in secondhand clothes.

SECONDHAND CLOTHES AND THE THEATRE

The players, I argued above, were crucially dependent upon the accumulation and circulation of clothes. Where did they get their clothes from?
Recent theatre historians have tended to minimize Henslowe's career as
a pawnbroker and as a dealer in secondhand clothes so as to rescue him
from the opprobrium with which Fleay treated him in the nineteenth
century. Fleay attacked Henslowe's "selfish hand-to-mouth policy" and

described Henslowe himself as a "pawnbroking, stage-managing, bear-baiting usurer."[28] The modern mission to "rescue" Henslowe, though, rests on a misunderstanding of the crucial role that pawnbroking and the trade in clothes and jewels played for rich and poor alike before the advent of modern banking systems.

In his business with the players, Henslowe profited both directly and indirectly from the trade in clothes. In the grievances of Lady Elizabeth's Men, probably dating from 1615, the players complained that Henslowe had retained ownership of their costumes and playbooks as securities for the money he had lent them. In other words, his relation to them was that of a pawnbroker, lending money upon the security of pledges. The players calculated that they would be able to pay off their debt over a period of three years, but, they claimed, Henslowe had deliberately broken up the company before they could repay him so as to keep the stock of clothes and playbooks.[29] If Henslowe made most of his money from the theatre by renting the buildings themselves and by taking a share of the profits, there is one record that shows that he was also capable of charging interest upon costumes. On 6 December 1602, Henslowe bought four cloaks for Worcester's Men for £4 each. He charged 5s. interest for each cloak, so that he made a profit of £1 on the deal.[30] It may be true, as Carson claims, that this was an unusual charge, but because of the illegality of high interest rates, Henslowe *usually* concealed the interest he charged. Another example where it seems that Henslowe was charging interest is in the case of "a damaske casock garded with velvet" which he records buying for 18s. in his "Note of all suche goodes as I have bought for the Companey of my *Lord Admirals men*, since the 3 of Aprell, 1598." On 7 April 1598, he "Lent vnto the company to by a damask cassocke garded wth velluet," which must surely be the same garment. But now he bills them for 20s., making a profit of 2s. or 10 percent.[31]

The list of the goods that Henslowe bought for the Admiral's Men in April 1598 also suggests that he was working as a fripper or secondhand clothes dealer. The clothes are fully made up, which means that, with the possible exception of a pair of woollen stockings, they are secondhand. It also suggests that he was buying clothes for the company on a larger scale than his *Diary* records. There are eighteen items of clothing on the list, nine bought from Henslowe's son-in-law, Edward Alleyn. Of the eighteen items, only the damask cassock is clearly identifiable from his other accounts as one that he lent the company money to buy. Two others have possible matches in the other accounts. But Henslowe is also spending substantial sums on clothes for the company of which no account remains. Somewhere between the purchase and their theatrical use, the clothes disappear from the records, so it is perhaps appropriate that one of the garments was "a robe for to goo invisbell," bought, together with a "gown for Nembia," for £3 10s. The clothes in all cost £53 11s.

As contemporary comments show, the business in secondhand clothes and pawnbroking constantly overlapped. Frippers dealing in cast-off apparel merged with brokers. Francis Bacon writes of "a Frippers or Brokers Shoppe; that hath ends of euerie thing, but nothing of worth"; and George Whetstone derides servants who, to get money upon "their owne, or [their] maisters apparell, brasse, pewter, sheetes, shirts, &c.," "finde Brokers, or fripperers."[32] In *Your Five Gallants*, the pawnbroker is given the name of Fripper, while the character named "Fripper" in Chapman's *Monsieur D'Olive* describes his trade as "*Fripperie* . . . or as some tearme it, *Petty Brokery*." Part of the trade of Chapman's Fripper is said to be burning gold lace, so as to regain the metal content. To D'Olive, frippery and broking are interchangeable professions: "Farwell *Fripper*, Farewell *Pettie Broker*." D'Olive assumes that Fripper wants to become his follower because "the Vulture smels a pray," the prey being not the bodies of the dead but their clothes:

S'light, I thinke it were my wisest course, to put tenne pounds in stocke with him, and turne pettie Broker . . . [I]f we be but a day or two out of towne heele be able to load euerie day a fresh Horse with Satten suites, and send them backe hither.[33]

Like usurers and brokers, frippers were treated with ambivalence. Were they making, as D'Olive assumes, easy profits, or did they deal in "nothing of worth"? Was the "frippery" they sold showy finery, even fashionable dress? Or was it worthless trumpery and trash? This ambivalence towards frippery rubbed off on the players, who mingled new finery and cast-off clothing, gold lace and copper lace.[34]

That players were repeatedly associated with the pawnbrokers with whom they dealt is not surprising, considering their dependency upon the circulation of clothes. John Stephens, in his satire on "a common Player," argues that "[t]he Statute hath done wisely to acknowledge him a Rogue: for his chief Essence is, *A dayly Counterfeite*." But that "dayly Counterfeite," in which the actor "professes himselfe, (beeing vnknowne) to bee an apparant Gentleman," is, according to Stephens, composed of the hybrid wares of the pawnbroker. The actor's thinne Felt, and his Silke Stockings, or his foule Linnen, and his faire Doublet, doe (in him) bodily reveale the Broaker: So beeing not sutable, he prooues a *Motley*: his minde obseruing the same fashion of his body: both consist of parcells and remnants: but his minde hath commonly the newer fashion, and the newer stuffe: hee would not else hearken so passionatly after new Tunes, new Trickes, new Devises: These together apparrell his braine and vnderstanding, whilest hee takes the materialls vpon trust, and is himselfe the Taylor to take measure of his soules liking.[35]

The player in this account is simultaneously a trickster who tailors himself, and a "motley," tailored from the "parcells and remnants" of others. The only difference between the composition of the actor's mind and his body is that his mind is made from the more recent fashionings of the playwright, the balladeer, and the actors themselves, whereas his body shows the wear of older "stuffe." But even the older "stuffe" sometimes passes muster as "fashion." If the thin felt and the foul linen openly betray their origin in the pawnshop, the silk stockings and fair doublet suggest, however misleadingly, a nobler origin.

The companies' circulation of secondhand clothes is only one way that the theatres functioned as engines of fashion. The actors provided a constant demand for clothes, but so too did the audiences who attended the theatres. Before the repeal of the sumptuary laws in 1604, it could be a risky undertaking to wear "unsuitable" clothes, particularly in church or the workplace, where one was most liable to surveillance and arrest. It is true that the sumptuary laws in England were more honored in the breech than the observance. But they were not completely without teeth. A Fellow of King's College, Cambridge was committed to prison in 1576 after a formal dispute with the Provost, when it was discovered that he was wearing "a cut taffeta doublet... and a great pair of galligastion hose" under his gown. And it was suggested that an attorney who appeared before the Privy Council in 1592 with a gilt sword, huge ruffs and other "unseemly apparel" be dismissed from the Court of Common Pleas.[36] But in the theatres, it was virtually impossible to regulate who wore what.[37]

This accounts for one of the central attacks upon the theatres: that audiences used the liberty of the theatrical space to rival the actors themselves in their dress. William Harison noted that "few of either sex come thither, but in theyr holy-dayes appareil, and so set forth, so trimmed, so adorned, so decked, so perfumed, as if they made the place the market of wantonnesse."[38] And in his *Characters*, Thomas Overbury describes "A Phantastique" as one who "withers his clothes on a Stage, as a Sale-man is forc't to doe his sutes in Birchin-lane; and when the Play is done, if you marke his rising, 'tis with a kind of walking Epilogue between the two candles, to know if his suit may passe for currant."[39] Henry Fitzgeoffrey decries both the unpatriotic luxury of an audience whose fashions come from Turkey, Spain, and France, and the extent to which such luxury bankrupts the young gallant:

> Enter *Tissue slop*!
> Vengeance! I know him well, did he not drop
> Out of the *Tyring-house*? Then how (the duse)
> Comes the misshapen *Prodigall* so spruce,
> His year's *Revenewes* (I dare stand unto't,)
> Is not of *worth* to purchase such a *Sute*.[40]

Attacks upon the acting companies combined a critique of the actors as shape-shifters with an awareness that the theatres staged and marketed new fashions in clothes through actors and audience alike.

No one was more aware, or more scornful, of the audience's clothes as a rival theatrical attraction than Ben Jonson. In "The Dedication to the Reader" for *The New Inn*, Jonson complains of the fastidious gallants who have decried his play:

What did they come for, then? thou wilt aske me. I will as punctually answer: To see, and to bee seene. To make a generall muster of themselues in their clothes of credit: and possesse the Stage, against the Play.[41]

And the plot of *The Devil is an Ass* is driven by Fitzdottrell's desire to cut a figure in the theatre. While Fitzdottrell insists that his wife wears fine clothes, he can only afford to furnish himself from the pawnbroker, Ingine. In a wonderful metatheatrical touch, Fitzdottrell has "a hyr'd suite" from Ingine to go to a play called... "the Diuell is an Asse."[42] But when Wittipol offers him his new cloak, which cost £50, in exchange for a quarter of an hour's conversation with his wife, Fitzdottrell cannot resist the offer, even if it means renting out his wife. The cloak (of plush, velvet and lace) will become, as Wittipol puts it, Fitzdottrell's "Stage-garment" in which he will be as much a spectacle as the actors. Fitzdottrell explains his transaction to Frances, his wife, by saying:

> Heere is a cloake cost fifty pound, wife,
> Which I can sell for thirty, when I ha' seene
> All London in't, and London has seene mee.
> To day, I goe to the Black-fryers Play-house,
> Sit i' the view, salute all my acquaintance,
> Rise vp between the Acts, let fall my cloake,
> Publish a handsome man, and a rich suite

> (As that's a speciall end, why we goe thither,
> All that pretend, to stand for't o' the Stage)
> The Ladies aske who's that? (For they doe come
> To see vs, Love, as wee doe to see them).

In the fiction of the play, as in the material practices of the actors and audience, clothes constantly circulate. Fitzdottrell wears Wittipol's cloak and imagines pawning or reselling it, and he rents clothes from the broker Ingine. Everill's clothes "[a]re all at pawne," and even Pug, the wretched devil, participates in the process of circulation, appearing as a human by stealing the clothes of Ambler, the gentleman usher of Lady Tailbush.[43] Ben Jonson presents this circulation with a mixture of irony, contempt, and delight. Although, like the anti-theatricalists, he scorned the mingle-mangle of social life, he himself depended upon the spectacle of the theatre, as his plays constantly remind us. Even Venetian visitors who could not understand a word of English were entertained by "gazing at the very costly dresses of the actors."[44]

There were different ways in which the actors could make a sumptuous display. First, like other servants, they could inherit the clothes of their masters as perks or favors. They were not regular household servants, though, and they were unlikely to be treated with the intimacy of domestics. Nevertheless they could and did acquire the cast-off clothing of the court. Ben Jonson mocks the gallant who, changing his clothes three times a day, teaches

> each suit he has, the ready way
> From *Hide-Parke* to the Stage, where at the last
> His deare and borrow'd Bravery he must cast.

And John Donne remarks on the passage of clothes from court to playhouse. Satirizing courtiers, he writes:

> As fresh, and sweet their Apparells be, as bee
> The fields they sold to buy them; "For a King
> Those hose are," cry the flatterers; And bring
> Them next weeke to the Theatre to sell.[45]

These literary anecdotes can be compared with the account of the Swiss traveller Thomas Platter. After visiting England in 1599, Platter wrote:

The actors are most expensively and elaborately costumed; for it is the English usage for eminent lords or Knights at their decease to bequeath and leave almost the best of their clothes to their serving men, which it is unseemly for the latter to wear, so that they offer them then for sale for a small sum to the actors.[46]

In Platter's version, the trade between court and stage is not as immediate as Jonson and Donne suggest. The clothes first pass from aristocrat to servant, and on then to the playhouse. The one thing to doubt in Platter's account is his claim that the clothes would be sold "for a small sum." We know from Henslowe's accounts that clothes made from expensive materials and dyes could be pawned for substantial sums, and there is no reason why servants would have sold their perquisites to the actors for less money than they could have got by pawning them to Henslowe. But the most striking aspect of Platter's account is the suggestion that it was primarily to actors that clothes of any station or gender could safely be rented or sold.

That the most extravagant of clothes and fabrics could end up in the theatre is clear from Henslowe's 1598 inventories of the Admiral's Men and from Edward Alleyn's undated inventory of theatrical apparel. The inventories include cloth of gold gowns, coats, venetians, and hose; a cloth of silver coat, jerkin, venetians, and hose; a scarlet cloak with two broad gold laces and gold buttons; "a crymasin sattin case [doublet or jerkin] lact w¹ gould lace all over"; a pair of red velvet venetians and a pair of green velvet venetians both "lact w¹ gould spanish"; and a satin doublet "layd thycke with gowld lace." Although there may be some repeats between Henslowe's and Alleyn's lists, there are thirteen records of cloth of gold or cloth of silver; thirty-two records of garments with gold or silver lace; and a number of other garments recorded as having gold or silver trappings (fringes, spangles etc.). Several of the garments have gold or silver buttons.[47]

There is even a crimson robe, striped with gold and faced with ermine.[48] This is remarkable not so much for the extravagant gold and crimson but for the ermine. Ermine was one of the most costly imports from Russia and Scandinavia; it was also a fur "principally used for ceremonial garments within royal and aristocratic circles."[49] The coronation portrait of Elizabeth I shows her in a magnificent gown lined throughout with ermine and with a collar of ermine.[50] In the "Ermine" portrait of Elizabeth, a white ermine, spotted with black, rests upon her left arm, a gold crown around its neck.[51] It is not only the crown that asserts the regal nature of this ermine, though. Ermines were in fact white, the only black being on the tip of their tails. Sumptuary legislation limited the use of these tails to the monarch alone. The white skins were "powdered" (as it was termed) by the furrier, who pulled the black tails through slits that he or she had made and sewed them in. The black-spotted ermine on Elizabeth's sleeve thus materializes the monarch herself – the only person who can be "powdered" with their black tails.[52] It is most unlikely that the player's robe had any such tails sewn in. But a crimson robe, striped with gold and faced with ermine, was probably a magnificent aristocratic garment that the theatre had acquired secondhand from the court.

Such transmissions of clothes mirrored the theatres' translations of the rituals of court and city alike from their "proper" locations to the Liberties, from which distance they could, as Steven Mullaney has argued, interrogate the solemnities of rule together with an audience which included the politically disenfranchised.[53] They also dislocated those rituals by making them nakedly dependent upon a cash nexus. Not having the deep pockets of some courtiers and merchants, players had to make do as best they could, and they intermingled their own fabrications with the cast-off paraphernalia of courtiers and citizens.

A striking example of such fabrications is to be found in the copper lace that players added to their costumes.[54] Gold and silver lace were a major item of expense for the aristocratic and wealthy, often costing as much as or more than the garments that they adorned. The players, on the other hand, while they bought secondhand garments made of cloth of gold and cloth of silver or richly embroidered with gold and silver lace, could rarely afford to buy such garments new. Yet they needed to display the finery of the court, and they also staged the latest extravagances of London fashion, particularly in city comedies. They did this by intermixing costumes containing gold and silver with garments faced and embroidered with copper lace. Copper lace was made in the same way as gold or silver, but it cost much less. It nevertheless represented a major expense for the companies. Between January and July 1599, Henslowe paid £17 1s 4d. for copper lace; between May and September 1601, he paid £20 5s 10d. for copper lace, although this was partly to account for old debts.[55] Copper lace had a special place in the theatre. Indeed, it became a metonymy for the professional players. In the "War of the Theaters," Jonson depicts the back-biter Tucca as fearing to be mocked "o' the stage":

you'll play me, they say: I shall be presented by a sort of copper-lac't scoundrels of you.[56]

Dekker responded in defence of John Marston with *Satiromastix* or "The Vntrussing of the Humorous Poet." Jonson, depicted as "Horace," will himself be exposed to ridicule in the theatre. In Dekker's play, Horace (i.e. Jonson) responds to this threat by saying that he will bring his own audience to the play to "distaste" the impersonation of himself:

me ath stage? ha, ha. Ile starue their poore copper-lace workmasters, that dare play me.

And Dekker's Tucca defends the players or "Stage-walkers" as "these charitable Copper-lac'd Christians."[57]

Dekker glosses this conflation of the players with copper lace in *The Gull's Hornbook*, where the gallant, eager to show off his "good clothes," pushes up onto the stage to display his "new satin." Having attained a stool upon the stage, he "examine[s] the playsuits' lace, and perhaps win[s] wagers upon laying 'tis copper."[58] But the gallant can only lay such wagers because of the hodge-podge of new and old, of gold lace and of copper simulating gold lace, which the theatre presented.

The undoing of clear boundaries between the court, the city, and the theatre is further demonstrated by an earlier record from the Office of the Revels. In 1572, Thomas Giles formally complained that the Revels was renting out its costumes. Giles was undoubtedly right. The previous year, among several other rentals, "yello clothe of golde gownes" were rented to Gray's Inn and to the Horsehead Tavern; black-and-white gowns were rented for the marriages of Edward Hind and Mr. Martin; copper "cloth of gold" gowns were rented for the marriage of Lord Montague's daughter; and red cloth-of-gold gowns were rented for a tailor's marriage. Giles, in his complaint, attributes an identity to the clothes themselves. He argues that they have suffered from the "soyll of the wereres / who for the most parte be of the meanest sort of mene" and that this soiling was "to the grett dyscredytt of the same aparell."[59] Here, as in the accounts of the guild theatres, the clothes themselves assume an identity, one which comes from their aristocratic point of origin. The clothes can thus be dishonored, soiled by circulation among "the meanest sort of mene." Giles was a haberdasher who lent out clothes and he was in competition with the Office of the Revels in the secondhand clothes trade. But despite his own business, he was alarmed by a circulation of clothes that unstitched apparel from social status, an unstitching that the theatre both staged within its fictions and encouraged in its audience.

There were, indeed, growing parts of London whose economy was founded upon the trade in secondhand clothes. Long Lane was recorded by John Stow in his *Survey of London* as "now lately builded on both the sides with tenements for brokers, tiplers, and such like."[60] The brokers and secondhand clothes dealers of Long Lane and Houndsditch provided dramatists and pamphleteers with an inexhaustible supply of satirical attacks on the very trade in which they were involved. In *The Puritaine*, an old soldier's weapons are "in *Long-lane* at Pawne, at Pawne"; in Dekker and Webster's *West-Ward Hoe*, Mistress Birdlime hires "three Liueries in Long-lane"; in their *North-Ward Hoe*, Doll tells Hornet that "if the Diuel and all the Brokers in long lane had rifled their wardrob, they wud ha beene dambd before they had fitted thee thus"; in their *The Wonder of a Kingdome*, a broker is said to have "a *long lane* of hellish Tenements / Built all with pawnes."[61] And in his pamphlets, Dekker writes of "Vsurers and Brokers (that are the Diuels Ingles, and dwell in the *long-lane* of hell)" and of "all the Brokers in Long-Lane, Hounsditch, or elsewhere, with all the rest of their Colleagued Suburbians, that deale vpon ouerworne commodities."[62]

The jibes at the long lane of hell are outdone by the ingenious wordplay upon Houndsditch. Stowe soberly noted that

[f]rom Aldgate Northwest to Bishopsgate, lieth the ditch of the Cittie, called Houndes ditch, for that in olde time when the same lay open, much filth (conueyed forth of the Citie) especially dead Dogges were there layd or cast.

Now, he writes, the houses "be for the most part possessed by Brokers, sellers of olde apparell and such like."[63] In Middleton's *Michaelmas Term*, Rearage, a London gallant, sneers at Andrew Lethe as

> One that ne'er wore apparel but, like ditches,
> 'Twas cast before he had it, now shines bright
> In rich embroideries.

Rearage plays upon "casting," meaning both the discarding of clothes and the clearing of ditches, but the two meanings are conflated in Houndsditch, simultaneously the ditch of dead dogs and the market of discarded clothes. In *Three Weekes, three daies, and three houres Obseruations and Trauel*, John Taylor describes a woman who defends the "honesty of brokers" as if she herself "like a desperate pawn had lain seven years in lavender on sweeting in Long Lane, or amongst the dogged inhabitants of Houndsditch."[64]

In the theatre, the unstitching and restitching of clothes by tailors and brokers was often represented ambivalently as materializing the unstitching and restitching of the social fabric. That process, so brilliantly analysed by Stephen Greenblatt in his work on the professional playhouses, was materialized in the piecemeal nature of the players' clothes.[65] The clothes, new and cast-off alike, were translated across geographical divisions, across class divisions, across gender divisions, across "national" divisions. And these boundary crossings provided a rich repository of stories for the playhouses to stage.

STAGING CLOTHES

The circulation of clothes (including their pawning and their theft) is repeatedly referred to in Renaissance drama, sometimes as a central aspect of the plot, sometimes as a mundane aspect of personal finances. Middleton's *Your Five Gallants* begins in a pawnshop with Frippery (the "broker-gallant," his very name testifying to the centrality of clothes to pawnbroking) going over his stock of gowns, petticoats, jackets, suits. The opening scene emphasizes the significance of pawnbroking in the play as a whole. Goldstone (the "cheating-gallant") steals the cloak of Fitzgrave ("a gentleman") and pawns it to Frippery, who then wears it himself; Goldstone also pawns a diamond and a sapphire; Tailby (the "whore-gallant"), losing at gambling, pawns his weapons, his hat, and his satin doublet; Bungler tries to pawn his grandfather's seal-ring (engraved with a "great codpeice, with nothing int") to Frippery; and, at the end of the play, Pursenet (the "pocket-gallant") gives Tailby the pledge of a chain of pearl to rent masquing costumes.[66]

The play revolves around the circulation of this pearl chain. It changes hands no fewer than twelve times, and its migrations illuminate the social life of other forms of clothing and jewelry as they move from gifts and material memories to commodities that can be cashed in. At the beginning of the play, Fitzgrave (the "gentleman") has given the chain to Katherine ("a wealthy orphan") as the material form of his love. The pearls are "The hallowed beades, whereon I iustly kept / The true and perfect number of my sighs." The chain is stolen by Pursenet's Boy, who gives it to Pursenet. Pursenet gives it to the First Courtesan, who in turn gives it to Tailby. Tailby, losing at gambling, wants to pawn the chain, but he doesn't have it with him. Pursenet takes the chain back, and attacks the First Courtesan for allowing it to be "wound on a strangers arme." Pursenet pawns the chain, but later pays £40 to redeem it, only to drop it on the ground. Goldstone picks it up, mistakenly thinking it belongs to Mistress Newcut and that she "dropt it from her arme / For a deuice to toale me to her bed." Tailsby then confronts Goldstone for stealing the chain, but it is in fact restored to Pursenet. Pursenet pawns it again to Frippery (whom he calls "Iewe") as a security for the furnishing of masquing suits. Frippery gives it to Katherine in an attempt to woo her, but she declares that it is "[t]he very chaine of Pearl was filcht from me!" And so the chain is returned to Katherine, to whom it had been given at the beginning of the play. As the chain changes hands, it changes its life-form, but its own persistence as a materialized relation between giver and receiver challenges any clear opposition between "love" and "lust" (between Fitzgrave and Katherine, Pursenet and the First Courtesan, the First Courtesan and Tailby, Fripper and Katherine) or between memorial object and exchangeable commodity.[67]

We do not need to read Fripper as an allegory of Philip Henslowe to note that the circulation of clothes that was necessary to the formation of the professional theatres was also an irresistible topic for dramatists. In Jonson's *Every Man in His Humour*, Brainworm begins by disguising himself as a soldier with clothes purchased from a broker. He later steals the clothes of Justice Clement's clerk and pawns them to raise cash. And when he promises aid to Matthew and Bobadill, they raise the necessary money by pawning a jewel, silk stockings, and a pair of boots.[68] Clothes are simultaneously a banking system, moveable objects to be stolen, and the materials out of which an identity is constructed.

If the theatres staged the circulation of clothes via the pawnbroker, they also paraded their own function as renters of clothes. In Jonson's *The Alchemist*, Face tells Drugger to rent the costume of Hieronimo (of Kyd's *The Spanish Tragedy*) from the players:

> Thou must borrow,
> A *Spanish* suite. Hast thou no credit with the players?
> DRUGGER: Yes, sir, did you neuer see me play the foole?
> FACE: I know not. NAB: Thou shalt, if I can helpe it.
> HIERONYMO's old cloake, ruffe, and hat will serue,
> Ile tell thee more, when thou bringst 'hem.

The costume itself appears an act later, when Subtle announces to Face, "Here's your HIERONIMO's cloake, and hat," and it migrates again when Lovewit puts on the costume for his marriage to Dame Pliant.[69] The costume hovers between a fetishized identity from the past (the specific role of Hieronimo) and its new possibilities once it has been appropriated (its generalized nature as a disguise and as a sign of "Spanishness").

There's a further joke in this recirculation of the clothes of Hieronimo from *The Spanish Tragedy*. For Jonson himself had, according to Dekker, played the part of Hieronimo: "thou hast forgot," says Tucca to Horace (i.e. Jonson) in *Satiromastix*, "how thou amblest (in leather-pilch) by a

[margin handwritten note: Metatheatrical .]

play-wagon, in the high way, and took'st mad Hieronimoes part, to get seruice among the Mimickes."[70] Dekker derides Jonson as a strolling player who will "weare anything," including "a Plaiers old cast Cloake." Having played the part of a Hieronimo, run mad for the death of his son, he is said to have borrowed "a gowne of *Roscius* the stager" and sent it back "lowsie."[71] No doubt, many actors did indeed supplement their personal wardrobes both from other players and from the companies' stocks, despite the prohibitions against the latter practice.

But the implication that "a Plaiers old cast Cloake" is worthless frippery is itself a self-conscious mockery of the illusions that the theatre performed and critiqued. In fact, the clauses that theatrical entrepreneurs and sharers in the professional companies drew up show that their "frippery" was far from worthless. Henslowe drew up Articles of Agreement between himself and Robert Dawes, specifically stating that Dawes should not at any time after the play is ended

depart or goe out of the [howse] with any [of their] apparell on his body, or if the said Robert Dawes [shall carry away any propertie] belonging to the said company, or shal be cosentinge or privy to any other of the said company going out of the howse with any of their apparell on his or their bodies, he . . . shall and will forfeit and pay unto the said Philip and Jacob . . . the some of ffortie pounds of lawfull [money of England].[72]

The circulation of clothes was a theme for comedy, history, and tragedy. But it was also a carefully controlled economic practice, for the theatres were founded upon the regulated vagrancy of moveable goods. Clothes as theatrical properties were simultaneously economic capital, material memory-systems, and trangressors of every social boundary.

QUOTE.

NOTES

1. This essay is a reworking of materials and arguments in Ann Rosalind Jones and Peter Stallybrass, *Renaissance Clothing and the Materials of Memory* (Cambridge: Cambridge University Press, 2000).
2. Lawrence Stone, *The Crisis of the Aristocracy 1558–1641* (Oxford: Clarendon Press, 1965), p. 509.
3. The lawsuit is printed in Alfred W. Pollard, *Fifteenth Century Prose and Verse, An English Garner* (Westminster: Constable, 1903), pp. 307–21. It has recently been re-edited by Janette Dillon in "John Rastell v. Henry Walton," *Leeds Studies in English*, n.s. 28 (1997): 57–75. See also Dillon's "John Rastell's stage," *Medieval English Theater* 18 (1996): 15–45, and William Ingram, *The Business of Playing: The Beginnings of the Adult Professional Theater in Elizabethan London* (Ithaca: Cornell University Press, 1992), p. 71.

4. Henry Medwall, *Fulgens and Lucers*, in *Tudor Interludes*, ed. Peter Happé (Harmondsworth: Penguin, 1972), p. 82.

5. A. W. Reed, *Early Tudor Drama: Medwall, the Rastells, Heywood, and the More Circle* (London: Methuen, 1926), pp. 17–19.

6. See G. E. Bentley, *The Profession of Dramatist in Shakespeare's Time, 1590–1642* (Princeton: Princeton University Press, 1971), p. 259.

7. Albert Feuillerat, *Documents Relating to the Office of the Revels in the Time of Queen Elizabeth I* (Louvain: Uystpruyst, 1908), p. 22.

8. Elizabeth McClure Thomson (ed.), *The Chamberlain Letters* (London: Murray, 1965), p. 75.

9. John Downes, *Roscius Anglicanus*, ed. Judith Milhous and Robert D. Hume (London: Society for Theatre Research, 1987), pp. 53, 101, 94, 89.

10. R. A. Foakes and R. T. Rickert (eds.), *Henslowe's Diary* (Cambridge: Cambridge University Press, 1961), p. 104.

11. Foakes and Rickert (eds.), *Henslowe's Diary*, pp. 77, 81, 86, 88, 89, 98. Was this "mr. langley" Francis Langley, draper, alnager, and proprietor of the Swan theatre?

12. For an excellent edition of the Henslowe documents associated with the Rose, see Carol Chillington Rutter (ed.), *Documents of the Rose Playhouse* (Manchester: Manchester University Press, 1984). Rutter notes that "over a period in which they repaid Henslowe some £92 from the gallery receipts, the Admiral's Men took loans of £142 in thirty-seven payments. They spent nearly twice as much on costumes (£88. 1 s.) as on playbooks (£45. 10s.), partly because they had reached an agreement with Francis Langley about the costumes he had evidently been withholding since Pembroke's Men decamped from the Swan in the summer of 1597, partly because they 'exsepted into the stocke' two expensive cloaks that had been in pawn since the previous November, and partly because they spent heavily on costumes for Drayton and Dekker's *Civil Wars in France* trilogy: in the second week of October, £10 for *Part I* and in late November, £20 for *Part II* just about the time *Part III* was being commissioned. Lavish costumes were likewise bought for Chapman's *Fount of New Fashions*...By 14 November £17 had been spent to costume that play. Some of these costumes were enormously costly. Langley's 'Riche clocke' cost £19" (pp. 152–3). Rutter notes that the outlay for costumes was not always so large, but it was normally a substantial part of performance costs.

13. Neil Carson, *A Companion to Henslowe's Diary* (Cambridge: Cambridge University Press, 1988), pp. 22–3; Jeremy Boulton, *Neighbourhood and Society: A London Suburb in the Seventeenth Century* (Cambridge: Cambridge University Press, 1987), pp. 88–91.

14. Raymond de Roover, *Money, Banking and Credit in Mediaeval Bruges: Italian Merchant-Bankers, Lombards, and Money-Changers: A Study in the Origins of Banking* (Cambridge, MA: The Mediaeval Academy of America, 1948), p. 121.

15. The figures are drawn from Boulton, *Neighbourhood and Society*, p. 91.

16. Melanie Tebbutt, *Making Ends Meet: Pawnbroking and Working-Class Credit* (Leicester: Leicester University Press, 1983), p. 33. On the crucial significance of pawnbroking, particularly to the poor, see also Kenneth Hudson, *Pawnbroking: An Aspect of British Social History* (London: The Bodley Head, 1982) and Peter Stallybrass, "Marx's coat," in Patricia Spyer (ed.), *Border Fetishisms: Material Objects in Unstable Spaces* (New York and London: Routledge, 1997), pp. 183–207.

17. Roover, *Money, Banking and Credit*, especially pp. 113–65. On European pawnbroking more generally, see Brian Pullan, *Rich and Poor in Renaissance Venice: The Social Institutions of a Catholic State, to 1620* (Oxford: Blackwell, 1971); Frederic C. Lane and Reinhold C. Mueller, *Money and Banking in Medieval and Renaissance Venice*, vol. 1, *Coins and Moneys of Account* (Baltimore: The Johns Hopkins University Press, 1985); Reinhold C. Mueller, *The Venetian Money Market: Banks, Panics, and the Public Debt, 1200–1500* (Baltimore: The Johns Hopkins University Press, 1997); Carol Bresnahan Menning, *Charity and the State in Late Renaissance Italy: The Monte di Pietà of Florence* (Ithaca: Cornell University Press, 1993). On the problems of Christians charging interest, see Jacques Le Goff, "The usurer and purgatory," in *The Dawn of Modern Banking*, Center for Medieval and Renaissance Studies, University of California, Los Angeles (New Haven: Yale University Press, 1979), pp. 25–52; and Richard A. Goldthwaite, *Banks, Palaces and Entrepreneurs in Renaissance Florence* (Aldershot: Variorum, 1992), pp. 31–9. On the Lombards as bankers/pawnbrokers, see Michael Prestwich, "Italian merchants in late thirteenth and early fourteenth century England," in *The Dawn of Modern Banking*, pp. 77–104. On goldsmiths and early banking in England, see R. D. Richards, *The Early History of Banking in England* (London: Frank Cass, 1958), especially pp. 24–35.

18. Lawrence Stone, *The Crisis of the Aristocracy*, p. 517.

19. Carson, *A Companion*, p. 23.

20. Foakes and Rickert (eds.), *Henslowe's Diary*, pp. 151, 149, 151, 158.

21. Foakes and Rickert (eds.), *Henslowe's Diary*, pp. 159, 259, 152.

22. Thomas Middleton, *Your Five Gallants, A Critical Edition*, ed. Clare Lee Colegrove (New York: Garland, 1979), [1. 1].

23. I am deeply indebted to Natasha Korda's "Household property/stage property: Henslowe as pawnbroker" (*Theatre Journal* 48 [1996]: 185–95) for her analysis of the role of women in the theatre. See especially 187–8, 191–3, and also her "Household Kates: domesticating commodities in *The Taming of the Shrew*," *Shakespeare Quarterly* 47: 2 (1996): 109–31. See also her "Women's theatrical properties" in this volume.

24. Sue Wright, " 'Churmaids, Huswyfes and Hucksters': the employment of women in Tudor and Stuart Salisbury," in Lindsay Charles and Lorna Duffin (eds.), *Women and Work in Pre-Industrial England* (London: Croom Helm, 1985), pp. 100–21, p. 111.

25. See Daniel Roche, *The Culture of Clothing: Dress and Fashion in the "Ancien Régime"* (Cambridge: Cambridge University Press, 1994), pp. 346–7.

26. On the preponderance of women's clothes as pledges in the nineteenth century, see Tebbutt, *Making Ends Meet*, p. 34 and chapter 5; Ellen Ross, *Love and Toil: Motherhood in Outcast London 1870–1918* (New York: Oxford University Press, 1993), pp. 46–8 and 81–4; and, for anecdotal evidence, Stallybrass, "Marx's coat," pp. 196–8. For a fine account for women's pledges in the twentieth century, see Annelies Moors, "Wearing gold," in Spyer (ed.), *Border Fetishisms*, pp. 208–23.

27. See Amy Louise Erickson, *Women and Property in Early Modern England* (London: Routledge, 1993), particularly pp. 17–20, 61–78, 223–36. Erickson's account not only challenges the view that women did not inherit property but also establishes the financial value of the moveable goods that women owned and circulated.

28. Frederick Fleay, *Chronicle History of the London Stage 1559–1642* (London: Reeves and Turner, 1890), p. 94. See also Natasha Korda's excellent account of the critical handling of Henslowe in "Household property/stage property," pp. 185–9.

29. Carson, *A Companion*, pp. 31–2.

30. Foakes and Rickert (eds.), *Henslowe's Diary*, p. 220. See also Bernard Beckerman, "Philip Henslowe," in Joseph W. Donohue (ed.), *The Theatrical Manager in England and America* (Princeton: Princeton University Press, 1971), pp. 19–62, p. 41 n. 33, and Carson, *A Companion*, p. 27.

31. *Henslowe Papers*, ed. Walter W. Greg (London: A. H. Bullen, 1907), p. 122; Foakes and Rickert (eds.), *Henslowe's Diary*, p. 88.

32. Francis Bacon, *The Advancement of Learning* (London, 1605), p. 66 [2.17.14 in modern editions]; Whetstone, *A Mirour for Magestrates*, sig. ki^v.

33. Middleton, *Your Five Gallants*; George Chapman, *Monsieur D'Olive*, ed. Allan Holaday, in *The Plays of George Chapman: A Critical Edition*, general ed. Holaday (Urbana: University of Illinois Press, 1970), 3.2.76, 81, 88–9, 169–75.

34. For a fuller account of gold lace, see Jones and Stallybrass, *Renaissance Clothing*, pp. 24–6.

35. John Stephens, *Satyricall Essayes* (London, 1615), pp. 244–5. I am indebted to Crystal Bartolovich for finding and sending me a copy of Stephens' character of a player.

36. N. B. Harte, "State control of dress and social change in pre-industrial England," in D. C. Coleman and A. H. John (eds.), *Trade, Government and Economy in Pre-Industrial England: Essays Presented to F. J. Fisher* (London: Weidenfeld and Nicolson, 1976), p. 147.

37. For a fine account of the "idolatry" of clothes in the theatre, see Jean E. Howard, " 'Satan's Synagogue': the theatre as constructed by its enemies," *The Stage and Social Struggle in Early Modern England* (London: Routledge, 1994), pp. 22–46.

38. Quoted in Andrew Gurr, *Playgoing in Shakespeare's London* (Cambridge: Cambridge University Press, 1987), p. 234.

39. Sir Thomas Overbury, *A wife now the widdow of Sir T. Overbury ... Whereunto are added many witty characters* (London: A. Crooke, 1638), M4; Gurr, *Playgoing*, p. 228.

40. Henry Fitzgeoffrey, *Satyres: and Satyricall Epigrams: With Certaine Observations at Black-Fryers* (London: Miles Patrick, 1617), F2v; Gurr, *Playgoing*, pp. 231–2.

41. Ben Jonson, *The New Inn* (acted 1629), in C. H. Herford, Percy and Evelyn Simpson (eds.), *Ben Jonson* (Oxford: Clarendon, 1938), vol. VI, p. 397.

42. For the play's dependence upon old costumes, even as it emphasizes Fitz-dottrell's craving of the new, see Jean MacIntyre, *Costumes and Scripts in the Elizabethan Theatres* (Edmonton: University of Alberta Press, 1992), p. 309. Her book gives an excellent account of the significance of clothes in the professional theatres.

43. Ben Jonson, *The Devil is an Ass* (acted 1616), in Herford (ed.), *Ben Jonson*, vol. VI, 1.4.16–25, 1.6.187, 1.6.28–38, 3.3.19.

44. Quoted in G. E. Bentley, *The Jacobean and Caroline Stage* (Oxford: Clarendon Press, 1941), vol. I, p. 136.

45. Ben Jonson, "An Epistle to a Friend, to Persuade Him to the Wars," *The Vnder-wood* no. 15 in Herford (ed.), *Ben Jonson*, vol. VIII, ll. 107–10; John Donne, *Satire IV*, in *The Satires, Epigrams, and Verse Letters*, ed. W. Milgate (Oxford: Clarendon Press, 1967), ll. 180–4. I am indebted to Susan Cerasano for both these references. See her excellent " 'Borrowed Robes,' costume prices, and the drawing of *Titus Andronicus*," *Shakespeare Studies* 22 (1994): 45–57.

46. Clare Williams, *Thomas Platter's Travels in England, 1599* (London: Jonathan Cape, 1959), p. 167.

47. Greg (ed.), *Henslowe Papers*, pp. 52–5 and 113–23.

48. Greg (ed.), *Henslowe Papers*, p. 53.

49. Valerie Cumming, " 'Great vanity and excesse in Apparell': some clothing and furs of Tudor and Stuart royalty," in Arthur MacGregor (ed.), *The Late King's Goods: Collections, Possessions and Patronage of Charles I in the Light of the Commonwealth Sale Inventories* (London: Alistair McAlpine, 1989), pp. 322–50; p. 328.

50. Roy Strong, *Portraits of Queen Elizabeth I* (Oxford: Clarendon Press, 1963), p. 56, P. 7 (plate IV). See also P. 93 (the frontispiece), P. 87, M. 1, D. and I. 7, D. and I. 12, E. 8, W. 2, W. 7.

51. Strong, *Portraits*, P. 86 (plate XXI [b], which is mislabeled as referring to P. 85).

52. By the mid-seventeenth century, however, Vermeer owned a yellow satin jacket with a trim of white fur, powdered with black fur (either powdered ermine or a simulation of it in lamb's wool). Such a jacket is recorded in the inventory of Vermeer's possessions (see John Michael Montias, *Vermeer and his Milieu: a Web of Social History* [Princeton: Princeton University Press, 1988], pp. 221, 340). This jacket appears in several of Vermeer's paintings: see Albert Blankert, John Michael Montias, and Giles Aillaud, *Vermeer* (New York: Rizzoli, 1988), pp. 113, 131, 132, 133, 144.

53. Steven Mullaney, *The Place of the Stage: License, Play and Power in Renaissance England* (Chicago: University of Chicago Press, 1988).

54. I am deeply indebted to Jonathan Gil Harris for bringing the significance of copper lace to my attention and for references.

55. Foakes and Rickert (eds.), *Henslowe's Diary*, ff. 63–63v and 87–94. On 3 July 1601, Henslowe paid the copper lace man £4 for an "owld deate" (f. 91), and on 6 July of the same year he settled "the whole deat" for £12 2s. 10d (f. 91v).

56. Ben Jonson, *Poetaster*, in Herford (ed.), *Ben Jonson*, vol. 4, 3.4.197–8.

57. Thomas Dekker, *Satiro-Mastix, or the Vntrussing of the Humorous Poet*, ed. Hans Scherer (Louvain: Uystpruyst, 1907), ll. 409–12, ll. 2010–12.

58. Thomas Dekker, *The Gulls Hornbook*, ed. R. B. McKerrow (London: De la More Press, 1904), pp. 50, 51.

59. Feuillerat, *Documents*, pp. 409, 410.

60. John Stow, *A Survey of London*, ed. Charles Kingsford (Oxford: Clarendon Press, 1908), vol. II, p. 28. In his additions to Stowe, John Strype wrote that Long Lane was a "Place of Note for the sale of Apparel, Linen, and Upholsters Goods, both Second-hand and New, but chiefly for Old, for which it is of note" (John Stow, *A Survey of the Cities of London and Westminster... Corrected, Improved, and very much Enlarged by John Strype* [London: A. Churchill et al., 1720], Book II, p. 122).

61. Thomas Dekker and John Webster, *West-Ward Hoe* (1607), in *The Dramatic Works of Dekker*, vol. II, 2.2.45–6; Thomas Dekker and John Webster, *North-Ward Hoe* (1607), in *The Dramatic Works of Dekker*, vol. II, 2.1.13–15; Thomas Dekker and John Webster, *The Wonder of a Kingdome* (1636), in *The Dramatic Works of Dekker*, vol. III, 4.2.56–7 (my emphasis); W. S., *The Puritaine or The Widdow of Watling-streete* (1607) in *The Shakespeare Apocrypha*, ed. C. F. Tucker Brooke (Oxford: Clarendon Press, 1918), 2.1.7–8;

62. Dekker, *The Wonderfull Yeare*, in F. P. Wilson (ed.), *The Plague Pamphlets of Thomas Dekker* (Oxford: Clarendon Press, 1925), p. 12 (my emphasis); Dekker, *Newes from Hell* (London, 1606), sig. F4v. See also Anon, *Muld Sacke*: "This [broker] is so cruell, that he will incroch vpon the very garments that shelter the poore and fatherlesse. I doe know (*Clinias*) a poore Widdow dwelling by me, neere Long-lane, that hath foure young Children, who for want hath beene forced to engage (to one of those Cormorants) the Couerlet of her bed, for twelue pence, and comming at night to haue it backe, she could not haue it without foureteene pence, and so in defect of two pence, shee and her Children were exposed to the extremitie of cold" (sig. B4).

63. Stowe, *Survey*, vol. I, pp. 128–9.

64. Francis Beaumont and John Fletcher, *The Woman's Prize, or The Tamer Tamed*, ed. Fredson Bowers, in *The Dramatic Works in the Beaumont and Fletcher Canon*, general ed. Fredson Bowers (Cambridge: Cambridge University Press, 1979), 2.2.37–9, 53–4; Thomas Middleton, *Michaelmas Term* (1607), ed. Richard Levin, Regents Renaissance Drama (Lincoln: University of Nebraska Press, 1966), 1.1.63–5; John Taylor, *Three Weekes, three daies, and three houres Obseruations and Trauel* (1617) in *The Works of John Taylor, the Water Poet*, ed. Charles Hindley (London: Reeves and Turner, 1876), p. 1. In Jonson's *Every Man in His Humour*, Brainworm disguises himself as a soldier, down on his luck, getting his clothes from "a *Hounds-ditch* man, sir. One of the devil's

neere kinsmen, a broker" (in Herford [ed.], *Ben Jonson*, vol. III, 2.3 and 3.5.31–2). See also Samuel Rowlands' *Doctor Merry-man: or, Nothing but Mirth* (London, 1616), where a "professed Courtizan" mocks those who "goe to Houns-ditch with their Cloathes / To pawne for Money lending" (sig. C4); and Rowlands' "Satyre 2" in *The letting of humours blood* where he depicts a gentleman bowing to his "Liuing-griper":

> And farre to fetch the same I will not goe,
> But into *Hounds-ditch*, to the Brokers row:
> Or any place where that trade doth remaine,
> Whether at *Holborne Conduit*, or *Long-lane*:
> If thyther you vouchsafe to turne your eye,
> And see the Pawnes that vnder forfayte lye,
> Which are foorth comming sir, and safe enough
> Sayes good-man Broker, in his new print ruffe:
> He will not stand too strictly on a day,
> Encouraging the party to delay,
> With all good wordes, the kindest may be spoke,
> He turnes the Gentleman out of his Cloake.
>
> (sig. D2v)

65. See Stephen Greenblatt, *Renaissance Self-Fashioning: from More to Shakespeare* (Chicago: University of Chicago Press, 1980); *Learning to Curse: Essays in Early Modern Culture* (New York: Routledge, 1990), particularly pp. 161–83; *Shakespearean Negotiations: The Circulation of Social Energy in Renaissance England* (Berkeley: University of California Press, 1988).

66. Middleton, *Your Five Gallants*, [1.1] ll. 2–6; [4.1] ll. 1915–31; [4.2] ll. 1946–53; [2.3] ll. 1141–48 and 1176; [2.3] ll. 1200–13; [4.6] ll. 2569–73.

67. Middleton, *Your Five Gallants*, [1.2] ll. 366–7 and ll. 414–15; [2.1] l. 619 and 806; [2.3] ll. 1138–40; [3.5] l. 1749; [4.6] ll. 2290–91, 2319–20, 2341–48, 2412, 2432–37, and 2569–73; [5.2] ll. 2920–22.

68. Ben Jonson, *Every Man in His Humour* (acted 1598, 1616 text) in Herford (ed.), *Ben Jonson*, vol. III 3.5.31–32, 4.9.45–50.

69. Ben Jonson, *The Alchemist*, in Herford (ed.), *Ben Jonson*, vol. V, 4.3.63–73, 5.4.68, 5.4.84–88. I am indebted to Michael Warren for drawing this passage to my attention.

70. Thomas Dekker, *Satiromastix*, in *The Dramatic Works of Thomas Dekker*, ed. Fredson Bowers (Cambridge: Cambridge University Press, 1953), vol. I, 4.1.129–32.

71. Dekker, *Satiromastix*, 1.2.352–58.

72. Greg (ed.), *Henslowe Papers*, p. 125.

CHAPTER 8

Women's theatrical properties

Natasha Korda

Studies of the relationship between "the market and the theatre" in early modern England have largely ignored questions of gender: What roles did women play in the networks of commerce surrounding early modern theatrical production? How were the types of female labor associated with the theatre and its environs divided by social status? What gendered division of labor obtained within the families of theatre people? How many of the men involved in theatrical production had wives, mothers, daughters or servants who collaborated with them? Were there any widows or unmarried women working independently in or around the theatres? How did theatrical properties circulate among women? Were women involved in the production of stage-props and costumes? How did the relationship between the theatres and the guild-companies affect such production?[1]

That such questions have remained unexplored may be attributed to three factors: 1. the long undisturbed assumption among scholars that the early modern English stage was an entirely male preserve; 2. the difficulty of recovering historical evidence about the forms of female labor in the period (which may have contributed to the prior assumption); and 3. an overly abstract and ungrounded notion of "The Market" as "transcend[ing] not only exact definition, but indeed the physical loci of exchange."[2] Unanchored in the complex and heterogeneous forms of economic exchange that surrounded the theatres, and the diverse, material practices contributing to stage production, this overly abstract and monolithic view of "The Market" has likewise ignored the socially differentiated and gendered subjects who produced, circulated, and invested in theatrical properties.

Recent materialist feminist criticism of the early modern stage seems poised to take up this challenge. Rejecting on the one hand the reductive economism of traditional Marxist aesthetics, and on the other, the "radical re-prioritizing of ideology" that came to replace it,[3] such critics have turned their attention to the material culture and practices of the early modern theatre, arguing that dramatic representations cannot be understood in isolation from the material conditions in which they were produced and consumed.[4] Such scholarship has begun to topple the myth of the "all-male stage" by pointing to the many instances of aristocratic female patrons, playwrights, and performers during the period.[5] In focusing primarily on aristocratic women, however, such criticism has thus far paid little attention to the role of ordinary women in theatrical production, having considered the latter only in their status as playgoers or consumers of theatrical commodities.[6]

In what follows, I will attempt to redress this omission by considering ordinary women's involvement in the networks of commerce surrounding the early modern stage. More particularly, I will examine evidence regarding women's productive relations to, and proprietary interests in, theatrical properties. I intentionally construe the term "properties" broadly here to underscore the status of costumes, stage-props, and sets as forms of *property*, as valuable assets that could be readily converted back into cash. This inclusive definition of theatrical properties is crucial in detailing the many roles women played in the production and circulation of goods in and around the theatres.

A more complex picture of the diverse types of market activity in which the commercial theatres and professional playing companies were engaged may be found in recent work by Ingram, Bristol, Stallybrass, and Jones, who have highlighted the playing companies' peculiar status as transitional economic formations, in certain aspects retaining the residual structure of the guilds while at the same time assuming the emergent form of innovative capital ventures.[7] While many of those involved in the "early entertainment industry," in Bristol's terms, sought status and protection by gaining their freedom from the established guild companies, they were also "freelancing entrepreneurs in an underground economy," who took maximum advantage of the many forms of "de-racinated" and ad hoc economic activity thriving in early modern London.[8]

Clothing was one of the most important and valuable theatrical properties in the period, as Ann Rosalind Jones and Peter Stallybrass have demonstrated; it stood at the nexus of these overlapping institutions. The "commercial theater," they provocatively argue, was "simply a new and stunning development" of England's "cloth economy," an economy in which clothing was both an industrial base and a staple currency in its own right. Jones and Stallybrass offer a spectacular account of the theatre's imbrication within an economy defined by the material culture of cloth: a theatre company's greatest expense in the period was the purchase of costumes;[9] players were often paid in clothing instead of cash, gained their freedom from the clothing guilds, wore the livery of their noble patrons, owned stock in the company wardrobe, and when they died left such stock, and their privately owned costumes, to their families, fellows, and apprentices.[10] In addition, theatrical entrepreneurs like Philip Henslowe often acted as "suppliers and retailers of the [new and secondhand] clothes which the theater staged."[11] While Jones and Stallybrass argue that the theatre participated in "a massive capitalist development in the circulation of clothing,"[12] like Ingram and Bristol, they recognize that it was also a "new industry" in its own right, one which had an opportunistic relation to older economic structures "even as it clearly violated them."[13]

In what follows, I shall argue that the commercial theatres' status as innovative, capital ventures with residual ties to the guilds, in particular the clothing guilds, and their marginal status on the cusp of formal and informal market activities rendered them particularly open to women's economic participation. Women were by no means excluded from production regulated by the guilds, and were active in the clothing and textile trades; and those whose economic activity was hampered by the licensed guilds[14] often turned to London's "shadow" economy of unregulated crafts and trades, becoming secondhand clothing dealers, pawnbrokers, peddlers, hawkers, etc.[15] By bringing together documents of Elizabethan stage history with evidence concerning the many types of economic activity in which urban women were engaged, my hope is to contribute to our understanding of their productive relations to and rights in property more generally.

The most serious obstacle confronting this type of investigation is the problem of evidence. Our understanding of the history of women's work is certainly hampered by the legal and economic institutions of the period, such as the legal fiction of "coverture," according to which a married woman's legal status and right to own property were suspended during marriage. Yet our knowledge of women's work has also "frequently been overshadowed and its characteristics obscured," as Beverly Lemire has argued, by our own prejudices, particularly when these characteristics deviated "from the standard male paradigms of employment."[16] Women, she observes, "found work where they could, flourishing in ad hoc businesses"; and while such "irregular household-based trade" was disapproved of by the guilds, "historical evaluation should not end with the guildsman's assessment." For these " 'disorderly' commercial practices were as common as they were reviled," and formed a "vast network of commerce, which must be integrated into our concepts of the market."[17]

It has long been assumed that the purportedly "all-male stage" grew out of the all-male guilds upon which the professional theatre companies were ostensibly modeled. This assumption is based on a number of fallacies that have been identified and methodically dismantled by Stephen Orgel. "Even where the stage was a male preserve," he argues, "the theater was not." The theatre, he contends, "was a place of unusual freedom for women in the period," insofar as women made up a large proportion of the audiences. This "meant that the success of any play," and therefore of the theatrical representations themselves, depended "to a significant degree on the receptiveness of women."[18] I would like to further extend Orgel's qualification, and suggest in what follows that if we take into account the full range of social and economic interdependencies and collaborations that went into stage production, the stage itself should not be conceived as an entirely male preserve but as a network of commerce between active (and not merely "receptive") economic agents of both genders. Orgel further suggests that the notion of the playing companies as "modeled" on the guilds is fallacious insofar as their imaginary relationship to the guilds was far more agonistic than straightforwardly mimetic. "If the adult playing companies were modeling themselves on the guilds," he maintains,

...the relationship between the two was always an uneasy one. The persistent complaint of London commercial interests that theatres are subversive, that the existence of theatres interferes with business, particularly that theatre seduces apprentices away from their craft, must have included a sense that the theatrical companies were in effect operating as unlicensed guilds, and even as antiguilds.[19]

I would like to add that the theatres were not alone in their marginal status as pseudo- or anti-guilds: they were entangled in an immense web of unlicensed commercial activity in London, many of whose strands, I hope to show, were taken up and woven into innovative enterprises by women. It is thus crucial that we attend not only to the theatre's metaphorical similitude to the guilds, but also to its quite material or metonymic ties to such commercial enterprises. Finally, Orgel challenges a fallacy of historical fact: even if we grant that the theatres were to some degree modeled on the guilds, he asserts, this in itself would only weaken, rather than strengthen, the myth of the theatre as an exclusively male preserve, since recent historical evidence suggests a much higher degree of involvement by women in the licensed guilds than was previously imagined.

Orgel here relies on the work of historian K. D. M. Snell, who has studied female apprenticeship as evidenced by parish registers in southeast England in his *Annals of the Laboring Poor*.[20] Snell's work is particularly important to our understanding of women at the lowest levels of society, since those listed in parish registers were charity, rather than paid, apprenticeships. His findings are quite stunning: as many as 41.2 percent of the apprentices listed in parish registers for the seventeenth century, in eighteen different occupations, are female.[21] The Poor Child Register of Southampton for the seventeenth century lists 22.9 percent of all apprentices as female, in such occupations as tailors, glovers, weavers, woolcombers, cordwainers, feltmakers, clothiers, cloth workers, cobblers, button makers, and sempstresses in the clothing trades, but also including joiners, barbers, musicians, basket makers, carpenters, chapwomen, and farriers.[22] It should come as no surprise that women were involved in such physically demanding occupations: early in this century, Alice Clark's groundbreaking *Working Life of Women in the Seventeenth Century* and Ivy Pinchbeck's *Women Workers and the Industrial Revolution* documented early modern women working as armorers, braziers, boot- and shoe-makers, goldsmiths, pewterers, upholsterers, gilders, furniture makers, and in virtually all of the retail and provision trades.[23] The levels of female apprenticeship studied by Snell among those whose families were able to afford payment of a premium were lower (at under 10 percent), though still by no means entirely negligible, and were concentrated in the needle and textile trades.[24]

Snell also refutes the claim of his predecessors that female apprentices were ordinarily "taught and employed in 'housewifery' (skilled though that could be) rather than to learn a craft," an assumption that "anachronistically applies Victorian middle- and upper-class assumptions on the roles of women to an earlier lower-class environment featuring very different female work."[25] He argues that housewifery was listed as such in apprenticeship registers when this was its intended aim, and that in such instances the premiums given were much lower (£1–2 as compared with £7–14 for other trades).[26] When wives' names are indicated along with their husbands in apprenticeship indentures, he maintains, this indicates not that the skill to be learned was housewifery, but rather that both husband and wife practiced the trade, and either both or (less commonly) the wife alone would instruct the apprentice. A Custom of London during the period would appear to support the latter claim; it states:

"Married women who practise certain crafts in the city alone and without their husbands, may take girls as apprentices to serve them and learn
their trade, and these apprentices shall be bound by their indentures of
apprenticeship to both husband and wife, to learn the wife's trade as
is aforesaid, and such indentures shall be enrolled as well for women
as for men."[27] Trades in which, according to Snell, there is firm evidence of mistresses taking apprentices themselves include: blacksmith,
carpenter, tin-plate worker, founder, mason, cooper, shipwright, vintner,
glazier, tallow-chandler, barber, butcher, soap maker, apothecary, miller,
gloveress, mercer, cordwainer, and all the textile and clothing trades.[28]

More work needs to be done on female apprenticeship records in
London, as evidence gathered hitherto is conflicting.[29] At the very least,
Snell's revisionist scholarship on female apprenticeship in southeast
England suggests that whether we view the theatre's relation to the
guilds metaphorically (as a mimetic rivalry) or metonymically (through
the networks of commerce that materially linked them), this relation
was probably not *entirely* exclusive of women.[30] This assertion is further
strengthened when we recall that female apprenticeship figures represent only a fraction of actual levels of female employment in crafts and
trades, since the majority of women working in guilds are likely to have
gained entrance not through formal apprenticeship, but through patrimony or marriage.[31] The labor-power of wives and daughters was indispensable to the guild family economy, being both unremunerated and
evading many of the restrictions to which journeymen and apprentices
were subject.[32] Women who worked within this largely unrecorded, yet
crucial, shadow economy thereby gained valuable "properties of skill"
which, in the case of daughters as in that of female apprentices, could
serve as a form of dowry, and in the case of widows, as a form of dower.
Masters' daughters who married journeymen within their craft at once
conferred privileges on their spouses (lowering the entrance fee journeymen had to pay and shortening the length of time necessary to gain their
freedom), and were themselves permitted to continue working within the
craft.[33] Masters' wives are known to have worked actively alongside their
husbands, either in manual labor or taking charge of the financial end
of the business, receiving payments, acting as buyers, etc.[34] Accustomed
to running the shop in their husbands' absence, these women inherited
the tools, stock and apprentices of the business in their widowhood.[35]
While masters' widows were highly sought-after commodities on the
marriage market (many married men much younger than themselves
in the same or allied crafts), some continued to work as independent

craftswomen, and others deployed their inherited capital and financial acumen as rentiers, mortgage brokers, money lenders, and general "facilitators of urban credit."[36]

Having briefly surveyed the general landscape of women's work in guild-regulated crafts and trades, I would like to turn now to evidence regarding how such work may have intersected with the networks of commerce surrounding theatrical production. My observations in what follows are not intended to be exhaustive, but merely to provide some suggestive examples of ordinary women working in and around the theatres, and to offer a preliminary sketch of possible paths for future research regarding women's productive relations to, and proprietary interests in, theatrical properties. Given the female apprenticeship figures cited above, perhaps we should begin by asking: Were girls ever apprenticed to or by the families of theatre people, or more particularly, to married or single women working in and around the theatres? Given the theatre's dependence on the clothing and textile trades, it seems likely that this would have been an attractive option for theatre families who wished to apprentice their daughters. We know that many theatre people were themselves members of the clothing guilds; their wives and children would have gained the right to work in these guilds through marriage or patrimony, rather than through formal apprenticeship.[37] The wives and widows of such men would have had the right to take on apprentices themselves.

A fascinating example of female apprenticeship within a theatre family occurs in the "diary" or account book of Philip Henslowe, who was himself a member of the Dyers' Company. Having assumed responsibility for the upbringing of the orphaned children of his brother, Edmund, Henslowe brought them to London in February 1595 and several months later apprenticed his nephew, John, to a dyer named Newman for forty shillings. At the same time, he apprenticed his niece, Mary, to John Griggs for seven years for the sum of £5, "to Learne to sowe al maner of workes & to Lerne bonelace."[38] Precisely from whom Mary was to learn these skills, however, is not entirely clear. It seems unlikely that it would have been from Griggs himself, who is listed in the deed of partnership between Henslowe and Cholmley for the building of the Rose Theatre as the carpenter responsible for erecting "the saide playhouse wth all furniture therunto belonginge."[39] It may be that Mary was to learn sewing and lacemaking from Griggs's wife. The couple were close friends of both the Henslowes and Alleyns (Griggs was also involved in building the Alleyns' house).[40] The wives of guildsmen often worked and took apprentices in crafts and trades other than those practiced by their husbands; a Borough Custom of the City of London allowed such women, who were known as "feme sole" traders, to conduct business as if they were single women. Of twenty-one girls apprenticed to the Carpenters' Company between 1654 and 1670, according to Alice Clark, nine were apprenticed to Richard Hill and his wife "to learn the trade of a sempstress." Rebecca Perry was apprenticed to William Addington "to learne the Art of a Sempstress of his wife," and another girl "to Anne Joyse sempstress & sole merchant without Thomas Joyse her husband." Clark also cites several examples of girls apprenticed to the wives of carpenters to learn the trade of millinery.[41] In general, there was a great deal of fluidity in the crafts practiced by guildsmen and their wives; Griggs himself, although practicing the craft of carpentry, describes himself in a loan agreement with Henslowe as "John griggs cyttezin and Butcher of London."[42] This fluidity was crucial in the rise of the public theatres and professional playing companies in London, allowing traditional artisans the flexibility to adapt their "properties of skill" to new commercial enterprises. This may be precisely what Henslowe had in mind in apprenticing his niece: given the exorbitant sums of money laid out in the account book for making up new and adapting old costumes, and for the purchase of lace (mostly copper, but sometimes gold and silver) to adorn them, Mary's skill as a sempstress and lacemaker would have been a valuable commodity in Henslowe's new theatrical ventures.

In what capacity and to what degree were the wives of theatre people involved in the business? Did their involvement reflect the apparently high degree of collaboration of wives in guild-family crafts and trades? Did it extend to the manufacture and circulation of theatrical properties (theatres, costumes, props, etc.) or was it concentrated in the purely financial end of the business? Did women (whether single, married or widowed) ever work independently in the networks of commerce surrounding and permeating the theatres? Evidence regarding women's involvement in theatrical affairs is scarce but by no means nonexistent; what evidence we do have has often been ignored, or its significance diminished, by the prejudices of stage historians.

Thus, for example, Margaret Brayne's contribution to theatre history has been limited to her financial dealings and litigation with James Burbage, following the death of her husband (and Burbage's partner), John Brayne. As Skiles Howard has argued, according to the records of this litigation (in which Margaret was attempting to recover her widow's share of the profits of the Theatre from Burbage), Burbage rhetorically casts Margaret as a scold or shrew, a depiction that has stuck to her like glue in subsequent criticism.[43] Moreover, in focussing solely on Margaret's financial dealings with Burbage, Howard notes, stage historians have ignored the significance of her collaboration with Brayne in the building of the Theatre. For, according to Robert Miles's testimony in the litigation with Burbage, John Brayne, who was the primary investor in the project, although a financially successful grocer, was soon overwhelmed by the building expenses, and forced to sell his house and stock, and give up his trade as a grocer, pawn his own clothes and Margaret's, and "to run in debt to many for the money to furnishe the said Playe house / & so to employe himselfe onlye uppon that matter / ... / to his utter undoing / for ... in the latter end of the fynishing therof / the said Braynes and his Wyfe ... were dryven to labor in the said workes / for saving some of the charge / in place of ii laborers."[44] While the once wealthy Brayne and his wife were clearly driven to this arrangement by the extremity of the situation, the testimony suggests a pattern of collaboration between husband and wife that may have carried over from the Braynes' years as grocers. Nor was it unheard of for women to work as carpenters or joiners in the period.[45] The Braynes, like the Griggs, are good examples of the kind of flexibility and improvisation required of crafts- and tradesmen and women to launch these new theatrical enterprises.

Evidence about women's involvement in the production of stage properties, costumes and other accessories, may be found in the account books kept by the Office of Revels during the reigns of Edward VI, Mary and Elizabeth.[46] While these accounts concern the production of masques and other revels at court, which were far more lavish and expensive than performances in the public theatres, the evidence they afford may be pertinent to the public stage as well, insofar as there is clear evidence that these costumes and props were often handed down to the professional players as payment for court performances when they were no longer deemed "serviceable" for the latter, and as there is also clear evidence that the Yeoman who worked in the Office was in the habit of renting them out to players and others to make money on the sly. There is no way of telling precisely how many female artisans worked in and around the Office, since many of the entries of payments to craftspersons do not indicate gender.[47] Those that do indicate that the artisans in question were women thus probably represent only a portion of the actual number employed by the Office. In addition, the participation of craftsmen's wives in work done for the Revels Office is almost entirely hidden to view; yet the accounts do on occasion make clear that such participation did occur. During the reign of Elizabeth, for example, the accounts include the following payment to a property-maker:

The Propertymaker To John Carow in his lyfe tyme not long before his death – vi^{li} And to his wyfe after his deathe in full satisfaction for all the wares by him delyvered this yeare into the said office or is to be by him the saide Carow his executors or admynistrators demawnded for any dett due before the third of ffebruary 1574[/5] or not entred in this booke – vi^{li} xiiii^{s} iiii^{d} as which grew by propertyes videlicet Monsters, Mountaynes, fforrestes, Beastes, Serpentes, Weapons for warr as gunnes, dagges, bowes, Arowes, Bills, holberdes, borespeares, fawchions daggers, Targettes, pollaxes, clubbes headdes & headpeeces Armor counterfet Mosse, holly, Ivye, Bayes, flowers quarters, glew past, paper, and suche lyke with Nayles hoopes horstailes dishes for devells eyes heaven, hell, & the devell & all the devell I should saie but not all xii^{li} xiiii^{s} iiii^{d}.[48]

Carow is listed as "propertymaker" (and sometimes as "Karver" or "Joyner," which may have been the crafts in which he was licensed) to the Revels Office over a period of twenty-five years, beginning in 1550 during Edward's reign. In addition to the rather impressive array of properties fabricated by his shop as listed above, he fashioned such elaborate contrivances as "hedpeces...mowlded lyke Lyons heddes the Mowthe devowringe the mannes hed helmetwise...Counterfett Apes of paste and Cemente mowlded to sytt upon bagpypes lyke minstrells," and other headpieces "doble vizaged thone syde lyke a man and thother like deathe."[49] It appears that he ran a thriving business, given his longevity in the account books and the large sums paid to him; at times he appears to have fabricated the props in his own shop and delivered them to the Office, in which case he was paid "by greate" or by the piece. At other times he did the work at the Revels Office or at Court as needed and was paid by the day. On one such occasion he brought five employees to the Office to work with him.[50]

What was Carow's wife's involvement in his business affairs? Did it extend no further than the collection of his debts, and possibly the execution of his will, after his death? Men who appointed their wives executors of their estates (a not uncommon practice) often did so because their wives had been actively involved in their business and financial affairs while they were alive. Such was the case with Christopher Beeston, the actor and theatre manager, who appoints his wife "full and sole executrix" of his estate "by reason I doe owe many greate debtes, and am engaged for greate sommes of money, which noe one but my wife understandes, where or how to receave pay or take in."[51] It is impossible to say whether

Carow's wife had the same degree of involvement in his business affairs during his lifetime (collecting debts, receiving payments, overseeing the delivery of merchandise, etc.), whether she worked in his shop with his other employees, as was often the case with craftsmen's wives, or whether she may have carried on running his shop after his death. There are no subsequent records of payments to Carow's wife, although there are payments for "propertye makers parcelles" for which no name is given. We do know that it was not unheard of for the Revels Office to deal financially with tradesmen's wives in the procurement of stage properties, however, as it lists a payment to "Brydgett the Bagpypers wyfe for one pere of lowde pypes... and for one pere of softe pypes... of her bowghte and provided."[52]

Other examples of women involved in the production of stage-props include confectioners who worked on the elaborate, moulded, "banquetting stuffs," also called "voids" or "empty dishes," which were ceremonially displayed and then destroyed at masques and banquets.[53] The Revels accounts list a payment to "Thomas Blagrave esquier for more mony by him payde for Mowldes to cast the frutes & ffishes in / & to the weemen that tempred the stuf & made up the same."[54] The previous entry makes it clear that the props in question were banqueting stuffs: "Banketting frutes necessaryes... Thomas Blagrave esquier for mony by him disbursed in Reward... ffor suger for Marchepane stuf... Gowlde leaves to gilde the Marchepane stuf... Dishes of suger... ffrutes counterfete bowghte of Brayne thappoticary."[55] The women confectioners in question may thus have worked for Brayne, or been hired separately by Blagrave, the Clerk of the Revels. Women had at least indirect involvement in the production of larger stage properties as well: such properties were often made out of canvas, and one of the primary suppliers of canvas to the Revels Office was a linen draper named Mistress Dane. One entry of payment to her reads: "The Lynnen draper Mistris Dane for Canvas to paynte for howses for the players & for other properties as Monsters, greate hollow trees & suche other."[56]

Because women worked in great numbers in the textile and clothing trades, they were particularly actively involved in the manufacture and retail of costumes, props made out of fabric, and other fashion accessories. There are many instances in the Revels Office accounts and in Henslowe's "diary" of women involved in millinery, in the manufacture of both head attire and perukes.[57] On several occasions, foreign women were hired to accompany boy actors to such destinations as Hampton Court and serve as head- and hairdressers. Thus, in 1573/4 the accounts list "An Italian Woman &c. to dresse theier heades."[58] The "&c." may refer to the Italian woman's servants or assistants, since the next record makes clear that she was not working alone: "Expences at Kingston on Munday Nighte...Lodging, ffyer, & vittells for the children & Women [tha]t wayted tattyer them with other [tha]t were appointed to stay till the Mask were showen and for their dynners the next daye."[59] The record for the following day ambiguously refers to expenses "for the childrens suppers & the Womens suppers with the Rest of their attendantes." Were these attendants also women under the charge of the Italian woman? We do know the identity of at least one of the women who accompanied her, since a later record refers to her daughter: "Rewardes & hier of womens heares for the Children...To the Italian women & her dawghter for Lending the Heares &c. & for their service & attendaunces – xxxiii[s] iiii[d]."[60] These records provide a fascinating example of a woman working independently in theatrical production, possibly with hired employees, and certainly with a daughter whom she had trained in her trade. This trade included not only the provision of perukes and head attire for the children but service as their theatrical dresser. The records likewise paint a picture of women working intimately with boy actors, dispelling the assumption that theirs was an entirely homosocial world.[61]

This kind of arrangement was not unique, for the accounts list a similar example of a mother-and-daughter team of hairdressers from France: "The Hyer of Heares for headdes and Rewardes To the french woman for her paynes and her Dawghters paynes that went to Richemond & there attended upon Mr hunnyes his Children & dressed their heades &c. when they played before her Magestye."[62] There is also a husband-and-wife team of head-attirers listed in the Revels Office accounts, a "John Bettes & his wife" who worked "for one daye & one nighte spangling...hedpeeces."[63] Another woman involved in work related to millinery hired by the Revels Office was "Alys perkyns," who was paid for "turnynge of iii headblockes to fasshion and Trymme hattes uppon."[64] It appears that, as in the case of Bettes's wife, such women sometimes worked in the Office and were paid by the day, and sometimes out of their own homes or workshops, in which case they were paid by the piece. The latter was the case with a "Mistris Swegoo," who was paid "to garnishe ix heades and ix skarfes for the. ix. Muzes owte the office. videlicet Spanish silke of sundry cullers," for "Heades of Heare drest and trymmed," and "Boxes to put the heades and skarfes in."[65]

Silk was the preferred fabric for headpieces, perukes and other fashion accessories for court masques, and was provided to the Revels Office

almost exclusively by women. There are numerous instances in the
accounts of "silkwomen," who provided a diverse range of products
(buttons, fringe, tassels, lace, etc.) and fabrics (silk, sarcenet, taffeta, velvet, lawn, etc.) for the production of head attire, adornment of costumes
and fabrication of small props. Some typical entries read as follows:

Sylke for here of weemens heddes byllymente lace frenge buttons tarsells and
other parcells bowghte of the Sylkewemen as by her bills aperethe...[66]

Silkwooman for Buttons and flowers for Maskers heddes vii & one silk tree for
A device in one of the Candlelstickes & a box to put them in...[67]

Maskes iiii[or] one of Argus & ii[or] of women wherof one of moores wth black
scalloppes upon tynsell & thother of Ammazons women of warre...for [th]e
making and garnishing whereof was...bowght and provyded of the Silkwomen
ffrenge buttons & tarsells of redd sylke Sylver & golde of dyverse Sortes for
garnishinge...[68]

The "dyverse Sortes" of garnishings in which these silkwomen specialized (referred to by one historian as "trappings" and "lesser silk" wares)
were by no means trivial to the Revels Office, for they were crucial in
the process of "translating" or renovating old costumes to make them
appear new. This process was one of the Revels Office's primary pre-
occupations, since costumes were only supposed to be worn once for
performances at Court. The cost of making up each and every garment
new from scratch would have been prohibitive, however, so the Revels
Office chose instead to take apart older garments and remake them in
a new form, or simply to "garnish" older costumes to give them a new
veneer. Two entries in the Revels Office accounts for 1564 makes the
importance of the silkwomen in this process clear:

1564 The ixth of June Translattinge new makinge of thre masks and other
devisses Agaynst the french Embassitours cominge to Richmond wages or dieats
of the officers and Tayllors payntars workinge uppon the Castle and other
devisses & mercers ffor Sarsnett and other stuf and Lynen drappars ffor canvas
to cover yt with all and Silkwemen for ffrenge & tassals to garnesh the old
garments to make them seme fresh Agayne...

1564 Shroftid ffollowinge wages or dieats of the officers and Tayllors paynters
working uppon the Townes and charretts ffor the goodesses & divers devisses
as the hevens & clowds and foure masks...with thare hole furniture which be
verie fayr and Riche of old stuf butt new garnished with frenge and tassells to
seme new...Silkwomen for ffrenge and tasselles...[69]

Indeed, the very distinction between which materials are "greater" and
which "lesser," or those which are deemed essential and those which

are considered mere "trappings," seems alien to the milieu of the court masque, which was, in its essence, about the staging of social ornament. Within the context of cultural performances centered around the conspicuous consumption of superfluous wealth, "ffrenge and tasselles" were hardly a mere distraction or sideshow; they were arguably the main event.

Moreover, as mentioned above, the London silkwomen not only provided such instruments of ornamentation as fringe, tassels, lace, buttons, and silk flowers to the Revels Office, they also sold an array of fine fabrics. Such was the case with "The silkwoman Ales Mowntague," who provided the Office with "Lawne of fine white Netwoorke,"[70] or the "sylkwoman Mistris Wyett," who vended "carnacion and sylver Lawne."[71] The term "silkwoman," according to Marion K. Dale, was used in the period to describe women "who were in any way interested in the production or sale of the commodity," and whose stock-in-trade covered a "whole range of goods, from colored silks or gold and silver thread sold by the ounce, to the more elaborate decorative articles or ribbons and similar woven silks," to "articles of clothing" which "came sometimes from their own workshops."[72] The silk industry, according to Dale, was one in which women worked very actively: they had a virtual monopoly beginning in the fourteenth century and extending at least to the sixteenth, she maintains, on "selling the lesser [sic] silk articles," and probably "were also mainly responsible for the manufacture of these goods."[73] Moreover, they often traded in large quantities of goods: Jane Langton, for example, who is described as a silkwoman in her will of 1475, was "involved in transactions with two merchants of Genoa, in which she agreed to become bound for payment for silk goods to the value of £300 15s." Her daughter-in-law, Elizabeth, also worked in the trade, and is known to have supplied "quantities of silk and other goods amounting to £101 17s. $\frac{1}{4}$d. for members of the royal family" in 1503.[74] Although the London silkwomen were "not recognized as a definite guild," Dale demonstrates that in many respects they modeled their industry along "the lines of the craft guilds of male workers":[75] the silkwomen were sufficiently organized to present petitions to Parliament resulting in acts passed to protect their work from foreign competition,[76] they took on apprentices and employed workers,[77] and they practiced their craft independently supplying the market either as wage earners, or in the case of many wealthier women of the "middling sort," as sole merchants.[78]

Thus far I have dealt mainly with women's involvement in regulated or semi-regulated crafts, and its impact on the production of stage-props, costumes, and scenery for masques and other court entertainments staged by the Revels Office. I would now like to turn my attention to their involvement in other forms of economic activity such as retailing, and in the many unregulated forms of commerce which played such an important role in the staging of plays in the public theatres. Craft and trade cannot easily be separated in many of the above examples of women's work in and around the theatre; as is clear from the example of the silk craft/trade, women often worked both on the production and the retailing ends of a particular industry. Scholars have long suggested that women played an active role in retailing across a wide range of social strata, from merchants to shopkeepers to women who kept stalls at markets to itinerant peddlers, hawkers, petty chapwomen, badgers, regraters, etc.[79] There are numerous examples in the Revels Office accounts (some of them cited above), of women selling cloth, clothing and other accessories, such as Mistress Dane, the linen draper, Ann Mallerye and Alice Montague, the silkwomen, and several widows who worked as mercers ("Mersers...knowles wyddo for xlviiiti yardes di. of Changable taffita"; "Julian hickes wydowe for iii yardes iii quarters di. redd sarsenet...white and black sarsenet...white taffita...black vellvat").[80] As mentioned above, such women represent only a portion of those who actually sold goods to the Office, since many of the entries for retailers (including mercers, haberdashers of small wares, and other trades in which women were actively involved) offer no indication as to gender.

To gain a more complete picture of women's involvement in stage production for the pubic theatres, we will need to turn to a different sector of the market. For the professional playing companies and the entrepreneurs who backed them could ill afford the kind of lavish expenditure on new costumes and properties exhibited by the Revels Office accounts. As mentioned above, these sumptuous garments often found their way to the public stage as hand-me-downs, as the players were often paid for their court performances in costumes instead of cash. We also know from a complaint lodged by a haberdasher named Thomas Giles that the Yeoman of the Revels Office participated in London's thriving, shadow economy in secondhand clothes by renting out costumes in the Office wardrobe to players and citizens in need of masking attire.

This shadowy world of used clothing and other goods, according to Beverly Lemire, was populated by "many of the same retail players as in the new: tailors, shopkeepers, salesmen and saleswomen, menders and makers of clothes," who were joined by "legions of petty and professional thieves, receivers, pawnbrokers and all classes of sellers and recyclers."[81]

Thanks to Lemire's work on the secondhand clothing trade, Margaret Spufford's on the itinerant vendors who served as "mercers for the poor," selling textile wares and related items (coifs, stockings, cravats, capes, scarves, stomachers, ribbons, lace, sewing silks, threads, etc.) in networks of commerce that extended across England,[82] and Garthine Walker's on the way these networks intersected with "the world of stolen goods," we now know what a vital role women played in every aspect of these illicit forms of trade.

The high levels of female participation in these unregulated industries in the sixteenth and seventeenth centuries are generally attributed to increasing restrictions placed on female labor in the licensed guilds. In the case of the clothing guilds, Merry Weisner notes, limitations imposed on female sempstresses, bleachers and dyers applied only to their work on new cloth and clothing; articles of clothing that were already used and were being remade were not (at least initially) covered by these restrictions.[83] In the face of such restrictions on their work by the guilds, according to Lemire, women "frequently depended on a judicious cobbling together of opportunities, taking advantage of the commercial niches in the urban landscape."[84] One of the niches which presented a host of opportunities for such women in London's urban landscape, I would like to argue, was the commercial theatres, which themselves depended heavily on the shadow industries in secondhand goods that were so dominated by women.

Wealthy widows frequently turned to pawnbroking in the period as a "business, open to, and fit for, single women with cash in hand to use for stock in trade."[85] Yet the trade was also carried out on a more informal level as well by the wives of landlords, inn- and tavern-keepers, and theatre people.[86] William Ingram cites the case of William Downell, one of the eight original members of the Queen's Company, who with his wife had taken up lodging with his fellow player, John Singer and his wife, Alice. Downell brought a complaint against the Singers in the Court of Requests, claiming that Alice Singer had taken several pounds out of a chest in which he had stored the £200 dowry he had just received from his wife's family. Alice maintained that "shee had leant" the money "to a Neighbour of hers upon a good quantitye of plate pawned and engaged for that money," and assured him that "the daye followinge or not above two or three dayes at the most he should have it againe."[87] Insofar as Alice needed to "borrow," if not steal, money from her tenant in order to subsidize her pawnbroking activities, hers was most probably a small-scale, ad hoc operation.

This kind of illicit brokering of secondhand, and sometimes stolen, goods between women, according to Garthine Walker, was quite common in the period. Walker persuasively argues that we should therefore not separate analyses of early modern women's work and economic status from a consideration of the forms of female criminality in the period. Indeed, she argues, insofar as women were often excluded from "skilled, paid work defended by urban guilds," and "their appearance in records was usually as transgressors of the guild and borough regulations which sustained the male monopoly...our definition of 'criminality' must surely be redefined...to include female participation in the various economic and social networks of exchange and interaction which provided the backdrop to prosecutions for property crime."[88] Viewed from this perspective, the many forms of unregulated female labor, ranging from the licit to the illicit, should be placed on a continuum. The fact that women were far more likely than men to steal cloth, clothing, and household goods (including linen, plate and other utensils), may thus be attributed to the very same expertise in assessing the value of such objects in the marketplace that made them such adept appraisers and pawnbrokers as well.[89]

There is no doubt that theatre people, whether wittingly or unwittingly, participated in the circulation of stolen, as well as used, costumes and props. Thus, in 1614, Henry Udall, a linen-draper in Drury Lane, accused John Shank, then a member of the Prince Henry's–Palsgrave's company, of "buying four network bands and a pair of cuffs at the Playhouse at an under-rate, being part of the goods which were stolen from the said Henry."[90] Theatre people were not only receivers of stolen attire, but were sometimes accused of stealing costumes themselves. In 1619, Christopher Beeston was charged by his fellows in Queen Anne's company with stealing or "carriing awaie" all of the company's "furniture & apparell" after it disbanded several years earlier.[91] It is worth recalling in this context that Beeston's wife, Elizabeth Hutchinson, was intimately involved in his theatrical affairs including his procurement of costumes. As mentioned above, Beeston appointed her executrix of his estate because he believed no one but she understood his financial affairs; his will also directs "that my said executrix shall...provide and finde for the said Companie [the King's and Queen's Young company], a sufficyent and good stock of apparell fitting for their use."[92] It seems unlikely that Beeston would have entrusted his wife with this task, if she had had no prior experience in the procurement of costumes for the stage.

Further evidence that women, including the wives of theatre people, were involved in pawnbroking and the circulation of secondhand costumes and props in and around the commercial theatres may be found in Henslowe's "diary." Some thirty pages of the manuscript of the "diary" are devoted to records of a pawnbroking business Henslowe appears to have managed from 1593 to 1596.[93] These accounts have long been ignored by stage historians, who have deemed them "of no conceivable interest to anyone."[94] Indeed, Sir Walter Greg found them so immaterial to Henslowe's theatrical affairs that he simply excised them from his otherwise complete and highly influential edition of the "diary" in 1904.[95] The segregation of Henslowe's pawnbroking accounts from his theatrical accounts has had the effect of occluding not only the connections between these two networks of commerce, but also the quite significant role that women played within and between them.

The great majority of customers listed in the pawn accounts were women: of the 312 loans in which the debtor's identity is known, 244 or 78 percent were made to women and 68 or 22 percent to men.[96] It appears from those entries in which the debtor's occupation is given that many of these women were tradesmen's wives who pawned mainly cloth and articles of clothing. Thus, for example, a "chapmanes wiffe" pawns "A stamell peticote wth iii laces" for 10s., a "taylers wife" pawns a "bufen gowne" for 15s., and a "buchers wiffe" pawns "A bufen gown wth A cape of vellvet & A petticotte of brode cloth wth iii laces" for 20s., which the accounts tell us was left unredeemed in the storage "Rome."[97] There were also market women or "regraters," such as "the womone wch selles earbes in the market," who pawns "A Remnant of brode clothe" for 12s., and "the womon wch sealles Reasones," who pawns "A kearttell of buffen" for 12s. Even lower down the social strata is the "poor womon dwellinge in theveng lane" (a poor street in Westminster by which thieves were conveyed to the Gatehouse prison and which "was chiefly occupied by dealers in second-hand goods");[98] she pawns "A Reamnant of Brod cloth" (stolen, perhaps?) for 10s.

These accounts provide a fascinating glimpse into the day-to-day economic activities of tradeswomen and market women in and around the theatre, and help to remind us that the webs of commerce in which the theatres were intertwined were hardly "all-male preserves." Many of the peddlers, hawkers, regraters, and dealers in secondhand clothing on the Bankside were women who turned to pawnbroking, either as a means of informal, urban credit or as a way to make a living. For the high incidence of women in Henslowe's pawn accounts may be attributed not only to the needs of market women to find ready cash, or of housewives to balance the household economy; for some of these women appear to have had a financial interest in the pawnbroking business as well.

For example, a "goody Watson" is listed fifty-three times in the accounts, often pledging more than one, and sometimes up to four items in a single day. In the four-month period between September 1594 and January 1595, she is listed forty-six times – or once every two and a half days, on average. It thus seems quite likely that goody Watson was herself an independent broker, who was either hired by Henslowe as an agent, or as a partner in his business. She is also listed as selling clothes for Henslowe in the secondhand clothing market, which may indicate she had expertise in this area.[99] Scholars have pointed to three such women who may have collaborated with Henslowe in his pawnbroking business: in addition to goody Watson, there was an "anne nockes" who appears often in the acounts from 9 December 1593 to 9 December 1594 (perhaps under an agreement to work for one year?), and a "mrs grante" who reckons accounts for him from January through May of 1594.

There are other instances in the accounts of women who may have turned to pawnbroking on a more ad hoc basis, such as "goody harison," who is listed five times in a single day, on 16 September 1594, pawning a diverse range of goods ("chyldbedlynen," "a bybell," "x peces of lynen tyde in & apkine [napkin]," "ii corse smockes," "a womons gowne of Blacke clothe playe wth a cape of vellvet," "a cuberd cloth of turckey worke," "vii peces of calecow," and "a womones gowne offfrenshe Rossett playne wth a cape of vellvet & lyned wth ashcoler bayes") for over 87 s.[100] There is also a "mrs Rysse a tayllers wiffe," who appears to have been in the practice of pawning remnants of cloth and other clothing from her husband's business: she pawns "A lynynge for a clocke of branched vellvet & a changable tafitie fore pte & a petticote of scarlete garded wth vellvet & a pece of weved worcke" for £5, and "a manes gowne unmade up," a "payer of fyne sheates," and a "cuberdcloth," "face cloth" and "beringe clothe" for £3. Mrs. Rysse, the ad hoc pawnbroker, and her husband, the guild-licensed tailor, provide an excellent example of the division between regulated male labor and unregulated female labor in the clothing trade in the period. There is evidence as well that Henslowe's wife, Agnes, may have been actively involved in his pawnbroking and money lending, as she is listed several times in the "diary" lending money to actors (as well as friends, family, and other employees); an entry for the 13 March 1601/2, for example, reads: "Lent unto Thomas towne by my wiffe...upon a payer of sylcke stockens tenneshellens."[101]

These are only some of the ways in which ordinary women worked productively in and around the early modern stage. There are many potentially fertile avenues of research which I have not even touched on (such as women's work as performers in the provinces,[102] or their work in the printing and book trades).[103] My focus here has been on women's productive labor on, investment in, and exchange of, theatrical properties, broadly construed. Nevertheless, this preliminary research strongly suggests that we need to rethink our assumptions about the "all-male stage," as well as our conceptualization of relations between "the market and the theater," in ways that will allow us to account for the full range of female participation in theatrical production. To accomplish this reconceptualization, it is crucial that we attend not only to the theatre's metaphorical similitude to the guilds, but to its quite material, metonymic ties to an entire matrix of unlicensed commercial activities in which working women in early modern London played such a vital role.

NOTES

1. These are only a few of the questions formulated by participants in a seminar on "Women and early modern theatrical production" I directed at the 1998 annual meeting of the Shakespeare Association of America. I am very grateful to the members of this seminar for the valuable new research they produced (some of which I discuss here) and for helping me to focus my thoughts on the material that follows. I would also like to thank the SAA for recognizing the importance of this subject.

2. See Jean-Christophe Agnew, *Worlds Apart: The Market and the Theater in Anglo-American Thought, 1550–1750* (Cambridge: Cambridge University Press, 1986) and Douglas Bruster, *Drama and the Market in the Age of Shakespeare* (Cambridge: Cambridge University Press, 1992), p. 15. See also Michael Bristol's critique of the "placeless" market in *Big-Time Shakespeare* (New York and London: Routledge, 1996), pp. 32–3.

3. In her introduction to *The Matter of Difference: Materialist Feminist Criticism of Shakespeare* (Ithaca: Cornell University Press, 1991), p. 8, Valerie Wayne thus explains the predominantly ideological focus of the essays in the volume, citing Michèle Barrett's *Women's Oppression Today: Problems in Marxist Feminist Analysis* (London: Verso, 1980), pp. 30–1.

4. It is no longer sufficient for materialist feminist criticism to attend to "theatrical representations qua representations," Jean E. Howard has argued, such representations must be viewed in light of "the material practices and conventions of the stage and of theater going." Jean E. Howard, "Scripts and/versus playhouses: ideological production and the renaissance public stage," in Wayne (ed.), *The Matter of Difference*, p. 228. This dual methodological focus is admirably demonstrated in a recent volume

entitled *Renaissance Drama by Women: Texts and Documents*, edited by Susan P. Cerasano and Marion Wynne-Davies (New York and London: Routledge, 1996). As its title indicates, the volume is divided into two parts: the first devoted to dramatic "texts" written by female playwrights, and the second to "documents" of stage history, detailing attitudes towards female playgoing, instances of female performers, and women's involvement more generally in theatrical affairs.

5. See for example, Susan Westfall, *Patrons and Performers: Early Tudor House-hold Revels* (Oxford: Oxford University Press, 1990) and David Bergeron, "Women as patrons of English Renaissance drama," in Guy Fitch Lytle and Stephen Orgel (eds.), *Patronage in the Renaissance* (New Jersey: Princeton University Press, 1981), and Cesarano and Wynne-Davies (eds.), *Renaissance Drama By Women*.

6. On female playgoers, see Michael Neill, " 'Wit's most accomplished senate': the audience of the Caroline private theaters," *Studies in English Language* 18 (1978): 341–60; Richard Levin, "Women in the Renaissance theater audience," *Shakespeare Quarterly* 40 (1989): 165–74; Alan H. Nelson, "Women in the audience of Cambridge plays," *Shakespeare Quarterly* 41 (1990): 333–6; Jean E. Howard, *The Stage and Social Struggle in Early Modern England* (London and New York: Routledge, 1994), p. 13.

7. William Ingram's beautifully researched book, *The Business of Playing*, has gone a long way towards offering a more historically grounded and lo-calized view of the "network of social . . . and economic, interdependencies that formed among the men" involved in early modern theatrical produc-tion, but fails to consider the possibility that women may have played a role in these social and economic interdependencies. William Ingram, *The Business of Playing: The Beginnings of the Adult Professional Theater in Elizabethan London* (Ithaca and London: Cornell University Press, 1992), p. 15. Ingram's book, together with Michael Bristol's recent *Big-Time Shakespeare* and Ann Rosalind Jones and Peter Stallybrass's *Renaissance Clothing and the Materials of Memory*, while not directly focusing on women's involvement in theatrical production, provide fertile ground for such research in ways that I shall at-tempt to delineate below. See Bristol, *Big-Time Shakespeare*, pp. 31–40; Ann Rosalind Jones and Peter Stallybrass, *Renaissance Clothing and the Materials of Memory* (Cambridge: Cambridge University Press, 2000), esp. pp. 31–2, 232–44; see also Peter Stallybrass, "Worn worlds: clothes and identity on the renaissance stage," in Margreta De Grazia, Maureen Quilligan, and Peter Stallybrass (eds.), *Subject and Object in Renaissance Culture* (Cambridge: Cambridge University Press, 1996), pp. 289–320.

8. Bristol, *Big-Time Shakespeare*, p. 38.

9. G. E. Bentley, *The Profession of Player in Shakespeare's Time, 1590–1642* (New Jersey: Princeton University Press, 1984), p. 88, cited in Stallybrass "Worn worlds," p. 295 and in Jones and Stallybrass, *Renaissance Clothing*, p. 178.

10. The will of Simon Jewell, an actor in the Earl of Pembroke's men, is il-lustrative of the importance of clothing as a theatrical property; in it he

describes what is owed to him by his "fellowes for my share of apparrell," and for certain "apparrell newe boughte." He also leaves Roberte Nicholls, a fellow actor in Pembroke's company, his personal stock of costumes and props ("all my playenge thinges in a box") and a pair of "velvet shewes." E. A. J. Honigman and Susan Brock, *Playhouse Wills, 1558–1642* (Manchester and New York: Manchester University Press, 1993), p. 59.

11. Stallybrass, "Worn worlds," p. 300; see also Stallybrass and Jones, *Renaissance Clothing*, pp. 181–92.
12. Stallybrass, "Worn worlds," p. 295; see also Jones and Stallybrass, *Renaissance Clothing*, esp. chapters 1 and 7.
13. Stallybrass, "Worn worlds," p. 293, and Jones and Stallybrass, ibid. See also Stephen Orgel's discussion of the theatre companies as "unlicensed guilds" or "antiguilds" in *Impersonations: The Performance of Gender in Shakespeare's England* (Cambridge: Cambridge University Press, 1996), p. 67.
14. Guilds restricted women's economic activity at the local level when there was a real or perceived labor surplus. David Herlihy thus cites a town ordinance in Bristol in 1461 forbidding weavers to employ their wives, daughters or maids at the loom "lest the king's people [i.e. male subjects] ... should lack employment." Cited in David Herlihy, *Opera Muliebria: Women and Work in Medieval Europe* (New York: McGraw Hill, 1990), p. 178.
15. Orgel argues that the "theater was a place of unusual freedom for women in the period," though he is referring here to women's ability "to go to the theater unescorted and unmasked," and to evidence that "a large proportion of the audience consisted of women." *Impersonations*, p. 10.
16. Beverly Lemire, *Dress, Culture and Commerce: The English Clothing Trade Before the Factory, 1600–1800* (New York: St. Martin's, 1997), p. 118.
17. Ibid., p. 120.
18. Orgel, *Impersonations*, pp. 10–11.
19. Ibid., p. 67.
20. K. D. M. Snell, "The apprenticeship of women," chapter 6 of *Annals of the Laboring Poor: Social Change and Agrarian England: 1660–1900* (Cambridge: Cambridge University Press, 1985). See also discussion of Snell in Orgel, *Impersonations*, pp. 72–3.
21. Snell, "Apprenticeship of women," p. 282.
22. Ibid., p. 286.
23. See Alice Clark, *Working Life of Women in the Seventeenth Century* (New York: A. M. Kelley, 1919), chapters 4 and 5, and Ivy Pinchbeck, *Women Workers and the Industrial Revolution, 1750–1850* (New York: A. M. Kelley, 1930).
24. Snell, "Apprenticeship of women," pp. 292–4.
25. Ibid., p. 295.
26. Ibid.
27. Cited in Clark, *Working Life of Women*, pp. 194–5.
28. Snell, "Apprenticeship of women," p. 300.
29. According to Vivien Brodsky, "apprenticeship records of fifteen London companies between 1570 and 1640 indicated an absence of female

apprentices from the records of 8,000 odd apprentices in the provisioning, textile, shoemaking and metal-working crafts and the retail trades." V[ivien] B[rodsky] Elliott, "Single women in the London marriage market: age, status and mobility, 1598–1619," in R. B. Outhwaite (ed.), *Marriage and Society* (London: Europa Publications, 1981), p. 91; see also Vivien Brodsky, "Widows in late Elizabethan London: remarriage, economic opportunity and family orientations," in Lloyd Bonfield, Richard M. Smith, and Keith Wrightson (eds.), *The World We Have Gained: Histories of Population and Social Structure* (Oxford: Basil Blackwell, 1986), p. 141. An older study by Jocelyn Dunlop, however, found girls bound as apprentices in the Carpenters', Wheelwrights', and Clockmakers' companies in early eighteenth-century London. Jocelyn O. Dunlop, *English Apprenticeship and Child Labor* (London: Unwin, 1912), p. 151. See also Amy Erickson's introduction to Alice Clark, *Working Life of Women in the Seventeenth Century* (New York and London: Routledge, 1992), p. xxxi.

30. Indeed, if we assume that levels of female employment in and around the London theatres are reflective of levels of female employment in crafts and trades elsewhere during the period, it would, using Snell's figures as a rough guide, be somewhere between 3 and 41 percent. The high concentration of women in the textile and clothing trades, and the theatre's interdependence on these trades, suggests that the figure might be closer to the latter than the former.

31. According to Snell, "most female involvement [in crafts and trades] took place outside the apprenticeship system. That is, women were massively involved in familial artisan production as the wives and daughters of apprenticed men, and most had never been apprenticed themselves. We have little access to the extent of their involvement in the family, but it was certainly most marked before the intensified capitalization of skilled trades, and before the split between home and place of production became more apparent after the mid-eighteenth century." Snell, "Apprenticeship of women," p. 277. See also Clark, *Working Life of Women*, pp. 150–1; for a comparison with early modern Germany, see Merry Wiesner, "Guilds, crafts and market production," chapter 5 of her book, *Working Women in Renaissance Germany* (New Jersey: Rutgers University Press, 1986).

32. See Clark, *Working Life of Women*, p. 156.

33. See Clark, *Working Life of Women*, pp. 150–1, 160; cf. Wiesner, "Guilds, crafts and market production," pp. 156–7.

34. Clark, *Working Life of Women*, p. 156.

35. Ibid., pp. 153–4.

36. Vivien Brodsky, "Widows in late Elizabethan London," p. 144.

37. See Stallybrass, "Worn worlds," pp. 292–7, and Stallybrass and Jones, *Renaissance Clothing*, pp. 175–6.

38. Philip Henslowe, *Henslowe's Diary*, ed. R. A. Foakes and R. T. Rickert (Cambridge: Cambridge University Press, 1961), fol. 123r. It is notable that a second entry on fol. 41v lists the amount paid to Griggs for Mary's apprenticeship as £3 instead of £5.

39. Dated 10 January, 1586/7, it states: "the saide Phyllipe...shall...wth as muche expedicon as may be ereckte fynishe and sett upp or cause to be erected finished and sett upe by John Gryggs Carpenter his servants or assignes the saide playhouse wth all furniture therunto belonginge." Foakes and Rickert (eds.), *Henslowe's Diary*, appendix: Muniment no. 16, p. 304.
40. See Foakes and Rickert (eds.), *Henslowe's Diary*, appendix: Articles 10, 11, 14 on pp. 275–6, 281 and f. 237.
41. Clark, *Working Life of Women*, pp. 174–6.
42. He does so in a loan agreement with Henslowe in the same year that he works as carpenter on the Rose. See Foakes and Rickert (eds.), *Henslowe's Diary*, fol. 12r.
43. Skiles Howard, "In praise of Margaret Brayne," unpublished paper presented at a seminar on "Women and early modern theatrical production," at the 1998 annual meeting of the Shakespeare Association of America.
44. Charles William Wallace, *The First London Theatre: Materials for a History* (London and New York: Benjamin Blom, 1913, 1969), p. 141. I am indebted to Skiles Howard for drawing my attention to this document. For the purposes of legibility, I have modernized the orthography of the documents cited in this paper, though have done so conservatively, expanding contractions, interchanging v and u, j and i, and substituting ſ with s, in accordance with modern orthography.
45. The parish records for Southampton between 1609 and 1708 list two female apprentice carpenters (as compared with seven male), three female apprentice joiners (as compared with five male) and one female apprentice bricklayer (as compared with two male). Snell, "Apprenticeship of women," p. 286.
46. See Albert Feuillerat (ed.), *Documents Relating to the Revels at Court in the Time of King Edward VI and Queen Mary (The Loseley Manuscripts)* (London: David Nutt, 1914), and Albert Feuillerat (ed.), *Documents Relating to the Office of the Revels in the Time of Queen Elizabeth* (London: David Nutt, 1908).
47. For example, an entry describing payments for artisans who worked on several masques performed during Christmas 1552/3 reads: "Maskes. one of covetus men with longe noses with a maske for babions faces of tinsel blak & tawny one other maske of pollenders with a mask of soldiours to their torchberers & one maske of women of Diana hunting with a mask of matrons to their torchberers for which was Bought and provided of the Mearser sarcenet of divers colours for attier of hedpecis...Draper red & white cottons for lynings of garmentes...Silke woman frenges & flours of silk & other garnitures...Myllener ribben gloves & other necessaries for maskes...ffethermaker plumes of phesauntes & capons tailes...Skynner savage heads and caps for maskes...Glover gloves for handes & feete like cattes fete & paws...Grocer colours gum Arabek & other painters stuffe...Carver swordes & bottons of wood for maskes...Turner ii head blockes to trym hattes & garnish hedpeces...propertie maker one mask of satires & ii doz. counterfet aglettes," Feuillerat (ed.), *Revels Edward and Mary,*

p. 116. One might argue that the entry for "Silke woman" should be taken as an indication that women artisans were so unusual that their gender was remarked upon, and that we should therefore assume that all of the ungendered artisans were male. However the term "silkwoman" was the standard term used to refer to women who worked in the silk industry in the period (see my discussion of this below), whereas most other artisans' names were gender neutral. Moreover, entries that do specify gender in the accounts offer many examples of female mercers, drapers, and milleners, so we should not assume that the artisans listed here were male. The turner referred to is quite likely a woman, since an earlier record for the same year lists "Alys perkyns for turninge of iii headblockes to fasshion and Trymme hattes uppon"; ibid., p. 108.

48. Feuillerat (ed.), *Revels Elizabeth*, p. 241.

49. Feuillerat (ed.), *Revels Edward and Mary*, p. 133.

50. "Karvers & propertye makers by the daye & by the greate with there stuffe/ John Carrowe ... at xx d the daye and fyve others at xii d the daye browghte with him woorkinge in the Revells one daye." Feuillerat (ed.), *Revels Elizabeth*, p. 81.

51. Honigmann and Brock (eds.), *Playhouse Wills*, p. 192.

52. Feuillerat (ed.), *Revels Edward and Mary*, p. 136.

53. Patricia Fumerton, *Cultural Aesthetics: Renaissance Literature and the Practice of Social Ornament* (Chicago and London: University of Chicago Press, 1991), pp. 130–3. See also my discussion of "voids" as signifiers of superfluous expenditure in Natasha Korda, "'Household Kates': domesticating commodities in *The Taming of the Shrew*," *Shakespeare Quarterly* 47:2 (1996): 126.

54. Feuillerat (ed.), *Revels Elizabeth*, p. 176.

55. Ibid.

56. Ibid., p. 197. See also pp. 160, 227, 306. An ambiguous entry, which may be evidence of women's work in the fabrication of stage-props for a masque performed for Elizabeth at Whitehall in 1559, reads: "Wages of taylours karvars propertie makers wemem and other woorking and attendinge theron." Ibid., p. 110.

57. Evidence from the first half of the eighteenth century gleaned by Snell from apprenticeship indentures in the Board of Inland Revenue for the counties of Surrey, Wiltshire, Warwickshire, Sussex and Bedfordshire gives millinery as the third most populous craft requiring skill with a needle after mantua-making and tailoring. See Snell, "Apprenticeship of women," pp. 292–3. On women milliners, see also Clark, *Working Life of Women*, pp. 176, 234, 293.

58. Feuillerat (ed.), *Revels Elizabeth*, p. 219.

59. Ibid.

60. Ibid.

61. In this context, it is worth noting that while at Kingston, the boys stayed with a "Mother sparo," who provided them with "lodginges with ffyer & foode that nighte & in the Morning." Ibid.

62. Ibid., p. 241. This kind of elaborate head attire, in which women appear to have specialized, may have been more common in performances at court than at the public theatres. Henslowe's account book lists a payment to a "mrs calle for ii curenets for hed tyers for the corte the some of xs." Henslowe also lists two payments "at the apoyntment of the companye [i.e. the Admiral's Men]" of twelve shillings in 1601/2 to a "mrs gosen" for "head tyer[s]," which do not specify that they are for court performances. Foakes and Rickert (eds.), *Henslowe's Diary*, fol. 118v.

63. Feuillerat (ed.), *Revels Elizabeth*, p. 180.

64. Feuillerat (ed.), *Revels Edward and Mary*, p. 108.

65. Feuillerat (ed.), *Revels Elizabeth*, p. 156.

66. Ibid., p. 110.

67. Ibid., p. 209; see also pp. 90, 93, 116–17, 156, 161.

68. Feuillerat (ed.), *Revels Edward and Mary*, p. 85; see also pp. 19, 70, 116.

69. Feuillerat (ed.), *Revels Elizabeth*, pp. 116–17.

70. Ibid., p. 156.

71. Ibid., p. 161.

72. Marian K. Dale, "London silkwomen of the fifteenth century," *Economic History Review* 4 (1932–4): 331–3. See also Clark, *Working Life of Women*, pp. 138–42. For a comparison with silkwomen elsewhere in Europe, see Judith C. Brown and Jordan Goodman, "Women and industry in Florence," *Journal of Economic History* 40:1 (1980): 73–80; Daryl M. Hafter, "Women who wove in the eighteenth-century silk industry of Lyon," and Patrizia Sione, "From home to factory: women in the nineteenth-century Italian silk industry," in Daryl M. Hafter (ed.), *European Women and Preindustrial Craft* (Bloomington and Indianapolis: Indiana University Press, 1995); and Merry Weisner, *Working Women in Renaissance Germany*, pp. 183–4.

73. Dale, "London silkwomen," pp. 332–3.

74. Ibid., pp. 327–8.

75. Ibid., p. 324.

76. "Between 1455 and 1504," Dale maintains, "five acts were passed forbidding the importation of certain silk goods for periods ranging from four to twenty years," the first being sent on behalf of the "Sylkewymmen and Throwestres of the Crafts and occupation of Silkewerk." Ibid., p. 324.

77. Ibid., pp. 325–7. According to Dale, silkwomen often remembered their apprentices in their wills, as was the case with Isabel Fremely, who left her female apprentice "a pair of sheets and her girdle of green silk garnished with silver" in 1456. Another silkwoman, Agnes Brundyssch, in addition to leaving her female apprentice, Alice Seford, certain goods, pardons her "the rest of her term of apprenticeship to me." Ibid., pp. 326–7.

78. Dale gives several examples of silkwomen who were or had been married to well-off citizens and operated as "feme sole traders." Ibid., pp. 328, 334–5.

79. According to Alice Clark, women took "a prominent part in every branch of Retail Trade." Clark, *Working Life of Women*, pp. 197ff. According to Merry Weisner, "Women conducted most of the business that went on at th[e]

market; they handled almost all retail distribution of food, used clothing, household articles, and liquor... In addition, the market place served as a gathering place for women, who were the majority of customers as well as vendors." Merry Weisner, "Spinning out capital: women's work in the early modern economy," in Renate Bridenthal et al. (eds.), *Becoming Visible: Women in European History* (Boston: Houghton Mifflin Co., 1987), pp. 235ff.

80. Feuillerat (ed.), *Revels Edward and Mary*, p. 69, and *Revels Elizabeth*, p. 90.

81. Lemire, *Dress, Culture and Commerce*, p. 2.

82. Margaret Spufford, *The Great Reclothing of Rural England: Petty Chapmen and their Wares in the Seventeenth Century* (London: Hambledon Press, 1984), p. 58.

83. Weisner, *Working Women in Renaissance Germany*, pp. 179–80. As the market in used goods continued to expand over the course of the sixteenth century, however, attempts were made to restrict this sector of the market. In the late sixteenth century, for example, the council of the Borough of Leicester attempted to prohibit the city's "brogers or pledge women" from practicing "the trade of sellinge of apparel & howshold stuff... hawkinge abrode from howse to howse." These women, according to Lemire, had not gained their freedom from any guild, and wandered about selling "goods that were neither uniform nor subject to inspection," offering "credit for some pieces of clothing and accept[ing] goods in pawn as well." Because they threatened "commercial proprieties," Lemire maintains, the city fathers determined that henceforth the trade would be "conducted by its new male appointees... 'and none other.'" Lemire, *Press, Culture and Commerce*, p. 100.

84. Ibid., p. 114.

85. B. A. Holderness, "Widows in pre-industrial society: an essay upon their economic functions," in R. M. Smith (ed.), *Land, Kinship, and Life Cycle* (Cambridge: Cambridge University Press, 1984), p. 439.

86. Henry Chettle, in his *Kind-Hartes Dreame*, speaks of landladies who, if their tenants "wanted money," would "on munday lend them... upon a pawne eleven pence, and in meere pittie aske at the weekes end not a penny more than twelve pence." Henry Chettle, *Kind-Hartes Dreame*, in George Bagshawe Harrison (ed.), *Elizabethan and Jacobean Quartos* (New York: Barnes and Noble, 1966), p. 47. Garthine Walker cites many instances of women acting as informal, neighborhood pawnbrokers, and maintains that "small-scale pawning was commonplace" in alehouses and inns by women; Walker, "Women, theft and the world of stolen goods," in Jenny Kermode and Garthine Walker (eds.), *Women, Crime and the Courts in Early Modern England* (Chapel Hill: University of North Carolina Press, 1994), pp. 81–105, see esp. pp. 91–3.

87. Ingram, *The Business of Playing* p. 58.

88. Walker, "Women, theft and the world of stolen goods," p. 98.

89. Ibid., pp. 85–90; see also Weisner, "Spinning out capital," p. 238.

90. G. E. Bentley, *The Jacobean and Caroline Stage*, vol. II (Oxford: Oxford University Press, 1941, 1968), p. 564.

91. Ibid., p. 367.

92. Honigmann and Brock (eds.), *Playhouse Wills*, p. 193.
93. The bulk of these records may be found on fols. 55r–61r, 73r–81r and 133r–136r; however, there are other references to actors pawning their costumes with Henslowe scattered throughout the "diary," some dated well after 1596 (see 19v, 28v, 37r, 41v), one as late as 1602. For a more extended discussion of Henslowe's pawnbroking records see Natasha Korda, "Household property/stage property: Henslowe as pawnbroker," *Theatre Journal* 48:2 (1996): 185–95. See also Jones and Stallybrass, *Renaissance Clothing*, esp. chapters 1 and 7.
94. Frederick Fleay, *Chronicle History of the London Stage 1559–1642* (London: Reeves and Turner, 1890), p. 95.
95. Philip Henslowe, *Henslowe's Diary*, ed. Sir Walter Greg, vol. 1 (London: A. H. Bullen, 1904).
96. Of the total number of loans, 55 percent were to women, 15 percent to men, and 30 percent to anonymous debtors.
97. Foakes and Rickert (eds.), *Henslowe's Diary* fols. 57r, 73r, 57v.
98. Edward H. Sugden, *A Topographical Dictionary to the Works of Shakespeare and His Fellow Dramatists* (New York: Longmans, Green & Co., 1925), p. 512.
99. Foakes and Rickert (eds.), *Henslowe's Diary* fol. 19v.
100. Ibid., fol. 79r; see also fols. 57v, 78v, 79v, and 133v.
101. Ibid., fol. 28v; see also fols. 28r, 38v, 83r and 124r.
102. For fascinating discussions of certain non-aristocratic female performers in ad hoc theatrical activity see Shirley Graves, "Women on the pre-Restoration stage," *Studies in Philology* 22, (1925): 184–97 and Ann Thompson, "Women/'women' and the stage," in Helen Wilcox (ed.), *Women and Literature in Britain, 1500–1700* (Cambridge: Cambridge University Press, 1996).
103. See Clark, *Working Life of Women*, pp. 161–7. Kathryn Murphy Anderson is currently working on this subject, and presented her research at the 1998 Shakespeare Association of America seminar on "Women and early modern theatrical production," in an essay entitled "Investigating women's work in early modern printing houses: the case of Frances Simson Read Eld."

CHAPTER 9

Staging the beard: masculinity in early modern English culture

Will Fisher

In August 1605, James I paid a visit to Oxford University as part of his progress that year.[1] While he was there, some of the students performed a play for his entertainment. In order to try to make a good impression on the King, the students rented a number of costumes and props for their production from suppliers in London. Even though there is nothing particularly noteworthy about this performance (as a matter of fact, James apparently fell asleep in the midst of it), it is nevertheless of considerable interest to theatrical historians because the inventories and receipts documenting the rental have survived to this day. They contain a fairly precise list of costumes and props used in the production. This is one of the few instances where we know exactly what items were used to perform a particular play. There are certainly other extant inventories from the period, but they are usually not connected with any specific performance or play. Instead, they are usually simply lists of costumes and stage properties belonging to a specific company (such as Henslowe's inventories for the Lord Admiral's Men)[2] or to a specific institution (such as the Revels Office).[3]

For my purposes, the crucial thing to note about the Oxford inventory is that it indicates that twenty-two false beards were hired for the performance. These include:

1 blewe hayre and beard for neptune.
1 black smooth hayre and beard for a magitian.
1 white hayre and beard for nestor...
2 hermeits beards the on graye th'other white...
3 beards one Red one blacke th'other flexen.
10. satyers heads and berds.[4]

Another "4 berds" were also sent along at a later date. A duplicate inventory states that these were "for Heremits." Both the number of beards used in this production and the wide range of colors are astounding. Other theatrical inventories give some insight into how the false beards might have been made and how the variety of color might have been achieved: a document from Cambridge describes "iiij beardes of cone skinnes & white fur & fox."[5]

I begin with this brief discussion of the Oxford students' performance in order to suggest the importance of false beards in early modern theatrical practice. Yet why were so many beards used for this performance? What were they used for? Although it is difficult to answer these questions in detail without reference to the play itself (the text of *Alba* has not survived), I will argue that in general, prosthetic beards were used to produce masculinity on the early modern stage.[6] As such, they were not unlike the dresses and wigs that were used to produce femininity. The beards would have been particularly important for student performances like the one at Oxford, or for plays performed by the boys' companies. In fact, I will argue that boy actors were as much "in drag" when playing the parts of men as when playing the parts of women.

In order to better understand the role of beards on the early modern stage, we first need to recognize that in English culture at large, facial hair was an important means of materializing masculinity. Put simply, the beard often made the man. We can begin to get a sense of the cultural investment in the beard if we consider that in a wide range of English sources from the Renaissance, being a man is virtually equated with having facial hair. For example, Thomas Hill's late-sixteenth-century physiognomy book sets out to explain why "men are lone bearded, & not women."[7] Similarly, the poet Hugh Crompton writes that "in each man's face appears / A beard extending upward to his ears... But every female beardless doth remaine, / both old and young her face is still the same."[8] In these texts, men are imagined as being bearded and women beardless. While these statements purport to describe a physiological truth, they imagine the difference between males and females to be much more clear-cut and dichotomous than it actually is, and are therefore really more prescriptive than descriptive.

One of the most striking indications of the cultural centrality of beards in early modern England is their prevalence in portraits. It is a largely unappreciated art-historical fact that English portraits from the sixteenth and seventeenth centuries routinely portray men with facial hair. As I have argued in more detail elsewhere, this phenomenon starts around the 1530s and continues for at least a century after that.[9] During this time period, approximately 90 percent of men in portraits are depicted wearing facial hair (and usually a full moustache and beard). The point I want to make in citing this evidence is not, however, that a large percentage

of men "actually" wore beards during the Renaissance. Instead, what I
want to argue is that these portraits – along with physiognomy books,
poetry, and other texts – helped to produce an idealized vision of the
male body, and that that idealized vision included facial hair. Moreover,
I also want to suggest that the early modern theatre played an important
part in this process: in short, I believe that the theatre was an important
cultural site where ideologies of masculinity were (per)formed.

If all of these sources begin to suggest that facial hair was an integral
part of early modern masculinity, we need to recognize that materializing
masculinity through a prosthetic part has significant ramifications for
how gender was conceptualized. Most importantly, it would mean that
masculinity would have been imagined as something that was, at least to
some extent, alterable. This is, in part, because beards are detachable.
As such, they are paradoxical entities that slide between many of the
categories we use to think about both identity and the theatre. It is not
clear, for example, whether false beards should be considered props or
costumes (the rubrics used to organize this volume). Can a beard really
be called a prop, given that it is portable and attached securely to the
body in a way that a bed, or even a handkerchief is not? If it does not
fit easily into the first category, then should we instead call it a part
of the actor's costume? Although early modern writers do sometimes
refer to the beard as "a garment for manly chekes,"[10] facial hair is not
usually considered an article of clothing on account of its "corporeality."
If it therefore doesn't really make sense to call facial hair an element of
costume, it can't really be called a part of the body either. The uncertainty
here is ultimately the result of the beard's detachability. How can facial
hair be considered a part of the body if it is not always present, or if it
can be removed? The detachability of the beard was foregrounded on
the stage (where beards were often put on or taken off in the course of
a performance), but all facial hair can, of course, be detached through
shaving and other means.

Given the difficulty of classifying beards, it is hardly surprising to find
that early modern writers link them to a wide range of items. For example,
in *The Loathsomeness of Longe Hair*, Thomas Hall compares facial hair to
"Nailes, Meate, Drink, [and] Cloaths."[11] In this description, Hall begins
with another detachable part of the body ("Nailes"). He then moves to
external objects that are brought into the body ("Meate" and "Drink"),
before ending with one that is simply attached to it ("Cloaths"). The
beard thus moves between what might appear to be different categories
of objects. In the end, passages like this therefore have the effect of
highlighting the ambiguous materiality of facial hair.

If early modern masculinity was materialized through features like beard growth, it was also produced around a certain set of social roles. In other words, to be a "man" meant not only to have a certain physiology, but also to perform certain activities such as fighting in battle and begetting children. These corporeal forms and social roles were themselves linked; beard growth was consistently associated with the "masculine" social roles of soldier and father.

Facial hair was often described using martial terms or imagery. It is, for instance, frequently called an "ensigne": Helkiah Crooke labels it an "ensigne of majesty"[12] in his anatomy book, *A Description of the Body of Man*, and John Bulwer calls it the "natural Ensigne of Manhood" in his proto-anthropological treatise, *Anthropometamorphosis*.[13] An "ensigne," as the *OED* explains, is "a military or naval standard." Thus, the beard is understood to announce a man's "Manhood" or social position (his "majesty") in the same way that an "ensign" announces the military identity of a group of soldiers. These formulations transpose the earlier descriptions of facial hair as a "signe of manhood" into a specifically military register.

Martial language is also used to describe the beard in the *Haec Vir* pamphlet (1620) – a tract explicitly concerned with the production and regulation of sexual difference. The narrator claims that effeminate men

... curl, frizzle and powder [their] hairs, bestowing more hours and time in dividing lock from lock, and hair from hair ... than ever Caesar did in Marshalling his Army. [And what's more, they have] so greedily engrossed [the Art of face painting] that were it not for that little fantastical sharp-pointed dagger that hangs at [their] chins, and the cross-hilt which guards [their] upper lip, hardly would there be any difference between the fair Mistress and the foolish Servant.[14]

According to the passage, curling, frizzling and powdering the hair have replaced "properly" masculine activities like "Marshalling [an] Army." The beard is quite literally imagined to be the last line of "defense" against effeminization – the only thing that separates the "fair Mistress and the foolish Servant." Given these codings, it is hardly surprising to find that the beard is here figured as a weapon (a "sharp-pointed dagger" with the mustache as a "cross-hilt"), thus recalling the "properly" masculine activity of combat.

If the *Haec Vir* pamphlet suggests that facial hair continues to signal masculinity, even when other traditional markers of masculinity such as clothes or the hair on the head have failed, it is also clear that, within the pamphlet, beards do not announce "Manhood" in a transparent or uniform manner. Indeed, in this text, the tenuousness of that production is insistently foregrounded; the beard appears to be under threat of imminent erasure (it is described as "fantastical" and "little"). We might therefore say that facial hair is not imagined to produce masculinity in a permanent or unalterable way. Moreover, masculinity itself seems to be more a matter of degree than simple presence or absence. Hence, differing styles of facial hair seem to confer differing degrees of masculinity. When seen from this perspective, it is appropriate that the beard is likened to a "dagger" in this passage, for even though the dagger is a "masculine" weapon, it is hardly the most potent martial implement.

Just as beard growth was partially correlated with martial ability, it was also partially correlated with reproductive capacity so that the growth of facial hair is seen as a sign that the wearer is capable of reproducing. The correlation between beard growth and reproductive capacity was not only symbolic; it was also quite "real." In medical books from the Renaissance, the growth of facial hair is explicitly linked to the production of semen. This "explanation" for the appearance of facial hair in men is most exhaustively articulated in Marcus Ulmus's *Physiologia Barbae Humanae* (1603), a three-hundred-page book devoted solely to the physiology and social significance of beards.[15] The book argues "that Nature gave to mankind a Beard, that it might remaine as an Index in the Face, of the Masculine generative faculty."[16] The physiognomer Thomas Hill explains beard growth in similar terms. He writes:

The bearde in man...beginnith to appeare in the nether jawe...through the heate and moysture, carried unto the same, drawn from the genitours: which draw to them especially, the sperme from those places.[17]

In this passage, Hill links the growth of facial hair to the "heat and moisture" arising from the production of semen in the testicles. The beard is thus figured as a kind of seminal excrement. This is fitting, for in the Renaissance, all hair was thought to be an "excremental" residue left by the "fumosities" as they passed out of the pores of the body:

...the immediate matter of Haires...is a sortie, thicke and earthy vapour which...passeth through the Pores of the Skin. For the vapor being thicke, in his passage leaveth some part of itself...where it is impacted by a succeeding vapor arising whence the former did, [and] is protruded or thrust forward.[18]

This description of hair growth is based on the model of soot building up in a chimney and eventually being pushed out of the body by the uprising fumosities: "we see by the continual ascent of Soot, long strings of it are gathered as it were into a chaine."[19] If hair is thus thought to be an excremental residue that is produced by the "fumosities" in general, the beard is described as a specifically seminal type of excrement, produced by the "sootie" excrement that is given off during the production of semen. As Hill explains: "Other Haires... [are bred] in Boyes when they begin to breed seed... come out in... the Chin and Cheekes."[20]

The language that Hill uses in his description of the beard clearly works to define it specifically as a marker of procreative potential. By calling the testicles the "genitours," Hill foregrounds their role in generation. The association of the beard with "the Masculine generative faculty" was forged in a more socially accessible form in Shakespeare's *Troilus and Cressida* through the common pun on "hairs" and "heirs." In the play, Pandarus describes how Helen had spied a white hair on Troilus's chin and said: "Here's but two and fifty hairs on your chin – and one of them is white." To which Troilus replies, "That white hair is my father, and all the rest are his sons" (1.2.150–62). In Troilus's response, he likens the hairs on his chin to his father (Priam) and his fifty sons. He thus associates his own production of facial hairs with his father's production of heirs (i.e. his fifty sons), in order to emphasize his own procreative potential. As in the medical texts, Troilus creates a direct link between the growth of his facial hair and his generativity. Finally, it is worth noting that the general connection between beard growth and generativity may help to explain why ten beards were hired for the satyrs in the student performance at Oxford University. It may seem strange that such effort was put into the costuming of these minor characters, but it seems that the beard was an integral part of the satyrs' image. Indeed, traditional iconography of these figures emphasized not only their hairiness, but also their lusty virility.

These sources demonstrate the extent to which the somatic and the social contours of "manhood" were imbricated in one another. I now want to shift my focus somewhat and suggest that facial hair was not simply a means of constructing sexual differences between men and women; it was also a means of constructing distinctions between men and boys. For boys were quite literally a different gender from men during the early modern period. Although we currently tend to see the difference between men and boys as being a matter of degree (boys are diminutive versions of men) and the difference between men and women as being a matter of kind (women are entirely distinct from men), we need to remember that in the Renaissance, all sexual differences were, as Thomas Laqueur has demonstrated, primarily conceptualized in terms of degree. Thus, the distinction between men and boys would have been analogous to that between men and women.[21]

In recent studies of Renaissance culture, there has been a burgeoning interest in the gender and sexuality of boys – especially boy actors. Stephen Orgel's *Impersonations*, for example, examines "why...the English stage [took] boys for women."[22] Similarly, Lisa Jardine has looked at the erotic interchangeability of boys and women, arguing that it was not so much the sex of the "submissive" partner that mattered, but the expectation of that very submissiveness.[23] Whereas this research has tended to focus on the eroticization of boys, I want to concentrate on their place within the sex/gender system. I will therefore be exploring how the gendered category "boy" was constituted, and especially how the gendered contrast between "boys" and "men" was produced.

Like the distinction between men and women, the distinction between men and boys was materialized through facial hair (though it was also materialized through a wide range of other attributes and parts). In Randal Holme's *Academy of Armory*, it is beard growth *alone* that separates the men from the boys. Holme lists the different stages of masculine development according to hair growth: he begins with the "child" who he says is "smooth and [has] little hair." Then, he defines a "youth" as having "hair on the head, but none on the face," and finally defines a "Man" as "having a beard."[24] Shakespeare offers a similar schema in *As You Like It*: in the "seven ages of man speech" given by Jaques, he speaks of the transition from "schoolboy" with a "shining morning face" to the "soldier" who is "bearded like the pard" (2.7.145–50).

Beardlessness was, however, by no means the only characteristic used to produce the opposition of boys and men.[25] Francis Bacon, for instance, remarks in his preface to *The Great Instauration* (1620) that "the characteristic property of boys" is that they "cannot generate."[26] As we have seen, however, it is not as if procreative capacity and beard growth were two unrelated ways of differentiating men from boys. These two gendered "traits" were insistently mapped onto one another insofar as facial hair was conceptualized as a kind of seminal excrement.

These two characteristics are used interchangeably to establish a distinction between a man and a boy in a scene from William Cartwright's *The Ordinary*. Simon Credulous reprimands Meanewell, telling him: "Leave off your flouting! You're a beardless Boy; I am a Father of Children" (5.4.2362–3).[27] Simon Credulous thus attempts to dissociate himself from the "boy" Meanewell (and to create a hierarchical power relation between them), by contrasting his own generativity with the beardlessness of Meanewell. In doing so, he forges an equivalence between the terms man–bearded–generative and the terms boy–beardless–non-generative, constructing, at the same time, an overarching opposition between these two sets of terms.

Marriage was one discursive site where the distance between boys and men was consistently accentuated. In Jonson's *Epicoene*, for example, Otter explains that "a boy or child under years is not fit for marriage because he cannot reddere debitum [literally 'pay the debt']."[28] In this passage, boys are marked as unsuitable husbands on account of their supposed non-generativity. In Massinger's *The Guardian* (1658), the beardless male is said to be similarly unfit for marriage: "to marry ... [i]n a beardless chin / 'Tis ten times worse then wenching" (1.1.62–4).[29] The implication of this statement is that marriage without a beard is even "worse" then heterosexual intercourse outside of marriage ("wenching"), presumably because such a marriage would not offer the possibility of reproduction and would thus have "degraded" the institution itself. Such a marriage might even be considered sodomitical.

Despite the insistent production of differences between men and "non-masculine" boys, beard growth did not absolutely determine gendered identity, nor was its production of masculinity completely seamless. In both Philip Sidney's *Arcadia* and William Shakespeare's *Coriolanus*, the protagonists are beardless, and yet they perform feats that are said to "demonstrate" that they are "men." In Philip Sidney's *Arcadia*, Pyrocles has "no hair of his face to witness him a man" and yet he performs martial exploits "beyond the degree of a man."[30] Similarly, in *Coriolanus*, Cominius describes Coriolanus's extraordinary feats of valor on the battlefield:

> [Coriolanus] fought beyond the mark of others ...
> When with his Amazonian chin he drove
> The Bristled lips before him: he bestrid
> An o'er-pressed Roman an i' the consul's view
> Slew three opposers ... in that days feats,
> When he might act the woman in the scene,
> He proved the best man i' the field ...
> His pupil age Man-entered thus.   (2.2.88–99)

On the one hand, Cominius indicates that Coriolanus might still seem to be a boy: he has a beardless "Amazonian chin" and might "act the woman in the scene" (something which Pyrocles actually does in the *Arcadia*). On the other hand, Coriolanus performs martial feats which quite literally confer masculinity: by fighting "beyond the mark" of the "Bristled lips" and thus "prov[ing] the best man i' the field" he "Man-enter[s]." This passage thus suggests that although differences between men and boys were materialized through facial hair, the beard (or lack thereof) did not absolutely determine gendered identity. Furthermore, it begins to pull apart the insistent conflation of masculinity, beard growth and martial capacity. Indeed, Coriolanus is said to be "Amazonian" and thus is associated with a tradition of non-masculine warriors.

These passages from Sidney and Shakespeare clearly suggest that facial hair did not necessarily materialize differences between boys and men in an unequivocal way. Moreover, they demonstrate that the social and somatic groundings for masculinity were not always consistent. Nevertheless, both of these texts might also be said to reiterate the normative ideals that equated masculinity with having facial hair, insofar as the beardlessness of each protagonist is put forward as being remarkable. In other words, we might say that these beardless men are meant to be the exceptions that prove the rule. In general, it would thus appear that the man was defined through the beard, and was defined against beardless women and boys. Indeed, Valerian reiterates this oppositional structure when he writes "[i]t is openly known amongst all kyndes of men, that chyldren [and] women...are ever sene withoute beards."[31] The implication is that these groups are alike in not having facial hair and in not being men.

Understanding the role that beards played in materializing sexual differences in English Renaissance culture will ultimately help us understand the role that they played on the early modern stage. Earlier, I suggested that beards were primarily a means of producing masculinity in the theatres, and that the boy actors who wore beards to play men were as much in drag as those who wore wigs and dresses to play the parts of women. It should now also be clear that the theatrical "production" of masculinity was particularly pronounced in plays performed by the boys. Yet how common was it for actors in the boy companies to wear false beards? Facial hair is mentioned in about half of the extant plays performed by the children's troupes.[32] Usually this means that within the play, an explicit reference is made to a character's beard, and in the process, the play draws attention to the character's "masculinity." In Nicholas Udall's *Thersites*, for example, Muliber asks Thersites "Would not thy blacke and rustye grym berde, / Nowe thou art so armed, make anye man aferde?"[33] In this question, Muliber draws attention to the specific color of Thersites' facial hair, and (albeit in an ironic way) to its masculinity. The latter is highlighted both through the martial analogy (he is "armed" with a beard) and through the fact that this beard makes men "aferde." Yet Muliber's question simultaneously foregrounds the temporary nature of Thersites' beard: he states that he is only so armed "Nowe." In other plays performed by boy companies, facial hair is even more conspicuous. For example, in Lording Barry's *Ram Alley* (a play performed by The Children of the King's Revels), there is a character who is actually named Lieutenant Beard, a moniker that again links the beard with the military context.[34]

While it is certainly possible that some of the beards mentioned in these plays were in fact "real," I believe that many of them were prosthetic. It is, however, difficult to determine the exact extent to which these props were used. Although the students at Oxford, as we have seen, used twenty-two beards for their production, this may not have been typical of English stage practice in general. Nevertheless, there is some evidence that suggests that false beards were a fairly common theatrical property (and especially within the boy companies). The beards for the Oxford performance were supplied by two men from London who were involved in the management of the boys' company at Blackfriars – Edward Kirkham and Thomas Kendall. This obviously means that the boy actors at Blackfriars would have had access to a similar range of props and costumes for their productions. In fact, it is possible that the items used at Oxford were supplied from the stocks of the Blackfriars troupe (variously known as the Chapel Children, the Children of Blackfriars and Children of the Queen's Revels).[35] It is also possible, however, that the twenty-two beards were taken from the properties owned by the Revels Office. At the time, Kirkham was the Revels Yeoman, and as Yeoman, he was probably entitled to rent out the costumes and other goods in his care. One of Kirkham's predecessors, John Arnold, seems to have engaged in just such a practice. According to a complaint filed by Thomas Giles in 1572, Arnold "havynge allone the costodye of the garmentes / dothe lend the same at hys plesure." Giles, a haberdasher, complained to the Queen because his own business was being undermined by Arnold's activities: as he puts it, he was "hynderyde of hys lyvyge herbye [because]...havynge aparell to lett...[he could not] so cheplye lett the same as hyr hyghnes maskes be lett."[36]

The Revels Office would almost certainly have had enough false beards on hand to fulfill the Oxford order since these items were frequently purchased for the production of plays and masks at court.

Although Revels Office inventories for 1605 have not survived, inventories from the late sixteenth century include many beards. An inventory for 1572–3 lists the following acquisitions:

...viij long white Beardes at xx^d the peece – xiij^s iiij^s/Aberne Berdes ij & j blackfyzicians bearde – xiiij^s viij^d/Berds White & Black vj – viij^s/Heares for plamers ij – ij^s vij^d Berdes for fy shers vj – ix^s ... Redd Berdes vj – ix^s.[37]

Another twenty-two beards were bought for the following season:

vij Long Aberne beardes at xvj^d the peece – ix^s iiij/vij other berdes ottett at xiiij^d the peece for the haunces Mask at xvj^d the peece – viij^s ij^d/xij beardes Black & Redd for the fforesters Mask at like rate – xvj^s/Heare for the wy lde Men at xvjd the lb iij lb – iiij^s/One Long white Bearde – ijs viijd.[38]

As with the Oxford inventory, the variety of colors and shapes here is remarkable. If the acquisitions by the Revels Office in the 1570s were in any way typical, Kirkham would have had a large collection of prosthetic beards to choose from.

It is worth noting that the receipts from the Oxford rental suggest that it was not Kirkham, but Kendall who sent all the beards, wigs, and vizards. This may simply be an indication of who sent the materials to Oxford that particular day. Nevertheless, we should note that Kendall was a haberdasher like the complainant, Thomas Giles, whom I mention above, and he may well have trafficked in costumes and properties (either on his own, through connection to the Children of the Queen's Revels, or both). There are numerous records of haberdashers renting theatrical properties and costumes including beards. For example, Harry Bennet rented false beards in Coventry throughout the early 1570s.[39] Similarly, there was a London haberdasher named John Ogle who made all of the beards and wigs acquired by the Revels Office during the 1570s and 1580s, including the fifty-six prosthetic beards delivered in 1572–4 that I listed above. Like Bennet, Ogle probably rented out beards in addition to selling them. In fact, in *The Book of Sir Thomas More*, when the player goes to borrow the "long beard" for the play within the play, he goes "to Ogles" only to find that "Owgle was not with in, and his wife would not let [him] have the beard."[40]

Although it is ultimately impossible to tell exactly where the beards used in the Oxford performance came from, it wouldn't be surprising if more than one of these avenues were involved – if, for example, the stocks of the Blackfriars' company, the stocks of the Revels Office, and Kendall's own personal property, were not completely distinct. In the end, what is crucial for my project is that these documents, when taken together, begin to indicate that false beards were a common theatrical property and that there was a lively traffic in them. In fact, a few months after the Oxford performance, Kendall and Kirkham appear to have supplied beards for yet another student production: the Christmas play at Westminster School. An inventory indicates that "Crownes, hayres, and beards" were rented for performance. Although the inventory does not say where these particular items came from, the only people it mentions are Kendall and Kirkham (both of whom are said to have supplied costumes). Kendall is paid "for the Lone of the Apparrell" and another payment is made to "Mr Kerkeham Man for his paynes for bringing a dublet [and] breeches."[41]

Contemporary theatre historians have, for the most part, failed to examine the significance of false beards for theatrical performance. Indeed, W. Reavley Gair's *The Children of Paul's* maintains that the boy actors at Paul's "did not . . . use false beards or moustaches."[42] The evidence from the plays themselves, however, seems to contradict Gair's claim. There are at least five extant plays performed by Paul's boys that explicitly call for prosthetic beards (either in the stage directions or by having the character appear at one point in the play with a beard, and at another point without it), and another nine plays that feature characters who are said to be bearded.[43]

If scholars have not adequately explored the use of prosthetic beards by the boys' companies, it is not simply because they have failed to see them. Many critics refuse to take these items seriously; they assume that prosthetic beards could only be used in a farcical manner, and hence would not have been a significant part of everyday playhouse practices.[44] This assumption is explicit in Gair's book: he notes that prosthetic facial hair "on a fourteen year old [is] obviously comic."[45] While it is possible that these props were employed in a comical manner, I see no reason to assume that false beards would *always* have been humorous. Boys routinely wore dresses and wigs in order to play the parts of women and no one assumes that this was invariably farcical. Moreover, if we push deeper, a gendered discrepancy begins to emerge: while critics have readily acknowledged that femininity was produced prosthetically on the early modern stage, they've been much slower to acknowledge that masculinity might have been produced in a similar fashion.[46]

At this point, I want to look briefly at a boys' company play in which a prosthetic beard is explicitly used to construct masculinity – Thomas Middleton's *A Mad World, My Masters*. Although the plot of this play is typical of early modern cross-dressing narratives, in this instance it is boy/man transvestism that is presented.[47] At the beginning of the play, the boy (Follywit) dresses himself as a man (Lord Owemuch) in order to sneak into the house of his grandfather (Sir Bounteous Progress) and repair their strained relations. Follywit's disguise consists of "a French ruff, a thin beard, and strong perfume" (1.1.78).[48] These items are the hallmarks of the effeminate courtier; so although Follywit disguises himself as a man, he is only able to become an effeminate one. When Follywit/Lord Owemuch eventually speaks with Sir Bounteous Progress about Follywit, the dialogue foregrounds the distinctions between "Follywit" and "Lord Owemuch." At one point, Sir Bounteous Progress comments on Follywit's immaturity, describing him as an "Imberbis juvenis" (beardless youth), noting that "his chin has no more prickles than a mid-wife" (2.1.135–6).[49] With this comment, Sir Bounteous Progress calls attention to the beardless Follywit and the thinly bearded Lord Owemuch. Moreover, he indicates that he does not consider Follywit to be a real man: he has "no more prickles" (with the obvious pun) than a "mid-wife" (meaning "half-woman"). But, on the other hand, his formulation does allow for the possibility that Follywit – as well as "mid-wife[s]," for that matter – might indeed have some "prickles." Thus, instead of constructing absolute or categorical distinctions between men, boys, and women, Bounteous seems to imagine a gendered continuum. In fact, the males in Middleton's play are arrayed along just such a spectrum: Owemuch – the effeminate courtier – stands symbolically between Follywit and the more masculine Sir Bounteous. We might therefore say that although prosthetic facial hair is used to mark out sexual differences between boys and men in *A Mad World, My Masters*, those differences are a matter of degree, rather than kind. For my purposes, however, the crucial thing to note is the centrality of the beard both in Follywit's costume and in the subsequent dialogue.

If *A Mad World, My Masters* provides an instance of a boys' company play in which a false beard is used to stage masculinity, it is worth noting that such boy/man cross-dressing was probably much less common in the adult companies. In fact, beards in general would have had a slightly different resonance in those companies on account of their organizational structure. The members of the adult troupes were, of course, categorized as either "adults" or "boys"; and the roles assigned to an actor were largely predicated upon the actor's place within this hierarchy (boy actors, for instance, usually played the parts of women). To the extent that this professional division was mapped onto the more general cultural division between men and boys, it would have reinforced early modern ideologies of gender. An instance where this occurs is the metadramatic scene in *A Midsummer Night's Dream*. When the rude mechanicals prepare to stage their production of "Pyramus and Thisbe," Flute is assigned the role of Thisbe. He protests: "Nay faith let me not play a woman, I have a beard coming" (1.2.47–8). Flute thus implies that because he has a "beard coming" it would be inappropriate for him to play a woman, and perhaps, by extension, that it would be inappropriate to consider him a boy. The logic here seems to echo the gendered discourse about the difference between boys and men. As we have already seen, Cominius says that the beardless Coriolanus could "act the woman in the scene" (2.2.89–94).

My point here is not that beard growth actually *determined* the roles an actor would play in the adult companies, nor that it was necessarily a factor in deciding when an actor would shift from playing women to men. Instead, I am suggesting that to the extent that the divisions between adult and boy actors – especially the differences regarding what roles these actors would play – overlapped with the gendered divisions of the culture at large, the adult theatrical companies could be said to (re)produce gendered norms and categories. At the same time, however, the actors could also subvert those very norms and categories. In *A Midsummer Night's Dream*, for example, Flute ends up playing a woman *despite* his beard. Indeed, part of the humor of the rude mechanicals' metadramatic scene lies in the fact that their casting decisions are completely backwards. That is to say, they reverse the beard conventions of the adult companies by having Bottom put on a beard in order to play the "masculine" Pyramus, and Flute – the hairy boy-man – remove his in order to play Thisby. Thus, if the adult companies (as well as the boy companies) ultimately helped to do the cultural work of constructing sexual difference, they did not do so in a completely seamless way.

Moreover, theatrical performances often complicated matters further by calling attention to the prosthetic nature of the beard. In *A Midsummer Night's Dream*, this is done by having Bottom ask "What beard were I best to play it [the role of Thisby] in? ... your straw-color beard, your orange tawny beard, your purple-in grain beard, or your French-crown color beard, your perfit yellow" (1.2.90–6). Bottom's list here is meant to foreground the artificiality of these outrageously colored beards. In fact, the actor may even have held up each of them for consideration. Yet in the rude mechanicals' play, it is not simply the beard that is prosthetic; the smooth chin is equally artificial. When Flute goes to play the part of Thisby, he does not shave his newly grown beard for the role.

Rather, he "play[s] it in a mask" (1.2.49). The mask used in this particular instance may have been something like the eggshell vizards listed
in the inventories of the Revels Office.[50] However Flute's costume was
constructed, it is clear that his hairless face is just as artificial as Bottom's
beard. Consequently, we might say that the contrast between the bearded
and the beardless in this performance is presented not so much as a contrast between the artificial and the natural, or the prosthetic and the
non-prosthetic (or "real"). Instead, it is presented as the difference between two different types of prostheses.

   The Book of Sir Thomas More is another early modern play in which the
beard's detachability and transferability are emphasized, but in this case,
the beard is not simply a focus of attention in the metadramatic scenes.
Although the prosthetic nature of facial hair is indeed foregrounded in
the play-within-the-play (where the performance is held up because one
of the actors has gone to fetch "a long beard for young Wit"), it is also
subtly evoked in the rest of the play through the main character's on-
again-off-again antics with regard to his beard. In fact, More both grows
facial hair and removes it several times throughout the play. He first
describes himself as having a "thin" beard, but then after his alienation
from the King, he receives what he (ironically) calls "a smooth court
shaving" (4.2.56–7).[51] Subsequently, however, More's facial hair returns;
during his imprisonment in the tower, he contemplates having "a barber
for his beard" (5.3.98), but decides not to cut it. Finally, he appears on
the scaffold at the end of the play beardless, having removed the beard
after all.

   It is hardly surprising to find that the beard is so central in *The Book
of Sir Thomas More*, given that two of the best-known anecdotes about
the life of the illustrious statesman and author involved his facial hair.
The first of these is described in many early modern sources, including
John Harington's *Metamorphosis of Ajax* (1596). Apparently, while More
was in the Tower, he told a courtier who was visiting him that he had
had a change of heart. The courtier assumed that More was talking
about his refusal to subscribe to the Oath of Supremacy and Act of
Succession, and ran to tell the King. The courtier finally returned, saying
that More should put his recantation into writing. At that point, More
explained:

I have not changed my mind in that matter, but only this; I thought to have sent
for a Barber, to have bene shaven ere I had died, but now if it please the King,
he shal cut off head, and beard, and all together.[52]

The second anecdote is an incident that took place on the scaffold during More's beheading. It is recorded by both Foxe and Hollinshed. According to Foxe,

...even when he [More] should laie downe his head on the blocke, he hauing a great graie beard, stroked out his beard, and said to the hangman, I praie you let me laie my beard ouer the block, lest you should cut it.[53]

In the seventeenth century, More's biographers also included the quip: "My beard has done no offense to the King."[54]

Both of these incidents appear in somewhat attenuated form in the final scenes of *The Book of Sir Thomas More*. In the Tower, More addresses the following lines to his wife:

I thought to have had a barber for my beard,
Now I remember that were labor lost,
The headsman now shall cut off head and all.
(5.3.97–9)

A version of the incident on the scaffold also appears in the play. More tells the hangman "One more thing, take heed thou cutst not off my beard," but then he "remembers" that "execution [was] passed upon that last night, and the body of it lies buried in the Tower" (5.4.99–101). The apparent discrepancy between this speech and the one in the Tower has usually been explained as an effect of collaboration – a result of the fact that these two scenes were written by two different playwrights.[55]

What I want to suggest here is that the play's obsession with facial hair needs to be understood in relation to one of its primary themes: the mutability or transferability of identity. This theme is again appropriate for the historical subject-matter since the main drama of Sir Thomas More's life revolved around the question of whether he would change his religious affiliation/identity. Jeffrey Masten has analyzed the importance of this theme, pointing out that characters constantly modify or transform their identity in the course of the play, in part by identifying with, or as, others.[56] For example, in the opening scenes depicting the riots between the English and the "strangers," Doll Williamson participates in the violence and in doing so, identifies as a man.[57] In addition, Doll seems to identify across class lines since she transgresses sumptuary legislation by wearing a "ruff." Later in the same scene, More asks all of the rioters to perform a kind of collective cross-identification: he asks the English in particular to put themselves in the strangers' shoes, transporting them imaginatively to a foreign country. In the middle of the play, the servants Randall and Falkner also go through identity changes. Randall impersonates More, his master, for the interview with Erasmus, and Falkner radically transforms himself by cutting his hair. In fact, Falkner's metamorphosis is so complete that More is no longer able to recognize him. Finally, at the end of the play, More lives out, as Masten puts it, the kind of "estrangement or cross-identification" that he himself had conjured up in his earlier speech during the riot.[58] He goes from being a trusted advisor to a traitor and martyr. Indeed, his very name is altered to emphasize his transformation: he is (paradoxically) reduced to "More" by having his supplemental titles stripped from him.

If *The Book of Sir Thomas More* thus tends to figure identity as being malleable and transferable, the facial hair in the play draws attention to this. For example, in the metadramatic performance of *The Marriage of Wit and Wisdom*, there is a discussion of whether the beard is an integral part of Wit's identity. At first, it seems that Wit must be bearded since the performance is postponed on account of the missing beard (this is reminiscent of the way in which Folly wit and Bottom needed their beards in order to play the parts of men). Later, however, this initial perception is problematized. More states that the actor "may be without a beard till he come to marriage, for wit goes not all by the hair" (3.2.143–4); and in fact, the actors do eventually begin the performance without the beard. When More claims that "wit goes not all by the hair," he may be implicitly contrasting wit and wisdom, and suggesting that Wit does not need to wear a beard because it is wisdom that is traditionally associated with facial hair (as in the figure of the bearded philosopher). In this regard, we might notice that Good Council, who is the wisdom figure in the play-within-the-play, is played by the bearded More himself. Another interpretation, however, is that More is implicitly linking wit with wisdom, but drawing on the proverb that stipulated that "The beard does not make the philosopher," or more humorously, "if the beard made the wise man, then goats would be philosophers."[59] More himself makes a similar comment to Falkner after his haircut: he claims that Falkner "has less hair...but more wit," and thus implies that before his haircut, Falkner had, as the proverb goes, "more hair than wit." These two contradictory interpretations of the same line imply contrasting relationships between inside and out. In the former, the hair and beard materialize intelligence, whereas in the latter, they do not.

Whatever the meaning of the first part of More's statement, he eventually qualifies it by saying that although Wit "may be without a beard" at the beginning of the play, this can only be "till he come to marriage." In this line, More seems to be drawing upon the marriage discourse that I examined earlier – a discourse that equated having a beard with being marriageable. Although the discussions of beards in *Sir Thomas More* do not seem for the most part to link facial hair with masculinity, this is one instance in which the ideologies of masculinity surface. Moreover, we also need to recognize that the more general issue regarding facial hair in this scene (about whether the beard makes the wit) clearly echoes the issue I mapped out earlier (about whether the beard makes the man).

The metadramatic scene also echoes the scene that immediately precedes it. There, More has a long discussion with the "ruffian," Falkner, about his long locks, and the question is ultimately whether they too are integral. When Falkner refuses to have his hair cut (implying that they are in fact essential), More sends him to Newgate. So whereas More claims, in the later scene, that Wit's identity is *not* bound up with his facial hair, in this one, he makes the opposite point. Indeed, when Falkner identifies himself as the servant of the secretary Master Morris, More states that "A fellow of your hair is very fit / To be a secretary's follower" (3.1.83–4). More quibbles on the meaning of "hair" as "nature, or character," virtually equating the two.[60] Moreover, when Falkner eventually cuts his hair, More cannot believe he is still the same person: Falkner says that he is "a new man my lord" and More responds "sure this is not he" (3.1.225–6). Both of these statements imply that Falkner's hair is an integral part of his identity.

If these scenes seem to present contradictory viewpoints (from the same character) about whether beards and hair are essential, they also complicate this issue further by calling attention to the prosthetic nature of hair. In the metadramatic scene, this is done most obviously by showing that the "commodity of the beard" can be obtained from a haberdasher. In addition, More emphasizes the detachability of his own beard when he offers it as a replacement for the actor's missing beard: he says "I'd lend [Wit] mine" (3.2.167). More's offer here recalls the scene at the beginning of the act where he dresses his man Randall in his clothes. Whereas in the previous scene, More successfully shifted the markers of his identity to his servant, however, in this one, this seems to be an impossibility. More explains that he cannot loan his beard to the actor who will play Wit because it is "too thin." Interestingly, the impediment to the transfer here is not the fact that it is More's "real" beard that is in question (as might be expected); rather, it is simply its size.

More's proposal about the loan of his facial hair is a classic instance of Freudian negation: he imaginatively enacts the transfer of his beard even as he denies that it is a possibility. Moreover, by invoking his beard's transferability, More implicitly equates it with the "false" beard that the player has gone to get. Although More's beard is meant to be "real" in the scene, we should note that in reality it was almost certainly "false" (given the changes the actor had to go through in the course of the play). Thus, the scene flirts with unmasking its own theatrical artifice. For my purposes, however, the crucial thing to note is that in the process, the scene also powerfully foregrounds the prosthetic nature of all facial hair by suggesting that even the "real" beard is a commodity that might be lent from one person to another.

These issues are again conspicuously taken up in the final scenes of the play. In fact, an effective dramatic link could be constructed between these two sections of the performance by having the actor who plays More wear Wit's prosthetic beard at the end of the play. If this were done, it would visually underscore the parallels between the two characters – emphasizing the way in which More, in a sense, becomes Wit. Indeed, throughout the scene he banters in a jocular fashion. It would also draw attention to the transformation of More's identity. Whereas earlier More himself "married" both wit and wisdom, here he is reduced to wit because he is no longer considered a "wise" and respected statesman.

Moreover, having More wear *the actor's* beard would foreground the metadramatic qualities of the final scenes, indicating that More is being forced to perform a role in someone else's drama. He himself suggests such an interpretation when he says "my offense to his highness makes of a state pleader a stage player (though I am old, and have a bad voice) to act this last scene of my tragedy" (5.4.73–5). The image of More as a "stage player" already reverberates with the earlier play-within-the-play, where More takes on the role of Good Counsel and the players as a result are ready to convert him into an actor: "Would not my lord make a rare player? O, he would uphold a company beyond all ho, better than Mason among the King's players" (3.2.295–7). For his part, More, like Bottom, seems ready to play all the roles. Having More wear Wit's beard in the Tower would visually conjure up these connections.

Even if Wit's false beard was not used to strengthen the link between these two sections of the play, they would still resonate with one another thematically insofar as they both explore the beard's relationship to identity. The final scenes of the play describe More's imprisonment and eventual execution; the dramatic tension in them arises from the uncertainty about whether he will change his religious affiliation in order to save his life. More's constant references to his beard in these same scenes may, at first, simply seem to be comic relief; the gravity of the dilemma concerning his religious conversion is offset by the triviality of the dilemma concerning whether he should shave his beard. I want to suggest, however, that religious identity and beard growth are not completely unrelated. In part, this is because the religious differences between Catholics and Protestants were, at least in some instances, materialized through facial hair: Catholic priests were often figured without beards and Protestants divines often represented with them.[61] The clean-shaven faces of Catholic priests demonstrate that they have become "eunuchs for God."[62] By contrast, the Protestant preachers' facial hair materializes their marriageability. The distinction between the two groups is powerfully visualized on the title page of John Foxe's *Book of Martyrs*, where virtually all the Protestants on the left side of the page have beards and the Catholic monks on the right side of the page do not.[63] This contrast is particularly conspicuous in the two juxtaposed images at the center of the page. There, seven Protestant martyrs are shown burning at the stake with clearly defined and fully developed facial hair. Across the page from them, the corresponding Catholics are beardless and have traditional tonsure.

Understanding the beard's role in fashioning religious differences between Protestants and Catholics can help deepen our understanding of the scenes at the end of the play. In the Tower, for example, one of the jokes is that More changes his mind about his beard rather than about his religious beliefs. Although we might have initially seen these two decisions as antithetical, it should now be clear that they could also be linked. Moreover, the scene gains part of its resonance from the contrast with the earlier scene with Falkner. Whereas More has a change of heart about his haircut *instead* of about his conversion, Falkner's haircut *is* his conversion.

If the final scenes of *Sir Thomas More* become richer once we recognize that religious identity was materialized through facial hair, it is worth noting that they also continue to foreground the ambiguous materiality of this part. The beard is relentlessly corporealized in these scenes through its implicit comparison with – and connection to – the head. At the same time, however, both of these parts are shown to be detachable. The humor in these scenes derives from the fact that More treats the beard as if it were as much a part of his body as his head, and indeed there is a sense in which this is true for him. For example, More equates the two parts when he decides in the Tower that he will not clip his beard, but rather "The headsman now shall cutt off head and all" (5.3.99). While the primary thrust of jokes such as this is to emphasize the similarity between the head and beard and stress that the head can be detached just like the beard, they have the rhetorical side-effect of corporealizing the beard and making it seem just as integral as the head. More's comments on the scaffold continue in much the same vein. There, he warns the hangman to "take heed thou cutst not off my beard" (5.4.99). The humor again results from More's treating the beard as if it were a critical part of his body. In fact, in this instance, More is *more* protective of his beard than his head.

The corporeality of More's beard is also evoked by the language he uses to describe it. For example, More "remembers" on the scaffold that he need not protect his facial hair because he left "the body of it... buried in the tower" (5.4.101). When More speaks of the "body" of his beard, his language not only resonates with his comments treating the beard as if it were as much a part of the body as the head, it also resonates with Falkner's language in the earlier scene. There, when More mentions his disbelief about Falkner's identity, Falkner claims that if More needs proof that he is who he says he is, "the barber shall give you a sample of my head" (3.1.227–8). If he thus confers a kind of corporeal status on his hair, by referring to it as a "sample of [his] head," he does so while simultaneously foregrounding its detachability (much as More does in the execution scenes).

What is odd, from my perspective, about *Sir Thomas More* is that although the beard is central throughout the play, and although it is generally linked to identity, it is, for the most part, not linked with masculinity or masculine identity. While the beard obviously worked to materialize all sorts of early modern identities, in this essay, I have focused on the way in which it worked to materialize gendered identity. Moreover, I have tried to demonstrate that the theatre was an important cultural site where the early modern ideologies of masculinity were (per)formed. But even if *Sir Thomas More* does not explicitly address the beard's relationship to masculinity, it is nevertheless of interest because of the way in which it foregrounds the paradoxical materiality of facial hair: while this part is, as we have seen, relentlessly corporealized in the play, it is also conspicuously detachable. Moreover, it is worth noting that the play also calls attention to the malleability of identity materialized through this prosthetic part. In fact, the jokes about More's "change of heart" make it clear that one's identity can always be modified just as a beard can always be modified. As a result, both are in need of constant reconfirmation or rematerialization.

In the end, I believe that this is the point that will be hardest for modern readers to comprehend. While we may readily acknowledge the importance of beards on the stage, and in English Renaissance culture in general, it is harder to appreciate exactly what it would mean to say that masculinity was bound up with a prosthetic part. The false beards of the early modern theatre, however, force us to grapple with these issues, for they were often deployed in a way that called attention to their liminality and transferability. Moreover, once we have recognized this characteristic in stage beards, it is only a small step to the realization that "real" beards are also extraordinarily liminal: as we have seen, there is a sense in which they both are and are not a part of the body. From there, we can perhaps begin to appreciate the fact that the identities constructed through these parts might at times seem fixed or naturalized, while at others they might seem completely malleable and provisional.

NOTES

I have been working on this project for quite some time now and have benefited greatly from the assistance of many people. First and foremost, I would like to thank Phyllis Rackin and Peter Stallybrass for all of their work and support. Each of them read numerous drafts of this essay and helped mould it into what it is today. I would also like to thank Gail Kern Paster and Patricia Parker for their encouragement as the project began to take shape and for suggestions on how to improve it. The comments of the members of the Folger seminar where I first formulated and presented this research were also quite helpful, especially those of Natasha Korda. Bruce Boehrer and Lucy Monroe both provided excellent references. Finally, I am grateful to Margreta De Grazia, Jeff Masten, and Valerie Traub for reading the paper and providing their own unique comments and insights.

Thanks to Jean Howard for accepting an early version for the MLA session on "Renaissance masculinities" and to the organizers of the "Body parts" conference, especially to Suzie Verderberer and Lynne Festa, for allowing me to present it in that forum. Thanks also to Joan de Jean for her helpful advice on that occasion. The revision of this essay for publication was aided by a generous grant from PSC-CUNY Grants Program and the Shuster Fellowship Program at Lehman College.

1. For an account of James's visit, including a contemporary description of many of the events including the performance of *Alba*, see John Nichols' *The*

Progresses, Processions, and Magnificent Festivities of King James the First (London: J. B. Nichols, 1828) 1: pp. 530–64.

2. R. A. Foakes and R. T. Rickert (eds.), *Henslowe's Diary* (Cambridge: Cambridge University Press, 1961). See especially Henslowe's inventories for the Lord Admiral's Men, pp. 317–25. It is worth noting that these inventories do not mention beards, but they tend not to be very detailed and therefore do not mention any smaller properties.

3. Albert Feuillerat (ed.), *Documents relating to the Office of the Revels in the time of Queen Elizabeth,* (Louvain: A. Uystpruyst, 1908).

4. *Collections (Malone Society)*, general editor W. W. Greg (Oxford: The Malone Society, 1909), 1.3: pp. 251–9. The documents include notes by F. S. Boas. The production at Oxford is also discussed by Jean MacIntyre in *Costumes and Scripts in the Elizabethan Theaters* (Edmonton: University of Alberta Press, 1992), pp. 72–5.

5. Alan H. Nelson (ed.), *Records of Early English Drama, Cambridge, Volume 1: The Records* (Toronto: University of Toronto Press, 1989), p. 127.

6. There has been a lot of work in recent years on the construction of masculinity in early modern England. The following are only a few of the most important studies. S. D. Amussen, " 'The part of a Christian man': the cultural politics of manhood in early modern England," *Political Culture and Cultural Politics in Early Modern England: Essays Presented to David Underdown* (Manchester: Manchester University Press, 1995); A. Bray, "To be a man in early modern society: the curious case of Michael Wigglesworth," *History Workshop Journal* 41 (1996); Mark Breitenberg, *Anxious Masculinity in Early Modern England* (Cambridge: Cambridge University Press, 1996); Lynn Enterline, *The Tears of Narcissus: Melancholia and Masculinity in Early Modern Writing* (Stanford: Stanford University Press, 1995); A. Fletcher, *Gender, Sex and Subordination in England 1500–1800* (New Haven: Yale University Press, 1995); Elizabeth A. Foyster, *Manhood in Early Modern England: Honour, Sex and Marriage* (London: Longman, 1999); Coppélia Kahn, *Man's Estate: Masculine Identity in Shakespeare* (Berkeley: University of California Press, 1981); David Kuchta, "The semiotics of masculinity in Renaissance England," in James Grantham Turner (ed.), *Sexuality and Gender in Early Modern England: Institutions, Texts, Images* (Cambridge: Cambridge University Press, 1993), pp. 233–47; Bruce Smith, *Shakespeare and Masculinity* (New York: Oxford University Press, 2000); Andrew P. Williams (ed.), *The Image of Manhood in Early Modern Literature: Viewing the Male* (Westport, CT: Greenwood Press, 1999).

7. Thomas Hill, *The contemplation of mankinde, contayning a singular discourse of phisioqnomie. In the ende is a little treatise of moles, by Melampus* (London, 1571), p. 148.

8. Hugh Crompton, *The Glory of Women . . . first written in Latine by Henricus Cornelius Agrippa, Knight* (London, 1652), p. 14.

9. Will Fisher, "The Renaissance beard: masculinity in early modern England," in *Renaissance Quarterly* 54 (2001): 155–87.

10. See John Valerian, *A Treatise Which Is Intitled in Latin Pro Sacerdotum Barbis* (London, 1533), p. 7.

11. Thomas Hall, *The Loathsomeness of Longe Hair* (London, 1653), p. 8.

12. Helkiah Crooke, *A Description of the Body of Man. The second Edition Corrected and Enlarged* (London, 1631), p. 70.

13. Bulwer, *Anthropometamorphosis*, p. 193.

14. *Haec Vir* is printed in Katherine Usher Henderson and Barbara F. Mc-Manus (eds.), *Half Humankind: Contexts and Texts of the Controversy about Women in England, 1540–1640* (Urbana: University of Illinois Press, 1985), p. 286.

15. Marcus Antonius Ulmus, *Physiologia barbae humanae* (Rome, 1602).

16. This is Bulwer's description of Ulmus's argument. Bulwer, *Anthropometamorphosis*, p. 208.

17. Hill, *The Contemplation of Mankinde*, pp. 145–6.

18. Crooke, *A Description of the body of man*, p. 67.

19. Ibid., p. 67.

20. Ibid.

21. If this is the case, then the early modern sex–gender system would have been organized around a tripartite set of distinctions between men, women, and boys, as opposed to the modern binary arrangement. It may well be, however, that there was a corresponding split in the production of femininity in the early modern period, in which case sexual distinctions would have been fourfold. This question requires further investigation.

    It seems clear, however, that boys, women, and castrati were all alike in the fact that they were not bearded "men." This is not to say that there were no differences *between* boys, women and castrati, or in other words, that boys and women, for example, were interchangeable or identical. As Jonathan Goldberg has trenchantly observed, collapsing these different categories runs the risk of turning all eroticism into heteroeroticism. See Goldberg's *Sodometries: Renaissance Texts, Modern Sexualities* (Palo Alto: Stanford University Press, 1992).

22. Stephen Orgel, *Impersonations: The Performance of Gender in Shakespeare's England* (Cambridge: Cambridge University Press, 1996).

23. Lisa Jardine, "Twins and travesties: gender, dependency, and sexual availability in *Twelfth Night*," in Susan Zimmerman (ed.), *Erotic Politics: Desire on the Renaissance Stage* (New York: Routledge, 1992), pp. 27–38.

24. Randal Holme, *The Academy of Armory* (Chester, 1688), p. 391.

25. Facial hair was not the only way in which this difference was produced: others important "signs" might include the voice, swords, testicles, skin, and armor.

26. In *Francis Bacon: A Selection of his Works*, ed. Sidney Warhaft (New York: The Odyssey Press, 1965), pp. 302–3.

27. *The Plays and Poems of William Cartwright*, ed. G. Blakemore Evans (Madison: University of Wisconsin Press, 1951), p. 347.

28. Ben Jonson, *Epicoene, or The Silent Women*, ed. L. A. Beaurline (Lincoln: University of Nebraska Press, 1966), 5.3.171–2.

29. *The Plays and Poems of Phillip Massinger*, ed. Philip Edwards and Colin Gibson (Oxford: Oxford University Press, 1976), vol. IV, p. 119.

30. Sir Philip Sidney, *The Countess of Pembroke's Arcadia*, introduction by Carl Dennis (Kent, Ohio: Kent State University Press, 1970), p. 36.

31. Valerian, *Pro Sacerdotum Barbis*, p. 7.

32. This is based on examination of many of the extant plays listed in appendix C of Michael Shapiro's *Children of the Revels*. In addition to the plays performed by The Children of Paul's (which I discuss in more detail below), I examined twenty plays performed by other companies and discovered that eight of them explicitly describe characters as having beards. *Children of the Revels: The Boy Companies of Shakespeare's Time and their Plays* (New York: Columbia University Press, 1977), pp. 261–8.

33. Nicholas Udall, *Thersites* (London, 1537), p. 43.

34. Lording Barry, *Ram Alley* (London, 1607–8).

35. Boas suggests – in the Malone Society documents – that the costumes came from the properties of The Children of the Queen's Revels. Both Kirkham and Kendall were associated with this company beginning in 1602. MacIntyre, however, believes that it may well have been from the Revels stock that the order was filled.

36. *A Complaint of Thomas Gylles against the Yeoman of the Revells* (c. December 1572). This document is included as an appendix in Feuillerat (ed.), *Documents relating to the Office of the Revels in the time of Queen Elizabeth*, p. 409.

37. Ibid., p. 177.

38. Ibid., p. 199.

39. A weaver's account book from Coventry in 1570 lists payments "for ye hyer of ij beardes to harry benet." Virtually identitical entries appear a couple of times in the following years. In 1572, for instance, we find: "Item paid for ye hyer of ij beardes to hary benete." R. W. Ingram (ed.), *Coventry: Records of Early English Drama* (Toronto: University of Toronto Press, 1981), pp. 252, 255, 258.

40. *The Book of Sir Thomas More* (Oxford: Malone Society Reprints, 1990), p. 38.

41. The inventory of the items hired for the Christmas performance at Westminster School is included in Lawrence E. Tanner's *Westminster School: A History* (London: Country Life Ltd, 1934). The other information comes from the Cambridge volume of the *Records of Early English Drama*, ed. Alan H. Nelson (Toronto: University of Toronto Press, 1989), pp. 223–4. My thanks to Lucy Munroe for telling me about this inventory.

42. Reavley Gair. *The Children of Paul's: The Story of a Theater Company, 1553–1608* (Cambridge: Cambridge University Press, 1982), p. 143.

43. Gair does qualify his claim by limiting the beard prohibition to 1599–1602. Although the plays that would have necessitated false beards do indeed fall outside Gair's date frame, I don't see why those props wouldn't have been used during that period as well. The five plays which would have required the use of prosthetic beards are *Endemion, A Mad World, My Masters, Antonio's Revenge, The Phoenix, North-ward Hoe.* Gair does acknowledge that

false beards must have been used in *Antonio's Revenge* and *The Phoenix*, but he dismisses these incidents as anomalies in which the false beard is utilized as a comic prop. This "explanation," however, does not account for the four plays in which the prosthetic beard is not simply part of a gag; nor, for that matter, does it really effectively account for the two in which the beards were used humorously. Even if false beards were used as a comic prop in these plays, this does not mean that the boys did not normally wear them. In fact, I would argue that these comic interludes might just as easily suggest that the wearing of prosthetic beards was *customary*. When seen from this perspective, the humor would result from the deliberate unmasking of a theatrical convention.

There are at least nine other extant plays in which characters are described as having facial hair. While it is, of course, possible that the parts in this second category were filled by boys who had "real" facial hair, I believe that it is just as likely that false beards were used in at least some of these instances, especially since the color of the beard is often specified in the play. The nine plays that mention beards are *The Wisdom of Doctor Doddypoll* (1600), Lyly's *Mother Bombie* (1589), *The Maydes Metamorphosis* (1600), Marston's *Antonio and Mellida* (1599) and *The Fawn* (1605), Middleton's *A Trick to Catch the Old-One* (1604) and *Family of Love* (1605), Dekker's *Satiro-Mastix* (1601), and Dekker and Webster's *Westward Hoe* (1604).

I am not the first one to recognize the limitations of Gair's argument. R. E. R. Madelaine contests Gair's claim about the boys' use of false beards, discussing Lyly's *Endemion* and Marston's *Antonio and Mellida* in "Boys' beards and Balurdo," *Notes and Queries* 228 (1983): 148–50.

44. A similar assumption seems to be behind Giorgio Melchiori's comment about the possible use of a false beard in *The Book of Sir Thomas More* (and it is not even about a boys' company play): "an obviously false beard in the last few scenes would have damaged [More's] credibility with the audience." In "The contextualization of source materials: the play within the play in *Sir Thomas More*," *Le Forme del Teatro* (Rome: Edizioni di storia e letteratura, 1984) III: 86.

45. Gair, *The Children of Paul's*, p. 143.

46. Margorie Garber has suggested, in *Vested Interests*, that there is a particularly modern anxiety about the artifactuality or detachability of masculinity: "traditionally, transvestism . . . has turned on the artifactuality of women's bodies – balloon breasts, fluffy wigs, makeup. Is it possible that this overt acknowledgement of artifice – often a source of consternation to women and to feminists – masks another (I hesitate to say, a deeper) concern about the artifactuality and the detachability of maleness?" Margorie Garber, *Vested Interests: Cross-Dressing and Cultural Anxiety* (New York: Penguin Books, 1992), p. 125.

47. The more common boy/woman transvestism is also presented.

48. *A Mad World, My Masters*, in *The Works of Thomas Middleton*, ed. A. H. Bullen (London: John C. Nimmo, 1885), vol. III: 256.

49. Ibid., p. 274.

50. The account books list payments "for egges to trymme vyzerdes...iid." Feuillerat (ed.), *Documents relating to the Office of the Revels in the time of Queen Elizabeth*, pp. 236 and 263.

51. All subsequent references to *The Book of Sir Thomas More* are from the Gabrieli and Melchiori edition. Anthony Munday and others; revised by Henry Chettle... [et al.], *Sir Thomas More: a Play*, ed. Vittorio Gabrieli and Giorgio Melchiori (Manchester: Manchester University Press, 1990).

52. John Harington, *Metamorphosis of Ajax*, ed. Elizabeth Story Donno (London: Routledge, 1962), p. 101.

53. John Foxe, *The Ecclesiastical Historie, conteining the Acts and Monuments of Martyrs* (London, 1583), p. 1069. See also *The Third Volume of Chronicles... first compiled by Raphael Holinshed* (London, 1586–7), p. 938.

54. Doyle claims that it was Francis Bacon who first gave the anecdote this punchline in his *Apophtegmes New and Old* (1625): he writes "Sir Thomas Moore...at the very instant of his death, having a pretty long beard, after his head was upon the block, lift it up again, and gently drew his beard aside, and said, This hath not offended the King." See Charles Clay Doyle, "The hair and beard of Thomas More," *Moreana* 18 (1981): 5–6.

55. More recently, Giorgio Melchiori has argued that the "discrepancy" may also have been the result of confusion about how to portray More. He says that the playwrights may have been "uncertain between the traditional iconography of a beardless More and the reports of his having grown a beard during his imprisonment," with the consequence that they portrayed him without facial hair in the final scene, but bearded in the tower scene. See "The contextualization of source materials," p. 86.

 In the end, I don't find either of these explanations completely satisfying. I believe that the "inconsistency" probably has more to do with a decision to privilege humor and thematic resonance over logic and realism. As we will see, the two final scenes (and their jokes about More's beard) resonate with each other in a number of different ways.

56. Jeffrey Masten, "*More* or less: editing the collaborative." Paper presented in the "Editing Shakespeare revisited" panel of the Shakespeare Association of American Annual Meeting, 2000. As will be clear from the following discussion, I am deeply indebted to this article. I thank Jeff for sharing it with me.

57. It is worth noting, however, that this is an imaginary identification – not because Doll is a woman, but because the men, at least according to Doll, are not behaving like real men.

58. Masten, "*More* or less," 12.

59. See Charles Clay Doyle's discussion of this line in "The hair and beard of Thomas More," 7.

60. As the note in the Vittorio and Melchiori edition points out, this is the sixth definition listed in the *OED*.

61. I don't mean to imply that this actually worked out in practice. In fact, there were debates within the Catholic church about whether the clergy should wear beards or not. On this issue, see Valerian's *Pro Sacerdotum Barbis*.
62. My thanks to Peter Stallybrass for these observations and this formulation.
63. The 1610 title page can be viewed on the Center for Electronic Text and Image database at the University of Pennsylvania, http://library. upenn.edu/etext/furness/foxe/index.html. John Foxe, *Actes and monuments of matters most speciall and memorable* ... (London, 1610).

PART IV

Hand Properties

Properties of marriage: proprietary conflict and the calculus of gender in Epicoene

Juana Green

In *Epicoene* (1609), Ben Jonson exploits the ability of stage properties to materialize, in spectacular form, early modern cultural concerns about shared marital property. Through his calculated choice of props, he exposes marital property's ability to create domestic discord. Jonson manifests concerns about marital property by reversing cultural expectations regarding gendered property relations, positioning Captain Otter as a husband without property rights. Having married for money and, in exchange, conceded control of the household to his wife, Otter must petition her to use the very things by which he identifies himself: animal-shaped carousing cups. These fashionable drinking vessels, which were popular among members of the Jacobean court, function within the play as status objects that blur distinctions of class and gender. Shaped in the forms of a bull, a bear, and a horse, the cups serve as visual referents to Captain Otter's former occupation as a bearwarden; thus, when the Captain and his wife battle for their control, the animal cups, through their reference to the Bear Garden, turn the Otter household into a theatricalized space. The Otters are a dramatic exaggeration, but as such their situation reveals real social tensions between husbands and wives regarding marital property.

In early modern England, a married woman's property rights were circumscribed by law and custom: unless it was protected by a trust for separate estate, any property a woman owned at marriage or acquired during marriage became her husband's. While under coverture, a woman could acquire and use property, but legally she could not exercise complete ownership rights over it without her husband's permission. Nevertheless, such absolute rules were often ignored; and safeguards did exist to protect certain categories of property.[1] In practice, wives exercised considerable control over property, especially everyday household things. Legally, she may not have had proprietary rights to the things themselves, but economically, the huswife's careful management of marital property contributed significantly to the household's wealth and to her reputation.[2]

The gap between a married woman's legal rights in property and a wife's practical management of property created a potential site for conflict between husbands and wives, and Jonson carefully locates the Otters' battle over drinking vessels in this gap. Read in relation to early modern conduct discourses, Mrs. Otter represents a stereotypical shrew, and the Otters' topsy-turvy marriage serves as an object of satire. The disordered Otter marriage functions also as an object lesson to Morose whose belated and hasty marriage, undertaken to thwart his nephew's expectation of inheritance, results not in an heir as Morose plans, but in public humiliation and alienation from his own property. In its multiple representations of marriage's role in determining property relations, *Epicoene* displays a cultural anxiety about women's control of property, an anxiety that gets staged when the Otters contend for control of the carousing cups.

At first glance, drinking vessels may seem too mundane an object over which to stage a marital conflict, and the critical tendency to overlook or discount the Otter narrative may be in part because the Otters battle over seemingly trifling things. Yet everyday objects were the stuff of domestic arguments; and arguments over practical things say much about the people who argue over them as well as about the issues at stake. Cups, however, were not merely practical objects. Philippa Glanville asserts they "had the highest status of any item of precious metal in Tudor and early Stuart England. Cups formed the core of the New Year's gift exchange, and passed as marks of honor from monarch to foreign prince or envoy, at weddings and christenings, and when a man entered into the higher ranks of office."[3] Jonson could rely, therefore, upon his audience's understanding of cups as icons of cultural significance, and the centrality of cups as stage properties makes them exemplary objects for considering how the materiality of stage properties can add to our understanding of a play. The conflicting meanings the play produces for these particular stage properties make visible the ways in which the play is inflected by cultural concerns about property and women's roles in its transmission. When Jonson associates animal cups with the Otters and their disordered marriage, he demonstrates the inextricable bond that links together the multiple meanings of the term "property," which can refer at once to ownership or proprietorship, a specific thing one owns, a characteristic attribute of a person or thing, an appropriate or suitable behavior, and a stage property.[4]

My aim in this essay is to examine the complex web of signification that surrounds these properties by suggesting possible meanings the cups might have held for contemporary theatergoers. My methodology moves between what Jonathan Gil Harris and Natasha Korda have called in the introduction to this volume "the qualitative analysis of the stuff of material culture" and the "quantitative analysis of patterns of production, consumption, and ownership of the world of goods." The first two sections adumbrate the cultural values and significances of these objects within the world of the play and early modern London life, whereas the third section links the material and symbolic attributes of the cups to the economic framework of early modern property law. Conceptually, what hold these sections together are materialist theories of consumer culture that understand objects as not only carriers of cultural values but also catalysts for creating new values. When an object appears on stage, it both acquires meaning and imparts significance to its present context. The stage life of an object thus becomes part of what Appadurai calls an object's "cultural biography." To read the culturally specific meanings for an object it is necessary to trace the trajectory of an object's life as it "moves through different hands, contexts, and uses."[5] In what follows, I create a brief "cultural biography" for animal cups, tracing the passage of these stage properties through the narrative of *Epicoene* and from the Whitefriars stage into London shops and affluent households. Attending to the material attributes of the cups, I shall argue, elevates the Otter narrative from its subordinate status; for in considering the cups as a type of property that was subject to the early modern law of coverture, rewritten in *Epicoene* to place men's property rights in abeyance instead of women's, we can recognize this neglected part of the play not as one more early modern shrew narrative, but as a culturally nuanced representation of the potential ills contemporaries associated with shared marital property. At stake in the conflict over women's control and ownership of marital property are the stability of gender relations and the balance of conjugal power within the household.

MATERIAL PROPERTIES

The carousing cups occupy a central position in the two scenes of domestic conflict between Captain and Mrs. Otter. Initially the cups are aligned with the Captain by Truewit who, introducing Otter to Dauphine, Clerimont, and the audience, explains how Otter marshals his bull, bear, and horse at home (2.6.57–64):[6]

Why, sir, he has been a great man at the Bear Garden in his time, and from that
subtle sport has ta'en the witty denomination of his chief carousing cups. One
he calls his bull, another his bear, another his horse. And then he has his lesser
glasses, that he calls his deer and his ape, and several degrees of 'em too, and
never is well, nor thinks any entertainment perfect, till these be brought out and
set o' the cupboard.

Dauphine and Clerimont, who are anxious to observe this spectacle, are
escorted to the Otters' home where the cups are "brought out and set
o' the cupboard" by the Captain. As promised, they witness the Otters
haggling over the bull, bear, and horse until Mrs. Otter's threat, "I'll take
away your exhibition" (3.1.54), concludes the scene. The cups reappear
when the action shifts to Morose's home where Captain Otter, the former
bearward, recreates a bear-baiting by staging a drinking bout, complete
with drum rolls and trumpet calls. The spectacle foregrounds the cups
and the Captain's command over them, at least until Mrs. Otter starts
beating her husband and Morose stops her (4.2.107, s.d.). The scene ends
after the defeated Captain, having searched somewhat pathetically for
his "bull-head" (4.2.125), finds the lid to his cup and carries it offstage.

Given the prominence of the carousing cups in these two scenes we
need to ask what the actor playing Otter carries offstage. And what was
set on the cupboard that made up Captain Otter's "exhibition"? The
lack of evidence for the small properties used in staging the period's
many banqueting and tavern scenes presents a conundrum,[7] especially
for *Epicoene*, in which the audience is asked to participate imaginatively
in the Captain's staged drinking bout (4.2) and in the wedding dinner
served by La Foole (3.7), for which the Otters supply not only the food and
wine but also the "silver dishes" (3.3.104). Unlike banqueting and tavern
scenes that call for generic stools, cushions, and cups, *Epicoene* demands
drinking vessels of a distinctive type, and savvy theatergoers would have
understood the cups within the cultural matrix of London material life.
Thomas Heywood offers a glimpse of that life in *Philocothonista, or, The
Drunkard, Opened, Dissected, and Anatomized* (1635) when he catalogues, in a
rather lengthy passage, the vessels available to the discriminating English
drinker (F3r–v):

...divers and sundry sorts wee have, some of *Elme*, some of *Box*, some of
Maple, some of *Holly*, &c. *Mazers*, broad-mouth'd dishes, *Noggins*, *Whiskins*,
Piggins, *Crinzes*, *Ale-bowles*, *Wassell-bowles*, *Court-dishes*, *Tankards*, *Kannes*, from
a Pottle to a Pint, from a Pint to a Gill: other Bottles wee have of Leather, but
they most used amongst the Shepheards, and haruest people of the Countrey;
small Iacks wee have in many Alehouses of the Cities, and Suburbs, tipt with

siluer, besides the great black Iacks, and bombards at the Court [...]; wee have besides, cups made of hornes of beasts, of Cocker-nutts, of Goords, of the egges of *Estriches*, others made of the shells of divers fishes brought from the *Indies*, and other places, and shining like mother of *Pearle*: Infinite there are of all measures, and fashions [...]: some I have seene made in the forme or figure of beasts, as of Doggs, Catts, Apes, and Horses, others of Fishes, as Dolphins, &c. But the most curious and costly, either for Workmanship, or Mettall, are brought from *China*: Of glasses to quaffe in, the fashions and sizes be almost without number, some transported hither from Venice, and other places, some made in the Citie by strangers; besides the ordinary sort, I have seen some like Shipps under-sayle, accomodated with Mastes, Sayles, Ordnance, Cable, Anchor, and saylors to man her: others like boates, Lyons, Ratts, Trumpets, and indeede what not?

Clearly, if men or women chose to be "in their cups," as Otter does, they had a plethora of cups from which to choose. Reading this passage is like walking through London's streets and Exchanges, surveying the goods available for sale. Once we recognize that drinking vessels could be had in a seemingly endless variety of sizes, shapes, and materials, and that Jonson has not fabricated a clever conceit but purposefully chosen a style of cup available for sale in London shops, we need to evaluate the potential reasons for, and the effects of, this choice.

In choosing this particular style of cup, Jonson relies on his audience's familiarity with zoomorphic drinking vessels, objects that were highly fashionable in Jacobean London. The rearing bull reproduced in figure 10.1 is an example of the cup Captain Otter might marshal.[8] Of German rather than English manufacture and standing between seventeen and thirty-six centimeters high, this style of partially gilt cup has a hollow body and a removable head that serves as the vessel's cover. The bear in figure 10.2 wears a collar encircled with rings that originally had bells attached. Thus outfitted, the cup would "allude to the sport of bear-baiting, the situation in which the animal would have been familiar to most German people of the time."[9] This style of metalwork was known in early modern England as "Nuremberg plate." The expert workmanship and inventiveness of its design appealed to status-conscious Londoners who bought the more fashionable Nuremberg plate before the English product, thus creating conflict among retailers of foreign plate and the Goldsmiths' Company between 1600 and 1620.[10]

Quite possibly many of the audience members or their friends had the same style of cups standing on their cupboards at home. The Earl of Somerset, Robert Carr, owned several pieces of "Norrombrig worke": a basin with an ewer in the shape of a falcon, a "Bason and Ewer

Figure 10.1 Bull-shaped Nuremberg drinking vessel.

Norrombrig worke gilt the Ewer like an Olophant," and a basin and snail ewer. Inventories of Somerset's belongings document the social and economic framework within which Nuremberg plate fits, and they offer insight into how such fashionable objects may have made their

Figure 10.2 Bear-shaped Nuremberg drinking vessel.

way to the stage. In 1615, Somerset wanted to add to his collection but, short of funds, he delivered 755 ounces of plate to the goldsmith "to bee pauned for 500 [pound] to Get made into plate for the Earles vse." This "old" plate included three gold cups with covers, two gilt cups with covers, and a gilt basin and ewer. Along with the plate sent to pawn, one "Bason & ewer Noremberk" and another "Noremberk" set were delivered to the goldsmith "for paterne for those hee was to make."[11] The objects sent as patterns were possibly, given their respective weights, the elephant and falcon documented in other inventories of the Earl's effects. Nuremberg work was not limited to objects fabricated in animal shapes, however, and without additional documentation it is impossible to determine what types of objects the goldsmith was commissioned to make from these patterns. Yet, in light of *Epicoene* and the courtly aspirations of its characters, it is tempting to visualize animal drinking cups standing on the Earl's cupboard, and I will return to the cultural significance of this possibility later.

The first performance of *Epicoene* occurred midway through the conflict over imported Nuremberg plate, and although I am convinced that Jonson's choice of stage properties is calculated, I cannot confirm that "real" Nuremberg animal cups stood on the cupboard at the Whitefriars performance in 1609/10. Imitation bull, bear, and horse cups could have been fabricated by property-makers and then gilt by painters. The Revels documents show, for example, that property-makers and painters worked closely with one another, constructing props of all sizes.[12] The commercial stage companies could have employed property-makers and painters to fashion the things needed for banqueting scenes. Philip Henslowe recorded in his *Diary* that on 27 June 1602, he "Lent vnto the company" the sum of twenty-five shillings "to paye vnto hime w[hi]ch made ther propertyes for Jeffa."[13] Henslowe also lent money to purchase unspecified "things."[14] What exactly were these "propertyes" and "things"? And where were the "things" bought? Certainly "things" could include the props which are so glaringly absent from theatre records. And if the companies bought and then resold the small properties required for household scenes, this practice would offer one explanation for their absence.

A likely source for small properties was the market in secondhand goods. There was, according to Glanville, "a flourishing trade in secondhand plate in London and the provinces, at all levels of society." Goldsmiths "sold indiscriminately both newly-made items and secondhand plate, which could be easily refurbished and re-engraved to the customer's order."[15] The secondhand market seems to have been connected to the flourishing business of pawnbroking; and if the business practices of John Williams, Robert Carr's goldsmith mentioned above, can be read as paradigmatic of the trade, then the goldsmiths who dealt in secondhand goods might also have been in the business of pawnbroking.[16] When Carr delivered 755 ounces of plate to Williams, he expected Williams to pawn it for 500 pound, money that was then to be used as payment for the making of more fashionable plate. But what happened to the plate that was pawned? Natasha Korda's analysis of Philip Henslowe's pawn-broking accounts suggests that the unwanted or less fashionable plate may have found its way to the stage.[17]

When plays call for specific props like animal cups, however, the players likely followed customary court practices, either borrowing from friends or hiring from goldsmiths.[18] Consequently, goldsmiths, pewterers, and members of other London guilds may have played a crucial role in fur-nishing properties for the stage. Peter Stallybrass's discoveries about the interconnectedness of the commercial theatre and the clothing trade might profitably be used to consider the theatre's connection to other trades, for as Stallybrass points out, "from a legal point of view, the boy actors were not theatrical trainees but apprentice bricklayers, butchers, drapers, goldsmiths, and so on."[19] The relationship between goldsmiths and the commercial theatre warrants further exploration, especially in light of Jonathan Gil Harris's essay in this volume about product placement in early English artisanal drama. Foregrounding consump-tion rather than production, the play-world of *Epicoene* constructs the stage into a "convenient display case" or "shop window" from which to advertise a product. Robert Keysar, an organizer of the Children of the Queen's Revels, the company that first performed *Epicoene*, was also a master goldsmith. Might not he, or one of his guild brethren, have participated in an early modern form of advertising and supplied the fashionable animal cups – and silver dishes – used in *Epicoene*?[20]

So far I have proposed some rather uncertain trajectories for these dis-tinctive stage properties: imported from Germany or copied in London; bought, borrowed or rented from a Cheapside goldsmith, pawnbroker, or friend; then displayed at court, placed on cupboards in wealthy house-holds, and/or carried onto the commercial stage by an actor playing a henpecked husband. Each use, exchange or movement creates new meanings for the object itself. In some cases, the reputations of those who engage in exchange modulate in response to the object's trajec-tory. For example, New Year's gift exchanges at court endowed gifts with added value for both the object and its recipient, but what about the plate Robert Carr sent to the local pawnbroker? Could the past life of this unwanted or unclaimed plate confer cultural capital on both the plate and its next owner in its new context? If bought secondhand by a would-be élite or middle-class consumer, its new owner might conceivably gain reputation among his or her friends, and in its new social setting the plate no longer desired by the Earl could still function as a status object. London's commercial theatres would be one site where new cultural meanings and values are created for the things that appear in performance. But what happens to the cultural capital of luxury objects exhibited on the commercial stage? Would the Earl's pawned plate re-acquire its aura of wealth, and for whom? How might the trajectory from market to theatre and its circulation on stage affect the cultural capital and significance of such things? Would Robert Keysar and other goldsmiths want their ware featured on stage as a form of advertising, and would they care what meanings were created as long as consumers bought their products?

While important, the answers to these questions about the larger cultural value of zoomorphic cups would depend largely upon conjecture. Evidence about the number of Nuremberg objects sold from the Jewel House in 1626 suggests, however, that their status at court remained high throughout James I's reign.[21] If the report of Charles II christening his henpecked brother "Tom Otter" is true, the symbolic capital attending on Captain Otter and the cups survived even longer,[22] and I now want to explore the symbolic meanings the play creates for the animal cups. Examining the uses and trajectories of the cups within the play itself suggests that Jonson intentionally chose this particular stage property in order to complicate early modern ideas about gender and property ownership, although Charles II's pet name for his brother indicates the intransigence of such ideas.

SYMBOLIC PROPERTIES

Truewit's initial description of Captain Otter and his cups (2.6.57–64), quoted above, weaves together cultural beliefs about property ownership and its relationship to identity and social class, thus binding the Captain to the cups in a web of discursive and material associations. Despite his retirement from that anything but "subtle sport" of bear-baiting (2.6.58), Otter continues to construct his identity around the markedly working-class occupation at which he labored prior to his marriage. Employing cups that represent the animals he formerly marshaled in the Bear Garden, Otter stages bouts with these surrogate beasts for the entertainment of courtier pretenders like Truewit who frequent the Otters' home to watch the spectacles.[23] Otter's power to control the cups bespeaks

an authority the play quickly undermines, however, when it uses them
to stage the contested relationship between Otter and his wife. While
the Captain's bouts might please the courtiers, they anger Mrs. Otter
who argues with her husband against the riotous behavior they occasion
(3.1.5–7) and the impropriety of the cups' shapes: "Is a bear a fit beast,
or a bull, to mix in society with great ladies? Think i' your discretion, in
any good polity?" (3.1.16–18). The horse, however, Mrs. Otter approves:
"[great ladies] love to be well horsed, I know. I love it myself" (3.1.20–1).
Exploiting the sexual innuendo, Otter suggests that the bull, too, should
please the ladies since Jupiter himself assumed this form. However, his
insubordination goes too far, and Mrs. Otter, who earlier had threatened
to chain up her husband with the "bull-dogs and bear-dogs" (3.1.2–3),
now threatens: "By my integrity, I'll send you over to the Bankside, I'll
commit you to the master of the Garden, if I hear but a syllable more.
Must my house, or my roof, be polluted with the scent of bears and bulls,
when it is perfumed for great ladies?" (3.1.25–7).

The heated verbal exchange between husband and wife in act 3, scene
1, which foreshadows the physical battle of act 4, scene 2, establishes the
gendered conflict over the cups. In arguing with his wife regarding their
control, Otter declares what's at stake for him: "these things I am known
to the courtiers by. It is reported to them for my humour, and they receive
it so, and do expect it. Tom Otter's bull, bear, and horse is known all over
England, in *rerum natura*" (3.1.11–14). For the Captain, the cups signify his
identity, his independence from an overbearing wife, and his inclusion –
albeit marginalized – in the male community of "courtiers" whom he
entertains. Otter's argument fails, however, to convince his wife, for she
understands how the Captain's staged bouts equate the Otters' home to
a Bear Garden. For Mrs. Otter, the carousing cups signify her husband's
slovenliness and drunkenness, characteristics that expose his lower-class
origins. The Captain's control of the cups undermines her authority
and threatens her efforts to civilize both the Captain and their home.
Furthermore, her inability to control the cups – and by analogy her
husband – threatens her precarious position as "pretender" to the lady
collegiates.

Haggling over the animal cups in this first scene in which the couple
appear together, the Otters display how both the cups and their name fit
their "animal nature." Animals in this period, Claudia Lazzaro argues,
"are cultural signs, embodying a complex of ideas about nature which
also define and sustain contemporary notions of civilization and culture.
In this society, the paradigms of nature and culture, wild and civilized,

were both in opposition and interlocked."[24] Otter's phrase "*rerum natura*"
draws attention to the play's ironic natural order of things: whereas binary gender divisions typically align men with culture and women with
nature, Mrs. Otter's dual concerns for good governance in a polity and
decorum in the presence of ladies aligns her with culture and civilization; Otter's unmannerly habits align him with the wildness of animals.
Jonson's choice of animals makes clear that the Otters' marriage resides
outside the contemporary notion of natural order.

A contemporary understanding of animals would be shaped in part by
natural history treatises such as Edward Topsell's *The History of Four-Footed
Beasts* (1607), itself based upon classical authority. The otter, according
to Topsell, "is a sharp biting Beast, hurtful both to men and dogs, never
ceasing or loosing hold after he hath laid his mouth upon them, until
he make the bones to crack betwixt his teeth [...] Otters are most accomplished biters."[25] The play represents both Mr. and Mrs. Otter as
accomplished biters, but Mrs. Otter is portrayed as the more tenacious
because Mr. Otter requires assistance in extracting himself from her grip,
first from Truewit (3.1.47, 51), then from Morose (4.2.108), and finally
from Dauphine (5.4.203–4). Their family name, R. V. Holdsworth states,
"suggests their sexual topsy-turviness, since the creature was a byword for
the unclassifiable," and he points to Falstaff's remark about the Hostess in
Henry IV Part One (3.3.123–8) as support: she "is an otter [...] she's neither
fish nor flesh, a man knows not where to have her."[26] Otters defy clas-
sification because they confuse established boundaries: "Their outward
form is most like unto a Beaver, saving in their tail, for the tail of a Beaver
is fish, but the tail of an Otter is flesh," writes Topsell.[27] The animal's
tail serves as the physical locus for Topsell's classificatory dilemma as
well as the metaphorical locus for Falstaff's sexualized remark about the
Hostess. As an insulting term, "tail" figured regularly in the period's slander and defamation cases. Whereas men's members were "described with
exactitude," Laura Gowing explains, women's genitals were not: "The
broad word 'tail' is the only one used with any regularity." Tails were
a "key focus," she explains, because tails "were imagined as the locus
of sexual pleasure, and the acts women were supposed to have engaged
in to satisfy that pleasure were visualized with bawdy exaggeration."[28]
Gowing found, however, that abusive words "related only opaquely to
actual sex." Instead, "gendered insults marked off the outlines of gender
roles in sexual, marital, and social relations."[29]

The carousing cups and the conflict they occasion outline the boundaries crossed by Captain and Mrs. Otter. Like the creature whose ability

to traverse boundaries renders it ambiguous, the Otters confuse sexual, gender, and social boundaries in that their marriage effeminates Mr. Otter and positions him as a wife. Despite Mrs. Otter's efforts to control them, the carousing cups are associated symbolically with the Captain, as referents both to his bear-baiting past and to his drunken impropriety. Although female drunkenness occurred, men were the ones stereotypically portrayed as "cupshot" by moralists who inveighed against the "swinish sin." Drunkenness, Edward Bury writes in *England's Bane* (1677), "is such a Sin, as takes away the use of reason and turns a Man into Beast, yea makes him worse than a Beast."[30] The title page to Heywood's *Philocothonista* (1635) (figure 10.3) epitomizes the sin's beastliness in its banquet scene of drunkards with animal heads: the swine vomits onto the floor, the lion threatens the ass with an upraised cup, the sheep stinks up the air with a pipe, while the goose and goat, oblivious to the riot that surrounds them, drain their cups. The scene asks pictorially what Bury asks rhetorically: "what is it that differenceth a Man from a Beast but the use of Reason, but if Reason be drowned, as it is in the Drunkard where lies the difference[?]" Responding to his own question, Bury claims, "'tis true they retain the shape of Men, and that is all, for they much resemble Swine in this also, in their nasty behaviour, wallowing in their Vomit, and moiling themselves in their Dung, and dirt, but they are very brutes in their understanding."[31] In *Philocothonista*'s banqueting scene, the replacement of the drunkard's head with an animal's characterizes his brutishness. Thus anatomized, the drunkard becomes "worse than a Beast" because he blurs the distinction between "man" and beast. Through his clever choice of stage properties, Jonson breathes life into the tired rhetoric of the sin's beastly nature and literalizes Otter's drunken beastliness in a most fashionable way.

In choosing the conceit of animal cups to characterize the Otters, Jonson purposefully selects objects that would appeal to both Mr. and Mrs. Otter, although they would appeal in differing ways to each. The Captain's use of the bull, bear, and horse to entertain the courtiers corresponds to the functionality of German welcome cups used by the nobility,[32] and their forms suit their use by the former bearwarden. As fashionable objects, the cups would appeal to the socially aspiring Mrs. Otter, who prides herself on her courtly taste. She would have been familiar with such tastes since she made her own fortune selling imported commodities in London's "China houses." Jonson may have conceived the idea for these stage props when, earlier the same year, he wrote an entertainment to celebrate the royal visit to the New Exchange at its

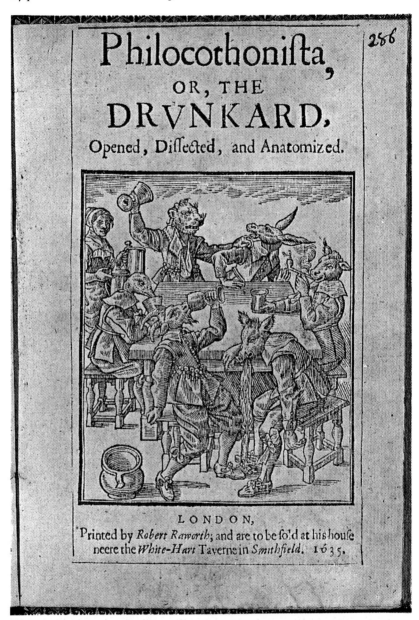

Figure 10.3 Title page to Thomas Heywood, *Philocothonista* (1635).

formal opening on 11 April 1609. The entertainment, known as either *The Key Keeper* or *The Entertainment at Britain's Burse*, is thought to be the one commissioned by Robert Cecil, Earl of Salisbury, who built the New Exchange in the Strand.[33] In *The Key Keeper*, a "China Man" offers an array of imported commodities, including a " 'conceited saltcellar' in the shape of an elephant," Indian mice and rats, silk flowers, wax fruit, hourglasses, and such things as "Basins, Ewers, Cups, Cans, Voyders, Toothpicks."[34] Perhaps the elephant-shaped saltcellar was gilt "Nuremberg-work" since Robert Carr owned one of these;[35] if so, the play's audience may have recognized Mrs. Otter's mercantile connection to the fashionable cups, an association that may have given her an equally strong claim to the cups in their minds.

Cups and silver serving dishes (3.3.104) are two of many signs of the Otter household's affluence and its pretensions to courtliness, and their cupboard of plate signifies that affluence in a culturally expected form. Thomas Heywood comments on the practice of conspicuous display in *Philocothonista* when he discusses plate drinking vessels (F3v–4r):

Come to plate, Every Taverne can afford you flat bowles, French bowles, Prounct Cups, Beare-bowles, Beakers, and private houshoulders in the Citie, when they make a Feast to entertaine their friends, can furnish their cupbords, with Flagons, Tankards, Beere cups, Wine-bowles, some white, some percell guilt, some guilt all over, some with covers, others without, of sundry shapes and qualities. Many can make showes of 50. pounds, or an hundred Mark-worth of plate upon his Table, when hee hath scarce an hundred shillings to dance in his pocket, and that makes the proverbe to grow so common amongst them. *A good pawne never shames his master*. But come to a great mans Invitation in the Citie, the varietie and value of their plate, were it not so common, might to some appeare wonderfull: what then may wee imagine the estate of the Nobilitie, and the Court to be in that kind: No question without valuation [. . .]

While regarded as an important indicator of wealth and status, the once wondrous effects of these sumptuous "showes" were now tarnished, Heywood suggests, because they had become "so common." Heywood blames the city's householders and tavern-keepers who imitated the nobility in the purchase, pawn, and display of plate for the debasement of this form of cultural capital. But might not the theatre share some of the blame when plays dramatize how the middle class apes courtly pretensions using the same objects? Surely the Otters' holdings could not compare to the massive quantities of plate owned by England's peers, livery companies, and wealthy citizen families, and the paucity of the stage display must comprise part of the satire aimed at the Otters, at least for those spectators who had ever witnessed such wondrous shows.

When the Captain and his friends carry the cups to Morose's house to celebrate the bridal, however, the cups take on new meanings. Customarily, cups and other types of plate were given as wedding presents; such gifts were constitutive of the newly formed social relationship. The trajectory of the carousing cups can be related to what Appadurai identifies as "socially regulated paths and competitively inspired diversions."[36] If they were gifts from the Otters to Morose, the cups would be following a socially regulated path to perform their part in gifting. However, the cups become a vehicle for symbolizing the impropriety of Morose's marriage and the absurdity of his wedding, a diversion from customary usage that becomes evident when Morose's wedding is compared to customary bridal practices.

At court, elaborately celebrated weddings featured several days of banquets, masques, dances, tournaments, and fireworks. Among the middling sort, the less costly but no less festive celebration typically included dinner, music, and dancing. Proper weddings were public events. By contrast, private weddings invited censure. When Lord Cranbourne married Katherine Howard "very privatly at the Lady Walsinghams lodging by the Tilt Yard," for example, John Chamberlain commented on the wedding's impropriety: the wedding "was not so fit, for holy thinges shold be solemnised in holy places. There were few at yt." The impropriety is partially overcome, Chamberlain implies, because "there was much plate provided to be geven."[37] In *Epicoene*, Lady Haughty voices a similar displeasure when she chastises Morose: "We see no ensigns of a wedding here, no character of a bridal: where be our scarfs and our gloves? I pray you give 'em us. Let's know your bride's colours and yours at least" (3.6.65–7). Haughty's criticisms, which become increasingly caustic, eventually rest on the absence of gifts: "You that have sucked the milk of the court . . . been a courtier . . . and you to offend in such a high point of ceremony as this, and let your nuptials want all marks of solemnity! How much plate have you lost today – if you had but regarded your profit – what gifts, what friends, through your mere rusticity?" (3.6.72–9). While comic, Haughty's remarks nevertheless inscribe the customary importance of signs to signify ceremony, solemnity, and validity: no gloves and garters for the guests, no plate for the bride and groom, no marriage. Chamberlain repeatedly emphasizes plate's importance to the symbolic and monetary economies of marriage when he reports wedding news in his letters, for he almost unfailingly recounts gifts of plate and their value. At the 1608 wedding celebration for Lord Haddington – for which Jonson wrote a masque – Chamberlain describes how "the King dranck a carouse in a cup of gold, which he sent to the bride, together with a bason and ewer, two livery pots and three standing cuppes all very fayre and massie, of silver and guilt."[38] The presents from King James to Lady Haddington may have been displayed on her cupboard, but by law these expensive gifts were her husband's property. Chamberlain's comments lend credibility to Lady Haughty's chastisement of Morose's "rusticity," and Jonson's audience would probably not quibble with Lady Haughty: plate could translate easily into the groom's "profit."

At Morose's bridal the absence of customary signs marks the marriage as invalid even before the "nullity." No one raises a gold cup to toast the health of Morose and his bride. There are no gifts. Instead, courtesy of Truewit and Dauphine, the Otters parodically supply the feast, music, and revels necessary to make Morose's "hymen high and happy" (3.5.49–50). At this bridal, the animal cups function as the stage properties of an antimasque in which a raucous drinking bout – complete with the "music" of drums and trumpets – recreates the spectacle of a bear-baiting in Morose's home by using the cups to replace live animals. Furthermore, the drinking scene cleverly dramatizes the challenge Mrs. Otter verbalized earlier when she and the Captain argued over the cups' appropriateness: "You were best bait me with your bull, bear, and horse!" (3.1.4–5). In the drinking bout, Daw believes that he and La Foole act as the dogs who bait Otter's "bull" when, in actuality, Dauphine and Clerimont "bait" the Captain who in his drunkenness unwittingly "baits" his wife. Mrs. Otter, watching the action from the side with Truewit, eventually breaks free (4.2.75) and beats her husband, thus becoming one of the "nasty, slutish, animals" Otter claims all wives to be (4.2.50–1).

The two strands of the play's narrative intersect when Dauphine and Truewit orchestrate this ritual of rough music to punish simultaneously Otter, who has abdicated his patriarchal duties, and Morose, whose marriage to Epicoene is aberrant on a number of counts: "she" is a boy, the clandestine marriage takes place without license or banns, and Morose marries solely to hinder his nephew's rightful claim to Morose's property.[39] Immediately following the marriage, Morose had exclaimed, "Oh my felicity! How I shall be revenged on mine insolent kinsman and his plots to fright me from marrying! This night I will get an heir and thrust him out of my blood like a stranger" (2.5.96–9). Morose figures marital felicity in terms of property and revenge. Ironically in view of the play's outcome, Morose considers his marriage felicitous only because it will disinherit his nephew. Earlier, Morose had offered a litany of reasons for why Truewit's harangues of Morose's upcoming marriage were unjustified: "Good Sir! Have I ever cozened any friends of yours of their land? bought their possessions? taken forfeit of their mortgage? begged a reversion from 'em? bastarded their issue? What have I done that may deserve this?" (2.2.41–4). Morose recognizes that each of these crimes against the proper transmission of property warrants punishment. In effect, Morose is attempting to cozen Dauphine from what should rightfully become "his" land. Fittingly, then, for someone who makes a mockery of marriage by marrying merely to thwart another's right in property, the punishments Dauphine and Truewit devise for Morose parody bridal celebrations.

MARITAL PROPERTIES

Through the use of stage properties, *Epicoene* represents how social disorder in one household can produce disorder in another when the Otters, battling over the cups, march into the Morose household. Morose belatedly and exaggeratedly asserts his patriarchal power. Still, by restoring order in his home, Morose performs the duties expected of early modern householders, and his action draws attention to the duties which Captain Otter has abdicated to his wife. The play's satire, therefore, is directed at men and women who do not behave appropriately, and so far I have read the play's symbolic uses of the cups from the perspective of dominant ideologies that attempted to regulate gender behavior.[40] Now, however, I want to offer an additional position from which to read the Otter narrative, a position many audience members may have occupied: that of the husband and wife who, like the Otters, executed a marriage settlement prior to marriage. Reading the marital conflict from this perspective complicates reading Mrs. Otter merely as shrew. Moreover, foregrounding the materiality of the carousing cups makes visible the practical effects of property law, and it demonstrates how the play displays cultural concerns about women's control of property.

The origin of the Otters' disordered marriage is revealed when Captain Otter "misbehaves" and Mrs. Otter threatens to send her husband back to the Bear Garden (3.1.29–36):

Is this according to the instrument when I married you? That I would be princess and reign in mine own house, and you would be my subject and obey me? What did you bring me, should make you so peremptory? Do I allow you your half-crown a day to spend where you will among your gamesters, to vex and torment me at such times as these? Who gives you your maintenance, I pray you?

Mrs. Otter claims authority over her husband through "the instrument" – the marriage settlement – executed prior to their marriage. Here the satire depends upon the audience's shared knowledge of property law and the use of legal instruments to evade the law of coverture, which governed property transmission at marriage. Broadly, the rules governing property transmission relate either to inheritance or marriage, and *Epicoene* reproduces the binary divisions of property and its transmission in the plot's structure: the Otter narrative dramatizes proprietary conflict in a middle-class household over moveables conveyed at marriage, whereas the Morose–Dauphine narrative dramatizes the conflict in a gentry family over an entailed estate and its revenues, which upon death should be conveyed to Morose's heir. While the "strict settlement" entailing an estate in the male line has received the most attention among historians, Amy Louise Erickson argues that "for most people marrying in early modern England, the principal purpose of a marriage settlement was the protection of the wife's property. And it was *this* type of settlement which was regularly employed by ordinary people with ordinary wealth."[41]

A marriage settlement established the details of portion and jointure, and it could be used to protect three other categories of the woman's personal property: "separate estate" held specified property "in trust for a wife's use during coverture, which was to be at her disposing"; "pin money," the maintenance money allowed yearly to a woman for outfitting herself and her household; and "paraphernalia," which included "a wife's clothes, jewels, bed linens and plate."[42] When arranging a settlement, the bride and groom could not contract directly with each other; therefore, trustees – parents, guardians, family or friends – were necessary to protect the woman's property. Trusts could also be established "by deed of gift or by will during the course of the marriage,"[43] as John Ive did when he left for his daughter, "20 marks yearly towards her maintenance, and my son-in-law Mr. Robinsonne her husband not to meddle with it,"[44] or as Robert Glascock did when he left "The reside of my goods to Anne my beloved wife; if she marry her husband shall have nothing to do with them more than their use, and after her decease to be divided equally between my niece and my wife's two daughters."[45]

Truewit's warning to Morose, therefore, needs to be read as only partially tongue-in-cheek: the woman "you are to marry, may have made a
conveyance of her virginity aforehand, as your wise widows do of their
states, before they marry, in trust to some friend" (2.2.119–20).

In theory, by giving women rights in property, marriage settlements
enabled wives to evade the law of coverture and thus alienated husbands
from the rights they expected in their wives' property. Settlements shifted
the balance of power between husband and wife regarding protected
properties: in effect, settlements reversed gendered property relations in
these households, positioning husbands as wives by placing men's right
to property in abeyance. In practice, however, Mr. Robinsonne may
well have "meddled" with his wife's maintenance, and Anne Glascock's
next husband may have sold or damaged some objects that her previous
husband had bequeathed as legacies. Martha Howell points to how "the
practicalities of everyday household management derailed the quest for
clarity and order" that people sought by dividing marital properties into
the husband's, the wife's, and the household's:

Property brought to a marriage might technically belong to one spouse or
another, and the conjugal fund might be carefully divided into "discretionary"
and "non-discretionary" accounts, but in reality bushels of grain, vats of dye,
piles of bedcovers, chests of coin, flocks of geese, wagons, looms or wall-hangings
could not be fully separate . . . In practice, there could have been no stable, fully
separate accounts – his, hers, theirs.[46]

Furthermore, the wife's position as the day-to-day manager of the household invested her with authority over marital property. William Gouge's
dedicatory epistle to *Of Domesticall Duties* (1622) recalls the strife created
when he addressed in his sermons the disposition of goods within marriage: he admits that "much exception was taken against the application
of a Wiues subiection to the restraining of her from disposing the common goods of the Family without, or against her Husbands consent."
Gouge's treatise marks the significant contestation surrounding marital
property. The effort Gouge exerts, moreover, demonstrates the ideological work needed to protect men's monopoly over household goods. As his
epistle suggests, conflict was most likely to focus on the everyday things
that made up the household's "common goods," the "moveables" that
could be readily sold in the secondhand market or be sent to pawn when
the household needed influxes of ready money.

In her research on domestic disorder, Gowing found that "[i]n the
house, violent disputes often centered on material goods, and particularly
the goods which women kept locked away, in their own chests." She

cites the example of William Phillips, who destroyed his wife's chest with a hatchet when she refused to give him a clean shirt that she had locked away; in the chest he also found " 'bras[s] and pewter which she had stolen from him and previously sworne that she had... soulde and given... away.' "[47] In more affluent households, jewels and plate were the objects wives "stole" from their husbands.[48] Eleanor Hubard's husband, Edward, expressed his shaky confidence toward her regard for "his" property in his will: "I earnestly request her as I have always found her to have a good conscience that she would not hide or keep anything of mine from my executor, and do take that which of right appertaineth to her and no more; and therefore I appoint her to have all such coin of gold as I now have, with such gilt plate that she brought to me."[49] The phrase "brought to me" recurs repeatedly in men's wills, and it inscribes the unstable status of moveables, a status that changes in relation to a woman's change in legal status: as a widow, the woman may – depending upon the will of her husband – get back the plate that she "brought" to the marriage; yet, while she remains a wife, the plate belongs to her husband. In domestic conflicts over everyday things, Gowing asserts "[b]oth husbands and wives regularly accused each other of taking and selling the household goods: it was the final expression of a collapsed economic union. At issue was the central question of shared marital property, an ideal whose full implications many of these women apparently refused."[50] Many early modern women, it seems, disregarded the law of coverture and considered as their own the goods they had brought to marriage. These women, perhaps, were Gouge's intended audience. It is not unreasonable to assume that most audience members had experienced or witnessed rifts over marital property, and when Jonson chooses gilt cups to stage the conflict between the Otters, he counts on his audience's awareness of the disputed place these objects might occupy as shared marital property.

Epicoene dramatizes the conflict over marital property in an exaggerated form; certainly settlements did not stipulate who would govern. While the play satirizes Mrs. Otter's unconventional use of the "instrument" to authorize a wife's tyrannical rule over her husband, the invocation of the instrument brings to mind the unrepresented but conventional aspects of marriage settlements and the conflicts often associated with their customary uses.[51] Jonson arguably chose gilt cups because plate was symbolically and monetarily important to the economy of marriage and it was a "real" object of domestic contention. In the practical workings of the household, plate is more easily divisible than bushels of grain, but it inhabited – along with the wife's clothes, linens, and jewels – the confused category of "paraphernalia." Today these objects seem "personal" or sentimental, and they seem, therefore, to be easily divisible into "hers": the pillowcases embroidered in anticipation of marriage; her mother's ring; the jewel received from her husband upon the birth of a child. Yet even these objects were subject to the early modern law of coverture. As Gouge states, "Yea, her necessary apparell is not hers in property."[52] If paraphernalia was protected in a settlement, it became, once again in Gouge's words, "the proper goods of a Wife," and her husband had no right in it. In the topsy-turvy world of *Epicoene*, the Captain's clothes are not his (3.2.37), and when Mrs. Otter asks her recalcitrant husband, "What did you bring me, should make you thus peremptory?" (3.2.32–3), her "bring me" echoes the "brought to me" phrase that occurs so frequently in early modern men's wills. The phrase therefore implies that the cups are not Captain Otter's "in property."

By employing animal-shaped carousing cups as stage properties to manifest the conflict in the Otter household, *Epicoene* puts into motion the multiple meanings of "property" and thereby creates new associations and new meanings for the cups. Tracing the trajectory of the cups through the play's narrative and into London's shops and affluent households produces a complex cultural biography for these seemingly trifling things. As a characteristic attribute, the animal-shaped cups exemplify simultaneously the "beastliness" of the Captain and his wife, the Captain's drunkenness, and Mrs. Otter's courtly aspirations. Performing their role as moveables, the cups represent a type of property that could belong to either a husband or wife. In their gendering, the carousing cups so clearly characterize the Captain that it is hard to imagine them as Mrs. Otter's personal property, until we recall her wealth and the marriage settlement. Moreover, early modern spectators who would have been familiar with the stuffs sold in China houses may have recognized a strong connection between Mrs. Otter and the cups because of her role in marketing such commodities, an association that remains less visible today. When the cups move from Otter's house to Morose's, their journey between households links the two narratives, and the cups become signifiers for what is improper or unsuitable about the marriages of both men: the Otter narrative is thereby set in relation to the main narrative in which Morose is punished for endeavoring to control the conveyance of his entailed estate. Yet, reading the Otter narrative next to the main one produces more questions than answers regarding the play's representation of cultural concerns about property.

Both Otter and Morose marry for proprietary interests: Otter to acquire property; Morose to keep property in his immediate line. These

reasons for marrying were highly conventional, yet both men are punished by marrying women who can be read as shrews. After his marriage
to the silent "woman" turned shrew, Morose admits to Dauphine, "strife
and tumult are the dowry that comes with a wife . . . I have perceived the
effect of it, too late, in Madam Otter" (4.4.21–6). The analogy between
Morose and Otter works, however, only if one aligns the characters by
gender and buys into the male assumption deployed within the play, that
a wife is by definition a shrew. However, if property is used to construct
analogies, Morose's position bears a greater resemblance to Mrs. Otter's:
they bring the property to marriage; they ground their authority on that
property; and they experience the "strife and tumult" that come with
a spouse. The play offers little hope for happiness to either the Otters
or Morose. At the play's end, the Otter marriage continues unchanged.
And Morose's "marriage" to Epicoene ends only after Morose "contracts" himself to his nephew. Offering to help Morose extricate himself
from his predicament, Dauphine petitions his uncle for what may be
read as maintenance: "You know I have been long a suitor to you, uncle,
that out of your estate, which is fifteen hundred a year, you would allow
me but five hundred during life, and assure the rest upon me after, to
which I have often by myself and friends tendered you a writing to sign,
which you would never consent or incline to. If you please but to effect it
now—" (5.4.164–9). Desperate, Morose pleads with Dauphine: "Come,
nephew, give me the pen. I will subscribe to anything, and seal to what
thou wilt, for my deliverance. Thou art my restorer. Here, I deliver it thee
as my deed" (5.4.183–5). Discursively, the play produces this "marriage"
between men as a less tumultuous, more appropriate means of conveying
property than a marriage between a man and a woman; nevertheless,
the contract he signs alienates Morose from his property. Furthermore,
the play's production of an "instrument" in this marriage recalls its use –
or abuse – in the Otters'.

Conjugal power relations, which functioned to structure not only early
modern gender relations but also social relations,[53] fail to perform according to cultural expectations in *Epicoene*, and Jonson locates the cause
of such failure in relation to women and property. Women's right in property, the play implies, troubled gender relations, social relations, social
order, and individual identity. Evidence from court cases lends further
support to the play's representation of how marital property destabilized
conjugal power relations that depended upon the proper functioning of
gender. How else to explain, for example, the cultural implications of the
remarks Edward Cleter uttered to his wife Alice just one day after their
marriage: " 'Thinkst thou that I can love such a mustie rustie widdow

as thou art thou hast a face that loketh like the back of a tode I married the[e] but to be mayntayned like a man and so I will be'."[54] Cleter
articulated his demand in a dispute over the debts he had brought to
the marriage. Alice Cleter had withheld economic power from her new
husband by refusing to pawn her household goods to pay his debts and
by refusing to turn over the lease of her house to him. Cleter's claim to
his new wife's economic assets demonstrates his gendered expectations
regarding marital property. Yet, Cleter's use of the term "mayntayned"
implies his financial dependence upon his wife, and its use by Cleter
recalls Mrs. Otter's claims for dominance over her husband (3.1.35). In
this "real" world marriage, as in the Otters' play-world marriage, rights
in property confer power and status to the woman. Cleter's claims to
masculinity, therefore, do not fit neatly into the schema of early modern
gender differences as constructed by ideological discourses and laws of
coverture: what did it mean in this instance to be "mayntayned like a
man"?

Epicoene, in effect, asks the same question when it uses stage properties to dramatize the problems created by women's control of property.
Unlike Edward Cleter, who retaliated against his wife's economic power
by stabbing the pewter, slashing the pillows, and cutting her face, Otter
reluctantly accepts his subordinate status, demanding to captain nothing
more than a few seemingly insignificant cups. But as I hope this analysis
has shown, the carousing cups' embeddedness within a complex web
of cultural signification materializes the gender and class confusions and
anxieties surrounding shared marital property in early modern England.
In its representation of cultural concerns about women's control of property and women's roles in its transmission, Epicoene demonstrates how
gender complicated the status of shared marital property and how a
woman's right in property further complicated the calculus of gender
relations within marriage.

NOTES

1. Amy Louise Erickson's *Women and Property in Early Modern England* (London:
   Routledge, 1993), informs my discussion of property law.
2. See Natasha Korda, " 'Judicious oeillades': supervising marital property in
   The Merry Wives of Windsor," in Jean E. Howard and Scott Cutler Shershow
   (eds.), *Marxist Shakespeares* (London: Routledge, 2001), pp. 82–103.
3. Philippa Glanville's *Silver in Tudor and Early Stuart England: A Social History and
   Catalogue of the National Collection 1480–1660* (London: Victoria and Albert
   Museum, 1990), informs my discussion of plate; quotation at pp. 243–4.

4. *OED*, "property."
5. Arjun Appadurai, "Introduction: commodities and the politics of value," in *The Social Life of Things: Commodities in Cultural Perspective* (Cambridge: Cambridge University Press, 1986), p. 34.
6. Ben Jonson, *Epicoene or The Silent Woman*, ed. R. V. Holdsworth (New York: New Mermaids, 1990). All quotations are from this edition.
7. Neil Carson, *A Companion to Henslowe's Diary* (Cambridge, 1988), p. 53.
8. I would like to thank the Schroder Collection for providing photographs of the bull and bear drinking vessels. I am especially grateful to Barbara Pugh, Executive Assistant to Mr. Bruno L. Schroder. For other examples of cups, see Timothy Schroder, *The Art of the European Goldsmith: Silver from the Schroder Collection* (New York, 1983); *Silber und Gold: Augsburger Goldschmiedekunst für die Höfe Europas* (Munich: Bayerisches Nationalmuseum, 1994); Lorenz Seelig, *Silver and Gold: Courtly Splendour from Augsburg* (Munich and New York: Prestel, 1995).
9. Schroder, *Art of the European Goldsmith*, p. 99.
10. Glanville, *Silver*, pp. 108–15.
11. Robert Carr inventories, Folger Shakespeare Library, Ms. L.b. 638, "A note of Such plate as was Delivered to M. williams goldsmith the 19th of Sept 1615."
12. Albert Feuillerat (ed.), *Documents Relating to the Office of the Revels in the Time of Queen Elizabeth* (Louvain: A. Uystpruyst, 1908), p. 157.15; p. 158.1–10; p. 359.7–9.
13. R. A. Foakes and R. T. Rickert (eds.), *Henslowe's Diary* (Cambridge: Cambridge University Press, 1961), p. 203.
14. Foakes and Rickert (eds.), *Henslowe's Diary*, p. 213.
15. Glanville, *Silver*, p. 75; p. 71.
16. T. F. Reddaway, "Elizabethan London: Goldsmith's Row in Cheapside, 1558–1645," *Guildhall Miscellany* 2 (1963): 181–206.
17. Natasha Korda, "Household property/stage property: Henslowe as pawnbroker," in *Theatre Journal* 48 (1996): 185–95; 194.
18. Glanville, *Silver*, pp. 40, 66, 211, 216.
19. Peter Stallybrass, "Worn worlds: clothes and identity on the Renaissance stage," in Margreta De Grazia, Maureen Quilligan, and Peter Stallybrass (eds.), *Subject and Object in Renaissance Culture* (Cambridge: Cambridge University Press, 1996), p. 292.
20. For Keysar's multiple careers, see William Ingram, "Robert Keysar, playhouse speculator," in *Shakespeare Quarterly* 37:4 (1986): 476–88.
21. Glanville, *Silver*, pp. 115–16.
22. Holdsworth provides this anecdote in his introduction to the play (p. xxi).
23. In reading the play's characters as social aspirers, I follow Mary Beth Rose, *The Expense of Spirit: Love and Sexuality in English Renaissance Drama* (Ithaca: Cornell University Press, 1988), pp. 51–2.
24. Claudia Lazzaro, "Animals as cultural signs: a Medici menagerie in the grotto at Castello," in Claire Farago (ed.), *Reframing the Renaissance: Visual*

Culture in Europe and Latin America, 1450–1650 (New Haven: Yale University Press, 1995), p. 197.

25. Edward Topsell, *The History of Four-Footed Beasts* (London, 1607), p. 445.
26. Footnote for Thomas Otter in "The Persons of the Play."
27. Topsell, *History*, p. 444.
28. Laura Gowing, *Domestic Dangers: Women, Words, and Sex in Early Modern London* (Oxford: Clarendon Press, 1996), p. 81.
29. Ibid., p. 59.
30. Edward Bury, *England's Bane, Or The Deadly Danger of Drunkenness* (London, 1677), p. 4.
31. Ibid., p. 4.
32. Lorenz Seelig, *Silver and Gold*, p. 15.
33. See James Knowles, "Cecil's shopping centre: the rediscovery of a Ben Jonson masque in praise of Trade," *Times Literary Supplement*, 7 February 1997, 14–15. For the masque itself, see James Knowles, "Jonson's *Entertainment at Britain's Burse*," in Martin Butler (ed.), *Re-Presenting Ben Jonson: Text, History, Performance* (New York: St. Martin's, 1999), pp. 114–51.
34. Knowles, "Jonson's *Entertainment*," p. 134. In "Cecil's shopping centre," Knowles argues that for *The Key Keeper* Jonson carefully chose the commodities with his patron's political and economic interests in mind, commodities which "epitomized the height of fashion (hence the depiction of Mrs. Otter, the China woman in *Epicoene*, as part of Jonson's satire on female extravagance, material, intellectual and verbal)" (15).
35. Knowles, "Jonson's *Entertainment*" (p. 145n).
36. Appadurai, *Social Life of Things*, pp. 16–17.
37. John Chamberlain, *The Letters of John Chamberlain*, ed. Norman Egbert McClure (Philadelphia: American Philosophical Society, 1939), 1.105, p. 273.
38. Chamberlain, *Letters*, 1.97, p. 255.
39. Useful sources on marriage include Jeremy Boulton, "Itching after private marryings? Marriage customs in seventeenth-century London," in *The London Journal* 16:1 (1991): 15–34; Martin Ingram, "Spousals litigation in the English ecclesiastical courts c.1350–c.1640," in R. B. Outhwaite (ed.), *Marriage and Society: Studies in the Social History of Marriage* (New York: St. Martin's, 1981); and Diana O'Hara, " 'Ruled by my friends': aspects of marriage in the diocese of Canterbury, c.1540–1570," in *Continuity and Change* 6:1 (1991): 9–41.
40. Karen Newman's "City talk: femininity and commodification in Jonson's *Epicoene*," in *Fashioning Femininity and English Renaissance Drama* (Chicago: University of Chicago Press, 1991), has influenced my reading of the play.
41. Amy Louise Erickson, "Common law versus common practice: the use of marriage settlements in early modern England," *Economic History Review*, 2nd ser., 43:1 (1990): 21–39; 37.
42. Erickson, *Women and Property*, p. 26.
43. Ibid., p. 124.

44. F. G. Emmison (ed.), *Elizabethan Life: Wills of Essex Gentry & Merchants Proved in the Prerogative Court of Canterbury* (Chelmsford: Essex County Council, 1978); Essex Record Office Publication No. 71, p. 99. The will of John Ive, Esquire, is dated 9 July 1600.

45. Will of Robert Glascock of Manningtree, gentleman, dated 14 February 1596, in Emmison, *Elizabethan Life*, p. 44.

46. Martha Howell, "Fixing movables: gifts by testament in late medieval Douai," in *Past and Present* 150 (1996): 3–45.

47. Gowing, *Domestic Dangers*, p. 213.

48. Chamberlain, *Letters*, p. 262.

49. Emmison, *Elizabethan Life*, p. 97. Will of Edward Hubard, Esquire, 16 March 1601.

50. Gowing, *Domestic Dangers*, p. 214.

51. Mrs. Otter's tyrannical rule over her husband also brings to mind the more common tyrannical rule of husbands over their wives. See Barbara C. Millard, " 'An acceptable violence': sexual contest in Jonson's *Epicoene*," in *Medieval and Renaissance Drama in England* 1 (1984): 143–58.

52. Gouge, *Domesticall Duties*, p. 302.

53. Gowing, *Domestic Dangers*, p. 231.

54. Ibid., p. 215.

CHAPTER II

The woman's parts of Cymbeline

Valerie Wayne

In his introduction to *The Social Life of Things*, Arjun Appadurai proposes that "economic exchange creates value," and that focusing on the things that are exchanged rather than the forms or functions of exchanges, as Marxist critics have traditionally done, makes visible the political linkages between exchange and value.[1] Drawing on the insights of Georg Simmel, Appadurai explores the conditions under which objects circulate in different regimes of value in space and time. His approach "justifies the conceit that commodities, like persons, have social lives" (p. 3), and that "*specific* things, as they move through different hands, contexts, and uses" may be regarded as having life histories (p. 34). One can trace the "career" or life history of objects by noting their participation in various exchanges and their consequent shifts in value. Appadurai is especially interested in the phases and contexts during which things meet the requirement of commodity candidacy, since they may move into and out of the commodity state at different times in their careers.[2] Luxury goods have a special "register" of consumption that sets them off from other objects. They often exhibit a "semiotic virtuosity, that is, the capacity to signal fairly complex social messages" and offer "a high degree of linkage of their consumption to body, person, and personality" (p. 38).

In this essay I want to trace the histories of three stage properties in *Cymbeline* that are associated with women's bodies: the manacle given by Posthumus to Innogen, which is only named as a bracelet in the last act of the Folio text; Innogen's ring, which she gives to Posthumus and is the only trace of her natural mother; and the bloody cloth, which Posthumus takes as proof that Innogen has been murdered according to his command. I will draw on Appadurai's terms to explore the changes in value and signification that these stage properties take on in the course of the play, and the implications of their value for our understanding of the identities of those who exchange them, because this anthropological theory enables a fuller understanding of the circulation of commodities in social life and literary texts than has been heretofore available. My use of Appadurai differs from other essays in this volume because I apply his theory to the circulation of stage properties in the text and its sources, on the stage, and in reprintings of the text and programs over time. Rather than exploring the objects' pre-theatrical lives, I begin with the textual uses to which those objects are put and work backwards as well as forwards to develop a diachronic appreciation of how and what they are made to signify, especially in connection with class and gender. I also give particular attention to the theatrical uses made of these three properties when they are referred to, manipulated, and worn on stage. In closing, I take up the more recent career of the manacle on the cover and within the texts of *Cymbeline*, the programs of its performances, and the advertisements associated with its productions, since that stage property has so repeatedly been used to symbolize the play that it has become well qualified to advertise and commodify it.

In examining the difficult distinction between gift and commodity exchanges, John Frow reviews Chris Gregory's argument that "a gift economy depends upon the creation of debt, where what is at stake is not the things themselves or the possibility of material profit but the personal relationships that are formed and perpetuated by ongoing indebtedness. Things in the gift economy are the vehicles, the effective mediators and generators, of social bonds."[3] The manacle and the ring first appear in *Cymbeline* in a gift exchange between Posthumus and Innogen. Having received from Innogen a ring of some worth – "This diamond was my mother's. Take it, heart" (1.1.113)[4] after she has termed Posthumus a "jewel" (1.1.92) – Posthumus exhibits what Appadurai calls the "calculative dimension" of exchange (p. 13) when he reciprocates by giving her his bracelet:

> and sweetest, fairest,
> As I my poor self did exchange for you
> To your so infinite loss, so in our trifles
> I still win of you. For my sake wear this.
>   *He gives her a bracelet*
> It is a manacle of love, I'll place it
> Upon this fairest prisoner.   (1.1.119–24)

As he gives her the "manacle of love," Posthumus calls attention to the differential values of these luxury goods and how they reflect the donors' class differences. This first exchange in the play suggests how difficult it is to distinguish gift from commodity exchanges, because at the same time that the exchange values of these objects are supposed to be superseded in the gift exchange, Posthumus invokes them as signs of his own insufficiency.[5] As Frow suggests, the very structure of gift economies sets in motion "forms of calculation and indebtedness."[6]

A "manacle" was "a fetter for the hand" (*OED* sb. 1) and derived from *manus*, Latin for "hand." In early modern marriages, the "handfast" constituted a promise of marriage in a spousal that could range in meaning from what we now call an engagement to a formal marriage ceremony. One gave one's hand in marriage. The word "handfast" is used with this meaning in the first act of *Cymbeline* (1.5.78), but it is also used to signal restraint and even arrest in *The Winter's Tale* (4.4.744),[7] which was written around the same time: the *OED* records both meanings for the adjective, "contracted by the joining of hands; betrothed or espoused," and "bound, manacled" (1, 2). When the stage properties are exchanged in *Cymbeline*, the ring and the manacle become what Appadurai calls "incarnated signs" (p. 38) of the marital bond between this husband and wife. Posthumus does not expect to receive the gift of Innogen's ring and may even register surprise at his good fortune, but by way of response he calls attention to and then symbolizes the inadequacies of his own birth through the bracelet. Without his doing so, the audience would have no reason to assume that his gift has less material worth than hers. But his saying so makes it so in this theatrical context, and introduces the issue of differential market values even at the moment that the ring and manacle are made to signify marital union.

Thus the marriage is fractured by a discrepancy in exchange values of commodities precisely when it is symbolized on stage as a union through these stage properties. What the manacle actually looks like seems of much less importance: it has varied widely from one production to the next, and the audience is not enlisted in witnessing or attesting to its lesser value. Yet Posthumus's awareness of the discrepancy explains in large part his desire to compensate for his lower birth by fettering Innogen's hand through marriage. As a consequence of his gift, she is doubly imprisoned early on in the play, first by a father who rates birth over merit ("Thou took'st a beggar, wouldst have made my throne / A seat for baseness," [1.1.142–3]), and then by a husband who tries to make up for his lack of birth and his banishment by constraining his wife.

The clandestine marriage that occurred before the play began[8] was not a typically patriarchal exchange of a woman among men, because Innogen's father did not "give" her to Posthumus; on the contrary, when she gave herself, Cymbeline took her back again. But this gift exchange of

things as incarnated signs eventually enables another exchange of Innogen among other men, and it is that exchange that the play foregrounds
as a crucial problem. Appadurai refers to a category called "enclaved
commodities, objects whose commodity potential is carefully hedged"
(p. 24): through the early gift exchange, the manacle becomes a visual
sign of the enclavement of Innogen's sexuality in the play. It marks containment of the woman's part. The very object that Posthumus intended
as a means to reciprocate his wife's gift and simultaneously control her
sexuality then becomes a means for her being put into circulation. Appadurai provides a larger context for this development: "the politics of
enclaving, far from being a guarantor of systemic stability, may constitute
the Trojan horse of change" (p. 26).

This shift is enabled by what, in Appadurai's terms, is the play's first
"tournament of value" (p. 21), when Posthumus displays his pride in
Innogen and his conviction that her sexuality is fully enclaved. He is
lured into a wager by the conjunction that Iachimo makes between her
value and the diamond ring: "If she went before others I have seen, as
that diamond of yours outlustres many I have beheld, I could not but
believe she excelled many: but I have not seen the most precious diamond that is, nor you the lady" (1.4.68–72). The conjunction of woman
and ring becomes a means of commodifying the woman. Posthumus at
first refuses this conflation: "You are mistaken. The one may be sold
or given, or if there were wealth enough for the purchase or merit for
the gift. The other is not a thing for sale, and only the gift of the gods"
(1.4.78–81), but even he characterizes Innogen as a gift and hence as a
potential object, one that he thinks, as Iachimo makes explicit, "the gods
have given" to him (1.4.82). So Iachimo can reassert commodification
through the threat of theft: "You may wear her in title yours: but you
know, strange fowl light upon neighbouring ponds. Your ring may be
stolen too; so your brace of unprizable estimations" (1.4.84–7). Note in
this phrasing the trace of the bracelet, here counterpoised with the ring:
Innogen is constructed as and through Posthumus's "brace of unprizable estimations," with "brace" evoking a coat of arms and a buckle of
a girdle or belt, both current meanings at the time (*OED*, sb. 2, 1 and
11). Innogen's enclavement through the bracelet was supposed to effect
what Igor Kopytoff calls "terminal commoditization, in which further
exchange is precluded by fiat,"[9] so that she becomes literally priceless,
beyond price, "unprizable." But Posthumus fails to maintain her uncom-
modified status in the face of Iachimo's comparisons with the ring. Like
the bracelet, Posthumus's "brace of unprizable estimations" in the form

of his boast becomes the means by which she is accorded a price and put into circulation. When they make their wager, Posthumus and Iachimo initiate a commodity exchange that will further fracture the social bonds created by the gift exchange between Posthumus and Innogen,[10] and it is Posthumus's heightened sense of his indebtedness and his corresponding pride in Innogen's loyalty that make him especially vulnerable to the Italian's machinations.

This tournament of value also has some similarities to Baudrillard's account of an auction, whose essential function "is the institution of a community of the privileged who define themselves as such by agonistic speculation upon a restricted corpus of signs" (Appadurai, p. 21). The wager in which these men in Rome participate permits them to exercise the privilege of their gender by debasing women into sexual signs of questionable worth. Innogen is weighed here in relation not only to the ring, but to the women of France and Italy, who are defended by the Frenchman and the Italian as being at least equal to her value. This is a distinctively male tournament of value and a contest among nations, a kind of European Olympics of female worth and attemptability, given the added presence of a Spaniard and a Dutchman in the scene. When Iachimo wagers ten thousand ducats against Posthumus's ring, Italian currency against British jewelry, Posthumus says he prefers to bet gold against gold; but he is goaded into "lending" his diamond as part of the wager. Iachimo then confirms its terms: "If I bring you no sufficient testimony that I have enjoyed the dearest bodily part of your mistress, my ten thousand ducats are yours, so is your diamond too" (1.4.143–6). The manacle becomes testimony to and signifies that "dearest bodily part."

To provide such proof, Iachimo engages in a theft of the commodity that symbolizes the enclavement of Innogen's sexuality. Appadurai describes commodities as having paths and diversions, and a diversion "may sometimes involve the calculated and 'interested' removal of things from an enclaved zone to one where exchange is less confined and more profitable... [W]hereas enclaving seeks to protect certain things from commoditization, diversion frequently is aimed at drawing protected things into the zone of commoditization" (pp. 25–6). Innogen's sexuality, her "woman's part" (2.4.174), is that protected "thing" staged through the property of the manacle. Iachimo later identifies the generative locus of this plot in a more general way, but its association with a woman's body remains: "Your daughter's chastity – there it begins" (5.4.179). Theft, as Appadurai describes it, is "the humblest form of diversion of commodities from preordained paths" (p. 26). When Iachimo comes out of the trunk, he notes the adornment of Innogen's room and the objects present in it; then he takes the manacle ("Come off, come off," [2.2.33]), and observes the mole on her breast. He does not know the history of the manacle, so he thinks the mole will be the "secret / Will force him think I have picked the lock, and ta'en / The treasure of her honour" (2.2.40–2). But in taking the manacle, rather than seeing the mole, he is diverting the sign of Innogen's sexuality from the enclaved path of marriage.

The mole, or rather its counterpart, was the more important object in Shakespeare's sources. In the ninth book, second day in Boccaccio's *Decameron*, merchants wager on a wife's fidelity and one of them conceals himself in a trunk to spy on her while she sleeps. The objects in her room are described in the English translation of 1620 as a "small wart upon her left pappe," a ring, a purse, a light robe of silk, and a "girdle," a belt worn around the waist.[11] In *Frederyke of Jennen*, the objects are a purse made of pearls and costly stones worth eighty-four ducats, a "gyrdle of fyne golde set with costly perles and stoones, that was worth CCCC ducates," a ring "with a point of diamond, that was worth 1 ducates," and a black wart on her left arm.[12] The girdle becomes the manacle in *Cymbeline*,[13] retaining its associations with something that constricts the body but becoming smaller, more visually coherent, and more appropriate to the woman's part. Those girdles on display at the Victoria and Albert Museum from the early modern and earlier periods are made of metal, sometimes enamelled, and were to be hung around the hips, a connection with the lower body that suits Shakespeare's play. They are in effect large, flexible bracelets made of links, as distinct from bangles, which are inflexible circles or ovals. Reference to a girdle is made in *Cymbeline* when Cloten says to Caius Lucius following Britain's refusal to pay tribute to Caesar, "if you seek us afterwards in other terms, you shall find us in our salt-water girdle: if you beat us out of it, it is yours" (3.1.80–1), suggesting that the ocean itself is a defensive belt encircling the island. Thomas Dekker makes a similar reference to England wearing a girdle of waves in *The Whore of Babylon* of 1606.[14] The salt-water girdle, like the manacle, protects property from invasion, and Linda Woodbridge has emphasized how effectively the play presents a woman's body as a metaphor for the nation confronted with that threat.[15]

The description of objects from the wife's bedroom in the sources by Iachimo's counterpart has the effect of unsettling the husband in each narrative. But he remains unconvinced by them when they are described because, as Boccaccio's character says and *Frederyke of Jennen's* implies, "this may be gotten, by corrupting some servant of mine," or by some other means than sleeping with his wife.[16] It is the far less erotic wart in each story that convinces the husband, just as Iachimo expects the mole will do for Posthumus. When he first sees the mole, Iachimo says,

> Here's a voucher
> Stronger than ever law could make; this secret
> Will force him think I have picked the lock and ta'en
> The treasure of her honour.   (2.2.39–42)

But the mole is not as compelling a form of evidence in a dramatic context because it is not highly visible or portable, and the non-corporeal objects in the stories have not been exchanged between the married pair as they are in the play, so they have not come to signify their social relations. Upon hearing Iachimo's description of the bedroom, Posthumus remains unpersuaded for the same reasons as the husbands in the sources. When he sees the manacle, he loses his trust and gives Iachimo the ring. Then he retracts it at Philario's urging but returns the ring again after Iachimo swears, "By Jupiter, I had it from her arm" (2.4.121). The mole serves as additional confirmation – "If you seek / For further satisfying, under her breast – / Worthy the pressing – lies a mole" (2.4.133–5) – but Iachimo has already won the ring and the wager by the time he mentions it.

This second tournament of value is therefore more easily won than Iachimo could have anticipated, because he is unaware of the career of the manacle. An exceptionally lucky villain, like Iago, who says more than he could possibly know, he creates a fictional scene of a gift exchange between himself and Innogen while he is displaying the manacle that, for Posthumus, ruptures the bond created by the former exchange:

> She stripped it from her arm. I see her yet.
> Her pretty action did outsell her gift,
> And yet enriched it too. She gave it me,
> And said she prized it once.   (2.4.101–4)

Here the act of giving is accorded even more value than the commodity itself through the narration of the exchange and simultaneously increases its value in Iachimo's eyes. There could be few more eloquent accounts of how exchange creates value than this one – "Her pretty action did outsell her gift, / And yet enriched it too" – and it is this entirely imaginary scene that prompts Posthumus to give over the ring. The theft of the manacle diverts it and the ring from their previous paths and debases the value of both when they come into Iachimo's possession. Having been promoted from their status as "trifles" (1.1.121) to signifiers of the marital and sexual

bond, they then become trophies of Iachimo's conquest over another
man through his presumed sexual conquest of a woman. Posthumus
completes the diversion and consequent devaluation of Innogen by giving
Iachimo the ring. Both the manacle as a sign of Innogen's enclaved
sexuality and the ring as a confirmation of her maternal lineage have
become contaminated through this final exchange, because both confirm
and "purchase" women's illicit circulation. The word "contaminated" is
Kopytoff's: he applies it to objects having a purely aesthetic or scientific
value which are then made to circulate in a monetized commodity-
sphere.[17] When they are joined as Iachimo's possessions, the ring and
the bracelet become commodities of bad faith.

Once Posthumus is without both objects, he becomes convinced that
"We are all bastards, / And that most venerable man, which I / Did call
my father was I know not where / When I was stamped" (2.4.154–7).
Posthumus's own identity is shattered by his errant conclusion about
women as he comes to believe he has no identifiable father, no legitimate
name, and no certain country of origin. Since the structures of kinship
and nation depend upon women's fidelity, Posthumus's doubts expose
men's fragile dependence in patriarchy on the disposition of women's
sexuality, and show that the threat to women's physical bodies posed
through seduction and rape can also become a threat to personal and
national identity, especially when the heir to the throne is a woman.
Posthumus's father had fought against the Romans and received the title
of Leonatus from Tenantius, a British king, after his success in battle;
his two brothers died with swords in their hands. His status as a gentleman was therefore won through physical combat, and although the
First Gentleman who reports his lineage "cannot delve him to the root"
(1.1.28), what class position he has was won by his father's meritorious
actions, not by his birth.

The play poses the problem of Posthumus's class in relation to Innogen
in its very first lines; then it returns to the issue of his origin at the very
end when the soothsayer construes the prophecy of his identity. Once
Posthumus rejects the possibility of women's fidelity, he literally does not
know who he is, and his absence for two acts that is sometimes lamented
by critics is a dramatization of his status as a non-person on the stage and
in the text. His loss of the ring and the manacle, then, are fundamentally
related to the loss of his identity and confirm the inter-animating relations
of objects and identities: as Margreta De Grazia puts it, a play-text can
lock "persons into things, proper selves into property, subjectivity effects
into personal effects."[18] When Posthumus returns to Britain with the

Romans, he fights first for Britain and then presents himself as a Roman so he will be taken and executed. His changes in costume are an index of his lost identity and show how malleable he remains in his subject positions, although not in his loyalties. As the prophecy declares, the play's resolution depends on establishing the relation between Posthumus's origin, Britain's fortunes, and peace and plenty among the nations.

The class problems posed by the marriage are intensified by Innogen's position as heir to the throne. Cymbeline's objection that she "took'st a beggar, wouldst have made my throne / A seat for baseness" (1.1.142–3) contradicts the observations of the First Gentleman, made twice earlier in the scene, that Posthumus is a gentleman (1.1.7, 34). Yet both agree that the problems of this marriage are a function of class. (Thomas D'Urfey's 1682 adaptation of *Cymbeline* is usually referred to by its first title, *The Injured Princess*, but one of its alternate titles was *The Unequal Match*.[19]) Innogen anticipates the solution to the problem when she meets Guiderius and Arviragus and hears them refer to her as a brother:

> Would it had been so that they
> Had been my father's sons, then had my price
> Been less, and more equal ballasting
> To thee, Posthumus.   (3.6.73–6)

She wishes herself worth "less" so that she can be more equal to Posthumus, and as if in response to her wish, events in the play repeatedly demote her in status. From heir to the throne to appearance in "A riding-suit no costlier than would fit / A franklin's housewife" (3.2.76–7) and then to a male page for a Roman general, changing, as Pisanio says, "Command into obedience" (3.4.156), Innogen finally loses her claim to the kingdom at the very end.[20]

Yet she places little value on social position or even royal inheritance, and throughout the play she seems remarkably uninterested in exercising any kind of influence over the kingdom.[21] In her speech on Britain she shows a readiness to leave the country (3.4.137–41). Her loss of the throne is mentioned by Cymbeline almost as an afterthought (5.4.373–4). However resilient Innogen may be when under duress, and however attractive she appears in performance, her desires in this play are expressed primarily toward her husband, which is probably why the Victorians liked her so much. To her the manacle is no form of constraint: she calls it her "jewel" when she cannot find it after it is stolen (2.4.138), adding, "'Shrew me / If I would lose it for a revenue / Of any king's in Europe!'" (2.4.139–41). Here she anticipates the consequences of its exchanges, for she will eventually lose a European king's revenue by accepting it, but only after she has lost her husband, her sexual respectability, even her emotional stability. The vacancy of the manacle's interior signifies the state to which Innogen approaches, for she comes close to being "an O without a figure,"[22] and admits to Lucius, "I am nothing" (4.2.368), although her "nothing" has a specifically female valence.

The recovery of her newly discovered brothers then constitutes "two worlds" (5.4.375) to her, and is presented as more than sufficient when she is reunited with her husband. As Jodi Mikalachki has demonstrated, this is not a play that validates female autonomy;[23] instead, I would argue, it affirms the importance of marital and familial bonds. The decline in her status makes Innogen's marriage to Posthumus viable according to dominant ideologies of Renaissance unions, in which class positions of spouses were supposed to be relatively equal.[24] Her loss of emotional stability is also a direct reaction to the loss of her husband. Both Posthumus and Innogen fall apart when their marriage disintegrates, and the scene of Innogen mourning his supposed death while embracing Cloten's headless corpse dressed in Posthumus's clothing has a dramatic function similar to Posthumus's misogynist tirade: both scenes exhibit the characters' deeply mistaken and foolish judgment.

Posthumus's error has wider implications for his relation with Innogen. When he gives his misogynist speech at the end of act 2, he leaves his sentence unfinished: "Could I find out / The woman's part in me – for there's no motion / That tends to vice in man but I affirm / It is the woman's part" (2.4.171–4). The thought remains suspended because he cannot find that part in himself, that absence of women's genital space that is signified through the manacle; he cannot locate it even to violate it. Part of Posthumus's problem is that he looking for woman's lack, the unseen, on his own body, thereby misrecognizing sexual difference. Women's vaginal space was unlocatable on any body in the play's early, all-male productions, and it is equally unlocatable for Posthumus through the stage properties that represent it in text and performance. Just before these lines, Posthumus has imagined Iachimo mounting Innogen and finding "no opposition / But what he looked for should oppose, and she / Should from encounter guard" (2.4.169–71): he has visualized Iachimo penetrating her after her modest resistance.[25] Having lost her, as he thinks, he then looks for the "woman's part" in himself and, finding instead the presence of the phallus that signifies the original loss and separation from the mother, he enters into language as a speaking subject through the discourse of misogyny:[26] he distributes the woman's part into a catalogue of faults – lying, flattery, deceit, lust and rank thoughts, "All faults that man can name, nay, that hell knows, / Why, hers in part, or all, but rather all –" (2.4.179–80).

This catalogue still evokes woman's material body, but is more directly related to a body of texts in the early modern debate about women: discursive misogyny constituted by far the largest portion of publications in that debate. When Posthumus declares, "I'll write against them, / Detest them, curse them" (2.4.184–5), he is asserting his new-found identity as a common misogynist writer voicing his rage against women. His loss of Innogen and repressed desire for union with a woman prompt his entry into language as a writer of misogynist texts, and when he does not show up for a full two acts, we have been spared the performance of a Joseph Swetnam.

When we do encounter him again, his first words are, "Yea, bloody cloth, I'll keep thee, for I wished / Thou shouldst be coloured thus" (5.1.1–2). What is this bloody cloth but another sign of the woman's part? The supposed stain of Innogen's blood is designed to confirm her murder, but it also evokes the bloodstained sheets of a marriage bed – like the handkerchief spotted with strawberries in *Othello* – and has associations as well with menstruation. *Cymbeline*'s bloody cloth is related to *As You Like It*'s use of the bloody napkin as proof that Orlando has been faithful to Rosalind despite his being wounded by a lion, and it affirms a connection to the woman's body as the handkerchief does in *Othello*; but given this play's attention to "the dearest bodily part" (1.4.144) through the manacle and Posthumus's preoccupation with "the woman's part," the bodily associations with this stage property are more specific and graphic. The word "stain" first enters the play when Iachimo describes the mole to Posthumus: "You do remember / This stain upon her?" At that point, Posthumus, who is already convinced of Innogen's infidelity through the manacle, replies, "Ay, and it doth confirm / Another stain as big as hell can hold" (2.4.138–40). The mole is used to evoke the stain of womankind associated with Eve and original sin in the second wager scene. Yet when Iachimo first sees the mole on Innogen, he describes it as "cinque-spotted, like the crimson drops / I'th' bottom of a cowslip" (2.2.38–9): its red spots are delicately patterned like the inside of a flower. The flower image associated with the mole becomes a stain when Iachimo sullies it to entrap Posthumus, and those associations of the erotic body and sexual guilt migrate to the bloody cloth.

This stage property differs from the manacle and ring because it is never exchanged within the play's narrative. In his letter to Pisanio requiring Innogen's murder, Posthumus requests "some bloody sign" of its performance (3.4.126), and this is it. Yet the text obscures any means by which the cloth is conveyed, so its history in the play is mystified: it simply appears at the beginning of act 5, saturated with enigmatic significance.[27] Peter Stallybrass emphasizes that it is "a purely theatrical stain, invented by Pisanio."[28] Pisanio's counterpart in the *Decameron* delivers some of his mistress's clothes to his master as proof he has performed the murder. In *Frederyke of Jennen* the comparable character, having been commanded to deliver his mistress's tongue and a lock of her hair, kills a lamb that has accompanied her, uses the lamb's tongue and a lock of his mistress's hair, then anoints her clothes with the blood of the lamb and presents all three objects to his master.[29]

Traces of this source appear in *Cymbeline* when Innogen encourages Pisanio to dispatch her quickly and invites his knife with the words, "The lamb entreats the butcher" (3.4.96). The bloody cloth is associated with sacrifice, and it is more like a martyr's relic or a memento mori than a commodity.[30] It exhibits the limits of the Appadurian model in approaching this play's stage properties, for that theory seems unable to fully account for its use and signification. It has a history from sources to play-text, but within the text it functions entirely as Posthumus's token of Innogen's body, without any circulation, without any apparent exchange value, imputed importance primarily by memory and guilt. Martyrs' relics and mementos mori could and certainly did become commodities in medieval and early modern culture, but in this play the cloth is presented as an intensely private matter. It signifies not just any woman's part as Posthumus sees it; it is Innogen's.

Although the audience knows that this object does not have the history that Posthumus thinks it does, his taking it as proof of Innogen's death endows it with crucial significance in the narrative. When he re-enters in act 5 he has abandoned the ranting misogynist for the repentant husband, and this change is marked by an acceptance of a token of the woman's body as he blames all husbands who would murder their wives "for wrying but a little" (5.1.5). What Coppélia Kahn terms "Posthumus's astonishing forgiveness of Imogen without proof of her innocence" in those lines – a remarkable event in the context of *Much Ado About Nothing*, *Othello*, *The Winter's Tale*, early modern dramatic texts and even early modern culture – is the verbal counterpart to the visual accommodation that he holds in his hands.[31] When he then says, "Gods, if you / Should have ta'en vengeance on my faults, I never / Had lived to put on this" (5.1.7–9), "this" can be taken to refer to the bloody cloth mentioned eight lines earlier. Editors since Samuel Johnson have overlooked the stage property when they glossed the pronoun "it" as to instigate or assume responsibility for Innogen's murder,[32] and it may have that meaning as well; but the performance tradition has offered as an antecedent the cloth that Posthumus holds in his hand.

Having lost the ring and manacle, Posthumus wears that cloth like another token of his beloved. David Jones's 1979 production for the Royal Shakespeare Company directed Posthumus to put the cloth around his neck and tie it when he says "put on this."[33] In the National Theatre's 1988 production directed by Sir Peter Hall and the 1997–98 RSC production directed by Adrian Noble, Posthumus later wraps the cloth around his head.[34] Other productions make similar uses of it.[35] He is putting on what Peter Stallybrass refers to as Innogen's meanest garment, the last remnant of her as far as he knows, and, having killed her "is forced to learn the value of the trace."[36] In making this accommodation, Posthumus cherishes this sign of women's sexuality, a visual stain associated with the sex that bleeds at the loss of virginity and has a bloody discharge as part of the process of generation, but not because the cloth has any value in the world at large. The term "meanest garment" is first associated with the underwear that Innogen probably refers to when she uses it to insult Cloten,[37] but for Posthumus the cloth replaces the diamond ring that had belonged to Innogen's mother. It functions as a sign of women's role in establishing lineage, as a token of Innogen's body, and evidence of Posthumus's guilt.[38]

Through this stage property, the play provides some alternative to Janet Adelman's opinion that "the fantasy solution of *Cymbeline* was to do away with the female body altogether," and to Jodi Mikalachki's argument that it participates in a disincorporation of the feminine because the wicked Queen is killed off and Innogen remains in male attire at the end.[39] *Cymbeline* effectively stages woman's parts through the properties of the manacle, ring, and the bloody cloth. In this last instance the token functions to show Posthumus's repentance for his behavior and his acceptance of the woman's part in relation to his own body. Those parts are displaced onto objects in ways that distance them from the female body, but the female body was itself absent from the English Renaissance stage, and these stage properties register that absence and materialize women's exclusion, so that the circulation of and accommodation to women's (absent) bodies can be represented.[40] Posthumus and Innogen's marriage at the end does, as Mikalachki suggests, "emphasize the necessary subordination of the feminine within the patriarchal structures of marriage and empire,"[41] because Innogen's loss of her kingdom is presented as far less important than her union with Posthumus, and the social status of the partners is altered to make each more equal to the other.[42]

But marriage is not the only agent that contains Innogen's erotic power: Posthumus's form of instantiating his desire through marriage as ownership, his impulse to enclave Innogen's sexuality as figured in the manacle, intensifies that containment. The play also foregrounds the larger wrongs of misogyny through staging Cloten's desire to rape Innogen, Iachimo's slander of her, and Posthumus's outrage against all women: it dramatizes those abuses and punishes all three men. Misogyny is rebuked in *Cymbeline* even as the claims of patriarchy are reasserted,[43] and the corresponding changes in Posthumus become evident by means of the stage properties. Our attention as an audience is called to his manacle of possessive marriage. Through the bloody cloth, Posthumus's acceptance of the stain of womankind, his incorporation of it on his own body and admission of his greater guilt, are presented as resolutions to sexual and marital discord. The theatrical display of the cloth animates this accommodation and manifests it through performance.

After Posthumus has contributed to the British victory and changed to Roman attire so that he can be taken by the Britons, he finds himself in fuller bondage than he ever desired to place on Innogen, with "locks" on both his "shanks and wrists" (5.3.102–3). He considers this a "welcome bondage, for thou art a way, / I think to liberty" (5.3.97–8) and death. Then after the dream in which he recovers his family – including his mother and her other legitimate sons – the messenger advises the jailer, "Knock off his manacles" (5.3.284). Posthumus has to live the constraint of his own limbs before he can recover his identity through his family connections and be reunited with his wife. In the recognition scene that follows, Innogen, as Fidele, being granted a boon by Cymbeline, asks Iachimo to "render / Of whom he had this ring" (5.4.135–6), and the ring sets in motion a chain of discoveries in which the identities of Iachimo, Posthumus, Innogen, Belarius, Guiderius, Arviragus, and yet again Posthumus via the Soothsayer are recognized and revealed. Although Iachimo confesses his crime, he still retains both objects. Even after husband and wife are reunited in a long embrace, it is another 150 lines before those properties are returned.

This final exchange occurs principally between men. Iachimo says to Posthumus:

> Take that life, beseech you,
> Which I so often owe; but your ring first,
> And here the bracelet of the truest princess
> That ever swore her faith.   (5.4.415–18)

Posthumus's reply shows no trace of the calculative dimensions of these goods. He spares Iachimo's life and forgives him for his injustices:

> The power that I have on you is to spare you,
> The malice towards you to forgive you. Live,
> And deal with others better.   (5.4.419–21)

Cymbeline's response then marks his recognition of Posthumus's new status after he has just learned that Posthumus fought the Romans alongside Belarius, Guiderius, and Arviragus: "Nobly doomed!" he says (5.4.421). The general pardon that the king offers to everyone and his reference to Posthumus as a "son-in-law" (5.4.422) are the fullest signs we have of his acceptance of his daughter's husband.[44]

When the Soothsayer expounds the prophecy, he shows how fully Posthumus's identity and fortunes are intertwined with those of his wife, his family, and his nation. If it was a form of male pride, stemming from the inadequacy of his own origins, that prompted Posthumus to enclave his wife's sexuality and to participate in the tournaments of value earlier in the play, then the audience is shown by the end that Posthumus has neither the impulse towards possession nor the reason for it that he once had. His reward is a reunion with Innogen in a long embrace. When he associates her with fruit in the lines, "Hang there like fruit, my soul, / Till the tree die" (5.4.263–4), his revision of the marriage topos of the elm and the vine figures her as the dearest and best part, even the soul, of their union. The passage claims a full incorporation of husband and wife at this moment, one that achieves its intensity as a resolution of the earlier fragmentation of both persons, their union, even their bodies.[45]

In this final scene, most of the characters are looking pretty ragged. Cymbeline refers to "bloody hands" not yet washed in the play's last line (5.4.486), and in many productions everyone who has engaged in the fight shows signs of blood and dirt, including Posthumus, though he is not wearing the clothes in which he fought. Innogen is still dressed as a male page, and most of the other characters are in garments that show the effects of toil and conflict. This is no accident in a play that puts so much emphasis on clothing and class, calls the worth of all noble characters into question, and dramatizes with grotesque consequences how clothes can make the man. Nearly everyone except Cymbeline in the last tableau looks base rather than noble, as if the events of the play have reduced them to their lowest common denominator, the status that occasioned Posthumus's exile at the play's opening. They are so stained with the blood of war that the stain of womankind on the bloody cloth is no longer a visual exception to the scene but in keeping with the larger spectacle.[46]

Meanwhile the manacle, having swung so widely in value from signifying Innogen's sexual containment to marking all women's sexual license, can revert to the status of a bracelet, perhaps even a trifle, since its earlier associations and its commodifying potential have been nearly evacuated by the movement of this narrative. Once Posthumus and Innogen have recovered their identities and each other, there seems little need for those properties to mark their bond, and the nearly continuous connection between their physical bodies in the last scene in some productions becomes an even more obvious confirmation of their union. Unlike the ring which is named seventeen times in the play, or the handkerchief in *Othello* that is mentioned twenty-seven times, the bracelet is only referred to as such on two occasions, and then only in the last scene. Readers of modernized texts encounter it in editorial stage directions as early as the first gift exchange, but the noun is not *heard* in performance until the end. It is such a visible stage prop that the bracelet does not even have to be named, and the absence of a stable or repeated verbal signifier permits greater play with its signification.

As staged in most recent productions, it is simply a big ring, large enough to be seen from a distance and functioning as an exaggeration of the claims and commitments often associated with the smaller object. Bracelets are referred to rarely in Shakespeare, occurring only in a catalogue of finery in *The Taming of the Shrew* (4.3.58); as "bracelets of... hair" in *A Midsummer Night's Dream*, one of many love tokens that Lysander has given to Hermia (1.1.33); as the previously vended contents of Autolycus's pack in *The Winter's Tale* (4.4.587); and as "iron bracelets" or shackles that Palamon wears in *Two Noble Kinsmen* (2.6.8, 3.1.31). Manacles are mentioned in *Henry IV Part Two, Measure for Measure, Coriolanus,* and *The Tempest* as agents of constraint and imprisonment.[47] Only in *Cymbeline* does a bracelet actually appear on stage, but its size is even more appropriate than a ring as a sign of the woman's part, the visible presence of women's lack and a mark of their commodification, containment, circulation, and devaluation through exchange, as well as a materialization of their exclusion in early modern theatrical representation.

It is this stage property, especially in the context of the bedroom scene, that has repeatedly been used to represent the play. As early as the first edition of Shakespeare's plays to be published after the four folios, Nicholas Rowe positioned opposite the title page to the first printing of his 1709 edition an image of the bedroom scene with Iachimo coming out of the trunk. The manacle is not evident in this engraving, but it is visible in the frontispiece to Bell's 1773 printing of the play, where Iachimo is noting down details of the chamber while Innogen sleeps (figure 11.1). Nosworthy's 1955 Arden edition of the play reproduced this image in its earlier and probably original printing, until the cover was changed to a portly and grizzle-haired Posthumus placing a bracelet on Innogen's arm (figure 11.2). The slipcase for Roger Warren's 1989 book on the theatre history of *Cymbeline* in the Shakespeare in Performance series uses a photo from the 1962 RSC production that shows the bracelet on Vanessa Redgrave's arm with a cormorant Eric Porter about to take it off (figure 11.3). A different view of the play was created in 1987–88 by the program cover for the RSC production directed by Bill Alexander at The Other Place and The Pit, when a huge eagle spread its wings as the program unfolded. Yet when this production was recast, moved to Stratford's mainstage in 1989, and needed a larger audience, the cover was changed to reveal a seemingly naked Innogen, asleep, with her braceleted arm draped across her face. The viewer of this program is positioned like the voyeuristic Iachimo and invited to scan her body, its singular ornament in stark contrast to the smooth surface of her skin (figure 11.4). Still another RSC production changed its image of the play in the middle of the run: the 1997 Stratford performances used an orientalized drawing of characters in a landscaped setting for the program cover, but for the 1998 London performances the cover was altered to a steamy close-up of Innogen and Posthumus staring in unison at the bracelet he has apparently just placed on her arm (figure 11.5). Roger Warren's 1998 edition of the play published in the Oxford Shakespeare Series reproduces a portion of Titian's *Sleeping Venus*, naked from the breasts up, for its paperback cover, once again evoking the seduction scene and aligning the viewer with Iachimo's voyeurism.

There are exceptions to this tradition, especially on the American side: the Ashland Shakespeare Company used three overlapping images of an upright, clothed, and Celtic Innogen for the cover of its festival program in 1998, and the New York Shakespeare Festival's theatre program of the same year reproduced an engraving from Barry Cornwall's 1846 *Works of Shakespeare* showing two hands in a round, stone vault, one pointing

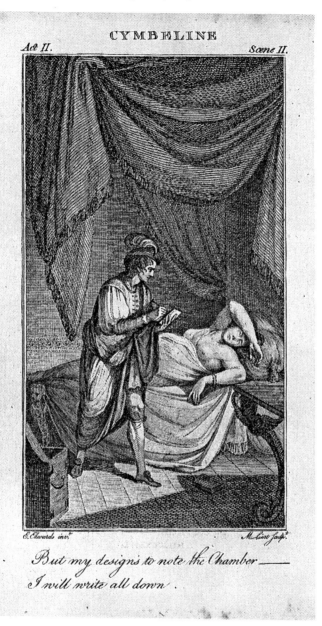

CYMBELINE

Act II.   *Scene II.*

E. Edwards inv.t   *M. Grire sculp.t*

But my design's to note the Chamber——
I will write all down.

Figure 11.1 Frontispiece opposite the title page from the 1773
performance edition of *Cymbeline* printed for John Bell.

Figure 11.2 The revised cover of the 1955 Arden edition of *Cymbeline*.

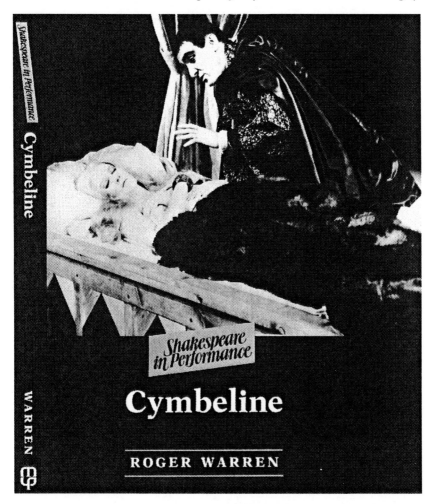

Figure 11.3 Slipcase cover of *Cymbeline* in the Shakespeare in Performance Series (Manchester University Press, 1989), showing Vanessa Redgrave and Eric Porter from the 1962 RSC production of the play.

to a ring on the other. Yet when the New York show was reviewed by *Shakespeare Bulletin* in its Fall 1998 issue, the photo used from the production was once again the scene of a recumbent, manacled Innogen and a predatory Iachimo. Shakespeare Santa Cruz's playfully postmodern production of 2000 imposed the head of a king of clubs from a deck of cards onto a Union Jack for its T-shirts and program, but the festival

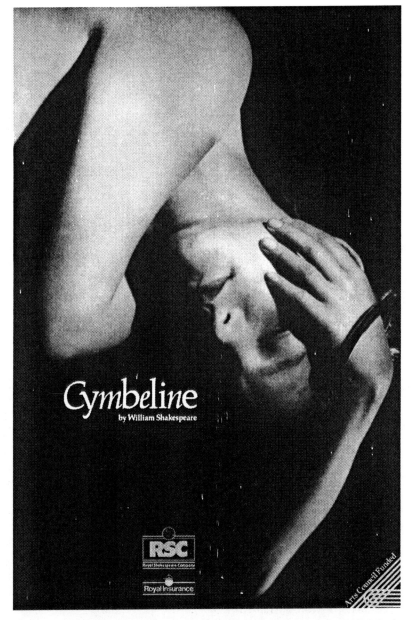

Figure 11.4 Program cover from the 1989 RSC mainstage production of *Cymbeline* in
Stratford, directed by Bill Alexander.

Figure 11.5 Revised program cover from the RSC production of *Cymbeline* at the
Barbican in Spring 1998.

also sold as a bracelet a wide purple rubber band on which was stamped, "For my sake wear this: it is a manacle of love. *Cymbeline* 1, i."

Theatre companies, booksellers, and their advertisers have been quick to see the erotic and voyeuristic appeal of the manacle and the seduction scene, so they have used it to commodify the text and lure consumers. As far as I know, the bloody cloth only served this function once, when it appeared along with the ring and bracelet as a russet-colored handkerchief, more dyed than stained, in the revised program cover for the RSC London production in 1998 (figure 11.5). That property is deemed representationally undesirable even at a time when books and art celebrate dislocation, grime, and grunge. Perhaps the *lack* of its use to signify the play is another indication that those in advertising still know a commodity when they see it, and when they don't.

NOTES

I am grateful to members of two seminars at the meetings of the Shakespeare Association of America in 1997 and 1998 for their responses to different versions of this essay, and to those who offered questions and comments when I presented it at the Shakespeare Institute, University of Birmingham; Froebel College at Roehampton Institute; and King's College, University of London, all in spring 1998; and the Medieval and Renaissance Consortium at the University of Hawai'i at Manoa in spring 2000. Those who were particularly helpful at various stages of this project include Laura Lyons, Tina Malcolmson, Helen Hackett, Joan Perkins, and Carol Rutter. Garrett Sullivan prepared a response to the essay for volume 1 of the electronic journal and seminar, *Early Modern Culture*, where an earlier version of it first appeared, and his astute critique led to a thorough revision. I have also benefited from information on productions provided by directors and dramaturgs: Cam Magee, Art Manke, and Ros King. Thanks to all.

1. Arjun Appadurai, "Introduction: commodities and the politics of value," in Appadurai (ed.), *The Social Life of Things: Commodities in Cultural Perspective* (Cambridge: Cambridge University Press, 1986), p. 3. Subsequent references to this source are given in parenthesis in the text.

2. Appadurai resists the notion that gift and commodity exchanges are fully separate from one another. He also finds commodities even in pre-industrial, non-monetary societies. In both respects he is revising the work of Karl Marx and other early political economists.

3. John Frow, *Time and Commodity Culture: Essays in Cultural Theory and Postmodernity* (Oxford: Clarendon Press, 1997), p. 125.

4. *Cymbeline*, ed. Roger Warren (Oxford: Oxford University Press, 1998), which will serve as the edition for subsequent citations to this play except those noted below. Warren modernizes Iachimo's name to Giacomo, but in this essay I have retained the Folio's spelling.

5. For this observation I am indebted to Garrett Sullivan.

6. Frow, *Time and Commodity Culture*, p. 124.

7. All references to Shakespeare's plays excluding *Cymbeline* are to *The Norton Shakespeare based on the Oxford Edition*, ed. Stephen Greenblatt et al. (New York: W. W. Norton, 1997).

8. See Ann Barton's discussion of the likelihood that this marriage is only a *spousal de praesenti*, a clandestine pre-contract, in " 'Wrying but a little': marriage, law, and sexuality in the plays of Shakespeare," chapter 1 of *Essays, Mainly Shakespearean* (Cambridge: Cambridge University Press, 1994), pp. 3–30; and Roger Warren's objections to Barton's argument that Innogen is still a virgin, in the "Introduction" to his edition, pp. 32–3, a portion of which is quoted at note 25 below.

9. Igor Kopytoff, "The cultural biography of things: commoditization as process," in Appadurai (ed.), *The Social Life of Things*, p. 75.

10. Frow quotes Lewis Hyde's *The Gift: Imagination and the Erotic Life of Property* (New York: Vintage Books, 1979): " 'the conversion of gifts to commodities can fragment or destroy such a group' " (p. 80). Frow presents Hyde's approach as the "simplest and purest model of the gift . . . against which all more complex versions," such as his own, "are set" (*Time and Commodity Culture*, pp. 103–4).

11. Geoffrey Bullough (ed.), *Narrative and Dramatic Sources of Shakespeare*, vol. VIII (London: Routledge and Kegan Paul; New York: Columbia University Press, 1975), p. 55.

12. J. M. Nosworthy (ed.), *Cymbeline* (London: Routledge, 1955), p. 196.

13. Bullough (ed.), *Narrative and Dramatic Sources*, vol. VIII, p. 11.

14. Thomas Dekker, *The Whore of Babylon* (London: Nathaniel Butter, 1607), sig. B1v, where the Empress of Babylon says, "Her Kingdom weares a girdle wrought of waves, / Set thicke with pretious stones, that are so charm'd, / No rockes are of more force."

15. Linda Woodbridge, "Protection and pollution: palisading the Elizabethan body politic," in *The Scythe of Saturn: Shakespeare and Magical Thinking* (Urbana: University of Illinois Press, 1994), pp. 45–85. A longer version of this essay appeared in *Texas Studies in Literature and Language* 33 (1991): 327–54.

16. Bullough (ed.), *Narrative and Dramatic Sources*, vol. VIII, p. 56.

17. Kopytoff, "Cultural biography," p. 78.

18. Margreta De Grazia, "The ideology of superfluous things: *King Lear* as period piece," in Margreta De Grazia, Maureen Quilligan, and Peter Stallybrass (eds.) *Subject and Object in Renaissance Culture* (Cambridge: Cambridge University Press, 1996), pp. 17–42; p. 21.

19. Thomas D'Urfey, *The Injured Princess* (1682; facsimile reprint, London: Cornmarket Press, 1970). The title of the play given on the page on which act 1 begins reads "The Unequal Match; or the Fatal Wager," sig. B1.

20. See Ann Thompson, "Person and office: the case of Imogen, Princess of Britain," *Literature and Nationalism* (Liverpool: Liverpool University Press, 1991), pp. 76–87.

21. Diana E. Henderson makes this point effectively in "Rewriting family ties: Woolf's Renaissance romance," in Sally Greene (ed.), *Virginia Woolf: Reading the Renaissance* (Athens: Ohio University Press, 1999), pp. 136–60: "Although Imogen's ultimate reunion with those blood brothers displaces her as royal heir, she celebrates it. Restoration of the male line of inheritance removes the impediment to her marriage with the commoner Posthumus Leonatus; that marriage is always her primary concern" (p. 137).

22. *History of King Lear*, 4.171; *Tragedy of King Lear*, 1.4.158.

23. Jodi Mikalachki, *The Legacy of Boadicea: Gender and Nation in Early Modern England* (London: Routledge, 1998), chapter 3. First published as "The masculine romance of Roman Britain: *Cymbeline* and early modern English nationalism," *Shakespeare Quarterly* 46 (1995): 301–22.

24. In *The Flower of Friendship*, Edmund Tilney's primary spokesperson in the dialogue advises that "equalitie is principally to be considered in this matrimoniall amitie... For equalnesse herein, maketh friendlynesse" (ll. 286–89). I have discussed how slippery this passage is and related it to issues of class in the introduction to my edition of the dialogue (Ithaca: Cornell University Press, 1992), pp. 50–9.

25. I find Roger Warren's discussion of these lines in his "Introduction," pp. 32–3, especially compelling. Countering Anne Barton's claim that the "opposition" refers specifically to Innogen's hymen and that she is a virgin, Warren says the quoted passage "simply means that Giacomo anticipated pleasurable physical 'opposition' to penetration, and that her behaviour was a mere prelude to intercourse ('encounter')." As for Posthumus's remarks at ll. 161–9, "any criticism is directed not at her [Innogen] but at Posthumus for a sexual demandingness that now, apparently humiliated, drives him to interpret her restraint as the behaviour of a professional 'tease'" (p. 33).

26. Lacan's account of the male child's discovery of the phallus as signifying separation and loss of the union with the mother, thereby prompting his entry into the Symbolic Order as a speaking subject, relates to Posthumus's loss and his discovery at this moment of a new discourse, one that is distinctly phallogocentric and governed by the Law of the Father. Posthumus's loss of Innogen triggers his earlier, infantile separation from his birth mother, since he was "ripped" from her via Caesarean section (5.3.139), and another separation from whoever nursed him as surrogate mother.

27. In a note to Posthumus's opening soliloquy in act 5, the Variorum editor observes: "ECCLES here expresses much and prolonged wonder over the difficulty of accounting for this 'bloody cloth'; since it must have reached the hands of Posthumus after his arrival in Britain. Eccles thinks that Posthumus must have privately dispatched a messenger with authority to receive it from Pisanio. And if this be so, Shakespeare should unquestionably have communicated some intelligence of it to the audience." *The Tragedie of Cymbeline*, ed. Horace Howard Furness (Philadelphia: J. B. Lippincott, 1913), pp. 349–50, n. 3. Shakespeare's failure to do what Eccles and Furness advise indicates how unimportant the conveyance of the cloth is in the play.

It is more mystified and resistant to commodification if it appears without explanation.

28. Peter Stallybrass, "Worn worlds: clothes and identity on the Renaissance stage," in De Grazia, Quilligan, and Stallybrass (eds.), *Subject and Object*, p. 310.

29. Nosworthy (ed.), *Cymbeline*, pp. 197–8.

30. Stallybrass connects it with the "senseless linen" (1.3.7) of Posthumus's handkerchief when he parted from Innogen, and sees it later as "the sentient material of the cloth which has 'clipt' her" (ibid.).

31. Coppélia Kahn, *Roman Shakespeare: Warriors, Wounds, and Women* (London and New York: Routledge, 1997), p. 168. Diana E. Henderson and James Siemon observe that "The most remarkable aspect of Posthumus's behavior, his repentance for killing his wife *prior* to learning of her innocence, in fact derives from Shakespeare's anonymous 'lowly' source, *Frederycke of Jennen*, rather than from Boccaccio" in "Reading vernacular literature," in *A Companion to Shakespeare*, ed. David Scott Kastan (Oxford: Blackwell, 1999), p. 220. While this is strictly correct and the repentance is prompted by the husband's seeing tokens of his wife's death, the stated reasons for his repentance are very different: "And whan Ambrose sawe theim [the tokens], than was he more sorier than he was before, because that he spake not with her before that he caused her to be put to death, to examyne her, wherfore John of Florence [Iachimo's counterpart] had the jewels" (Nosworthy [ed.], *Cymbeline*, p. 198). In the source the husband regrets not *confirming* her guilt before having her killed; he gives no indication that had she been guilty – wryed by a little – he would have regretted his order for her death.

32. Warren, note to 5.1.9 "**put on** instigate"; J. M. Nosworthy, note to 5.1.9, "put on usually explained as to instigate, incite (this crime), but assume, take on myself seems equally possible," in *Cymbeline*.

33. The promptbook indicates that Posthumus enters the act with "cloth in R hand," and at the line "put on this" the direction reads, "Cloth round neck and ties it" (Shakespeare Centre Library).

34. Of the National's 1988 production, Warren comments that "Posthumus's transformation was clinched by the very effective device of wearing the bloody cloth wrapped round his head, with eye-holes cut in it, like a guerilla's balaclava. By the time he had gone through the battle, his face and body not only caked in grime but streaming with blood, his own and other people's, it was no surprise that he was unrecognizable to anyone except the audience until he chose to reveal himself." Roger Warren, *Staging Shakespeare's Late Plays* (Oxford: Clarendon Press, 1990), p. 74. In Noble's 1997–98 production, Posthumus had the cloth tied around his head after he re-entered at 5.3. The production by the Los Angeles company A Noise Within in 2000 followed Peter Hall's use of the balaclava.

35. In the 1982 BBC production for television, directed by Elijah Moshinsky, Posthumus had the bloody cloth in his belt for much of act 5. The 1996 production for the Washington Shakespeare Company, directed by Joe

Banno with Cam Magee as dramaturg, had Posthumus tie the cloth around his neck at a later point in 5.1 and it was still there in the last scene. Innogen then took it off after they were reunited. A Noise Within's 2000 production in Los Angeles, directed by Art Manke, had Posthumus wrap the cloth around his head at 5.1.24. For the Shakespeare Santa Cruz production of 2000 directed by Danny Scheie, with Ros King as dramaturg, Posthumus returned from battle with the bloody cloth tied around his wrist.

36. Stallybrass, "Worn worlds," p. 310.

37. Warren (ed.), *Cymbeline*, n. to 2.3.130–1: "Posthumus' *meanest garment* is presumably his underwear, chosen by the now enraged Innogen because the point at which it *clipped* (encircled) Posthumus' body will be particularly provocative and humiliating to Cloten."

38. Coppélia Kahn remarks that "in his fifth-act soliloquy he internalizes that part and cleanses it of sexual contamination. Surely the play works as hard to enable Posthumus to accept 'the woman's part' as to foster manly virtue in him," in *Roman Shakespeare*, p. 168. I agree with this important observation and recommend Kahn's entire discussion, but I do not think that Posthumus is able to "cleanse" the woman's part of its sexual contamination. Instead, he accepts contaminated woman, the wife whom he thinks has wryed by a little. Neither he nor anyone else in the culture is capable of removing that stain from the bloody cloth.

39. Janet Adelman, *Suffocating Mothers: Fantasies of Maternal Origin in Shakespeare's Plays* (New York: Routledge, 1992), p. 219; Jodi Mikalachki, *Legacy of Boadicea*, p. 113.

40. See Dympna Callaghan, *Shakespeare Without Women: Representing Gender and Race on the Renaissance Stage* (London and New York: Routledge, 2000), especially pp. 26–43.

41. Mikalachki, *Legacy of Boadicea*, p. 113.

42. Jean Howard observes in her "Introduction" to the play in the *Norton Shakespeare* (New York: W. W. Norton, 1997), p. 2963, "In its narratives of nation, *Cymbeline* seems able to reprove the most virulent forms of misogyny only when it simultaneously removes women from public power, transforms them into chaste, domesticated wives, and reaffirms the dominance of husbands." While I agree with the first point, the play's emphasis on chastity is mitigated through Posthumus's forgiveness of Innogen when he believes she has committed adultery, and I see little evidence that it asserts Posthumus's dominance over her at the end. The emphasis is on their union, not on the hierarchical disparity between them.

43. I have explored the difficult distinction between patriarchy and misogyny in "Historical differences: misogyny and *Othello*," in Wayne (ed.), *The Matter of Difference: Materialist Feminist Criticism of Shakespeare* (Ithaca: Cornell University Press, 1991), pp. 153–79.

44. Barton emphasizes the reference to "son-in-law" in " 'Wrying but a little,' " p. 30.

45. I would also argue that this embrace, rather than the "masculine embrace" between Fidele and Lucius discussed by Mikalachki (*Legacy of Boadicea*, p. 112), is the more important embrace of the play.

46. The bloody cloth frequently reappears in production in the last scene. See note 34 for two instances.

47. *The Tempest*, 1.2.465, Prospero to Ferdinand: "I'll manacle thy neck and feet together"; *Henry VI Part Two*, 5.1.147, Clifford to York about Warwick and Salisbury: "We'll bait thy bears to death / And manacle the bearherd in their chains"; *Measure for Measure*, 2.4.90–4, Angelo to Isabella: ". . . that you his sister / Finding yourself desired of such a person / Whose credit with the judge, or own great place / Could fetch your brother from the manacles / Of the all-binding law"; *Coriolanus*, 1.10.55–6, Cominius to Coriolanus: "If 'gainst yourself you be incensed we'll put you, / Like one that means his proper harm, in manacles."

CHAPTER 12

Wonder-effects: Othello's handkerchief

Paul Yachnin

Many readings have taken the handkerchief in *Othello* as a symbol of something more momentous than the altogether practical and commonplace stage property that it must have been in the Globe playhouse. In this paper, I focus on the handkerchief as a prop first, and only then do I consider how it speaks about something beyond itself, and at that, not as a symbol, but rather as an object involved in a complex series of exchanges. In part, this approach allows me to suggest how theatrical practices and interests intersected with early modern English culture, while protecting against the tendency to read the playhouse as a window onto that culture. Localized interpretation helps to shift interpretation from an imaginary, totalized cultural field (with the handkerchief as a pass-key to historical understanding) to one that takes into account the relative autonomy of the stage (where the handkerchief emerges as a prop whose work within the play involves elements from the broader culture). I suggest that only by understanding how the handkerchief operated in the playhouse can we begin to grasp how it and the play operate within culture at large.

A localizing interpretation can help explain how a piece of cloth has become what might be called a magical property, and why Shakespeare might have wanted to transform a stage-prop into an object of wonder. Importantly, it can also provide the foundation for a longer-term account by suggesting how the playhouse's strategic representation of the handkerchief has contributed to the development of the "wonder-effects" of Shakespeare's works themselves: the process by which Shakespeare has come to be for modernity what the handkerchief is for Othello – a possession that possesses the possessor.

Because the story I seek to tell concerns the long-term development of Shakespearean wonder-effects, my essay can perhaps serve as a critical supplement to some of the emphases of this volume. I am suggesting that the literary qualities of wonderfulness (and the concomitant subjectivity-effects), which have seemed central to Shakespeare since at least the nineteenth century, are a long-term outcome of Shakespeare's own representational strategies rather than an imposition upon his plays. Instead of seeking to recover how things really were in Shakespeare's playhouse by invalidating two centuries of reception history, we need to attempt to situate ourselves in relation to the past in light of lines of continuity and transvaluation that lead from the Elizabethan playhouse, through intervening historical scenes of reception, up to the present moment. And more than that: while it is indubitable that the handkerchief and the play itself are far more sublime for us than they were for early modern playgoers (sublimity accruing to the property and the play over time and by dint of the contributions of many differently situated cultural producers), it is nevertheless not possible at this juncture to discard the sense of wonder by some extraordinary act of historical recovery. Even though it has been built up over time, wonder belongs to the handkerchief as an intrinsic feature because it is not in fact separable from the thing itself as its operations within the play are experienced by spectators (not to mention how it affects readers, who have solely an idea of a handkerchief to work with). Accordingly, I do not intend my history of theatrical and literary wonder-effects to vitiate the play's ability to affect us deeply (as if my argument could do that!) or indeed to impair its capacity to arouse within us a sense of wonder.

Beyond all that has been said about its social and psychosexual meanings, there are two remarkable features about the handkerchief. The first is that it starts off as unremarkable. Embroidered handkerchiefs were gentrified but unexotic love tokens in Shakespeare's day. The well-born Celia throws one down to the disguised Volpone; and in a later play, Jonson associates "perfumed napkins" with "silver dishes [and] gold chamber pots."[1] In Elizabethan upper-crust portraiture, subjects are often given fine "handkerchers" to hold.[2] Indeed, we might think that Desdemona must have felt a bit let down when her "extravagant and wheeling stranger" (1.1.136) bestowed on her, as his very first gift, a typically English-style, strawberry-spotted silk handkerchief.[3] We could, of course, argue that an unworldly Venetian girl would have found English embroidery strange and beautiful, but we could not easily maintain that Shakespeare's audience would have shared her admiration.

The second remarkable feature of the handkerchief is its transformation into something wonderful. Not only does the handkerchief acquire a myth of origin pungent with Egyptian magicians, Virgilian sibyls, and the dye of mummified maidens' hearts (3.4.55–75), but it also gathers an uncanny aura because of how its movement from hand to hand in the play links the characters in ways they are unable to apprehend – they merely handle the handkerchief, but *it holds them*, binding them to relations with others which remain invisible to them but which conduct them to their destinies.[4]

The transformation of the handkerchief involves the whole design of the dramatic action, Othello's claims about its magical power, and the other characters' recognition of its worth. Moreover, the playwright imports three weighty elements from the world outside the playhouse – social rank, cultural otherness, and heterosexual love. He can assume, of course, that the audience will associate silk handkerchiefs with gentrified wooing, which is what Celia's napkin connotes in *Volpone*. But that is just the beginning point for an elaborate infusion of charisma into this square of cloth, versions of which had been standard stage properties in plays such as Thomas Kyd's *The Spanish Tragedy*, where it reminds us of Horatio's murder by being stained with his blood, or *As You Like It*, where (also bloodied) it stands as a token of Orlando's faith. Shakespeare's transformation of the handkerchief in *Othello* draws in part on the traditional theatrical uses of bits of cloth (like Thisbe's mantle or Troilus's sleeve) and also on the Jacobean passion for cultural exotica – stories of peoples such as "the Anthropophagi, and men whose heads / Do grow beneath their shoulders" (1.3.144–5) or Egyptian charmers and two-hundred-year-old sibyls. Finally, the handkerchief is made to symbolize the problem of sexual love within patriarchal culture; indeed, it *becomes* the problem of woman's love so completely that Othello cries out against the (imagined) defection of Desdemona by calling for *its* return: "Fetch me the handkerchief, my mind misgives ... The handkerchief! ... The handkerchief! ... The handkerchief!" (3.4.89–96).

If the handkerchief has attracted extensive critical interest, that is because it was intended to be interesting. And if it repays study from social and psychological points of view, that is because Shakespeare has folded into it aspects of culture and human relations as part, first and foremost, of a theatrical project to arouse wonder in early modern playgoers. In *Othello*, Shakespeare maneuvers to make wonder out of the material he has to work with, which, among other things such as language, costume, and Othello's black-face makeup, includes the fabric of the handkerchief and the body of the boy actor who plays Desdemona. These two objects are constructed so as to enhance the cultural status of the play by raising it above the commercialism and materiality of actual play production.

My focus here is the operation of wonder in Shakespeare's playhouse. However, in order to link the local and the macrohistorical, I also examine the differences between playhouse wonder and later forms of wonder in Shakespeare as literature and in Shakespeare criticism. These versions are linked by their relationship with subjectivity, possession, and the nature of the object, but they are produced in different ways and toward different ends. Theatrical wonder is largely visual, processive, and collective; literary and critical wonder is "visionary," possessive, and directed toward the individual as individual.

Othello is an illuminating text in this discussion because it is both wonderful in itself and critical of how magical properties can enchant the eye and mind. By analyzing how *Othello* fetishizes theatrical properties, we can begin to understand the investments that the play wins from modern readers and critics. This is not to suggest that the play is magically prescient. Rather its fictions of possession and wonder imply the conditions of its production and make the contradictions in that production visible as ideology. Pierre Macherey tells us, "the book revolves around this myth [i.e., that the book is uncannily alive]; but in the process of its formation the book takes a stand regarding this myth, exposing it. This does not mean that the book is able to become its own criticism: it gives an implicit critique of its ideological content, if only because it resists being incorporated into the flow of ideology in order to give a *determinate representation* of it."[5]

To Macherey's insight into the book's capacity to imply a critique of its own ideological content, we should append Mikhail Bakhtin's ideas about literary language, which in effect provide the explanation of literature's critical power that is not articulated by Macherey. Recent materialist criticism often assumes that ideology is capable of becoming visible in literary texts because literature is a weak or neutral linguistic field – hence the putative interpretive "openness" of literature. Bakhtin, however, reminds us that literary texts generate extraordinary fields of semantic force; indeed, it is the persistent intentionality of the literary text that operates to objectify the intentionality of the sociolects that the text imports into its literary domain, transforming them from closed systematic ways of understanding the world into "*things*, limited in their meaning and expression."[6] Bakhtin explains how the novel "orchestrates" the social heteroglossia of the novelist's world:

all languages of heteroglossia . . . are specific points of view on the world, forms for conceptualizing the world in words . . . As such they all may be juxtaposed to one another and be interrelated dialogically. As such they encounter one another and co-exist in the consciousness of real people – first and foremost in the creative consciousness of people who write novels . . . these languages live a real life, they struggle and evolve in an environment of social heteroglossia. Therefore they are all able to enter into the unitary plane of the novel, which can unite in itself parodic stylizations of generic languages, various forms of stylizations and illustrations of professional and period-bound languages, the languages of particular generations, of social dialects . . . They may all be drawn in by the novelist for the orchestration of his themes and for the refracted (indirect) expression of his intentions and values.[7]

Shakespeare appropriates the languages of social rank, cultural other-ness, and heterosexual love and possessiveness – including the symbolism of silken love tokens – not for their own sakes, but rather to perform a set of tasks specific to the play. Iago's populist scorn for high rank (espe-cially for high-born women), Othello's proud claims about his own rank, Othello's reprisal of travel-literature exotica, and the play's retelling of the bliss and threat of romantic love – all these "languages" are orches-trated by Shakespeare to perform the work of thematic development, characterization, representation of social context, and the arousal of wonder. Since he is not discussing theatre, Bakhtin naturally ignores the "language" of stage properties, but his model of literary orchestration nevertheless describes well the operations of props in Shakespeare. The overall effect of orchestrated texts is wonderful but also critical, since the languages, together with their conceptualizations of the world, cut across each other in illuminating ways; in *Othello* itself, the production of the theatrical wonder of the handkerchief tends to reveal the real-life relationship among identity-formation, other people, and fetishized objects.

To move toward a historical understanding of Shakespearean wonder, let us consider two exemplary views of wonder by two leading Shakespear-eans of the present epoch. Where Northrop Frye views *The Tempest* as a play where wonder leads to self-knowledge, Stephen Greenblatt elabo-rates a troubled but similar account of the effects of wonder. Of course, new historicism arose in opposition to approaches such as Frye's, but humanist and anti-humanist forms of criticism share some surprisingly similar assumptions about the relationship between the literary text and the subject. Here is Frye, writing in 1959:

[T]he play is an illusion like the dream, and yet a focus of reality more intense than life affords. The action of *The Tempest* moves from . . . reality to realization.

What seems at first illusory, the magic and music, becomes real, and the *Realpolitik* of Antonio and Sebastian becomes illusion . . . When the Court Party first came to the island "no man was his own"; they had not found their "proper selves." Through the mirages of Ariel, the mops and mows of the other spirits, the vanities of Prospero's art, and the fevers of madness, reality grows up in them from inside, in response to the fertilizing influence of illusion.[8]

Greenblatt in 1991 sees wonder as "the central figure in the initial European response to the New World" – "something like the 'startle reflex' one can observe in infants."[9] Although his model of personhood is far more corporealized than Frye's, he nevertheless sees wonder as ineluctably inward:

Someone witnesses something amazing, but what most matters takes place not "out there" or along the receptive surfaces of the body where the self encounters the world, but deep within, at the vital, emotional center of the witness. This inward response cannot be marginalized or denied, any more than a constriction of the heart in terror can be denied; wonder is absolutely exigent, a primary or radical passion . . . The experience of wonder seems to resist recuperation, containment, ideological incorporation; it sits strangely apart from everything that gives coherence to Léry's universe [Jean de Léry, whose *History of a Voyage* (1585) Greenblatt is discussing here], apart and yet utterly compelling.[10]

Although connected with the violent harrowing of the self central to Christian visionary experience, Frye and Greenblatt's accounts generally understand wonder in terms of a modern idea of personhood, where wonder provokes what Frye calls "realization," the emptying out of the world and the concomitant expansion of the self. This view differs from Shakespeare's because he usually shows how wonder violates or nullifies the self rather than how it precipitates the self's expansive fulfillment. We remember Horatio "harrow[ed] . . . with fear and wonder" (*Hamlet*, 1.1.45) or Cleomenes reduced to nothing by "the ear-deaf'ning voice o' th' oracle" (*Winter's Tale*, 3.1.9). For Frye and Greenblatt, in contrast, our ability to grasp an authentic selfhood centrally has to do with possessing and with being possessed by a literary text. "*The Tempest*," Frye says, "is a play not simply to be read or seen or even studied, but possessed."[11] At the beginning of *Marvelous Possessions*, Greenblatt too declares his investments in the marvels of narrative: "I remain possessed by stories and obsessed with their complex uses."[12]

To be sure, the idea of being possessed by theatrical spectacle was current in the Renaissance. In his *Apology for Actors* (1612), Thomas Heywood, reiterating Shakespeare's emphasis on the invasive power of spectacle, praises theatre's capacity to refashion the members of the audience: "so bewitching a thing is lively and well-spirited action that it hath power to new mold the hearts of the spectators and fashion them to the shape of any noble and notable attempt."[13] But among eyewitness accounts of the drama, there are far fewer indications of the formative power ascribed to it by Heywood. We remember that the actors normally performed in the cold light of day and did not have the scenic resources of the court masque. Thomas Platter, in 1599, writes of the "marvelous" dancing that followed a performance of *Julius Caesar*; about the play he notes only that it was "very well acted."[14] In 1613, Sir Henry Wotton disapprovingly recounts the tawdry spectacle Shakespeare's company made of the history of Henry VIII: "The King's Players had a new play called *All is True*, representing some principal pieces of the reign of Henry VIII, which was set forth with many extraordinary circumstances of pomp and majesty, even to the matting of the stage . . . sufficient in truth within a while to make greatness very familiar, if not ridiculous."[15] While there were marvels in the theatre, they were usually greeted as something akin to mere showiness.

In accord with these views of theatrical spectacle, playgoers seem not usually to have been possessed by wonder.[16] The antitheatricalist writer and sometime dramatist Stephen Gosson writes scathingly about the fun audience members have at the playhouse:

In our assemblies at plays in London, you shall see such heaving and shoving, such itching and shouldering to sit by women. Such care for their garments that they should not be trod on, such eyes to their laps that no chips light in them, such pillows to their backs that they take no hurt . . . such tickling, such toying, such smiling, such winking, and such manning them home when the sports are ended that it is a right comedy to mark their behavior.[17]

Indeed a considerable part of the thrill of playgoing had little to do with the plays themselves, but was involved instead with the erotic and social gratifications of seeing and being seen by other spectators. In 1613, Henry Parrot satirized the practices of self-display characteristic of a theatre described by one antitheatricalist as "Venus' palace":[18]

> When young Rogero goes to see a play,
> His pleasure is you place him on the stage,
> The better to demonstrate his array,
> And how he sits attended by his page,
> That only serves to fill those pipes with smoke,
> For which he pawned hath his riding cloak.[19]

In view of the mirthful and eroticized atmosphere of Renaissance playhouses, it seems clear that the emphasis upon the conversional marvelousness of Shakespeare's drama must have been consequent upon its transformation into literature, a process that began in earnest only after Shakespeare's death. In the 1623 First Folio, Jonson lauds Shakespeare as "the wonder of our stage," but promotes his "book" as an embodiment of genius which makes an irresistible claim on all those who "have wits to read, and praise to give."[20] In the Second Folio (1632), Milton expresses similar "wonder and astonishment" at Shakespeare's "Delphic lines." In Milton's account, Shakespeare's astonishing book transforms the reader into a "livelong monument" – "thou our fancy of itself bereaving, / Dost make us marble with too much conceiving."[21] In commendatory verses prefixed to *Poems: written by Wil. Shakespeare* (1640) – twenty-four years after the playwright's death – Leonard Digges is able to remember "how the audience, / Were ravished, with what wonder they went hence," but invites the reader to look upon the "wit-fraught book, . . . whose worth / Like old-coined gold, . . . / Shall pass true current to succeeding age."[22] These tributes suggest that Shakespearean wonder, from the outset, was an experience which, while it might be imagined as the rapture of audience members possessed by a bewitching spectacle, in fact belonged to readers who owned the text. "[Y]ou will stand for your privileges . . . to read, and censure," urged John Heminge and Henry Condell, the actors responsible for the publication of the First Folio. "Do so, but buy it first . . . whatever you do, buy."[23]

But while there are differences, there is also a historical line to be traced from the spectacles performed in Shakespeare's playhouse to the visionary wonders of the First Folio to the evocation of literary wonder in recent criticism. These versions of the marvelous can be usefully related to the broader development of what Georg Lukács calls "reified consciousness," the idea that persons become objects to themselves because of their traffic in fetishized commodities – goods onto which are projected the realities of human labor and relations, and for whose commodified value real persons exchange their own worth. In "Reification and the consciousness of the proletariat," Lukács develops an analysis of the alienating effects of commodity fetishism:

The essence of commodity-structure . . . is that a relation between people takes on the character of a thing and thus acquires a "phantom objectivity," an autonomy that seems so strictly rational and all-embracing as to conceal every trace of its fundamental nature: the relation between people . . . The commodity character of the commodity, the abstract, quantitative mode of calculability shows itself here in its purest form: the reified mind necessarily sees it as the form in which its own authentic immediacy becomes manifest.[24]

When the commodity in question is a literary text supposed to be a source of wonder, and when such wonder is a possession that possesses and is the form in which the reader's mind finds its own "authentic immediacy," readerly investments will be both profound and unstable. A text like *Othello* will be to the engrossed reader as Desdemona is to her husband – an object whose capacity to arouse wonder in the beholder is seen to underwrite the beholder's selfhood. Kenneth Burke explains Othello's stake in Desdemona as "ownership in the profoundest sense of ownership, the property of human affections, as fetishistically localized in the object of possession, while the possessor is himself possessed by his very engrossment."[25] We want to bear in mind the differences between the spectacular marvels staged in the culturally lowbrow Shakespearean theatre and the visionary wonder produced in the highbrow province of Shakespeare as literature. We also should remember that a performance – unlike a book – cannot be owned. But we also want to consider the possibility that reading or writing about Shakespeare for his wonderful insights into the meaning of life or the operations of culture might constitute particular institutional transformations of spectacular, *commercial* theatricality.

In Shakespeare's London, Othello's handkerchief would have been marketable goods, a square of embroidered cloth in a nation whose primary industry was the production of textiles, a stage property in a theatre whose largest operating expense was for the purchase of costumes and draperies. Othello's mystification of the handkerchief within the play is of a piece with Renaissance Londoners' investments, both financial and psychological, in what even Caliban recognizes as "trash" – the "glistering apparel" (*Tempest*, 4.1.224, 193 s.d.) that advertised individuals' high social status in the real world and whose visual appeal in the theatre helped to make Shakespeare's drama so popular. The play's stake in the handkerchief registers the theatre's participation in English society's fetishized trade in textiles.[26]

In the world of the play, all the characters except Othello view the handkerchief as marketable goods; he defines it as a magical talisman. The effect of this definitional contest is twofold. One, the handkerchief emerges as wondrous – an object of great emotional and sexual energy. The napkin's enhancement serves the institutional project of valorizing drama over against the theatre's degraded world of work and its trade in play-texts and textiles. Two, the intensity of Othello's investments in this square of cloth works to reveal the fetish-character of commodities in general. Although everyone except Othello thinks of the handkerchief as an ordinary object, they fetishize it too. They turn it into a commodity, in Marx's sense: a thing that becomes "mysterious... simply because in it the social character of men's labour appears to them as an objective character stamped upon the product of that labour."[27] To understand the particular mystery the fetishized handkerchief evokes, however, we need to expand the field of labour and exchange so as to include the "work" of sex. That is necessary because the characters' projections of themselves onto the handkerchief run along lines determined by sex and gender. Moreover, to take sex and gender into account is to recognize their importance in the development of modern aesthetic fetishism. In this view, the art-object is the feminine beloved of the masculine owner – "a non-alienated object, one quite the reverse of a commodity, which like the 'auratic' phenomenon of a Walter Benjamin returns our tender gaze and whispers that it was created for us alone."[28]

For most of the characters, the handkerchief is reproducible, exchangeable, and has a certain cash value. Furthermore, although it circulates widely, everyone recognizes it as private property. Because it is private property, Emilia, Cassio, and Bianca all speak about making copies of it. In this regard, is it even clear that Emilia plans to keep it after having found it? She says, "My wayward husband hath a hundred times / Woo'd me to steal it... I'll have the work ta'en out, / And give't Iago" (3.3.292–6). Does she intend to give Iago the original or the copy? Does she prefer – as seems likely – robbing the handkerchief of its singularity to stealing the thing itself from Desdemona? For Desdemona, the handkerchief balances between the everyday and the sacred, becoming a hugely valued love token that is nonetheless commensurable with monetary value. "Where should I lose the handkerchief?" she asks, "Believe me, I had rather have lost my purse / Full of crusadoes" (3.4.23, 25–6).

Cassio and Emilia each intend to have the handkerchief copied because they recognize it as property that will be wanted by its owner. The strawberry-spotted handkerchief bears the print of the owner's possessive desire for it as a singular object, even though it is not necessarily unique, but potentially only the first of a series. It could be reproduced endlessly for an endless number of owners. This contradiction is paralleled by Iago's jealous ownership of his wife. She bears the imprint of his possessive desire for her as a unique prize even though he discounts her, with a sexual quibble, as "a common thing": "You have a thing for me? It is a common thing" (3.3.302).

The handkerchief's properties are continuous with the properties of love. Were Desdemona an object like the handkerchief, Othello could possess her, but so could anyone else and in any case she would then be a "common thing" like the handkerchief, certainly not the inimitable treasure for which Othello happily sacrifices his "unhoused free condition" (1.2.26). If she is not an object to Othello, then she is a subject, which is to say she is an object to herself. As self-possessed, she is free to give herself away to another. If she is her own private property, as Peter Stallybrass points out, then her defining attribute – her honour – becomes as detachable as her handkerchief:[29]

> IAGO: But if I give my wife a handkerchief –
> OTHELLO: What then?
> IAGO: Why then 'tis hers, my lord, and being hers,
> She may, I think, bestow 't on any man.
> OTHELLO: She is protectress of her honor too;
> May she give that? (4.1.10–15)

No possible permutation is able to unburden heterosexual love of the contradictions involved in the patriarchal ownership of women who are also required to be owners of themselves.

The handkerchief figures possessive male desire for the female "common thing" in ways that legitimize jealousy in terms of the "phantom objectivity" of the gender system. The operation of this system seems invisible to the characters and its effects cut across gender lines. Bianca returns the handkerchief to Cassio, refusing to "take out the work" since she thinks it was given to him by another woman. This other woman is a "hobby-horse" while Cassio is allowed the agential attributes of desire and deceitfulness:

> What did you mean by that same handkerchief you gave me even now? I was a fine fool to take it. I must take out the work? A likely piece of work, that you should find it in your chamber, and know not who left it there! This is some minx's token, and I must take out the work? There, give it your hobby-horse. (4.1.148–54)

Given the invisible influence that the handkerchief wields in its travels through the play, the claims Othello makes about both its sacred, feminine origins and its magical power to bind husband to wife through male desire seem not to belong to an enchanted world entirely foreign to Venetian civility, but rather to constitute a somewhat outlandish explanation of the handkerchief's actual operations. The play opens to analysis the fetish character of the handkerchief with regard to all the characters who touch it. It does so through Othello's explanation of its quasi-magical powers, but more so by the way Othello convinces himself into accepting it as "ocular proof" (3.3.360) against his wife (since it falls to the stage in his presence and as a result of his action some hundred and fifty lines before Iago reports having seen Cassio wipe his beard with it). Othello uses the handkerchief to prove something against Desdemona which the desirable thingness of the handkerchief has already inscribed as inevitable in heterosexual relations – the "destiny unshunnable" (3.3.275) of being made a cuckold. It is the fate of every man to invest his all in the vexed figure of Woman, she who is unique because she is a rare object and "common" because she is a subject. On this account, the vexing constitution of Othello's selfhood on the basis of heterosexual mutuality is no different from anyone else's – it is only that his terminology is strangely revealing.

But Othello's terms constitute more than an exotic account of the ordinary. In Othello's telling, the handkerchief is a different kind of thing – a wonder that possesses a particular history and a charismatic hold on its owner. Desdemona is reframed as just such a wonderful object. If she were like the handkerchief that Othello imagines, then he could possess her wholly yet she would become neither the "common thing" of marketplace exchanges nor the free trader of her own honour. Not, of course, that the handkerchief ever becomes convincingly magical. It is rather that its movements in the play suggest that there *could* be "magic in the web of it" (3.4.69). The handkerchief is held in hand after hand; but its significance is never grasped by any one possessor. Its power to generate an unseen network of connections over the heads of every character except Iago lends it a certain marvelousness. Even Iago cannot quite get hold of it. He is just lucky: it is surprising that Cassio is unacquainted with Othello's first and most valued gift to Desdemona, especially since Cassio went "a-wooing" with Othello "from first to last" (3.3.71, 96).

So while the play opens to examination the operations of fetishism, it also works to fetishize the handkerchief in the wonderful terms of Egyptian charmers, sibylline prophetic fury, and "mummy... / Conserved of maidens' hearts" (3.4.74–5). In order to understand the theatre's apparent need to redescribe its most important material resource, we do not need to follow Richard Wilson's spirited attack either on Shakespeare's theatre as "part of the apparatus of the English nation-state" or on

Shakespeare as a proto-capitalist enemy of the artisanal class of clothworkers.[30] But perhaps we do need to consider that costumes in the commercial theatre, while expensive and often gorgeous, were also redolent of the theatre's participation in trade and manual labor. Some costumes could project the somewhat grubby aura that went with being aristocratic cast-offs, but those costumes had themselves passed through the pawnbrokers' and the secondhand dealers' shops; and other costumes and all the rest of the cloth used in performances constituted at one level "ocular proof" of the theatre's material and class connections with the increasingly hard-pressed and riotous clothworkers.[31] In this view, the play endeavors to "take out the work" from textiles in order to purge theatre of the manual labor that made theatre possible, aligning drama thereby with the ethos of courtliness which itself was an important factor in the theatre's commercial success.

In 1610, Henry Jackson, member of Corpus Christi College, wrote of a performance of *Othello* he had witnessed at Oxford:

> They also had tragedies, which they acted with propriety and fitness. In which [tragedies], not only through speaking but also through acting certain things, they moved [the audience] to tears. But truly the celebrated Desdemona, slain in our presence by her husband, although she pleaded her case very effectively throughout, yet moved [us] more after she was dead, when, lying on her bed, she entreated the pity of the spectators by her very countenance."[32]

Jackson was a serious and religious young man, and Oxford probably provided a more attentive audience than did the Globe or even Blackfriars.[33] Yet his response to the boy actor, while deeply engaged, is equivalent to neither Frye's "realization" nor Greenblatt's "radical passion." In his account, the audience's response mirrors the shift within the play from the language-based relationship between the lovers at the outset to Othello's subsequent attempt to gain visual mastery over Desdemona. At first they woo each other through storytelling, hinting, and speaking (1.3.128–70); under Iago's instruction, however, Othello learns to "[w]ear" his eyes so as to be ever on the watch for signs of his wife's infidelity (3.3.198). As a consequence of this shift from an aural to an ocular axis of relationship, Desdemona is transformed into a spectacle of duplicity within Othello's theatre of the gaze. In similar fashion, the Oxford spectators are moved by the speaking and acting of the actors, but are more affected by the sight of the countenance of the dead Desdemona. Importantly, however, the audience resists the conversion of Desdemona into the iconic figure of purity exemplified by Othello's comparison of his wife to "such another world / Of one entire and perfect chrysolite" (5.2.144–5), or by A. C. Bradley's classic description – "her nature is infinitely sweet and her love absolute."[34] On stage at Oxford, not even death can transform her into the figure of "monumental alabaster" (5.2.5) envisioned by the text and by critics such as Bradley. Instead the murdered Desdemona remains like a speaking subject: her face "entreated the pity of the spectators" (*"spectantium misericordiam ipso vultu imploraret"*).

Plays such as *Othello*, *King Lear*, *Pericles*, *The Winter's Tale*, and *The Tempest* work to transform the bodies of the boy actors into sights of wonder. It is not surprising that Shakespeare and his theatre should use the actors in this way. The body as show-piece is simply more impressive than any other spectacular object, with the possible exception of the costly machines being developed by Inigo Jones for court masques or the fireworks or cannon-fire displays like the one that caused the destruction of the Globe in 1613. Yet however well woman-as-fetish works within the play-texts or in the context of the modern formation of aesthetic fetishism, it seems unlikely that the early modern audience would have agreed, for example, with Ferdinand's proprietary, already jealous awe at his first sight of Miranda: "My prime request, / ... is (O you wonder!) / If you be a maid, or no?" (*Tempest*, 1.2.426–8). This complex, critical response was underwritten no doubt by the gap between characters such as Miranda or the murdered Desdemona and the skilled boy actors who impersonated them. This gap, normally invisible to the spectators but always available to them, is exemplified also by the operation of stage-props like the handkerchief, which is both a contested wonder in the play-world and a piece of silk (or perhaps a less costly cloth!) in the playhouse.

Finally, let us consider the relationship between the handkerchief and Desdemona, as well as the idea that the play's infusion of charisma into the body of Desdemona operates in relation to the Renaissance difference between movable property and land.[35] That Desdemona's body replaces the handkerchief (not to mention Othello's blackness) as an object of wonder makes good sense because bodies are more evocative than textiles, but what I want to suggest is that the play *trades* the handkerchief for Desdemona's body. To understand the wonder of Desdemona as the profit accruing from a sequence of exchanges within the spectacular

economy of the play is to begin to grasp the production of theatrical wonder as continuous with ordinary life, rather than as something sacred set
over the ordinary.

Of course, the iconic power of Desdemona toward the end of the play
has to do also with how Iago's "odious, damned lie" (5.2.180) pushes
us to invest fully in her "sweetest innocen[ce]" (5.2.199). In terms of
Jacobean property values, however, Desdemona's amazing value is the
culmination of a series of trades involving land, cash and moveables,
women, and status. Roderigo, very much like a number of young, landed
gentlemen in Jacobean city comedy, converts his land into money in order
to buy jewels in order to win the love of a woman, a treasure, who will
bring him high status. But while Roderigo believes that Desdemona will
confer greater sexual and social status than his land, the play, like so
many city comedies, suggests the ideal that landedness is the only true
basis of high status. Land is different from commodities because, in this
somewhat nostalgic view, land possesses the possessor, who must live on
it in order to administer and preserve it. In medieval law, all land belongs
in principle inalienably to the king; general unease with the system by
which land becomes virtually as exchangeable as other commodities finds
expression in John of Gaunt's lament for the shameful binding of the
sacred "earth of majesty,... / This other Eden" within "inky blots, and
rotten parchment" (*Richard II*, 2.1.41–2, 64).[36] In the early seventeenth
century, furthermore, the duties of landholders to their property and
tenants were an acute social issue. The landed gentry flocked to London,
leaving the rural population without governance, judicial supervision,
or "hospitality"; some members of the gentry even lost their inherited
estates in the pursuit of status in the spendthrift circles around the court.[37]
Roderigo speaks for this group when he promises to invest everything
he owns in the chase after Desdemona: "I am chang'd... I'll sell all my
land" (1.3.380, 382). Since land itself has become a commodity like all
others, Desdemona, "full of most bless'd condition" (2.1.249–50), takes
its place (as the possession that possesses) in the conferring of social status
and personal worth.

So Desdemona is not merely a treasure, but the treasure of land.
With wicked irony, Iago says: "[Othello] to-night hath boarded a land
carract. / If it prove a lawful prize, he's made for ever" (1.2.50–1). Desdemona is as solid and valuable as land, Iago insinuates, but she is
also moveable and leaky like a boat. That irony possesses Othello, and
only by her murder can it be exorcised. Only at the end can he settle
into a view of Desdemona as the permanent, possessing possession that
land ideally was for the Jacobeans. This construction of Desdemona is

intensely tragic for Othello, since the idea that she is Othello's homeland means that her murder renders him irredeemably homeless:

> Where should Othello go?
> Now – how dost thou look now? O ill-starr'd wench,
> Pale as thy smock! when we shall meet at compt,
> This look of thine will hurl my soul from heaven,
> And fiends will snatch at it. (5.2.271–5)

From the shattered viewpoint of Othello's impending damnation, Desdemona's body shines out wonderfully as the promised land forever out of reach. We should perhaps bear in mind Othello's scattered, destroyed personhood when we, following indeed the play's hint, undertake to transvalue *Othello*, making it into "a play not simply to be read or seen or even studied, but possessed."[38] We might also remember Othello's fate when we attempt to exchange the moving sight of Desdemona's body for a "magical property," a visionary possession of Desdemona in which we try to find manifested our own "authentic immediacy."

The eighteenth-century writer and lawyer Arthur Murphy once imagined himself at Parnassus. He saw that the land had been divided by Apollo among the great writers of the classical and modern canons. Among these figures he found Shakespeare:

The great *Shakespeare* sat upon a cliff, looking abroad through all creation. His possessions were very near as extensive as *Homer's*, but in some places, had not received sufficient culture. But even there spontaneous flowers shot up, and in the *unweeded garden, which grows to seed*, you might cull lavender, myrtle, and wild thyme... Even *Milton* was looking for flowers to transplant into his own Paradise.[39]

Murphy's quaint description of Shakespeare as land and as landholder may remind us of the investments readers and critics make when they attempt to inhabit and be inhabited by a text such as *Othello*. Like the wandering court party on Prospero's island or the wonderstruck conquistadors in the New World, we attempt to stake a claim to territories that seem able to restore us to ourselves. Instead of possessing and being possessed by *Othello*, however, we might do better to love it for the multiplicity of its uses. As a useful rather than a sacred text, *Othello* would be, among other things, a work of literature, a script for actors, a text of considerable historical importance, and a powerful and moving instrument of social critique, by virtue of its implicit critique of ideology and its wonderful orchestration of a rich array of social languages, including the "language" of theatrical properties.

NOTES

1. Ben Jonson, *The Staple of News*, ed. Anthony Parr, *Revels Plays* (Manchester and New York: Manchester University Press, 1988), 3.4.54–5.

2. See Karen Hearn (ed.), *Dynasties: Painting in Tudor and Jacobean England 1530–1630* (London: Tate, 1995), esp. the following portraits: no. 17, Isabel de Valois (?1560), no. 49, Robert Dudley (c. 1564), no. 124, Archduchess Isabella Clara Eugenia (c.1599), no. 141, Alathea Talbot, Countess of Arundel (c.1618).

3. See Lawrence J. Ross, "The meaning of strawberries in Shakespeare," *Studies in the Renaissance* 7 (1960): 225–40. All Shakespeare quotations refer to *The Riverside Shakespeare*, ed. G. Blakemore Evans (Boston: Houghton Mifflin, 1974).

4. See Douglas Bruster, *Drama and the Market in the Age of Shakespeare* (Cambridge: Cambridge University Press, 1992), p. 84.

5. Pierre Macherey, *A Theory of Literary Production*, trans. Geoffrey Wall (London: Routledge, 1989), p. 64.

6. M. M. Bakhtin, "Discourse in the novel," in *The Dialogic Imagination: Four Essays*, ed. Michael Holquist, transl. Caryl Emerson and Michael Holquist (Austin: University of Texas Press, 1981), p. 289, italics in original. Note that Bakhtin does not claim that literary *language* is untouched by these imported dialects; on p. 294, he explains the process as "a dialogue of languages":

> As they enter and are appropriated to literary language, dialects in this new context lose, of course, the quality of closed socio-linguistic systems; they are deformed and in fact cease to be that which they had been simply as dialects. On the other hand, these dialects, on entering the literary language and preserving within it their own dialectological elasticity, their other-languagedness, have the effect of deforming the literary language; it, too, ceases to be that which it had been, a closed socio-linguistic system.

7. Bakhtin, "Discourse," pp. 291–2.

8. Northrop Frye, "Introduction," *The Tempest*, in *The Complete Pelican Shakespeare*, ed. Alfred Harbage (Baltimore: Penguin, 1969), p. 1370.

9. Stephen Greenblatt, *Marvelous Possessions: The Wonder of the New World* (Chicago: University of Chicago Press, 1991), p. 14.

10. Ibid.

11. Frye, "Introduction," p. 1372.

12. Greenblatt, *Marvelous Possessions*, p. 1.

13. Thomas Heywood, *An Apology for Actors* (London 1612; facsimile reprint. New York: Scholars' Facsimiles and Reprints, 1941), sig. B4.

14. The original German text, as well as the translation used here, is quoted in *Riverside Shakespeare*, p. 1839.

15. Quoted in ibid., p. 1842.

16. See Andrew Gurr, *Playgoing in Shakespeare's London* (Cambridge: Cambridge University Press, 1987), pp. 44–8.

17. Stephen Gosson, *The Schoole of Abuse* (London, 1579; fascimile reprint. New York: Garland, 1973), sig. C1v.
18. Phillip Stubbes, *The Anatomie of Abuses* (London, 1583; facsimile reprint Amsterdam: Theatrum Orbis Terrarum, 1972), sig. L7v.
19. Henry Parrot, *Laquei ridiculosi: or Springes for Woodcocks* (London, 1613), C6v.
20. Ben Jonson, *The Complete Poems*, ed. George Parfitt (Harmondsworth: Penguin, 1975), p. 264.
21. John Milton, *Complete Poems and Major Prose*, ed. Merritt Y. Hughes (Indianapolis: Odyssey Press, 1957), pp. 63–4.
22. Quoted in *Riverside Shakespeare*, p. 1846.
23. Quoted in ibid., p. 63.
24. Georg Lukács, *History and Class Consciousness: Studies in Marxist Dialectics*, trans. Rodney Livingstone (Cambridge: MIT Press, 1986), p. 83.
25. Kenneth Burke, "*Othello*: an essay to illustrate a method," *Hudson Review* 4 (1951): 166–7.
26. On clothes, fetishism, and identity in Elizabethan society, see Peter Stally-brass, "Worn worlds: clothes and identity on the Renaissance stage," in Margreta de Grazia, Maureen Quilligan, and Peter Stallybrass (eds.), *Subject and Object in Renaissance Culture* (Cambridge: Cambridge University Press, 1996), pp. 289–320.
27. Karl Marx, *Capital: A Critique of Political Economy*, ed. Frederick Engels, transl. Samuel Moore and Edward Aveling (New York: Modern Library, 1906), p. 83.
28. Terry Eagleton, The *Ideology of the Aesthetic* (Oxford: Basil Blackwell, 1990), p. 78.
29. Peter Stallybrass, "Patriarchal territories: the body enclosed," in Margaret Ferguson et al. (eds.), *Rewriting the Renaissance: The Discourses of Sexual Difference in Early Modern Europe* (Chicago: University of Chicago Press, 1986), p. 137.
30. Richard Wilson, "'A mingled yarn': Shakespeare and the cloth workers," *Literature and History* 12 (1986): 169.
31. For pawnbroking and the circulation of clothing/costume, see Natasha Korda, "Household property/stage property: Henslowe as pawnbroker," *Theatre Journal* 48 (1996): 185–96.
32. The original Latin text, along with the translation used here, is quoted in *Riverside Shakespeare*, p. 1852.
33. See *Dictionary of National Biography*, entry on Henry Jackson, for an account of his character and career.
34. A. C. Bradley, *Shakespearean Tragedy: Lectures on* Hamlet, Othello, King Lear, Macbeth (1904; rpt. London: Macmillan, 1964), p. 145.
35. On woman as land, see Stallybrass, "Patriarchal territories."
36. See Kenelm Edward Digby, *An Introduction to the History of the Law of Real Property* (Oxford: Clarendon Press, 1875).
37. See Felicity Heal, "The crown, the gentry and London: the enforcement of proclamation, 1596–1640," in Claire Cross et al. (eds.), *Law and*

Government under the Tudors (Cambridge: Cambridge University Press, 1988), pp. 211–26.

38. Frye, "Introduction," p. 1372.

39. Arthur Murphy, *Gray's-Inn Journal* (London, 1786), quoted in Mark Rose, *Authors and Owners: The Invention of Copyright* (Cambridge, MA: Harvard University Press, 1993), epigraph.

Appendix

Jonathan Gil Harris and Natasha Korda

The following inventory of properties was first printed in Edmund
Malone, *The Plays and Poems of William Shakespeare* (London, 1790), Vol. 1,
part 11, pp. 302–4. It was found in a bundle of loose papers at Dulwich
College, which have since disappeared. The inventory was subsequently
reprinted in W. W. Greg, *Henslowe Papers* (1907), pp. 116–18, and in R. A.
Foakes and R. T. Rickert (eds.), *Henslowe's Diary* (Cambridge: Cambridge
University Press, 1961), appendix 2, pp. 319–21.

> *The Enventary tacken of all the properties for my* Lord Admeralles men, *the*
> 10 *of Marche* 1598.
> *Item*, j rocke, j cage, j tombe, j Hell mought.
> *Item*, j tome of Guido, j tome of Dido, j bedsteade.
> *Item*, viij lances, j payer of stayers for Fayeton.
> *Item*, ij stepells, & j chyme of belles, & j beacon.
> *Item*, j hecfor for the playe of Faeton, the limes dead.
> *Item*, j globe, & j golden scepter; iij clobes.
> *Item*, ij marchepanes, & the sittie of Rome.
> *Item*, j gowlden flece; ij rackets; j baye tree.
> *Item*, j wooden hatchett; j lether hatchete.
> *Item*, j wooden canepie; owld Mahemetes head.
> *Item*, j lyone skin; j beares skyne, & Faetones lymes, & Faeton charete;
> & Argosse heade.
> *Item*, Nepun forcke & garland.
> *Item*, j crosers stafe; Kentes woden leage.
> *Item*, Ierosses head, & raynbowe; j littell alter.
> *Item*, viij viserdes; Tamberlyne brydell; j wooden matook.
> *Item*, Cupedes bowe, & quiver; the clothe of the Sone & Mone.
> *Item*, j bores heade & Serberosse iij heades.
> *Item*, j Cadeseus; ij mose banckes, & j snake.

335

Item, ij fanes of feathers; Belendon stable; j tree of gowlden apelles; Tantelouse tre; jx eyorn targates.

Item, j copper targate, & xvij foyles.

Item, iiij wooden targates; j greve armer.

Item, j syne for Mother Readcap; j buckler.

Item, Mercures wings; Tasso picter; j helmet with a dragon; j shelde, with iij lyones; j elme bowle.

Item, j chayne of dragons; j gylte speare.

Item, ij coffenes; j bulles head; and j vylter.

Item, iij tymbrells, j dragon in fostes.

Item, j lyone; ij lyon heades; j great horse with his leages; j sack-bute.

Item, j whell and frame in the Sege of London.

Item, j paire of rowghte gloves.

Item, j poopes miter.

Item, iiij Imperial crownes; j playne crowne.

Item, j gostes crown; j crown with a sone.

Item, j frame for the heading in Black Jone.

Item, j black dogge.

Item, j cauderm for the Jewe.

Index

Note: The following abbreviations are used in the index: *SH* for *The Shoemaker's Holiday*; *WKK* for *A Woman Killed With Kindness*; WS for William Shakespeare.

All plays are listed under the names of their authors, when known, except for those of William Shakespeare, which are listed directly under their titles, followed by (WS).

Locators *in italics* indicate illustrations.

Printed in the United Kingdom
by Lightning Source UK Ltd.
115506UKS00001BA/29